The Restless City Reader

"A superb compilation of essential documents spanning the tumultuous 400-year history of America's premier city. The selections crackle with their own restless energy and provide a riveting coherence to this epic story of conflict and possibility. Reitano's crisp commentary and probing questions invite real reflection and dialogue."
   —**Vincent DiGirolamo**, Baruch College, City University of New York

"*The Restless City Reader: A New York City Sourcebook* is a splendid teaching tool. Its well-chosen selections, including primary source documents, excerpts from historical monographs, biographies, autobiographies, historic pictures, and political cartoons, and the editor's clear, concise introductions to the material offer students a vivid picture of life in this vibrant, restless city from its earliest Dutch beginnings through 9/11/01 and its aftermath."
   —**Barbara Blumberg**, Professor of History, Pace University, and author of
     The New Deal and the Unemployed: The View from New York City

From Peter Stuyvesant to Mayor Bloomberg, New York City's history is full of vibrant characters, riveting events, and fascinating controversies that reflect shifting economic, political, social, and cultural currents within New York's long history. *The Restless City Reader: A New York City Sourcebook* uses primary and secondary sources from a variety of perspectives to illuminate the issues that have affected the city and its people.

The Restless City Reader can be used alone or with *The Restless City*, a short narrative history of New York from colonial times to the present. With a helpful introduction and document head notes, as well as study questions and suggestions for further inquiry, *The Restless City Reader* is a short, engaging, usable collection of sources for students, professors, and anyone interested in the city—its dreams, its challenges, its voices.

Joanne Reitano is Professor of History at La Guardia Community College, City University of New York. She is the author of *The Restless City: A Short History of New York from Colonial Times to the Present*.

The Restless City Reader

A New York City Sourcebook

Edited by

Joanne Reitano

Routledge
Taylor & Francis Group

NEW YORK AND LONDON

First published 2010
by Routledge
270 Madison Avenue, New York, NY 10016

Simultaneously published in the UK
by Routledge
2 Park Square, Milton Park, Abingdon, Oxon OX14 4RN

Routledge is an imprint of Taylor & Francis Group, an informa business

© 2010 Taylor & Francis

Typeset in Sabon by
HWA Text and Data Management Ltd, London

Printed and in the United States of America on acid-free paper by
Edwards Brothers, Inc.

All rights reserved. No part of this book may be reprinted or reproduced
or utilized in any form or by any electronic, mechanical, or other
means, now known or hereafter invented, including photocopying and
recording, or in any information storage or retrieval system, without
permission in writing from the publishers.

Trademark Notice: Product or corporate names may be trademarks or
registered trademarks, and are used only for identification and explana-
tion without intent to infringe

Library of Congress Cataloging-in-Publication Data
Reitano, Joanne R.
   The restless city reader : a New York City sourcebook /
Joanne Reitano.
      p. cm.
   Includes bibliographical references and index.
   1. New York (N.Y.)—History. 2. New York (N.Y.)—Social
   conditions. 3. New York (N.Y.)—History—Problems, exercises, etc.
   4. New York (N.Y.)—Social conditions—Problems, exercises, etc.
   5. Readers. I. Title.
   F128.3.R46 2010
   974.7´1—dc22   2009038266

ISBN 10: 0-415-80227-X (hbk)
ISBN 10: 0-415-80228-8 (pbk)

ISBN 13: 978-0-415-80227-7 (hbk)
ISBN 13: 978-0-415-80228-4 (pbk)

For Adam and Paul

Contents

Acknowledgments

Designing a reader is a humbling experience, especially if it is about as complex a city as New York. There is so much rich material available that any selection process is inherently inadequate. Finding sources that are engaging and clear further complicates the task. However, the more difficult the job, the greater is one's appreciation of the people who helped along the way.

As always, I am indebted to La Guardia Community College of the City University of New York for its continuing support. The La Guardia-Wagner Archives, directed by Richard Lieberman and located at La Guardia Community College, provided excellent resources and superb archival assistance, particularly from Douglas DiCarlo. In addition, I am grateful for the guidance of librarians at the New York Public Library, New York University, and the New York Historical Society. The three anonymous readers raised excellent questions and offered constructive suggestions that greatly improved the manuscript.

It is a privilege to continue working with Kimberly Guinta, History Acquisitions Editor at Routledge. She has consistently proven to be a wise and supportive professional with the highest possible standards of excellence. Senior Editorial Assistant for History, Matthew Kopel, skillfully and patiently (but firmly) guided me through the agonizing permissions process. My gratitude extends to the efficient production team in London, including Helen Dixon, Siân Findlay, John Hodgson and Alexa Richardson.

Each new book makes me increasingly aware of how strange my compulsively academic personality is to others. Therefore, I thank again the colleagues, friends and family, especially my sons, who have encouraged (or at least tolerated) me over the years.

CHAPTER 1

Introduction

The city that never sleeps is a restless city. It is fast-paced and exciting—ever-changing, ever-challenging, ever-fascinating. As the writer Morris Dickstein explained, "Only dying cities remain the same."[1] For better or worse, New York has never remained the same. From colonial times to the present, it has changed many times—rising to incredible heights, falling to unfathomable depths, but repeatedly recovering and reinventing itself. Shaped by a spirit of risk-taking and rebellion, by controversy and conflict, by wave after wave of new blood, New York City was constantly invigorated by its restless energy. Ironically, the city's main source of continuity has been its commitment to change.

Change breeds complexity and, by definition, complexity is hard to understand; but that is what makes it so interesting. Over time and within each historical period, different people have held different opinions about the individuals and events that have shaped New York City history. These varied voices reflect the multidimensional nature of the city as a place of perpetual conflict and change. Time and again, New Yorkers have argued about the meaning of opportunity and equality, individualism and community, freedom and order. Their debates reflected the challenge of creating the good society, not just in New York City, but everywhere. Could it be that, as a result, New York City history is a microcosm of human history?

This sourcebook invites the reader to participate in the debate over the meaning of New York City history. It combines primary sources (originating during the time period being discussed) and secondary sources (originating after the time period being discussed). The primary sources include letters, speeches, newspaper articles, drawings, cartoons, maps, public documents, and autobiographical excerpts. They help us see the past in its own terms. The secondary sources are selections from books and articles representing various fields—anthropology, economics, history, journalism, political science, sociology. They help provide perspective on the past. Together, the primary and secondary sources bring the past to life and make it relevant to the present. However, they do not solve the mystery of history. That remains for each reader to discover by wrestling with the questions that follow each source and by posing new questions.

Note that this reader can be used alone or it can be coupled with my companion text *The Restless City: A Short History of New York from Colonial Times to the Present.*[2] Like *The Restless City*, this reader emphasizes political, economic and social conflict. Each chapter examines four of the following five topics: urban development (city building), policy priorities (the public interest), conflict (law and order), social change (change and challenge) and activism (breaking barriers). One unit in each chapter is structured around a biographical sketch. The overall purpose is to make New York City history as provocative as the city itself, a theme that is reinforced by a final unit on the city's restless qualities over time.

This reader assumes that restlessness is a central characteristic of New York City. Furthermore, it suggests that restlessness is more often an asset than a defect because it reflects an energetic and ambitious resistance to limits. Consequently, said the sociologist Peter Berger, New York City has always represented "transcendence inasmuch as it embodies universalism and freedom."[3] Its restlessness can be observed and analyzed in many different ways. The following documents offer a small sample of how primary and secondary sources can empower everyone to decipher the past. Enjoy.

1-1.   THE RUSHING CITY: THEODORE DWIGHT, EDUCATOR, 1834

In 1834, Yale University's President Theodore Dwight commented on the spirit of the city.

Source: Theodore Dwight, *Things As They Are; or, Notes of a Traveler through some of the Middle and Northern States* (New York: Harper and Brothers, 1834), 31.

Whoever visits New York feels as he does in a watchmaker's shop; everybody goes there for the true time, and feels on leaving it as if he had been wound up or regulated anew. ... He hears clicking, as it were, on all sides of him, and finds everything he looks at in movement, and not a nook or corner but what is brimful of business. Apparently there is no inactivity; that is, no person is quiescent both in body and mind at once. The reason of this is, that the lazy are excited by the perpetual motion of the busy, or at least compelled to bestir themselves to avoid being run over.

1. How was comparing New York City to a watch both a compliment and a criticism?
2. Why did Dwight say that New York City represented "the true time"?
3. What phrases in this quote best convey the spirit of a restless city?
4. Explain why you are or are not surprised that this statement was written in the 1830s.

1-2.   THE CRUSHING CITY: A NINETEENTH-CENTURY TRAFFIC JAM

Cartoons hold up a mirror to society. They force us to think about our taken for granted worlds and are, therefore, interesting tools for analyzing reality. This cartoonist's version of a nineteenth century traffic jam captures and comments on some fundamental characteristics of the city.

Source: Henry Collins Brown (ed.), *Valentine's Manual of Old New York* (Hastings-on-Hudson, NY: Valentine's Manual, 1928), 397.

1. What positive and negative characteristics of New York City did the cartoonist emphasize?
2. How did the cartoonist suggest that restlessness breeds conflict?
3. How did the cartoonist reflect urban class and gender differences?
4. What are the similarities and/or differences between Dwight's statement and this cartoon?
5. How does this cartoon connect the 19th to the 21st-century city?

1-3. THE THRILLING CITY: WALT WHITMAN, POET, 1888

Walt Whitman was the nation's first urban poet. Written in 1860, his famous poem "Mannahatta" offers a ringing testimony to the author and the city he loved. The title of this primary source comes from the Mannahatta Indians and therefore is meant to suggest the city's original character.

Source: Walt Whitman, "Mannahatta" *New York Herald*, February 27, 1888, 4.

I was asked for something specific and perfect for my city,
Whereupon lo! Up sprang the aboriginal name.
Now I see what there is in a name, a word, liquid, sane,
  Unruly, musical, self-sufficient,
I see that the word of my city is that word from old,
Because I see that word nested in nests of water-bays, superb,

Rich, hemm'd thick all around with sailships and steamships, an island
    sixteen miles long, solid-founded,
Numberless crowded streets, high growths of iron, slender, strong. light,
    splendidly uprising toward clear skies,
Tides swift and ample, well-loved by me, toward sundown,
The flowing sea-currents, the little islands, larger adjoining islands, the
    heights, the villas,
The countless masts, the white shore steamers, the lighters, the ferry-
    boats, the black steamers well-model'd,
The down-town streets, the jobbers' houses of business, the houses of
    business of the ship-merchants and money-brokers, the river streets,
Immigrants arriving, fifteen or twenty thousand in a week,
The carts hauling goods, the manly race of drivers of horses, the brown-
    faced sailors,
The summer air, the bright sun shining, and the sailing clouds aloft,
The winter snows, the sleigh-bells, the broken ice in the river,
    Passing along up or down with the flood-tide or the ebb-tide,
The mechanics of the city, the masters, well-form'd,
    Beautiful-faced, looking you straight in the eyes,
Trottoirs throng'd, vehicles, Broadway, the women, the shops and shows.
A million people—manners free and superb—open voices—hospitality—
    the most courageous and friendly young men,
City of hurried and sparkling waters! City of spires and masts!
City nested in bays! My city!

---

1. How many different kinds of people and activities did Whitman describe?
2. What kind of people and activities did Whitman leave out of his poem? Why?
3. What key words in the poem best conveyed the restlessness of Whitman's New York City?
4. How was Whitman's city similar to and/or different from the city reflected in the watch metaphor and the traffic cartoon?

1-4.   THE EVOLVING CITY: THOMAS BENDER, HISTORIAN, 2002

In 2002, the historian Thomas Bender published a book about New York called *The Unfinished City*. Because the title suggests a place that is always in process, it reflects New York's restlessness. As a secondary source, Bender's book placed Whitman in the larger context of New York City history and suggested that the great poet embodied the true spirit of the city.

Source: Thomas Bender, *The Unfinished City: New York and the Metropolitan Idea* (New York: The New Press, 2002), xii, xvi.

No one has come closer than Whitman to capturing the soul of New York; his person and poetry (which are nearly indistinguishable) are part of a collective memory that sustains the city's metropolitan self-definition. ... Whitman was self-fashioned—and, like New York, an utterly unpredictable result. Who could have imagined that the undistinguished journalist, carpenter, writer Walter Whitman would or could make himself into Walt Whitman, poet of the city and the continuing fount of American poetry? Yet neither Whitman nor his poem was ever complete. That was his human and artistic strength, as it is New York's. He was always growing, absorbing more, and battling with the contradictions that his voraciousness forced upon him. Whitman was the poet of the intentionally unfinished poem. *Leaves of Grass* (1855 et seq.) was never finished or intended to be finished. It was perpetually in revision. So too the city. Both Whitman's poems and the city are deliberately collections of people, sights, things, ideas, feelings. Ordinarily, they seem to be merely miscellaneous, whether in poetry or in life. Yet episodically and magically they are fused into aesthetically powerful and morally compelling imageries and practices. ... New York defies the logic of closure, of resolution, and that is what produces both its special strengths and its weaknesses.

1. According to Bender, how were Whitman and New York City similar?
2. What is the relationship between being unfinished and being restless?
3. How did Bender's interpretation of Whitman echo the watch metaphor and the traffic cartoon?

1-5.   THE LIVING CITY: CHIANG YEE, CALLIGRAPHER, 1950

Chiang Yee (1903–1977) was a Chinese author, poet, painter and calligrapher who wrote and illustrated 24 books, including nine about cities in Europe and the United States. After moving to America in 1955, he taught at Harvard and Columbia. Much to his surprise, Chiang discovered that New York City defied its negative stereotypes. In particular, he was delighted by Times Square with its orderly crowds, varied diversions, "dazzling" signs, sundry food carts, numerous restaurants and ceaseless activity. New Yorkers, he observed, enjoyed being outside—eating, shopping, relaxing, or just walking. Chiang Yee admired their lively spirit and concluded that the city was a "place where every kind of impossibility is daily becoming possible."[4]

Source: Chiang Yee, *The Silent Traveller in New York* (London: Methuen, 1950), 48.

1. Explain the symbolism of the hourglass and the shape of Chiang Yee's drawing.
2. Analyze Chiang Yee's New Yorkers. Who was represented? Were they pushy, purposeful and/or polite?
3. How was Chiang Yee's concept of time in the city similar to and/or different from that of Dwight, the cartoonist, Whitman and Bender?
4. Based on these five sources, explain the characteristics of New York's restlessness and whether it was a strength and/or a weakness.

SELECTED GENERAL RESOURCES

Allen, Oliver. *New York, New York: A History of the World's Most Exhilarating and Challenging City*. New York: Atheneum, 1990.

Binder, Frederick M., and David M. Reimers. *All the Nations Under Heaven*. NewYork: Columbia University Press, 1995.

Burns, Ric, and James Sanders. *New York: An Illustrated History*. New York: Alfred A. Knopf, 1999. *New York: A Documentary Film* at http://www.pbs.org/wnet/newyork

Burrows, Edwin G., and Mike Wallace. *Gotham: A History of New York City to 1898*. New York: Oxford University Press, 1999.

Dodson, Howard, Christopher Moore, and Roberta Yancy. *The Black New Yorkers: The Schomburg Illustrated Chronology*. New York: John Wiley and Sons, 2000.

Ellis, Edward Robb. *The Epic of New York City*. New York: Old Town Books, 1966/ Kodnasha America Reprint, 1997.

Homburger, Eric. *The Historical Atlas of New York: A Visual Celebration of Nearly 400 Years of New York City's History*. New York: Henry Holt and Company, 1994.

Jackson, Kenneth T. (ed.). *The Encyclopedia of New York City*. New Haven, CT: Yale University Press, 1995.

Jackson, Kenneth, and David S. Dunbar (eds). *Empire City: New York Through the Centuries*. New York: Columbia University Press, 2002.

Lankevich, George. *New York City: A Short History*. New York: New York University Press, 2002.

Rock, Howard B., and Deborah Dash Moore. *Cityscapes: A History of New York in Images*. New York: Columbia University Press, 2001.

Still, Bayard. *Mirror for Gotham: New York as Seen by Contemporaries from Dutch Days to the Present*. New York: Fordham University Press, 1956/1994.

www.bronxhistoricalsociety.org: Bronx history
www.brooklynhistory.org: Brooklyn history
www.forgotten-ny.com: old lampposts, advertisements, signs, buildings, etc.
www.historymatters.gmu.edu: vast collection—specify NYC
www.gilderlehrman.org: vast collection—specify NYC
www.gothamcenter.org: various resources on NYC
www.historicrichmondtown.org: Staten Island history
www.lcweb2.loc.gov/ammem: vast collection—specify NYC
www.mcny.org: NYC history
www.nyhistory.org: NYC history with an e-museum of artifacts
www.nypl.org: digital collection—specify NYC
www.queenshistoricalsociety.org: Queens history

CHAPTER 2

1609–1799

New York supposedly began with a bargain when Dutchman Peter Minuit "bought" Manhattan Island from the Indians for a mere sixty guilders. It was literally and figuratively an investment in futures. Of course, the deal was deceptive because you could not "buy" land from people who had no concept of private ownership. Besides, there was no current real estate value for what would become an incredibly valuable site.

That was the point. It explains how an acquisitive, aggressive people developed an ambitious, competitive, colorful and highly profitable community on the banks of the Hudson River. It leads us to Wall Street, the Empire State Building, Rockefeller Center and, tragically, the World Trade Center. Because the almighty dollar seemed to have reigned supreme from the beginning, New York epitomized America's cash value culture. Of course, the story was much more complicated. New York was always an amalgam of many peoples and possibilities. Never dull, never irrelevant, never finished, New York was always restless because, like the nation, it rejected limits.

Conflicts have permeated New York's economic, political, social, and cultural life. They have exposed problems, compelled reforms, fomented riots, spurred strikes, and inspired artistic creativity. Conflicts in the colonial and revolutionary periods foreshadowed a vibrant history of urban growth, but they also made New York seem dangerous, threatening and, therefore, somewhat un-American. As historian Thomas Bender put it, New York's diversity and controversy made it "a center of difference" which also made it different from the rest of America.[1]

Conflicts tested New York. The city's fundamental dilemmas emerged in the colonial and revolutionary eras when settlers confronted the challenges of survival. In the process, the colonists tried to balance self-interest with the general good, morality with exploitation, order with freedom. This chapter investigates those dilemmas. It begins with an examination of tensions embodied in the colonial relationship between Europeans, Native Americans and Africans. By contrast, it then explores the meaning of freedom for Europeans in the colony and the development of New York's liberal traditions. Discussions of Peter Stuyvesant and of New York's Stamp Act Riots raise questions about leadership, economic development, self-government and civic priorities. For better or worse, New York's character emerged from the colonial experience.

UNIT 2-1. CHANGE AND CHALLENGE: COLONIZATION

From the start, the process of colonization was complicated by the interaction of three different groups—Europeans, Native Americans and Africans. The following documents reflect the attitudes of the settlers as they confronted people whom they exploited but on whom they depended for survival. The settlers recognized this contradiction and became increasingly anxious about it over time. In some cases, the dichotomy made them more defensive and therefore more brutal; in other cases, it made them more liberal. Because we live with this dual legacy today, it is particularly important to explore its origins.

2-1-1. STRUGGLING TO SURVIVE: DUTCH COLONISTS, 1643

Hailing from a small coastal country with few resources, the Dutch became explorers and traders. They ranged from the Far East to South Africa and were among the first Europeans to set roots in the New World. Sponsored by the Dutch East India Company in 1609, British-born Henry Hudson discovered a magnificent harbor leading to an inland river that he named after himself. By the 1620s, the Dutch West India Company was created to exploit the entire region. It established a small trading post called New Amsterdam, which was part of a larger colony called New Netherland.

The natural resources seemed limitless, but the human dynamics were complicated. As the Europeans struggled to secure a foothold in the New World, they clashed with the Native Americans' desire for self-sufficiency. The result was conflict. Dutch Governor William Kieft, who ran the colony from 1641 to 1645, fomented so many wars with the Native Americans that the Staten Island settlements were obliterated and 1643 was called "the year of the blood." The following letter was written in 1643 by eight male colonists to the Dutch West India Company. The text reflects not only the suffering of the colonists, but also the nature of Indian resistance.

Source: "Memorial of the Eight Men at the Manhattan to the States General," in E. B. O'Callaghan (ed.), *Documents Relative to the Colonial History of the State of New York Procured in Holland, England and France* by John Romeyn Brodhead, vol. I, (Albany, NY: Weed, Parsons and Company, 1856), 139–140.

Noble, High and Mighty Lords,
The Noble Lords of the States General of the United Netherland Provinces:

As no sacrifice is more acceptable to our God than an humble spirit and a contrite heart, so nothing should, in like manner, be more pleasing to all Christian princes and magistrates, than to lend an ear to their complaining, and to extend a hand to their distressed subjects.

It is then that we poor inhabitants of New Netherland were here in the Spring pursued by these wild Heathens and barbarous Savages with fire and sword; daily in our houses and fields have they cruelly murdered men and women; and with hatchets and tomahawks struck little children dead in their parents' arms or before their doors; or carried them away into bondage; the houses and grain-barracks are burnt with the produce; cattle of all descriptions are slain and destroyed, and such as remain must perish this Winter for the want of fodder.

Almost every place is abandoned. We, wretched people, must skulk, with wives and little ones that still survive, in poverty together, in and around the fort at the Manahatas where we are not safe even for an hour; whilst the Indians daily threaten to overwhelm us with it. Very little can be planted this autumn, and much less in the spring, so that it will come to pass that all of us who will yet save our lives, must of necessity perish next year of hunger and sorrow, with our wives and children, unless our God have pity on us.

We are all here, from the smallest to the greatest, devoid of counsel and means, wholly powerless. The enemy meets with scarce any resistance. The garrison consists of but 50 or 60 soldiers unprovided with ammunition. Fort Amsterdam, utterly defenseless, stands open to the enemy night and day. The Company hath few or no effects here (as the Director hath informed us). Were it not for this, there would have been still time to receive assistance from the English at the East (ere all had gone to ruin); and we wretched settlers, whilst we must abandon all our substance, are exceedingly poor.

These heathens are strong in might; they have formed an alliance with seven other nations; are well provided with guns, powder and lead, which they purchased for beaver from the private traders who have had, for a long time, free reign here. The rest they take from our fellow countrymen whom they murder.

In fine, we experience here the greatest misery, which must astonish a Christian heart to see or to hear.

We turn then, in a body, to you, High and Mighty Lords, acknowledging you as our Sovereigns and the Fathers of the Fatherland. We supplicate, for God's sake, and for the love your High Mightinesses bear your poor and desolate subjects here in New Netherland, that your High Mightinesses would take pity on us, your poor people, and encourage the Company thereunto, and command them (to whom we also hereby make known our necessity) to forward us, by the earliest opportunity, such assistance as your High Mightinesses will deem most proper, in order that we, poor forlorn people, may not be left all at once a prey, with wives and children, to these cruel heathens. And should suitable assistance not speedily arrive (contrary to our expectations), we shall, through necessity, in order to save the lives of those who remain, be obliged to betake ourselves to the English at the East, who would like nothing better than to possess this place. And that an account of the superior convenience of sea coasts, bays, and large rivers, besides the great fertility of this place; yea, which alone could of itself provision and supply yearly 20, 25 or 30 ships from Brazil or the West Indies with all necessaries.

Remaining, as we are, your High Mightinesses' faithful servants and subjects, lawfully chosen and authorized by the Honorable Director and Council and the entire Commonalty of New Netherland.

---

1. How did this letter reveal the strengths and weaknesses of the new settlement?
2. Why did the colonists both fear and respect the Indians?
3. What was the colonists' attitude toward the Dutch West India Company?
4. Was the letter designed to dramatize, beg and/or threaten?

2-1-2. DRAWING THE FIRST SETTLEMENT, 1651

In the days before photography, movies, and television, drawings provided essential records of places and people. Of course, drawings are not exact replicas of reality, but selective depictions of reality as perceived by the artist. Thus, they have a point of view. Dating from 1651, this first known drawing of New Amsterdam reflected the tenuous relationship between the European settlers and the Native Americans. Note that the words are in reverse because of an error in the original engraving. They read Fort nieuw Amsterdam of the Manhatans (an Indian tribe).

Source: Dingman Versteeg, *Manhattan in 1628* (New York: Dodd Mead, 1904), frontispiece, from Joost Hartger, *Beschrijvinghe Van Virginia, Nieuw Nederlandt, etc.* (Amsterdam, 1651).

---

1. How did this artist suggest and/or question the stability and growth potential of the colony?
2. How did this artist depict the relationship between the colonists and the Native Americans?
3. How did this drawing support and/or contradict the letter above?
4. Would this drawing have encouraged Europeans to join the colony? Was it propaganda?

2-1-3. FREEING SLAVES: THE DUTCH WEST INDIA COMPANY, 1644

Because New Amsterdam got off to a slow start, the Dutch West India Company was always concerned about securing workers. Already involved with the slave trade between Africa and Latin America, the Dutch promoted slavery in New Amsterdam. The first few slaves were brought to New Amsterdam in 1626 and the first significant shipment of slaves from Brazil were sold in 1645. By 1654, the slave trade with New Amsterdam had been formalized and regularized. Although the number of slaves under Dutch rule remained small, tensions abounded. The presence of slaves in a city dedicated to freedom and opportunity created conflict between economic interests and ethical concerns. One reflection of this dilemma was the policy called "half-freedom."[2]

Source: E. B. O'Callaghan (ed.), *Laws and Ordinances of New Netherland, 1638–1674* (Albany, NY: Weed, Parsons and Company, 1868), 36–37.

February 24, 1644:
Having considered the petition of the Negroes named: Paul D'Angola, Senion Congo, [et al], who have served the Company 18 to 19 years, to be liberated, especially as they have been many years in the service of the Honorable West India Company here and have long since been promised their freedom; also that they are burdened with many children so that it is impossible for them to support their wives and children as they have been accustomed to do, if they must continue in the Company's service. Therefore, we, the Director and Council do release them and their wives from slavery ... where they shall be able to earn their livlihood from Agriculture, in the land shown and granted to them ... on condition that they, the above named negroes, shall be bound to pay for the freedom they receive, each man for himself annually, as long as he lives, to the West India Company, or its Deputy here, 30 skepels of Maize, or Wheat, Peas, or Beans and one Fat Hog, valued at 20 Guilders ... on pain if any one shall fail to pay the yearly tribute, he shall forfeit his freedom and return to the Company's slavery."

---

1. Was the Dutch West India Company's justification for granting freedom and land to the slaves based in ethics and/or economics?
2. Why was this arrangement called "half-freedom"? Is that term an oxymoron?
3. What did the ruling reveal about the slaves themselves and their role in the colony?

2-1-4. BAPTIZING SLAVES: COLONIAL GOVERNOR, COUNCIL AND ASSEMBLY, 1706

Slavery grew after England took over the colony in 1664 and renamed it New York. Spurred by the British Royal African Company, New York shippers participated in the slave trade and a slave market flourished at the foot of Wall Street. The difference between the Dutch and English attitudes towards slavery was revealed by harsh laws authorized by the royal governor together with the colonial Council and Assembly. The new laws directly confronted the ethical contradictions of slavery. Note that mulatto refers to someone of mixed European and African descent. Mestee refers to someone of mixed European and Indian descent.

Source: State of New York, Report of the Commissioners of Statutory Revision, *The Colonial Laws of New York from the Year 1664 to the Revolution,* vol. I (Albany, NY: James B. Lyon, 1894), 597–598.

An Act to Encourage the Baptizing of Negro, Indian and Mulatto Slaves, October 21, 1706.

Whereas divers of Her Majesty's good Subjects, Inhabitants of this Colony, now are, and have been willing that such Negro, Indian, and Mulatto Slaves, who belong to them, and desire the same, should be Baptized, but are deterred and hindered thereof, by reason of a Groundless opinion that has spread itself in this Colony, that by the Baptizing of such Negro, Indian or Mulatto Slaves, they would be free, and ought to be set at Liberty. In order, therefore, to put an end to all such Doubts and Scruples as have, or hereafter at any time might arise, about the same; Be it Enacted by the Governor, Council and Assembly, and it is hereby enacted by the authority of the same, That the Baptizing of any Negro, Indian or Mulatto Slave, shall not be any Cause or reason for the setting them or any of them, at Liberty.

And be it declared and Enacted by the Governor, Council and Assembly and by the Authority of the same, That all and every Negro, Indian, Mulatto and Mestee bastard Child and Children who is, are, and shall be born of any Negro, Indian, Mulatto or Mestee, shall follow ye State and Condition of the Mother and be esteemed and reputed, taken and adjudged a Slave and Slaves for all intents and purposes whatsoever.

Provided, always and be it declared and Enacted by ye said Authority That no slave whatsoever in this Colony shall at any time be admitted as a Witness for or against any Freeman in any Case, matter or Cause, Civil or Criminal whatsoever.

---

1. Why was it significant that Document 2-1-3 used the names of individual slaves while this document used general terms such as Negro, Indian, Mulatto, and Mestee?
2. Why was it significant that the English definition of slave included these four categories?
3. Did the English colonists recognize any conflict between Christianity and slavery?
4. Beyond purely religious motivations, why might the colonists have wanted to encourage the baptism of slaves?
5. Why was a child's status determined by the status of the mother, not the father?
6. Why were slaves not allowed to testify against freemen (or freewomen)? Would they have been able to testify against other slaves?
7. In terms of tone and substance, how did these English colonial policies compare with the Dutch colonial policy cited above?

2-1-5. PROSECUTING SLAVES: DANIEL HORSMANDEN, JUDGE, 1744

Being in a busy, lively town rather than isolated on a plantation, the slaves had many opportunities to rebel against slavery by commiting minor crimes, participating in an underground economy and running away (see Document 10-4-1). In addition, slaves were often hired out and allowed to keep some of their wages, thus giving them a tangible taste of freedom. While moving about the city on their daily chores, slaves could easily fraternize with each other and with free blacks. Controlling them was difficult; resistance was inevitable.

A slave rebellion in 1712 resulted in 18 executions and the passage of severe codes designed to limit the slaves' ability to congregate, trade and possess arms. A robbery and several fires in 1741 spurred fear of a "Great Negro Plot" to murder whites and destroy the city. The result was the arrest and trial of 150 slaves along with several whites accused of being co-conspirators. Five whites were executed and eight were compelled to leave the colony. The 30 slaves considered most dangerous were either hung or burned at the stake. Over eighty others were deported to the Caribbean. Throughout the spring and summer of 1741, New York was gripped by a hysteria worse than the Salem Witch trials. Responding to criticism of the way the crisis was handled, the judge, Daniel Horsmanden, published a record of the trials embellished with his own commentary. One short excerpt conveys the spirit of the moment.

Source: Daniel Horsmanden, *Journal of the Proceedings Against the Conspirators, at New York, in 1741* (New York: James Parker, 1744), 60.

Monday, May 11: Caesar and Prince were executed this day at the gallows, according to sentence. They died very stubbornly, without confessing any thing about the conspiracy, and denied they knew any thing of it to the last. The body of Caesar was accordingly hung in chains.

These two negroes bore the characters of very wicked idle fellows; had before been detected in some robberies, for which they had been publicly chastised at the whipping-post, and were persons of most obstinate and intractable tempers; so that there was no expectation of drawing anything from them which would make for the discovery of the conspiracy, though there seemed good reason to conclude, as well from their characters as what had been charged upon them by information from others, that they were the two principal ringleaders in it amongst the blacks.

It was thought proper to execute them for the robbery, and not wait for the bringing them to a trial for the conspiracy, though the proof against them was strong and clear concerning their guilt as to that also; and it was imagined, that as stealing and plundering was a principal part of the hellish scheme in agitation, amongst the inferior sort of these infernal confederates, this earnest of example and punishment might break the knot, and induce some of them to unfold this mystery of iniquity, in hopes thereby to recommend themselves to mercy, and it is probable, that with some it had this effect.

---

1. Upon what evidence and for what crimes were the slaves Caesar and Prince executed? Could they be executed on such evidence today?
2. What seem to have been the real reasons for executing them?

3. What does this document tell us about slave resistance in colonial New York?
4. What does this document tell us about white New Yorkers' state of mind concerning slavery in the 1740s?

2-1-6. EXECUTING SLAVES

The institution of slavery was generally less harsh in the Northern city than on the Southern plantation. Nonetheless, the problems of enforced labor were the same. The inevitable slave resistance bred a psychology of prejudice, insecurity, fear and violence among slaveholders and non-slaveholders alike. It was a volatile emotional mix that could easily explode, as it did in 1712 and 1742. The result was brutal.

Source: "Slave Being Burned at the Stake in Colonial New York."

1. What aspects of this drawing suggest that colonial New York was a law and order town?
2. Why did the artist include the women and child?
3. Why did the artist include the flag, the building and the church?
4. What socio-economic element of the community was observing this execution? Were the observers an unruly, irresponsible, drunken mob of ruffians? Why does it matter?

UNIT 2-2. BREAKING BARRIERS: PRACTICAL TOLERATION

One of the major legacies of the colonial era was to establish New York's tradition of what historian Milton Klein called "practical toleration," an attitude of live and let live among European settlers. This ideology contrasted with the colonists' attitudes towards Native Americans and Africans, regarding whom, Klein noted, "colonial New York mirrored the national disease."[3] Ironically, the existence of oppression for some made the promise of freedom for others all the more precious. In that sense, Indians and slaves became negative reference groups, that is, what the colonists did not want to be. Under Dutch and British rule, the concept of freedom of conscience was applied to religion, the press and education. Although never fully realized, the ideal of freedom remained alive and made New York a haven for diversity and dissent.

2-2-1. PROMOTING TOLERANCE: RESIDENTS OF FLUSHING, 1657

Then, as now, diversity was controversial. The Dutch Governor Peter Stuyvesant and the ministers of the Dutch Reformed Church in New Amsterdam feared that the colony "would become a receptacle for all sorts of heretics and fanatics." Stuyvesant tried to keep Lutherans and Jews from settling in the colony, but the Dutch West India Company insisted that they be allowed to observe their faiths privately, as they did in Holland. The same policy was applied to the Quakers whom Stuyvesant not only banned from the colony but also had tortured. In 1663, Quaker John Bowne appealed to the Company for the right to practice his religion in New Amsterdam. The Company supported Bowne and directed Stuyvesant to follow a "maxim of moderation" that would attract and keep immigrants. A few years earlier, 31 non-Quaker residents from Flushing also had opposed Stuyvesant's policies. In 1657 they wrote the famous Flushing Remonstrance, which opened the door to religious freedom in America. [4]

Source: E. B. O'Callaghan, *History of New Netherland or New York Under the Dutch*, vol. II (New York: D. Appleton and Company, 1848), 350.

You have been pleased to send up unto us a certain prohibition or command that we should not receive or entertain any of those people called Quakers … We desire therefore in this case not to judge least we be judged, neither to condemn least we be condemned, but rather [to] let every man stand and fall to his own Master. We are bound by the law to do good unto all men ... The law of love, peace and liberty [extends] to Jews, Turks, and Egyptians, as they are considered the sons of Adam ... So love, peace and liberty extending to all in Christ Jesus, condemns hatred, war and bondage ... Our desire is not to offend one of his little ones, in whatsoever form, name, or title he appears in, whether Presbyterian, Independent, Baptist, or Quaker, but shall be glad to see anything of God in any of them, desiring to do unto all men as we desire all men should do unto us, which is the true law both of Church and state.

---

1. What were the most important phrases in the Flushing Remonstrance?
2. How did the Flushing Remonstrance promote "practical toleration"?
3. Did the Flushing Remonstrance lay the groundwork for the separation of church and state?
4. What are the similarities and differences between the Flushing Remonstrance and the slave policies in Documents 2-1-3 and 2-1-4?

2-2-2. DEBATING EDUCATION: WILLIAM LIVINGSTON, LAWYER, 1753

A century later, the issue of religious tolerance was applied to education. For four years, from 1752 to 1756, New Yorkers debated the relative merits of having a sectarian college controlled by the Anglican Church or a non-sectarian college open to all Protestants (but not other religions). William Livingston, who later became governor of New Jersey, was one of the three Presbyterian lawyers who opposed Anglican domination. He believed that a college committed to only one religious sect would undermine the civic fabric of a complex, multi-denominational city. In the end, King's College was established under Anglican auspices in 1756, even though it admitted other Protestants. After the American Revolution, King's College became officially non-sectarian and, in the spirit of independence, its name was changed to Columbia College. Livingston explained his position in his newspaper, aptly named the *Independent Reflector*.

Source: *The Independent Reflector*, Numbers xvii, xviii, xx (1753).

March 22, 1753: The true Use of Education, is to qualify Men for the different Employments of Life, to which it may please God to call them. 'Tis to improve the Hearts and Understandings, to infuse a public Spirit and Love of their Country; to inspire them with the Principles of Honour and Probity; with a fervent Zeal for Liberty, and a diffusive Benevolence for Mankind; and in a Word, to make them the more extensively serviceable to the Common-Wealth.

March 29, 1753: Should our College, therefore, unhappily through our own bad Policy, fall into the Hands of any one religious Sect in the Province; Should that Sect, which is more than probable, establish its religion in the College, show favour to its votaries, and cast Contempt upon others; 'tis easy to foresee, that Christians of all other Denominations amongst us, instead of encouraging its Prosperity, will, from the same Principles, rather conspire to oppose and suppress it. Besides English and Dutch Presbyterians, which perhaps exceed all our other religious Professions put together, we have Episcopalians, Anabaptists, Lutherans, Quakers and a growing church of Moravians, all equally zealous for their discriminating Tenets. Which-soever of these has the sole Government of the College will kindle the Jealousy of the Rest, not only against the Persuasion so preferred, but the College itself. Nor can anything less be expected than a general Discontent and Tumult, which affecting all Ranks of People, will naturally tend to disturb the Tranquility and Peace of the Province.

April 12, 1753: Instead of a [private] Charter, I would propose that the College be founded and incorporated by [a public] Act of Assembly. ... While the Government of the College is in the Hands of the People, or their Guardians, its Design cannot be perverted. ...Our college, therefore, if it be incorporated by Act of Assembly, instead of opening the door to universal bigotry and establishment in church, and tyranny and oppression in the state, will secure us in the enjoyment of our respective privileges both civil and religious. For we are split into so great a variety of opinions and professions, [that] had each individual his share in the government of the academy, the jealousy of all parties combating each other, would inevitably produce a perfect freedom for each particular party.

---

1. According to Livingston, what were the civic purposes of education?
2. According to Livingston, why was it dangerous to allow one religious group to dominate the colony's new college?
3. According to Livingston, what were the advantages of a publicly run college? Did he anticipate the separation of church and state?
4. How did Livingston's arguments reinforce the Flushing Remonstrance?
5. How did Livingston's arguments reflect the uniqueness of New York City?

2-2-3. DEFINING NEW YORK: MILTON M. KLEIN, HISTORIAN, 1978

In several ground-breaking works, the historian Milton Klein drew attention to New York's neglected role in founding the nation and shaping the American character. From his perspective, the very qualities which made New York seem un-American actually made it very American. Consequently, he urged historians to take "a new look" at the colonies like New York, which, he said, deserved "the honor of initiating the American tradition."[5] As Klein explained in 1978,

Source: Milton M. Klein, "Shaping the American Tradition: The Microcosm of Colonial New York," *New York History* 59 (1978), 173–197.

Englishmen, accustomed to the homogeneity of their own country, were irritated by New York's polyglot peoples. "Our chiefest unhappyness is too great a mixture of nations," one complained in 1692. Seventy years later, another Englishman was baffled by what he saw in the province: "Being ... of different nations, different languages, and different religions, it is almost impossible to give them [New Yorkers] any precise or determinate character."

The visitors could not appreciate that it was precisely this diversity which would give New Yorkers their distinctive cast as a tolerant, easy, practical, exciting, and unstable people—just as the rest of the nation became.

Neither the Dutch nor the English set out to establish a haven for the dispossessed of Europe on the shores of the Hudson. In matters of religion, the Dutch expected to extend the Reformed Church of the fatherland. And the English conquerors, although they granted religious liberty to the Dutch, made vigorous efforts to Anglicize the whole province after they became its possessors. However, both the Dutch and the English discovered that these intentions clashed with conditions that came to exist in their colonies.

When Peter Stuyvesant urged the removal of Lutherans, Jews and Quakers as threats to religious uniformity in New Netherland, the Dutch West India Company commanded him to shut his eyes to such eccentrics, "at least not force people's consciences, but allow everyone to have his own belief, as long as he behaves quietly and legally, gives no offence to his neighbors, and does not oppose the government." What Dutch officials were really suggesting was the policy that the good burghers of old Holland had long pursued. Officially, they stood for religious conformity, but as a practical matter they connived at all deviations from orthodoxy which were not disruptive of social order. It was this policy of practical toleration that had made Holland the wealthiest and most cosmopolitan of all European states; there was even more reason to follow it in their overseas plantation, where people were at a premium. ...

For historians as for contemporary observers of the New York scene from elsewhere, accustomed to the homogeneity of New England and Virginia, the mystery of colonial New York was why its heterogeneous society did not come apart at the seams. There was neither the sense of special mission of the New Englander nor the common racism of the Virginian to knit them together. But New Yorkers did have a bond of unity, perhaps only dimly perceived and certainly rarely articulated. It was their common interest in making money and a set of political values which caused them to immerse their energies and diffuse their hostilities in politics.

Colonial New Yorkers were widely regarded as a materialistic lot. Cadwallader Colden's criticism bespoke a broadly held sentiment: "The only principle of Life propagated among the young People is to get Money and Men are only esteemed according to what they are worth, that is, the money they are possessed of." Englishmen attributed the mercenary qualities of New Yorkers to their Dutch ancestry. Of the merchants of old Amsterdam it was once said that if they thought they could make a profit by passing through Hell, they would risk burning the sails of their ships to try. The Dutch surely set the tone of New York's commercial character; they came to the New World, it was said, "to enjoy life, not to establish creeds; to secure a domestic fireside, not to make converts to political opinions." Under English rule, New Yorkers continued to follow the practice of old Holland, where, a visitor reported as early as 1662, "Next to the freedom to worship God, comes the freedom for all inhabitants to make one's living. ..."

New York's prosperity was reflected in the stability of its paper currency, its numerous civic and social organizations, its ability to support its poor citizens and also to finance a variety of public improvements, and its hospitality to artists and craftsmen. There was little "high culture" in colonial New York and few prominent native authors, but then as now, creative talent flowed to its principal city. It was even then the "open market for ideas," the "glorious vehicle…for the cross-fertilization of minds," that it has been ever since. …

…But in New York, commerce was the handmaiden of a utilitarian culture that sheared off the rough edges of the wilderness from its inhabitants and introduced the embellishments of the arts to a broad spectrum of its people. The two combined to make New York a collection of individuals who were different but who had learned that both culture and commerce required hospitality to outsiders. The society that developed in colonial New York was no "melting pot" but rather a system of stable pluralism, individuals and ethnic groups contributing to the richness of the colony's material and cultural life while resisting the intrusion of the whole on their individual autonomies. …

And finally, then as now, it was politics that not only absorbed the attention of multitudes of New Yorkers but also taught them in still another sphere the virtues of compromise and accommodation. New York was not a democracy by modern standards, but its inhabitants early learned to play the game of politics in a way that enlisted large numbers of the citizenry. The province had its patricians, as did the other colonies, but they did not exercise unchallenged authority. The Dutch—who continued to be a sizable part of New York's population well into the eighteenth century—proved to be a contentious sort—"stubborn for liberty," as one recent historian describes them. Under English rule, they were in the courts for offense of "contempt of authority" more often than any other ethnic group, reflective of their highly individualistic temper and their traditional suspicion of the agencies of government. Presbyterians, Lutherans, Quakers, Jews, German Calvinists, Dutch Calvinists, and French Calvinists all eyed each other with a proper wariness, and all of them were suspicious of the Anglicans.

New Yorkers divided also on economic and sectional lines: wholesale fur traders and retailers; those who bought directly from the Indians and those who preferred to buy pelts in Montreal; city merchants desiring to monopolize the export of flour and up-river millers who fought such a monopoly; landowners who wanted taxes on trade and merchants who urged taxes on land; Long Islanders who wanted to carry on business directly with Connecticut and Massachusetts and New York City merchants who insisted that such commerce be funneled through its harbor.

What might have produced intense intergroup violence instead was converted into vigorous politicking. Men with similar interests organized into political factions, and factions became parties, employing much of the paraphernalia of modern politics: petitions to the legislature, appeals to the voters in newspapers and pamphlets, parades and mass meetings, electoral tickets and party platforms. New Yorkers were considered a "factious people," but their politicking was not meaningless or mindless. Elections were the battleground on which the province's pluralistic society competed for control over the legislative machinery. The extraordinary diversity of the colony's citizenry compelled its political leadership to build coalitions, court other interest groups, balance tickets, awaken political consciousness, and enlist the support of large numbers of voters. …

New York's arts and sciences may have languished during the colonial period, and its population and trade may have lagged behind those of some of its neighbors, but the tumultuous and pluralistic society that developed on the Hudson and on Long Island had taught the other English colonies a precious lesson: that free, popular government could thrive on the foundations of social diversity, religious difference, and humane cosmopolitanism. It was a lesson from which the new American republic profited and from which it drew the inspiration for its future greatness.

---

1. According to Klein, what made colonial New Amsterdam and New York unique?
2. According to Klein, what was the relationship between diversity and freedom?
3. According to Klein, why was being pluralistic better than being a "melting pot"?
4. According to Klein, how did New York's cultural, economic and political characteristics provide a positive model for the nation?
5. Which primary sources in units 2-1 and 2-2 support and/or contradict Klein's analysis?

2-2-4. MAPPING THE COLONIAL CITY, 1755

Maps are rich historical resources for understanding both geography and society. They help us see how economic, social, cultural and political power relates to the physical setting of a place. They provide tangible visual evidence of the dynamics of history and enable us to test the assumptions of primary and secondary sources.

Source: Thomas A. Janvier, *In Old New York: A Classic History of New York City* (New York: Harper and Brothers, 1894), 39.

Notes on interpreting the map using the legends:

"do" means ditto or also.

Wall Street was named after the wooden wall built in 1653 at the northern end of New Amsterdam to protect it against Native Americans and the British. As the city grew, a second line of defense called the Palisades was constructed in 1745.

The Fresh Water Pond, called the Collect, was the city's main source of water until the early nineteenth century when it was deemed polluted and filled in.

The Common is today's City Hall Park.

Golden Hill near Lyon's Slip was the site of the battle in 1770 over the fourth Liberty Pole resulting in the nation's first Revolutionary fatality.

Although the black square (10) at the foot of Wall Street is labeled as the meat market, other maps identify it as the slave market.

The executions of the "Great Negro Plot" of 1741 took place near the word Palisades at the northern end of the Common, right by the Negro Burial Ground.

Bridewell, the prison, was also at number 25.

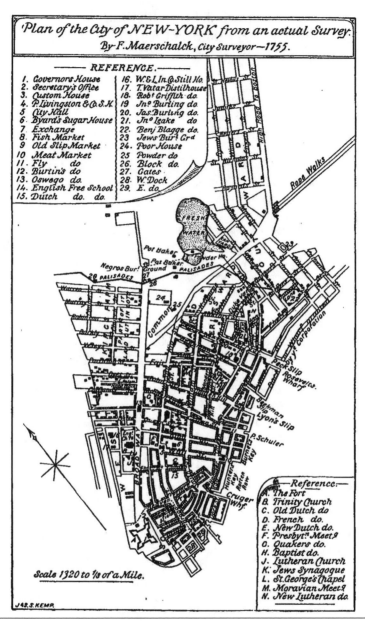

Plan of the City of NEW-YORK from an actual Survey. By F. Maerschalck, City Surveyor—1755.

1. How did the map reflect the city's economic diversity, vitality and growth in 1755?

2 How did the map record the colony's religious diversity?

4. Why were there separate burial grounds for Jews and Negroes?

5. What did the existence of a poor house say about the economic realities and the public policies of the colony?

6. How urban was New York in 1755?

UNIT 2-3. CITY BUILDING:
PETER STUYVESANT, DIRECTOR GENERAL

From the moment he landed in New Amsterdam in 1647, Peter Stuyvesant confronted controversy. The welcoming ceremonies were brief. Stuyvesant's formal greetings were received with polite applause, but parting words from outgoing Governor William Keift elicited jeers and curses from the crowd. After nine years of arbitrary taxes, rules, regulations and constant war with the Indians, the Dutch colonists were grateful for change, but hostile to all authority. Kieft was a petty, vindictive ruler who drank too much and enriched himself at the colonists' expense. He left a legacy of dissent, distrust and disorder.

Stuyvesant confronted these problems on behalf of his employers, the Dutch West India Company. Quite autocratic himself, Stuyvesant was a strict Calvinist who believed that his calling was to save New Amsterdam from itself. In the process, he made some of the same mistakes as Kieft, but he was sober and hard-working. Despite being arrogant and arbitrary, Stuyvesant earned a begrudging respect from his community and from history.

Born in 1610, Stuyvesant was the son of a minister, but was expelled from college for having an affair with his landlord's daughter. His father sent him to Amsterdam in 1630 where he rose rapidly as an agent of the Dutch West India Company. While serving as governor of Curacau in 1644, he lost a leg in a battle with Spain. The result was his famous peg leg (encircled with silver bands) and his appointment as governor of all the Dutch possessions in North America, including director general of New Amsterdam.

As Stuyvesant saw it, his mission was to "govern you as a father his children, for the advantage of the chartered West India Company, and these burghers, and this land." Although the residents of New Amsterdam shared his materialistic goals, they did not appreciate either his loyalty to the company or his paternalism. From the start they were suspicious of a man who, they said, behaved like "a peacock, with great state and pomp."[6]

Their suspicions were confirmed when Stuyvesant began issuing edicts. From his perspective, the free-wheeling town of New Amsterdam was too free-wheeling. Never a religious refuge like Boston, it had attracted restless, ambitious people from different nations speaking a variety of languages and professing a variety of religions. The only thing they shared was the desire to prosper. With a strong spirit of competitive individualism and an equally strong passion for Dutch beer, New Amsterdam contained the seeds of New York City; it was an exciting but unruly place.

Stuyvesant tried to impose order. First, he tackled personal behavior by closing taverns at nine and prohibiting the sale of alcohol to Indians. Believing that "the people are grown very wild and loose in their morals," he not only required that everyone attend church, but also banned drinking, doing business or socializing on Sundays. In order to reduce drunkenness and riot, public festivals were curtailed. Cohabitation without marriage was declared illegal. Fighting with a knife was punished heavily. Good intentions notwithstanding, these edicts fostered discontent, especially as the punishments became increasingly brutal, ranging from flogging to imprisonment to hanging.

Second, Stuyvesant addressed the physical city. Surveyors were appointed to mark out property lines and streets, which were required to be freed from garbage, animals, and privies. He banned wooden chimneys in order to reduce fires and established a night-time rattle watch to warn of fire, crime or Indian attacks. Fences and the fort were strengthened. In addition to erecting a wooden wall at the northern edge of the city in 1653, Stuyvesant built the first pier, first post office, first hospital, first school and a canal at Broad Street. The first paved street was appropriately renamed Stone Street. Although residents resented the tax on imported liquors that funded these developments, they knew that the city was being improved.

The third challenge was to bolster the economy, an objective that was critical to Stuyvesant's role as agent of the profit seeking Dutch West India Company. Accordingly, he set quality standards for bread, meat and beer as well as for wampum used as currency. Designating a place for a central market and announcing regular market days stimulated economic growth. So too, importing slaves brought profits to the Company and made New Amsterdam a major slave port. At the same time, when Stuyvesant allowed individuals to dominate certain businesses like brick making or limited the rights of traveling traders to sell in the city or claimed the right to inspect ships for smuggling, the Dutch West India Company objected. Such controls, they said, hurt the colony by diminishing opportunity and, therefore, discouraging immigration.[7]

Stuyvesant also faced opposition from Holland on the issue of religious freedom. Just as he was rebuffed by the Company and the residents for persecuting Lutherans and Quakers, so too he failed to eliminate Jews. "Liberty of conscience" was an article of faith in Holland and was protected in the colonial grant for New Netherland. However, Stuyvesant and his Dutch Reformed ministers claimed that liberty of conscience only applied to Christians. Time and again, the Jews appealed for the right to have their own cemetery, trade, own property, conduct business and serve in the militia. When Stuyvesant refused, they appealed to the Dutch West India Company which ruled jn their favor pointing out that Jews had similar rights in Holland, that Jews were financial backers of the Company itself, and that the colony needed as many settlers as it could get, regardless of religion.[8]

Stuyvesant's greatest test came on the question of government. Both he and the Company believed that strong leadership was essential for stability and profit, especially in a community characterized by diversity and prone to disorder. Furthermore, they assumed that since the Company ran the colony, the Company's interests should prevail. Democracy, they once explained, would "nourish serpents in our bosom, who finally might devour our hearts." Inevitably, these biases backfired because the more autocratic Stuyvesant became, the more the residents clamored for self-government.[9]

The outcome might have been different if Stuyvesant had been less arrogant and if his enemies had been less determined. As it was, Stuyvesant antagonized increasing numbers of residents by bullying his critics and punishing people who violated his edicts. Adrien van der Donck was a brilliant young lawyer intent upon dethroning Stuyvesant and obtaining popular rule. As their conflict intensified, Stuyvesant seized van der Donck's papers and arrested him. Supported by most of the colony's inhabitants, van der Donck took a Remonstrance to Holland condemning Stuyvesant as a despised "vulture" who was devouring the body politic.

The Dutch West India Company considered recalling Stuyvesant, but instead granted New Amsterdam its first form of municipal government. Established in 1653, it included five aldermen (*schepens*), two co-mayors (*burgomasters*) and one treasurer (*schout-fiscal*) to complement the director general and his already existing Board of Nine advisors. The only problem was that Stuyvesant insisted upon appointing the new officers himself, just as he already appointed the Board of Nine. He was somewhat chastened, but still in power.[10]

Gradually, however, his dominance diminished. Together with the Board of Nine, the new officers challenged Stuyvesant's control of the colony's taxes. New settlements on Long Island (today's Brooklyn and Queens) demanded the right to representative government. When Stuyvesant claimed "absolute" authority to deny their appeals, they complained to the Dutch about Stuyvesant's "arbitrary government." This time the Company sided with Stuyvesant, but they took away some of his taxing powers. Meanwhile, he faced challenges from the Indians, such as the Peach Tree War of 1655, plus threats from the ever-expanding English. [11]

In 1657 citizenship rights were redefined by creating a distinction between Great Burghers and Small Burghers. The Great Burghers were the colony's wealthiest, most prominent people (including one woman) who paid fifty guilders for the exclusive privilege of holding office. The Small Burghers included anyone who was born in New Amsterdam or who lived there for over a year or who paid twenty guilders. Now they too would be considered citizens and given full rights to engage in trade or business. Whereas few people applied for the status of Great Burgher, almost everyone applied to be a Small Burgher—shopkeepers, shoemakers and even chimney sweeps. Thus, although the new power structure was based on wealth, it was more inclusive than the English colonies where citizenship remained limited. Gradually, democracy seemed to be winning over autocracy. [12]

Undaunted, Stuyvesant pressed ahead. On the one hand, he won support by establishing a school, a hospital and an orphan asylum. A settlement called Nieuw Harlem was established in hopes of protecting the city's northern border from English invasion. On the other hand, he antagonized the community by imposing taxes and banning the driving of wagons on any street but Broadway in order to reduce accidents. He issued an endless series of edicts to reinforce earlier edicts and increased the punishments for transgressors. Consequently, there was a growing sense, as one official put it, that Stuyvesant was like a "wolf: the older he gets, the more inclined he is to bite." [13]

Despite all of his constructive contributions, Stuyvesant failed as a leader because of his utter disregard of public opinion. To be sure, he was an appointed, not an elected, official, but his staunch refusal to tolerate criticism was foolhardy. Although he accepted change when it was forced upon him, he never changed his ornery ways. Once he even declared that "We derive our authority from God and the Company, not from a few ignorant subjects." Ultimately, the discontent undid him. When the British challenged Dutch control of the colony in 1664, the residents (Stuyvesant's son among them) refused to defend it. Not only were they relieved to depose Stuyvesant and the Dutch West India Company, but they lacked the troops and the arms to resist. [14]

After the surrender, Stuyvesant was called back to Holland to report to the Company which, considering all of his efforts on its behalf, was surprisingly critical of his command. True to form, he pointed out their own shortcomings and inadequate support. Three years later, he returned to his old colony, now called New York, and retired to his farm (or *bouwerie*) which stretched from today's Fourth Avenue to the East River and from Fifth to Seventeenth Streets. Stuyvesant died in 1672 and was buried in a Dutch Reformed chapel on his estate. Reflecting the shift from Dutch to English dominance, it was replaced in 1799 by an Episcopal church, St. Marks in the Bowery, at today's 10th Street and Second Avenue, where a plaque, street names and a housing development provide meager memorials to Stuyvesant.

During his remarkably long 17-year tenure, Stuyvesant made a difference. Because of him, the colony established the basic institutions of urban living so essential to stability and prosperity. Although his edicts were often onerous, they acknowledged problems, sought solutions, and promoted civic order. Ironically, they also fostered patterns of democracy and tolerance. Stuyvesant's greatest shortcoming was seeing himself solely as an agent of the Dutch West India Company, rather than as the leader of a new community with a unique personality based on diversity, competitive individualism and the pursuit of profit. Although he failed on the interpersonal level, Stuyvesant succeeded in laying the groundwork for a city that would always seek new ways to grow and prosper while always wrestling with the tensions between order and freedom.

---

1. Why could Stuyvesant be considered an innovative and important city builder?
2. What were Stuyvesant's limitations as a leader?
3. In what ways did modern New York emerge from old New Amsterdam?

2-3-1. RULING NEW AMSTERDAM: PETER STUYVESANT *ET AL*, 1650s

Societies pass rules and regulations in order to meet specific challenges. Consequently, those rules and regulations reveal what was really going on in the community. By providing a window into a community's political, economic and social structure, rules and regulations reflect the character of a society—its problems as well as its priorities, the style of its leaders as well as the needs of its people.

Source: Bertold Fernow (ed.), *The Records of New Amsterdam from 1653 to 1674 Anno Domini*, vol. I. (New York: Knickerbocker Press, 1897), 1–11, 15, 21–22, 35–36, 42.

May 31, 1647: Petrus Stuyvesant, Director General of New Netherland and the Islands thereto pertaining, Captain and Commander of the Company's ships and yachts in West India cruising, to All, who may hear or see there presents read, Greeting:

Whereas we have experienced the insolence of some of our inhabitants, when drunk, their quarrelling, fighting and hitting each other even on the Lord's day of rest... to the annoyance of our neighbors and to the disregard, nay contempt of God's holy laws and ordinances, which command us, to keep holy in His honor His day of rest, the Sabbath, and forbid all bodily injury and murder, as well as the means and inducements, leading thereto,

Therefore, by the advice of the late Director general and of our Council and to the end, that instead of God's curse falling upon us we may receive his blessing, we charge, enjoin and order herewith principally all brewers, tapsters and innkeepers, that none of them shall upon the Lord's day of rest, by us called Sunday, entertain people, tap or draw any wine, beer or strong waters of any kind and under any pretext before 2 of the clock, in case there is no preaching or else before 4, except only to a traveler and those who are daily customers, fetching the drinks to their own homes,— this under penalty of being deprived of their occupation and besides a fine of 6 Carolusguilders for each person who shall be found drinking wine or beer within the stated time...

And to prevent the all too ready drawing of a knife, fighting, wounding and the mishaps resulting therefrom, therefore with the approval of the Very Wise, High Council of the City of Amsterdam, we command, that all who shall draw or have drawn their knives or swords rashly or in anger against one another, shall pay a fine of 100 Carolusguilders, or if they have not the money, be employed in the most menial labor for half a year with bread and water for food...

September 28, 1648: Great complaints are daily made to the Director general and Council by the Indians or natives, that some inhabitants of New Netherland set the natives to work and use them in their service, but let them go unrewarded after the work is done and refuse, contrary to all international law, to pay the savages for their labors. These Indians threaten, that if they are not satisfied and paid, they will make themselves paid or recover their remunerations by other improper means,

Therefore, to prevent all trouble as much as possible, the Director General and Council warn all inhabitants, who owe anything to an Indian for wages or otherwise, to pay it without dispute, and if in the future they employ savages, they shall be liable to pay upon the evidence and complaint of Indians (who for good reason shall be considered credible witnesses in such cases), under the penalty of such a fine, as the circumstances shall indicate as proper.

April 16, 1650: The Director General and Council have consented, on the request of the bakers, that provisionally for the accommodation of the community they may bake white bread, but not cakes or cracknels, provided that they bake said white bread to conform in weight with the rules of the Fatherland. The bakers are also charged that the common bread must only be baked from clean wheat or rye flour, as it comes from the mills, so that the community may not have cause to complain of the thinness and meagerness of the common bread.

February 26, 1656: Whereas the Burgomasters of the City of Amsterdam in New Netherland find that great many people within the City pay little attention to their fireplaces and chimney sweeping, which has already caused fires several times and will create further difficulties from conflagrations, especially as most of the houses are built of wood, some are roofed with reeds, have wooden and plastered chimneys, which is very dangerous, and which we must prevent as much as possible,

Therefore, ...we have appointed firemasters... to inspect, whenever they please, all houses and chimneys in the jurisdiction of this City and there to do for the prevention of fires what is necessary and to collect such fines, as are prescribed...

May 29, 1656: The Director General and Council of N. N., with the advice of the Burgomasters and the chief officers of the burghers, herewith inform and warn everybody, that nobody shall henceforth lodge any savages overnight between here and the fresh water under a fine of 25 fl. payable by everyone who hereafter harbors an Indian overnight without a pass signed by the Director General or the Secretary. ...

August 16, 1658: Whereas many, even the greatest part of the burghers and inhabitants of this City build their privies even with the ground with an opening towards the street, so that hogs may consume the filth and wallow in it, which not only creates a great stench and therefore great inconvenience to the passers-by, but also makes the streets foul and unfit for use,

Therefore, to obviate it the Burgomasters and Schepens herewith order and command that all and everybody, whoever they or he may be, shall break down and remove such privies coming out upon the street within 8 days of the publication hereof, rebuilding them in such places, that they give the least offense to the community under the penalty of 6fl. for the first time, double as much the second and arbitrary correction the third time.

Furthermore as the roads and streets of this City are by the constant rooting of the hogs made unfit for driving over in wagons or carts, the Burgomasters and Schepens direct and order, that every owner of hogs in or about the City shall put a ring through the noses of their hogs to prevent them from rooting, within 8 days under penalty of 2 fl. for each time that this ordinance is not obeyed...

January 7, 1659: Know ye, that for the convenience of everybody it has been deemed best and decided to establish in this City and jurisdiction a market of lean and fat cattle, oxen, sheep, goats, pigs, bucks and the like and with the approval of the Director general and the Council to have made and put up convenient stalls for the benefit of everybody bringing cattle to the market.

---

1. Which of these regulations were reasonable? Which were unreasonable?
2. How did the regulations reveal the strengths and weaknesses of New Amsterdam's economy?
3. Based on these regulations, what mixed feelings did the colonists have towards Native Americans?
4. How did these regulations reflect Stuyvesant's personality and his vision for New Amsterdam?

2-3-2. OPPOSING STUYVESANT: ADRIEN VAN DER DONCK, LAWYER, 1649

Adrien van der Donck was an ambitious young lawyer who led the resistance to Stuyvesant and the quest for democracy in New Amsterdam. His short-term goal was more participation by the inhabitants in local government, but his long-term goal was to free the city of control by the Dutch West India Company altogether. Thus, his objective was truly revolutionary. Stuyvesant considered him so dangerous that he had van der Donck arrested, but van der Donck would not be deterred and took his case to the Company itself. On October 16, 1649, he issued a formal remonstrance, or protest, against Stuyvesant's undemocratic leadership. Ultimately his efforts resulted in the first grant of self-government by the Dutch to the city, a concession that contributed significantly to the development of democracy in the new world.

Source: J. Franklin Jameson (ed.), *Narratives of New Netherland, 1609–1664*
(New York: Charles Scribner's Sons, 1909), 330–331, 344–345, 350.

Mr. Stuyvesant has almost all the time from his first arrival up to our leaving
been busy building, laying masonry, making, breaking, repairing and the like,
but generally in matters of the Company and with little profit to it; for upon
some things more money was spent than they were worth; and though at the
first he put in order the church which came into his hands very much out of
repair, and shortly afterwards made a wooden wharf, both acts very serviceable
and opportune, yet after this time we do not know that anything has been done
or made that is entitled to the name of a public work, though there is income
enough, as is to be seen in the statement of the yearly revenue...

Thus in a short time very great discontent has sprung up on all sides,
not only among the burghers, who had little to say, but also among the
Company's officers themselves... But it was all in vain, there was very little
or no amendment; and the greater the endeavors to help, restore and raise
up everything, the worse it has been; for pride has ruled when justice dictated
otherwise, just as if it were disgraceful to follow advice, and as if everything
should come from one head. ...

But there is always misunderstanding and discontent, and if anything is said
before the Director of these matters more than pleases him, very wicked and
spiteful words are returned. Those moreover whose office requires them to
speak of such things are, if he is in no good fit, very freely berated as clowns,
bear-skinners, and the like. ...

His Honor said, and openly asserted, that he was allowed, on behalf of the
Company, to sell powder, lead and guns to the Indians, but no one else could
do so. ... This begat so much discontent among the common people, and even
among other officers, that it is not to be expressed; and had the people not been
persuaded and held back, something extraordinary would have happened. ...

Besides this, the country of the Company is so taxed, and is burdened and
kept down in such a manner, that the inhabitants are not able to appear beside
their neighbors of Virginia or New England, or to take any enterprise. ...

Now as his Honor was not willing to convene the people however urgent our
request, or that we should do it, we went round from house to house and spoke
to the commonality. The General has, from that time, burned with rage. ...

1. How did van der Donck's criticize Stuyvesant's city building policies?
2. How did van der Donck criticize Stuyvesant's leadership style?
3. How much discontent did there seem to be in New Amsterdam?
4. Explain how this document reflected the quest for democracy in New Amsterdam

2-3-3. SURRENDERING TO THE BRITISH: EDMUND B. O'CALLAGHAN, HISTORIAN, 1848

The nineteenth-century historian, Edmund B. O'Callaghan, recounted New Amsterdam's surrender to the British in 1664. Although he covered the practical reasons for surrender, his real focus was on the relationship between Stuyvesant and the inhabitants of New Amsterdam. Like all historians, O'Callaghan had a point of view that enhanced the drama of the historical moment. Note that 93 male inhabitants signed the appeal including Stuyvesant's son

Source: E. B. O'Callaghan, *History of New Netherland or New York Under the Dutch,* vol. II (New York: D. Appleton, 1848), 521–531.

From the moment [British Colonel Richard] Nicolls cast anchor before New Amsterdam, that city might be said to have been virtually surrendered. ...The Schout, Burgomasters and Schepens, the officers of the Burgher Guard, and several of the citizens assembled at the City hall to learn how matters stood. Non-resistance was at once openly avowed. ...

Two commissioners from the New England colonies had joined the fleet and now, in the hope of making a favorable impression on the minds of the citizens, visited New Amsterdam under a flag of truce. They came, they said, to offer very favorable conditions, in the King's name, to all the inhabitants. Should these be refused, they must be held guiltless of any cruelties which might follow. Thereupon [Connecticut] Governor Winthrop placed a sealed letter in the Director-general's hands, and the commissioners took their leave.

On his return to the fort, Stuyvesant opened this communication in the presence of the Council and the Burgomasters. The latter demanded permission to communicate this paper to the other city magistrates; but as it was considered "rather disadvantageous than favorable to communicate such letter to the inhabitants," the Director-general refused the request. The Burgomasters declared, on the other hand, that "all which regarded the public welfare ought to be made public." The Director remonstrated, and endeavored to explain the pernicious effects of such a course. The Burgomasters would not be convinced, and Stuyvesant in a fit of indignation "tore the letter in pieces." The city fathers thereupon protested against "the consequences of dilacerating that paper," and took their departure in high dungeon.

The citizens now collected in numbers around the City Hall. "Suddenly the work of setting palisades on the land side of the city ceased," and three of the principal burghers presented themselves before the Council and demanded a copy of the letter, "not without a sinister and covert hint at something worse happening." They were deaf to all reason, and dissatisfied with the plea that the paper was destroyed. Stuyvesant, seeing the critical state of affairs, hastened in person to the City Hall "to animate the burghers to return to and continue the public work."... A general cry was now raised for "the letter!"... Fearful of a mutiny, Stuyvesant retired and reported to the Council what he had witnessed. To prevent all further difficulties, the pieces of the torn letter were collected and a copy of the communication made out, and delivered to the Burgomasters.

Though the power the Director-general exercised for seventeen years had now evidently passed away, and the truncheon he had so long wielded was shivered, he still considered it his duty to vindicate the right of his superiors to the country. In answer to the summons of Nicolls, he, therefore, returned a lengthy manifesto in which he…repudiated, in direct terms, the pretence now put forth in the name of his Britannic Majesty to "an indisputable right to all the lands in the north parts of America". …

Nicolls, now perceiving that the Dutch Governor was averse to the surrender, ordered two of his ships to disembark the troops below Breukelen, where a company of cavalry and a party of volunteers had already taken up a position. Hyde, the commander of the squadron, was directed at the same time, to lay the other two frigates broadside before the city. Stuyvesant was standing on one of the points of the fort, when he perceived the frigates approaching. It was the critical moment on which hung the fate of the city and the lives of its inhabitants. …

The greatest consternation prevailed throughout the city when this answer became known. Many of the inhabitants, with their wives and children, implored the Director, with tears, to submit. But Stuyvesant was obdurate. "He had rather be carried a corpse to his grave." The civic authorities, the clergy, and the commanders of the Burgher Corps now assembled at the City Hall, to hear the report of the Commissioners. All further resistance was considered not only useless but rash, and, on motion of the Reverend Joannes Megapolenses, it was resolved to… [appeal for] "an honorable and reasonable capitulation."

The position of Stuyvesant was now one of extreme difficulty. In front a determined foe, backed by constantly increasing numbers from New England; in his rear a disaffected burghery, headed, as it were, by his own son. The condition of the city was such as forbade all hope of withstanding a siege. It was open along the banks of both rivers; at the northern, or land side, its only defence was a hastily erected fence, composed of "old and rotten palisades, in front of which was thrown up a small breast-work, about three to three and a half feet high and scarcely two feet wide." . …

The stock of provisions was equally low; there were not more than a thousand schepels of wheat in store; the supply of meat and peas was much smaller, and as for water, there was not a well in the fort. To add to these difficulties, disaffection spread from the citizens to the soldiers, for the latter, finding that the burghers could no longer mount guard, cared little for the issue, and were heard speculating on the opportunities for plunder they should shortly have. "Now we hope to pepper those devilish traders who have so long salted us; we know where booty is to be found, and where the young women live who wear gold chains." Under all these circumstances, there was but one course to adopt, and that was to capitulate.

---

1. According to O'Callaghan, how well did Stuyvesant handle this crisis?
2. How many different factors influenced the surrender? Which factors made surrender inevitable?

3. Did O'Callaghan's account suggest that the struggle for democracy within New Amsterdam had succeeded?
4. How do the biographical sketch and the documents above support and/or contradict O' Callaghan's depiction of Stuyvesant?

2-3-4. DRAMATIZING SURRENDER

Considering that Stuyvesant was a proud man, a firm ruler and a dedicated employee of the Dutch West India Company, it must have been very difficult for him to surrender to the British in 1664 without a fight. The drama of his dilemma is captured by the following drawing.

Source: The Manhattan Company, *"Manna-hattin," The Story of New York* (Port Washington, NY: Ira J. Friedman, Inc., 1929), 47.

1. How did the artist convey Stuyvesant's personality through his facial expression, clothing, accessories and stance? What words best describe Stuyvesant?
2. How did the artist depict the relationship between Stuyvesant and the colonists?
3. How did the artist portray class and power differences in the colony?
4. Explain the advantages and disadvantages of the harbor.
5. How well does this drawing confirm or refute the evidence in Documents 2-3-1 to 2-3-3?

UNIT 2-4. LAW AND ORDER: THE STAMP ACT RIOTS

The debate over the meaning of freedom was central to the debate over the American Revolution in New York City. Issues of political freedom were interwoven with issues of economic freedom in a bustling city committed to expansion and hostile to all restraints. After the expense of waging the French and Indian War from 1757 to 1763, England increased taxes on the colonies starting with the 1764 Sugar Act followed by the 1765 Stamp Act. Even though the rates were low, they strained power relations not only between the colonists and the British Empire but also among the colonists themselves. The result was a multi-layered crisis.

While the Sugar Act was a tariff on imports that was mainly visible to merchants, the Stamp Act was a direct tax on a variety of items that were used by many people, rich and poor. It taxed diplomas, licenses and legal transactions such as wills, deeds, marriages, affidavits, court proceedings, playing cards and dice. Newspapers, pamphlets, calendars and almanacs had to be printed on special English paper with special stamps for advertisements, all of which raised the price for the consumer. The cost of the stamps varied with the items being taxed and was paid in cash, which was in short supply. To make matters worse, the revenue would be used to support the hated British troops who were stationed in the colonies.

Resistance was immediate. Nine colonial assemblies sent resolutions of protest to the British Parliament. Starting with Boston in August 1765, riots erupted across the colonies and, in early October, a Stamp Act Congress convened in New York City. As the first inter-colonial conference, the meeting was an important statement of protest and a significant (if still cautious) step towards independence. New York City initiated another form of protest in late October when merchants agreed not to trade with England and retailers agreed not to sell British goods. Instead of imported cloth, colonists vowed to weave and wear homespun.

It is often assumed that the local elite led the Stamp Act Riots, which paralyzed New York City for five days in early November 1865. However, the record is complicated. The riots were orchestrated by the Sons of Liberty, an ad-hoc group supported by sailors and other workers. Their leaders were upwardly mobile middle class merchants and sea captains, like Isaac Sears and Alexander McDougall, who were not part of the mercantile elite. Nonetheless, they cooperated with members of the elite who saw that popular protests could help their own cause and who, in turn, added status to the Sons of Liberty. The relationship between these three groups was delicate because the upper- and middle-class leaders often disagreed and because the working-class rioters often followed their own agendas. Whether together or separately, they moved the colony closer toward revolution.[15]

2-4-1. CONDEMNING THE RIOTS: JOHN MONTRESOR, BRITISH ENGINEER, 1765

One of the most interesting primary sources for the Stamp Act Riots was the journal of Captain John Montresor, a British engineer asked by British General Thomas Gage to strengthen the fort against possible attack by the rioters. (Note that Randall's Island was originally called Montresor's Island.)

Source: G. D. Scull (ed.), *The Montresor Journals/New York Historical Society Collections* XIV, (New York: New York Historical Society, 1882), 336–337.

23rd October 1765. Arrived the vessel with the Stamps...2000 people (mob) on the Battery expecting the Stamps would be landed, but were disappointed. However, they were secretly landed in the night and deposited in the fort and took charge of by the Governor. ... Many placards put up threatening the Lives, Houses and properties of any one who shall either issue or receive a stamp.

31st October 1765. Several people in mourning for the near Issue of the stamps and the Internment of their liberty. Descended even to the Bag-gammon Boxes at the merchant's Coffee House, being covered with Black and the Dice in Crape. This night a mob in 3 squads went through the streets crying "Liberty" at the same time breaking the Lamps & threatening particulars that they would the next night pull down their houses. Some thousands of windows broke. Major James of the Royal Artillery—threatened to be burned alive by the Populace as Commanding the troops in the Fort for the protection of the Stamps. Merchants of this place met to Know whether they shall carry on trade or not. Agreed in the negative till the 1st of May.

November 1st. ...This night the Rabble or rather Rebels assembled again early in the evening & Continued the Riot til 4 this morning, their numbers about 2000, during which time they broke open the Governor's coach house under the Fort fire & then took out his chariot & 2 Sleighs & a chair which they burnt in the Bowling Green with effigies & Gallows &c &c... 300 Carpenters belonging to the mob were collected & prepared to attempt to cut down the Fort Gate on the first shot fired from thence. From thence they proceeded to major James' House and there after breaking every window, cut down all the window shutters & broke all the Partitions—then they destroyed 91/4 casks of Wine & destroyed & Stole all his plate, Furniture, apparel, Books &c to the value of L1500. (Artillery officers & Guard to the Goal). The Mob got the permission to toll the Bells of the several churches, meetings and other Houses of worship except the churches of England, which they broke into & tolled the bells beginning at ½ after Nine.

---

1. According to Montresor, what methods did the rioters use to make their point? How destructive were they? How effective were they?
2. What is the difference between rabble and rebel? Was this a slip of the tongue?
3. According to Montresor, were the rioters well organized? Who was in control?
4. What words best reveal Montresor's point of view?

2-4-2. SEEKING PEACE: COLONIAL MERCHANTS, 1765

One reflection of the relationship between the elite and the rioters was the following appeal for calm posted at the Merchant's Coffee House on November 6, 1765 after five days of riot.

Source: *The Letters and Papers of Cadwallader Colden,* vol. VII (New York: New-York Historical Society, 1923), 91.

To the Freeholders & Inhabitants of the City of New York
Gentlemen:
We have now the Stamp'd Papers in our own Hands, so that there is a Prospect of our enjoying Peace once more; all then that we have to do is to promote this Peace; to do which we are under many Obligations; of which what follows will be a Proof:

1st We have entirely accomplish'd *all we wanted* in rescuing the Stamps from the Hands of our inveterate Enemy; to proceed any farther then would only hurt the good Cause in which we are engaged.

2nd As we have promised, both for ourselves & by our Representatives whom we ourselves have chosen, that if the Stamps were lodged in the Hands of these our Representatives (as they now are) we would be quiet & no Harm should be done, the Honour & Credit of the City lie at Stake, & shall we ruin our own Credit? I am persuaded no one would be so infatuated as to attempt it. Let us then as we have joined Hand in Hand in effecting the Peace that now subsists also join in preserving it. This will shew that we have Conduct as well as Courage, prove that we have acted, not as a Mob, but as Friends to Liberties & be as strong an Argument as we can use to obtain a Repeal of the Stamp Act.

---

1. What was the difference between "Freeholders and Inhabitants" and what did it reveal about the rioters?
2. If the rich controlled the mob, why did they need to post this appeal?
3. Did this letter suggest that there was cross-class cooperation and/or cross-class conflict?
4. Why did the authors distinguish between having "accomplished all we wanted" and going "any farther"? What might "farther" have meant? To whom? Did the authors fear it?

2-4-3. RECONSIDERING THE RIOTS: JESSE LEMISH, HISTORIAN, 1969

British General Gage claimed that "the sailors, who are the only People who may be properly stiled Mob, are entirely at the Command of the Merchants who employ them."[16] The historian Jesse Lemish disagreed and reassessed the role played by sailors in the Sons of Liberty and in the pre-revolutionary protests.

Source: Jesse Lemish, "The American Revolution Seen from the Bottom Up," in Barton J. Bernstein (ed.), *Towards A New Past: Dissenting Essays in American History*, (New York: Pantheon Books, 1968), 19-21.

The Stamp Act Congress had adjourned without answering the question, What is to be *done*? The Stamp Act riots showed that the mob had begun to think and reason. Historians have been hesitant to acknowledge it. Instead they have preferred to accept the testimony of British officials who attributed the riots to "the Wiser and better Sort," who stirred up the lower class in behalf of a cause in which that class had no real interest: thus they easily turned to plunder and violence for its own sake. But gentlemen of property associated themselves with mob violence only under the most extreme conditions. Those conditions had not been achieved in 1765.

British officials assumed that lawyers and property owners were the riots' secret leaders partly because of a bias which said that leaders *had* to be people of "Consequence." In addition, those officials were accustomed to confronting members of the upper class as political adversaries in the courts and the assembly halls. But a new politics—a politics of the street—was replacing the old politics of the assembly hall. British officials failed to understand these new politics. ...

The upper classes may not have been pulling the strings in the Stamp Act riots. The assumption that an uninterested mob had to be artificially aroused— created—disregards the ability of the people to think for themselves; like everyone else in the colonies, they had real grievances against the British. Unlike others, they had fewer legal channels through which to express their grievances. So they took to the streets in pursuit of political goals. ...

The struggle against the Stamp Act was also a struggle against colonial leadership. Declarations had not prevented the Act's taking effect. Those who had *declared* now had to *do*, but they could do no better than a boycott: the cessation of all business which required the use of stamps. This strategy put pressure on the English merchants, but it also increased the pressure on the American poor, the hungry, the prisoners in city jails who could not hope for release so long as the lawyers refused to do business.

Radicals protested against the absurdity of American blustering about liberty and then refusing to do anything about it: if a law was wrong, then it was no law and business ought to go on without the use of stamps. They urged disobedience. Upper-class leaders demanded legality and tried, sometimes by shady means, to suppress or distort this dissent. But the radicals continued their pressure, and they were supported by the self-defeating character of the boycott strategy. The more time that passed without ship sailings, the more attractive a policy of disobedience became to merchants, and they began to send their ships out without stamped papers.

British officials began to cave in; they were worried about "an Insurrection of the Poor against the Rich," united action by unemployed artisans, and the increasing numbers of unruly seamen who were pouring into the colonial cities and finding no way to get out. The seamen—"the...people...most dangerous on these Occasions"—especially worried customs officials. Instead of waiting for them to force their captains, the officials yielded, giving way before enormous pressures and allowing a radical triumph. Then the Parliament itself backed down, repealing the Stamp Act.

The poor people of the colonies had reason to congratulate themselves: word of their actions had thrown a scare into Parliament, and they might even suspect that the economic rationale which Parliament had offered for repeal covered its fear of a challenge not so much to its view of the constitution as to its actual authority in the colonies. Thus the meaning of the Stamp Act crisis goes beyond the pursuit of constitutional principles. The lower class had spoken out against the British, against deference, and against colonial leadership, and they had won.

---

1. According to Lemish, why did the British (and many historians) miss the real message of the Stamp Act riots?
2. According to Lemish, why were riots still deemed necessary after the Stamp Act Congress and the boycott against British goods?
3. What was the difference between the "politics of the street" and the "politics of the assembly hall"? Why was this distinction important for understanding the history of New York and the nation?
4. According to Lemish why and how were the Stamp Act riots truly revolutionary? Whose power did they challenge?

2-4-4. REPRESENTING NEW YORK, 1774

The Stamp Act crisis began a decade-long struggle over power between England and the colonies. Tensions increased in 1767 when Parliament taxed imports on tea, glass, paper, lead and paint. Although Parliament rescinded most of those taxes in 1770 and although the level of taxation was actually low, the principle of no taxation without representation became an increasingly powerful rallying cry across the colonies. In 1773, when Parliament reaffirmed the tax on imported tea and gave its East India Company a monopoly on trading tea, it sparked tea parties during which colonists threw tea from British ships into the harbors of Boston and New York. Dressing up like Native Americans not only camouflaged prominent participants, but also asserted a new sense of identity associated solely with the Americas.

In 1774, Parliament passed a series of acts so offensive that they were labeled the Intolerable Acts and the colonists began planning a Continental Congress to coordinate further resistance. New Yorkers were divided about how strongly how to oppose the British, setting moderate merchants, lawyers, and the De Lancey family against radical merchants, tradesmen, and the Livingston family. In May 1774, the latter group formed a Mechanics Committee to better articulate their position and challenge the power of the moderates, who were the colonial elite. The new committee marked a major step towards democratizing colonial politics. Although the Mechanics Committee continued to work with the moderates, they asserted their independence by rejecting two of the five Continental Congress delegates nominated by the moderates in favor of two of their own (Lispenard and McDougall). In the process, they showed how complicated the revolutionary struggle really was.[17]

(Note that because this 1774 document reflects colonial era writing conventions, the letter f should be read as an s.)

Source: "Advertisement. At a general Meeting of the Committee of Mechanicks, 1774," Broadsides and Other Printed Ephemera Collection, Library of Congress Prints and Photographs Division.

Advertiſement.

AT a general Meeting of the Committee of MECHANICKS, at the Houſe of EDWARD BARDIN, yeſterday Evening, the Nomination of the COMMITTEE of MERCHANTS, of Delegates to ſerve at the General Congreſs, was taken into Conſideration, and the Names of the Perſons reſpectively read for their Concurrence; when a Negative was put upon Meſſ. Duane and Alſop, and Mr. Leonard Liſpenard, and Mr. Alexander M'Dougall, were nominated in their Stead: And as the Committee of Merchants did refuſe the Mechanicks a Repreſentation in their Body, or to conſult with their Committee, or offer the Names of the Perſons nominated to them for their Concurrence, the Mechanicks of this City and County, and every other Friend to the Liberties of his Country, are moſt earneſtly requeſted to attend at the General Meeting, at the City Hall, to-morrow, (being Thurſday) at 12 o'Clock, agreeable to the Time propoſed by the Committee of Merchants, to give their Voices for the five following Perſons, or to chooſe ſuch others as they may think proper.

ISAAC LOW,
PHILIP LIVINGSTON,
JOHN JAY,
LEONARD LISPENARD,
ALEX. M'DOUGALL.

WEDNESDAY, July 6, 1774.

---

1. How much cooperation was there between the merchants and the mechanics over the nomination of delegates to the Continental Congress?
2. What role did the mechanics plan to play by attending the general meeting called by the merchants at City Hall? Why were they still meeting with the merchants at all?
3. How does this document confirm and/or contradict Lemish's analysis of the Sons of Liberty?
4. Overall, what economic, political and social factors promoted and/or retarded the spirit of rebellion in New York City?

SELECTED RESOURCES

Berlin, Ira, and Leslie M. Harris, (eds), *Slavery in New York*. New York: The New Press and the New York Historical Society, 2005.

Davis, Thomas J. *A Rumor of Revolt: The "Great Negro Plot" in Colonial New York*. New York: The Free Press, 1985.

Goodfriend, Joyce D. *Before the Melting Pot: Society and Culture in Colonial New York City, 1664-1730*. Princeton, NJ: Princeton University Press, 1992.

Headley, Joel Tyler. *The Great Riots of New York, 1712-1873*. New York: Dover, 1873/1971.

Hodges, Graham Russell. *Root and Branch: African Americans in New York and East Jersey, 1613-1863*. Chapel Hill, NC: University of North Carolina Press, 1999.

Ketchum, Richard M. *Divided Loyalties: How the American Revolution Came to New York*. New York: Henry Holt, 2002.

Lepore, Jill. *New York Burning: Liberty, Slavery, and Conspiracy in Eighteenth Century Manhattan*. New York: Knopf, 2005.

Schecter, Barnet. *The Battle for New York: The City at the Heart of the American Revolution*. New York: Penguin Books, 2002.

Shorto, Russell. *The Island at the Center of the World: The Epic Story of Dutch Manhattan and the Forgotten Colony that Shaped America*. New York: Doubleday, 2004.

www.conferencehouse.org/vtour: Revolutionary era house on Staten Island

www.frauncestavernmuseum.org: George Washington's farewell to his troops

www.morrisjumel.org: George Washington headquarters

www.nypl.org/research/sc/afb: African Burial Ground

www.slaveryinnewyork.org: Museum of the City of New York exhibit

www.theoldstonehouse.org: replica of Dutch farmhouse

CHAPTER 3

1800–1840

In 1809, the author Washington Irving named New York City Gotham after an old English town where the residents pretended to be crazy in order to keep the king from moving in and taking over. The label lasted because New Yorkers often seemed to be irrational, especially in the hectic, competitive early-nineteenth-century city. "The busy hum of commerce, the noise of revelry, the rattling equipages of splendid luxury, were unknown in the peaceful settlement of New Amsterdam." Irving regretted that the "sweet tranquility" of a golden age based on simplicity had been replaced by "the hardships, the labours, the dissentions, and the wars, occasioned by the thirst of gold."[1] Success bred its own evils.

The period from 1800 to 1840 was particularly tumultuous for New York City. In an era when democracy was developing and the national economy was expanding, anxiety and anger often accompanied optimism and opportunity. The port was booming, factories were emerging, banks and stores were multiplying geometrically. Finally more prominent than Philadelphia, Gotham was already settled up to Houston Street. When the city's fathers decided in 1811 to control Manhattan's growth with a grid of streets all the way up to 155th Street, they proclaimed their commitment to profit and practicality. Hills, rocks, trees and streams could give way to regularity and efficiency, but the city could never really be controlled.

The result was conflict over the roles of politicians and voters, men and women, blacks and whites, employers and workers. During the 1830s, these tensions came to a head. They are examined in this chapter through a riot, a sensational murder and a strike. In addition, a profile of John Jacob Astor provides perspective on the perpetual pursuit of wealth with which Gotham has always been identified. Reflecting on this period late in life, an old cartman acknowledged that New York was "a go-ahead place" dedicated to progress and prosperity. However, he feared that "New York has been growing *great*, without growing *good*." New Yorkers (and Americans) have always struggled with that dilemma.[2]

UNIT 3-1. LAW AND ORDER: THE ANTI-ABOLITIONIST RIOTS

Nineteenth-century New York City was a riotous place. Continuing the eighteenth-century concept of "a right to riot," protestors took their concerns to the streets and insisted on being heard. Such public theater was a form of democratic participation in public affairs, but it could also lead to what French observer, Alexis de Tocqueville, called the "tyranny of the majority." A seemingly endless series of small riots punctuated the early 1800s, including land, dog and hog riots, theater riots, election riots, ethnic riots, New Year's Eve riots, brothel riots, and gang riots. The peace that defined the nation's Era of Good Feelings (1816–1823) did not seem to apply to Gotham where rioting was almost a norm. 1834 was an especially violent year, so violent that it was called "The Year of the Riots." The emotions expressed by the riots were complex and have always perplexed historians. They illuminated the paradoxes of Jacksonian America.[3]

The anti-abolitionist riots started on July 4, 1834, just months after election riots had paralyzed the city for three days in April. Motivations for riots are always complex and the anti-abolitionist riots combined economic with social anxieties. Although slavery in New York State ended in 1827, the abolition of slavery nationwide was an increasingly controversial issue in New York City where black and white abolitionists were active. At the same time, anti-abolitionist sentiment was also strong because of New York's close trading ties with the South and because of concerns that emancipation would result in a flood of cheap black labor to the North. White workers' fear of black economic competition reinforced anxiety about racial equality and exploded into riot. No physical incident triggered the riots. Rather, there was an emotional trigger called amalgamation, or racial mixing.

For eight days, mobs controlled the city. They destroyed homes, stores and churches affiliated with white abolitionists and broke up integrated abolitionist meetings. The white abolitionists who were most reviled were Arthur and Lewis Tappan, founders of the New York Anti-Slavery Society, along with the Reverend Samuel H. Cox who supported integration and the Reverend Henry Ludlow who was accused of marrying mixed couples. African American homes, schools, stores and churches were targeted by the mob and the issue of amalgamation became the key rallying cry. By the time the riot was finally stopped by the state militia, it had exposed the tensions that lurked beneath the surface of urban civility. The "tyranny of the majority" seemed to have prevailed.[4]

3-1-1. DENOUNCING RIOTS: WILLIAM LEGGETT, NEWSPAPER EDITOR, 1834

On July 11, the reformer William Leggett, who was editing the *New York Evening Post* while the regular editor William Cullen Bryant was in Europe, stated that the paper did not support the "fanatical" element of abolitionism. Nonetheless, Leggett affirmed that all lawful American citizens, no matter how offensive their point of view, "have a right to be protected in their persons and property against all assailants whatsoever." Therefore, the *Post* blamed the riots on its rival papers—the *Commercial Advertiser,* edited by William Leete Stone, and the *Courier and Enquirer,* edited by James Watson Webb. Both had published inflammatory editorials linking abolitionism to amalgamation. Leggett claimed that Stone and Webb had "inflamed the public indignation" against abolitionism, thereby instigating "lawless violence highly disgraceful to this city." As the riot continued, the sense of crisis grew and on July 12 the *Post* urged the mayor to do whatever was necessary to restore order, even if it meant shooting the rioters "down like dogs." Also on July 12, Leggett, who was himself an abolitionist, described the violence, under the heading "DREADFUL RIOTS."

Source: *New York Evening Post*, July 12, 1834

The worst anticipations of the day have been realized. For five hours, our city has been the prey of an infuriated mob, or rather mobs, who have been carrying destruction before them in every direction. All the efforts of the Watch and of the Military as they were conducted, have not availed to stay the work of desolation, nor scarcely to retard its progress ... Affairs have come to such a pitch that severe measures must be adopted, or our government is at an end.

Mr. Tappan's store was attacked at half-past nine last evening by a number of boys and men, who fired volleys of stones and broke the upper windows, but did not attempt to force the doors. The mob were suspicious that things were behind the doors to which they did not wish to be introduced. ... On the first appearance of the Watch they scattered. ...

Between ten and eleven a large mob assembled at Doctor Cox's church in Laight street and smashed in the door and windows and demolished the interior of the building. ... The mob proceeded to Spring street and attacked Rev. Mr. Ludlow's church, the doors and windows of which they began to batter in, when a small party of watchmen arrived and put a momentary stop to their proceedings, and took one or two of the ringleaders into custody. Their companions, however, soon liberated them, beat the watchmen off and maltreated some of them....

As if the tragedy which had just been performed was not sufficient to satisfy the mob, a gentleman, whose name we believe is Wood, added a farce to it, by addressing the mob, outré style, commencing his discourse by saying that he was neither a civil nor military officer, and declaring that he would willingly cut the ears off any man who would propose to amalgamate a black man and a white woman ... .

Between 11 and 12 o'clock, a detachment of the mob proceeded from Spring street Church to Rev. Mr. Ludlow's house in Thompson street, between Prince and Houston, broke the windows and doors, but were prevented from going in by the arrival of a squadron of cavalry. Mr. Ludlow and his family were out of town.

About 11 o'clock, another mob attacked St. Phillips African Episcopal church in Centre street—Rev. Peter Williams, a colored man, pastor—and demolished it almost entirely, including a fine organ. The furniture they took out and burned it in the street.

The windows of the African Baptist church in Anthony street were broken to atoms.

The African school-house in Orange street, which is also used as a Methodist meeting house, was totally demolished.

Several houses where colored people resided, in Orange and Mulberry streets, between Anthony and Walker and about the Five Points, were greatly injured or totally destroyed. The mob compelled the [white] occupants of the houses to set lights at the windows, and wherever colored people were seen or no lights were shown, the work of destruction commenced. In one case, a colored woman advanced to the window with her light when, in an instant, some missile was sent which knocked her down and extinguished the light.

Two houses in Anthony street were attacked and the furniture brought out into the street and burned. One or two in Leonard street shared the same fate.

The distress occasioned by families in this vicinity, both whites and blacks, by this unexpected visit was very great. Although many of the inhabitants are of dissolute character, there are others, particularly of Irish families, whose only crime was that they were poor.

About 9 o'clock, a detachment of the mob at the Five Points commenced an assault upon a small wooden building in Orange, near Bayard street, occupied as a barber shop by a colored man named Marsh, the front and interior of which they soon demolished. The black intrepidly kept possession of his premises, discharging a pistol three times at his assailants, the last of which unfortunately took effect and severely wounded Elisha Spence in the leg as he was passing on the opposite side of the street on his way home. ...

The Military were on duty and the Mayor was at the Hall all night. It cannot be disguised, however, that the mob were complete masters of the city, and the City Government was overawed, and for the time at an end. ...

---

1. According to the *Post*, how large, organized and effective was the mob?
2. Based on the *Post*'s account, in how many ways was this riot "dreadful"?
3. Why did the mob attack African American churches, schools and stores, not just homes?
4. Based on the *Post*'s account, was New York City ungovernable in 1834? If so, why?

3-1-2. DEPLORING AMALGAMATION: WILLIAM LEETE STONE, NEWSPAPER EDITOR, 1834

William Leete Stone, editor of the *New York Commercial Advertiser*, was one of the abolitionists' strongest critics. His diatribes against amalgamation were widely credited with fomenting the 1834 anti-abolitionist riots.

Source: *New York Commercial Advertiser,* July 10, 1834.

Suffice it to say that public sentiment, in the ratio of more than an hundred to one, revolts at this unnatural amalgamation which is attempted to be forced upon by the Abolitionists—and when against such fearful odds they attempt to coerce and bring that public feeling to the standard of their own morbid taste, they must not only expect discomfiture, but assume the responsibility of consequences that at the beginning they would have shuddered to think of. We therefore repeat that the Abolitionists are the very worst enemies of the African race; for by fostering their hopes and jealousies in the way we have described, they create mutual hatred between the two races, which, if not prudently controlled, may cause such outbreaks as must ultimately lead to the worst possible consequences.

We all know that in a large city like this there is ever a body of men ripe for scenes of riot. They neither know nor care for causes or consequences. The pleasure of the row is all they seek. They scorn amalgamation with the blacks, and therefore are the more ready to resent the offensive proposal. It is to this class of men generally, so far as we have been informed, that the riots of last evening and on the preceding days are mainly to be ascribed. They accord in sentiment and feeling it is true, with the great mass of the white community, but the more respectable and orderly portion of our citizens disclaim, in all sincerity, recourse to violence and believe that these fanatics may and will be put down by the operation of the laws and the overwhelming power of public opinion. ...

1. What key words did Stone use to condemn amalgamation? How could they have incited riot?
2. Why did Stone blame the abolitionists for the riot?
3. Why did Stone believe that abolitionism harmed blacks?
4. How did Stone justify riot but distance himself from it?
5. In what ways did the *Commercial Advertiser* and the *Post* agree or disagree?

3-1-3. RIDICULING AMALGAMATION: EDWARD W. CLAY, CARICATURIST

Amalgamation was an emotional and volatile issue because voluntary interracial mixing implied equality, which undermined the basic assumptions of slavery and racism. Of course, as the abolitionist David Ruggles explained, African Americans were less interested in intermarriage than in obtaining their civil and legal rights. However, emphasizing intermarriage, with all of its sexual implications, was a clever way confuse the issue and distort the crusade for civil and legal equality.

As always, cartoons used ridicule to convey serious messages. The artist Edward W. Clay (1799–1857) trained for the law and was admitted to the bar in 1825, but then studied art in Europe for five years. Returning to the United States, he spent 20 years in New York City as a much admired caricaturist until failing eyesight forced him to give up drawing and become a court clerk. Note that the tall man with the hat in the doorway was probably the abolitionist William Lloyd Garrison.

Source: Edward W. Clay, "The Fruits of Amalgamation." .

THE FRUITS OF AMALGAMATION.

Publ'd by JOHN CHILDS 160½ Fulton St New York.

---

1. How did Clay use ridicule to promote stereotypes of African Americans?
2. In how many ways did Clay reverse conventional racial roles?
3. Explain the title of the cartoon and its relationship to the concept of "mongreliza-tion."
4. Explain how this cartoon reinforced Stone's editorial in Document 3-1-2.
5. What would have been the most shocking aspect and the most powerful message of this cartoon in the nineteenth century?

3-1-4. DEBATING AMALGAMATION: DAVID RUGGLES, ABOLITIONIST, 1834

In response to the riot, the abolitionists issued a public proclamation asserting that their purpose was to eliminate slavery, not to advocate amalgamation. Nonetheless, in the summer of 1834, a New York City physician, Dr. David M. Reese, published a pamphlet equating abolition with amalgamation. Reese supported the American Colonization Society, which advocated sending free African Americans back to Africa. David Ruggles, New York City's leading black abolitionist, criticized Reese in a counter-pamphlet which was the first pamphlet published by an African American. Ruggles also was America's first professional African American journalist and owned the first African American bookstore before it was destroyed by a mob.

Ruggles was best known for his work with the New York Committee of Vigilance which rescued and defended blacks who were being kidnapped in the city and sold South into slavery. Ruggles was a major conductor on the underground railroad, which was a secret network designed to help slaves escape from the South to the North. The houses in which fugitives hid were called stations and the people who hid them were called conductors. Ruggles may have aided as many as 400 slaves escape, including Frederick Douglass. Another measure of Ruggles' success was the contempt he aroused among slaveholders and slave catchers. It was so great that in 1836 they tried to kidnap Ruggles and ship him to Georgia, but he foiled the attempt. Radical to the end, Ruggles' life was cut short by illness at the age of 39 in 1849.[5]

Source: David Ruggles, A Man of Color, *The 'Extinguisher' Extinguished! Or David M. Reese, M.D. 'Used Up.'* (New York: D. Ruggles, Bookseller, 1834), 12–17.

Abolitionists do not wish "amalgamation." I do not wish it, nor does any colored man or woman of my acquaintance,…but I deny that "intermarriage" between the "whites and blacks are unnatural…"

Now "that no white person never did consent to marry a Negro without having previously forfeited all character with the respectable and virtuous among the whites," *is not true*, unless it is true that a man's character depends upon the color of his skin; if it does, which of the two races would "forfeit all character" by intermarrying, the white or the colored? The whites have robbed us (the blacks) for centuries—they made Africa bleed rivers of blood!—they have torn husbands from their wives—wives from their husbands—parents from their children—children from their parents— brothers from their sisters—sisters from their brothers, and bound them in chains—forced them into the hold of vessels—subjected them to the most unmerciful tortures; starved and murdered, and doomed them to the horrors of slavery! Still, according to Dr. Reese's logic, the whites have virtuous "characters" and we are *brutes*!…

What is the reason that a white man cannot marry a female of a different hue without expecting the execration of the majority of the whites? Prejudice is against it; we are human. Why is it argued that our elevation "to an equality" with other "Americans is incongruous and unnatural?" Simply because public opinion is against it. Now we don't want to alter public opinion respecting intermarriages, but we do respecting our "equality." Now we are degraded and ground into the very dust by prejudice. …

But why is it that it seems to you so "repugnant" to marry your sons and daughters to colored persons? Simply because public opinion is against it. *Nature* teaches no such "repugnance," but experience has taught that education only does. Do children feel and exercise that prejudice towards colored persons? Do not colored and white children play together promiscuously until the white is taught to despise the colored? …

How could "nature" excite such repugnance, and uneducated children know it not? The southern infant, I mean the white infant, is suckled at slavery's breast, and dandled on black slavery's knee, and if it was here that nature excited a "repugnance" in whites against the colored child, could they both suck at one breast? Now all this repugnance about which such repugnant ideas are entertained, is identified with public opinion. …

In South America, white and colored persons live together on terms of perfect equality; no "repugnance" exists natural or artificial; and certainly nature is true to herself. If the "repugnance" of N. America is natural, why is it not natural in S. America? The Dr.'s logic on this subject is false as I believe his heart to be. …

If prejudice is invincible, amalgamation can never take place by intermarriages between white and colored persons. Why then is all this rant and poetry about amalgamation, if the *races do not and will not incorporate?* Now as amalgamation seems to be the only bugbear that can be held up against abolitionists, let every candid man ask himself this question—What is the cause of amalgamation between white and colored persons? And after reviewing the North and South he must come to the conclusion that *slavery* is the cause. Then if he wished to check that base and damning prostitution that is fast making the United States "a nation of mulattoes and mongrels" would he not annihilate slavery? To me nothing is more disgusting that to see my race bleached to a pallid sickly hue by the lust of those cruel and fastidious white men whose prejudices are so strong that they can't come in sight of a colored skin. Ah no! His natural prejudices forbid it! Oh, delicacy thou hast run mad, and chased thy sister chastity out of the bounds of the Southern States! Thou hast frightened the Doctor too, for not a word does he say about the virtue of the Ebon virgins—virgins reared for _____. But I forbear, God knows the truth is appalling enough to make a devil start, disgraceful enough to crimson the face of the whole heavens and make the angels blush!

---

1. How did Ruggles challenge the racist assumptions of the anti-abolitionists?
2. How did Ruggles redefine the issue of amalgamation?
3. How did Ruggles redefine the issue of character?
4. What were Ruggles' most powerful points?
5. How does this statement help explain why Ruggles was despised by slavery's supporters?

3-1-5. APPEALING FOR HELP: A CITIZEN, 1834

Although the issue of amalgamation was polarizing and although discrimination was prevalent in the city, blacks and whites often interacted peacefully and constructively in social movements such as abolition, as well as in daily life. The following letter offers some evidence of the more positive aspects of African American survival and inter-racial cooperation. Written during the riot, it helps us understand the complex relationships between blacks and whites in ante-bellum New York City. It was sent to Mayor Cornelius W. Lawrence on July 12, 1834.

Source: The Miscellaneous Manuscripts, Riots Collection, The New York Historical Society.

Dear Sir: The bearer E. Davis a coloured man has for several years had charge of our store as porter and possesses our entire confidence in point of integrity + is civil + unobtrusive in his manner + deportment. By diligence + economy he has acquired a comfortable property which is vested in two houses. ...that in which he resides 121 Broome St. + the house 123 Forsyth St., both good two story brick buildings.

He is much alarmed in consequence of having been several times informed during the day that it was the intention of the rioters to destroy his houses in the ensuing night. We hope the danger may not be so great as he apprehends but his anxiety on the subject is so great that we take the liberty of stating his case to you.

> We are yours respectfully.
> H + A Averill

---

1. What did the letter reveal about the economic status of some New York City blacks in 1834?
2. What did the letter reveal about the racial attitudes of some New York City whites in 1834?
3. Suggest at least two possible reasons why Mr. Davis did not write the mayor himself.
4. How did this letter support the *Post*'s analysis in Document 3-1-1?
5. Altogether, how does this unit reveal the strengths and weaknesses of the city in 1834?

UNIT 3-2. CHANGE AND CHALLENGE: THE MURDER OF HELEN JEWETT

The murder of a 22-year-old prostitute named Helen Jewett rocked New York and the nation for three months in 1836. According to the historian Timothy Gilfoyle, it was "the city's most intensely covered story of the decade." Coinciding with the birth of the penny press, the case established the sex scandal as a major feature of popular newspapers. Most importantly, it challenged prevailing notions of women's role in society and promoted the image of Gotham as a dangerous, immoral place anathema to traditional American values. (Later, Gotham would be labeled "sin city.") National fascination with the murder fostered a fear of New York City.[6]

In April 1836, Jewett was brutally beaten and set afire in her brothel bed. A bloody hatchet and cloak found near the scene lead to the arrest of Richard Robinson, a 19-year-old clerk who was her steady customer. After a sensational trial during which the judge instructed the jury to disregard all testimony given by prostitutes, Robinson was acquitted on June 12.

Every aspect of the trial was covered at length in New York City's newspapers and in papers across America, twenty of which had reporters in the courtroom. Interest in the case derived not just from the fact that the victim was a working-class woman known to be beautiful and charming or that the accused was from a respectable Connecticut family or that his employers hired top lawyers to defend him. Rather it was that the murder brought to the surface the anxieties of the time regarding cities, class, female roles, male subcultures and sex.

During this period, the cult of female domesticity defined women's role in society. On the farm, women's work and family functions were intertwined, but in the city and the new industrial economy, male and female roles came to be seen as separate spheres. Whereas men were associated with wage labor outside the home, women were associated with unpaid domestic functions inside the home, even though such functions are a form of work and many women also worked from home doing laundry or sewing. Instead of monetary value, women's worth was increasingly measured in moral terms. The ideal woman was envisioned as pure, demure, pious, submissive and dependent. The prostitute defied these norms.[7]

The controversy over Helen Jewett's murder dovetailed with the controversy over and hostility toward radical feminist Fanny Wright. Although certainly not a prostitute, Wright was called the "red Harlot of Infidelity" because she advocated full equality for women, including sexual equality. Moreover, Wright defied conventional norms for female behavior in her dress, activism and public speaking tours. To Wright, "Ignorant laws, ignorant prejudices, ignorant codes of morals … condemn one portion of the female sex to vicious excess, another to as vicious restraint, and all to defenceless (sic) helplessness and slavery, and generally the whole of the male sex to debasing licentiousness, if not to loathsome brutality." The Helen Jewett murder involved precisely these issues.[8]

3-2-1. PUBLICIZING THE JEWETT CASE, 1836

Popular interest in the Jewett murder generated a flood of print materials about the case. Everyone had an opinion about it, as shown by this pamphlet cover. Note that there was some debate over whether Jewett's name was Helen or Ellen, but she is commonly referred to as Helen.

Source: Murder of Ellen Jewett, pamphlet printed in New York, 1836.

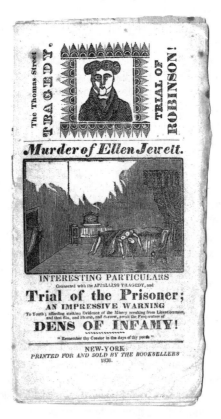

1. What social values were promoted by the words on this pamphlet's cover?
2. What messages were conveyed by the difference between Jewett and Robinson in terms of dress, position and size?
3. Did this image suggest that the tragedy was about Jewett, Robinson and/or licentiousness?
4. Why could this pamphlet be considered propaganda?

3-2-2. OBSERVING THE TRIAL: PHILIP HONE, DIARIST, 1836

Philip Hone was mayor from 1826 to 1828 and one of New York City's most prominent men. He became rich in the auction business and joined the elite whose opinions he represented. Nonetheless, he sometimes sympathized with the poor and was an acute observer of human affairs. His diary entries are a rich primary source for nineteenth-century New York City. In reading Hone's account, note that there were rumors that the judge and the jury were being bribed to acquit Robinson. Note also that Rosanna Townsend ran the brothel where Jewett worked.

Source: Allan Nevins (ed.), *The Diary of Philip Hone, 1828–1851*, vol. I (New York: Dodd Mead, 1927), 210–211.

Saturday, June 4, 1836—Robinson's Trial.

I succeeded in gaining admittance this afternoon to the courtroom where the trial of Robinson for the murder of Helen Jewett is going on. The crowd is very great and I found my position so uncomfortable that I stayed only a short time.

Yesterday the mob was so great and their conduct so disorderly that the court was compelled to retire into another room until order was in some degree restored. Every avenue was filled, and on the opening of the doors a general rush was made, in which the railings of the courtroom were broken down. ...

I think there is no doubt of the guilt of the wretched youth, but it is to be feared that he will escape punishment. The jury will not convict him, for circumstantial testimony, as is usually the case in trials for murder, can only be obtained, and the ingenuity of counsel can so mystify the minds of jurors as to create a doubt whether some other person may not by possibility have committed the crime; to say nothing of *other means* which may be successfully applied, as they have heretofore been in similar cases, to add *weight* to the doubts of some *conscientious* dispensers of the public justice. Robinson has the advantage of able counsel judiciously selected from the New York bar; Hoffman, Maxwell, and Price—if these gentlemen cannot get him off, his case must be very desperate.

I perceived in court a strong predilection in favor of the prisoner. He is young, good looking, and supported by influential friends. Sitting between his counsel and Mr. Hoxie his employer (who does not abandon his protégé in the hour of adversity), he certainly looks as little like a murderer as any person I ever saw. These are good reasons for public sympathy, but there are others less benevolent. There appears to be a fellow-feeling in the audience. I was surrounded by young men, about his own age, apparently clerks like him, who appeared to be thoroughly initiated into the arcane of such houses as Mrs. Rosanna Townsend's. They knew the wretched female inmates as they were brought up to testify, and joked with each other in a manner illy comporting with the solemnity of the occasion.

1. How did Hone's description of popular interest in the Jewett case reveal his own biases?
2. Why did Hone think that Robinson would be acquitted? Which reason was most important?
3. What did Hone think of young men like Robinson and their social mores?
4. Would Hone have agreed with the analyses of Bennett and Gilfoyle below?

3-2-3. QUESTIONING SIN CITY: JAMES GORDON BENNETT, NEWSPAPER EDITOR, 1836

By the 1830s, New York City was already the nation's communications center whose newspapers provided information for the entire country. In addition to six-penny papers for the upper classes, there were an increasing number of penny papers expressly targeted to the working classes, including Fanny Wright's radical but short-lived, *Free Enquirer*, and Benjamin Day's immensely popular and sensational *The Sun*. Helen Jewett's murder trial promoted the penny press as readers devoured accounts of the case. The penny press dramatized the testimony, embroidered on Jewett's biography, interviewed prostitutes, described brothels and exposed other licentious affairs. The public purchased so many papers that the sex scandal became a staple of popular journalism.

The New York Herald was the most successful of the penny press papers that arose in the 1830s. Edited by James Gordon Bennett, it targeted both the working and the middle classes. While upper-class papers like the *Post* avoided dealing with the specifics of the crime, Bennett dwelt on every detail, including his own visit to Jewett's room and an interview with her madam. Immediately, the *Herald*'s circulation tripled, and four years later it outpaced even the London *Times* to become the world's most widely read newspaper.

Aware of being, in his words, "accused of all sorts of crimes against taste—against morals—against propriety," Bennett also appealed to middle-class respectability by raising the larger questions posed by the Jewett case. Bennett was always controversial, often offensive, frequently perceptive.[9]

Source: *New York Herald*, April 13, 1836.

The question now before the public involves more than the guilt of one person—it involves the guilt of a system of society—the wickedness of a state of morals—the atrocity of permitting establishments of such infamy to be erected in every public and fashionable place in our city. *We are all guilty alike*—from the magistrate down to the scavenger—from the leader in society down to its follower. The courts of law have not alone a right to investigate this crime—this red-blooded atrocity. The whole community has an interest— the present generation are both court, jury, witnesses, culprit, and executioner. It has sprung from a state of society that we men, and ye women also, of this age have permitted to grow up among us, without let or hindrance.

Suppose Robinson is guilty—suppose he is tried—suppose he is found guilty—suppose he is carried out to Bellevue, and privately executed according to our bloody law—suppose all this—will that take away the awful guilt of the present age—of this city—of our leaders in society—of our whole frame of morals and manners in permitting such a state of things to exist in a respectable, moral, Christian city? Beauty and innocence—talent and accomplishment, such as are seldom seen commingled together, gave up its existence when the fatal axe penetrated the alabaster forehead of Ellen Jewett. But had not our morals—our manners—our unprincipled male sex, first inflicted a more fatal blow upon her spotless and innocent soul when she became the first victim of seduction, and gave up, in a moment of love and passion, the only ornaments and value of female character?

1. What phrases in this editorial reflected the sensationalism of the penny press?
2. What phrases in this editorial went beyond sensationalism to raise broad social issues?
3. How did Bennett reinforce the cult of female domesticity while also sympathizing with women's plight?
4. How did Bennett suggest that New York City was really a "sin city"?

3-2-4. ANALYZING GENDER ROLES: TIMOTHY GILFOYLE, HISTORIAN, 1992

The historian Timothy J. Gilfoyle examined the relationship of the Jewett case to changing ideas about male and female roles in a changing city and a changing nation. The immense amount of attention paid to the case proved that it touched a very sensitive cultural nerve.

Source: Timothy J. Gilfoyle, *City of Eros: New York City, Prostitution, and the Commercialization of Sex, 1790–1920* (New York: W. W. Norton & Company, Inc.) 96–99.

Jewett represented two contradictory fears of many nineteenth-century critics of prostitution. The loss of her virginity through innocent teenage sexuality and its devolution into prostitution embodied middle-class fears of downward mobility. … One erotic mishap, and the fall from respectability to social marginality was likely, if not guaranteed. Jewett's case saw the feared and final result—death. On the other hand, Jewett never truly suffered economic want. Rather, prostitution provided her with male paramours, a handsome residence, desirable possessions, and personal autonomy. In sum, she was wealthy, free and female. Jewett simultaneously represented the dangerous, "inevitable" results of sexual freedom alongside the tangible benefits of a career in commercial sex … .

To the American public in 1836, Richard Robinson was on trial for more than just the murder of Helen Jewett. As the boardinghouse, peer group, and market economy replaced the craft household, family, and "moral economy," young men frequented brothels … in growing numbers. … Robinson's promiscuous adventures aptly illustrated the restructuring of male sexual behavior in New York after 1820. Numerous young men courted prostitutes, "kept" women, paid their rent, and assumed aliases to hide such activities. Sexual desires were now expressed through institutions of public leisure and commercial exchange—the theater, the boardinghouse, and the brothel. More significantly, Robinson's behavior was defensible in the minds of his supporters. Jewett was a social leech out to ruin a rising but poor clerk, a female threat to "Young America." Indeed, "no man ought to forfeit his life for the murder of a whore," concluded some apologists. ...

In that tiny, overcrowded municipal chamber, New York and the rest of America confronted a changing sexual ethos. Robinson not only murdered a woman, but, more important, also challenged the emerging "respectable," bourgeois, Christian morality. In the years following the Second Great Awakening, the values of self-control, chastity, domesticity, sobriety, and frugality were espoused by Protestant and Catholic clergy, male and female moral reformers, and entrepreneur and small merchant alike. Severe social restrictions increasingly limited intimacy between young men and women as the nineteenth century progressed. Long before the phrase was popularized by a twentieth-century president, these groups admonished young Americans to "just say no."

Robinson's sexual behavior mocked these ideals. For the next decade, it was a national topic of discussion. More than any single person, Robinson put the tension of what constituted "respectable" sexuality on public view. Above all, his popularity among large numbers of urban youths represented the emergence of a "sporting male" culture. Organized around various forms of gaming—horse racing, gambling, cockfighting, pugilism, and other "blood" sports—sporting-male culture defended and promoted male sexual aggressiveness and promiscuity. For young men like Robinson, bachelorhood was the ideal. Prostitution, sexual display, and erotic entertainment brought excitement to a prosaic world. Respectable, reproductive heterosexuality, in contrast, was associated with femininity and female control. Self-indulgence, not self-sacrifice, meant freedom; unregulated sex was the categorical imperative for the sporting male."

---

1. According to Gilfoyle, how was the definition of respectability changing for both men and women in the Jacksonian era?
2. According to Gilfoyle, how did the Jewett case reflect those changes?
3. According to Gilfoyle, why were changing mores particularly evident in the city?
4. How could Gilfoyle have used the documents above to support or revise his interpretation of Helen Jewett's murder?

UNIT 3-3. ECONOMICS AND THE PUBLIC INTEREST: THE JOURNEYMAN TAILORS' STRIKE

The Great Fire of December 1835 raged for two days, wiped out over 700 buildings, simmered for two weeks and razed 13 acres below Wall Street. Of course, the city quickly rebuilt. Although the fire came to symbolize urban resilience, it was also a vivid reminder of urban vulnerability. Social ramifications smoldered beneath the physical devastation.

On the one hand, there were the poor who descended upon the wreckage to scavenge whatever goods remained. On the other hand, there were the rich (including Phillip Hone) who quickly reconstructed their businesses downtown or resettled further uptown causing an explosion of real estate values. Aid was provided to banks and businesses; the poor got nothing. The new Greek-revival Merchant's Exchange building signaled a new concentration of financial services on Wall Street and the movement of other businesses up Broadway. As the economy boomed, inflation took a toll on the poor and class differences were magnified. The city was combustible in more ways than one.[10]

Urban tensions were painfully exposed by the New York City journeyman tailors' strike of 1836, perhaps America's most significant and most extensive pre-Civil War labor protest. At issue was whether workers were entitled to try to improve their working conditions through labor organizations and job actions. The question was increasingly important as the old craft economy gave way to a new market economy characterized by large workplaces, unskilled labor and uncertain wages. The old system ,whereby men could rise from apprentice to journeyman to self-sufficient master craftsman, was rapidly becoming obsolete. As workers lost status, they fought back. During 1836 there were so many labor protests that the historian Sean Wilentz called it "the year of the strikes."

After master tailors reneged on earlier wage agreements, journeymen tailors struck in February 1836. Other workers followed and hundreds marched along the waterfront. They clashed with police and, for the first time in New York City's history, the militia was used against strikers. In response, skilled and unskilled workers overcame their differences to form an umbrella labor organization encompassing an astonishing 66 percent of New York's male workers. Employers formed counter-organizations. Violence between strikers, strikebreakers and the police mounted. When the tailors were sued for conspiracy against trade in March, the tailoresses joined the strike and thousands of workers from various trades marched up Broadway in protest.

The tailors lost the case. Although slightly delayed, because he was also presiding at the Helen Jewett trial, Judge Ogden Edwards' charge to the jury assumed that labor did not have the right to organize and that unions were illegal. The workers were furious and, a week later, 30,000 people (a fifth of the city's population) convened at City Hall in the largest meeting the nation had seen thus far. The workers hung the judge in effigy from the park's main gates, listened to speeches, and passed resolutions. For labor it was a moment of solidarity, but for many other New Yorkers it was a dangerous, irresponsible mob action.[11]

3-3-1. CONDEMNING STRIKES: OGDEN EDWARDS, JUDGE, 1836

Judge Edwards' statement at the sentencing represented the prevailing opinion that labor organizations were un-American.

Source: *New York Evening Post*, June 13, 1836.

Associations of this description are of recent origin in this country. Here, where the government is purely paternal, where the people are governed by laws of their own creating; where the legislature proceeds with a watchful regard to the welfare not only of the whole, but of every class of society; where the representatives even lend a listening ear to the complaints of their constituents, it has not been found necessary or proper to subject any portion of the people to the control of self-created societies. ...

In this favored land of law and liberty, the road to advancement is open to all, and the journeymen may by their skill and industry, and moral worth, become flourishing master mechanics. Combinations, which operate to the injury of the employers or of the trade, will in the regular course of events be found injurious to the journeymen. Our trades and tradesmen have hitherto flourished without any such aid. Every American knows, or ought to know, that he has no better friend than the laws, and that he needs no artificial combination for his protection. Our experience never manifested their necessity, and I may confidently say that they were not the offspring of necessity. They are of foreign origin, and I am led to believe are mainly upheld by foreigners.

1. Why did Edwards consider labor organizations unnecessary?
2. Why did Edwards consider labor organizations self-defeating?
3. Why did Edwards consider labor organizations un-American?
4. Why did Edwards condemn labor organizations as "self-created societies" but praised the fact that in a democracy "the people are governed by laws of their own creating"?

3-3-2. DEFENDING STRIKES: THE JOURNEYMEN TAILORS, 1836

After the guilty verdict, the journeymen tailors distributed a handbill around the city asking supporters to come to City Hall Park on the day of the sentencing. The image of a coffin on the handbill symbolized the death of workers' rights.

Source: *New York Herald*, June 7, 1836.

THE RICH AGAINST THE POOR: —Judge Edwards, the tool of the Aristocracy against the People.—Mechanics and Workingmen! A deadly blow has been struck at your Liberty! The prize for which your fathers fought has been robbed from you! The Freemen of the North are now on a level with the Slaves of the South!—with no other privilege than laboring that Drones may fatten on your lifeblood!

Twenty of your brethren have been found guilty for presuming to resist a reduction of their wages! And Judge Edwards has charged an American Jury, and agreeably to that charge they have established the precedent, that Workingmen have no *right to regulate the price of labor*! Or in other words, the Rich are the only judges of the wants of the Poor Man!

On Monday, June 6, 1836, at 10 o'clock, these freemen are to receive their sentence to gratify the hellish appetite of the Aristocracy! On Monday the Liberty of the Working men will be interred!—Judge Edwards is to chant the requiem! Go, go, go every Freeman! Every Workingman, and hear the hollow and melancholy sound of the earth on the Coffin of Equality! Let the Courtroom, the City Hall, yeah! the whole Park be filled with Mourners! But, remember, offer no violence to Judge Edwards! Bend meekly, and receive the chains, wherewith you are to be bound! Keep the peace! Above all things, keep the peace! '76"

---

1. What words in the handbill support the Coffin of Equality metaphor? How appropriate was the coffin metaphor?
2. How well did the strikers understand the changing relationships between worker and employer? How class conscious were the strikers?
3. How and why did the strikers link workers' rights to broader American concepts of freedom?
4. Why was their reference to slavery particularly significant?
5. Explain whether or not this handbill was a convincing response to Judge Edwards.

3-3-3. QUESTIONING THE SICK CITY: JAMES GORDON BENNETT, NEWSPAPER EDITOR, 1836

As in the Jewett case, James Gordon Bennett, editor of *The New York Herald,* played both sides of the fence in the tailors' strike by appealing simultaneously to working-class and middle-class concerns. He also placed the strike in context by linking it to specific events such as the 1834 riots and the 1835 fire as well as general factors such as the American character and the American economy. Bennett seemed to understand that the 1836 strike was part of broader developments in the city and the nation.

Source: *The New York Herald*, February 25, 1836.

RIOTS—STATE OF THE CITY
We are in a remarkable condition. Having just passed through a series of the severest snowstorms and the greatest conflagration ever known to befall a city in a single winter, we are on the verge of domestic riot, bloodshed and local revolution. The general thaw has commenced indeed—a thaw that melts snow, ice, the human heart, and all the worst and best principles of human nature. At one and the same moment, we have committees of charity perambulating the streets to collect money for the poor—Trades Unions associations spreading bloodshed and devastation around—journeymen tailors combining against their employers—landlords uniting in putting up rents enormously high and lease takers bidding over each other to get places of business—fights between

the police authorities and the stevedores—military regiments ordered out in arms—snow melting—business resuming—crowds collecting, &c, &c, &c.

Ever since the fatal day when certain assemblages of this city, led on by the *Courier and Enquirer,* gave an example of lawless mob violence, and were cheered to the destruction of Mr. Tappan's house and furniture, the spirit of insubordination has only increased—spread around the country—and may almost be now considered a settled element of the American character. Occasionally the blame is thrown upon the poor devils of Irishmen, on the Popish religion, or on the fanatics and abolitionists, but the unhappy trait now developed is not confined to any section or to any season. ...

What is the matter? Can any body tell the radical cause of the diseased state of society? ... The evil of our present state of society springs from both sides— from the rich and the poor—from the employer and the employed—from the master and the journeyman. It grows out equally of the grasping nature of the human heart. No calamity will teach the rich moderation—no suffering, the poor discretion. The great fire and its consequent events, the removal of the post office, the increase of rents, have caused much of the present state of things. Landlords, forestallers and employers are the avaricious. Take for instance the master tailors. No class of traders make higher profits or charge higher prices than they. Yet the journeymen do not get a fair remuneration for their labor. There is no class of men more liberal than the merchants. On no one occasion have the persons employed by them just cause of complaint. The principal oppressors of the working people are your small aristocrats—those who have just got a little property together and commence shaving in miniature.

The expenses of living and rents have all advanced enormously. So great has this rise been that many families are preparing to emigrate from New York to the great West. We know many respectable men, clerks in banks, who cannot afford to live on a good salary during the present increase of expenses. They say, "come let us go west, we can always get a living there, and lay up something for a rainy day." If the present high rates of living continue, let our men of wealth take care they don't depopulate the city.

On the side of the journeymen and labourers, there is as great a fault to be found as on that of their employers. These Trades Unions are nuisances—these riots ought to be at once put down by the military power. The whole system of combination is vicious and illegal in the extreme. On any occasion, a calm and general remonstrance from journeymen to employers, backed by public opinion, would always gain its ends. Lawless violence, bloodshed, and riot, never.

---

1. How did Bennett's first two paragraphs convey a sense of urban crisis?
2. According to Bennett, how many different factors created "the diseased state of society"? Which factor was most important?
3. How did Bennett both support and criticize the journeymen tailors?
4. According to Bennett, what was the connection between the anti-abolition riots, the journeymen tailors' strike and the American character?

3-3-4. DEPICTING THE DEPRESSION OF 1837: EDWARD C. CLAY, CARICATURIST

The economic depression that started in 1837 killed the fledgling labor organizations and fostered a nation-wide depression that lasted until 1843, making it America's first major depression. In New York City, hundreds of businesses failed, land values plummeted, the stock market plunged and 50,000 people were thrown out of work. Unable to pay rent, many ended up crowded in cellars or roaming the streets. The usually busy port was eerily still.

When banks stopped giving new loans and started calling in old loans, the crisis got wider and deeper. There was a "run" on the banks and such chaos on Wall Street that the mayor called out the militia to maintain order. Even Philip Hone lost much of his wealth and wondered "What is to become of the labouring classes?" Indeed, the combined effect of unemployment, a shortage of flour and rampant inflation caused the 1837 flour riot. The city's response was inadequate. Instead of providing jobs or food for the poor, it formed an investigative committee chaired by Hone and hired more watchmen to control protest. Charities failed to meet the need; people starved. The suffering is depicted overleaf in an 1837 lithograph called "The Times" by Edward C. Clay (see also Document 3-1-3).[12]

Source: Edward W. Clay, "The Times."

Notes on interpreting the image:

- The peaches and flour are selling at inflated prices.
- The billboard is offering cheap credit.
- The hotel is for sale.
- The Customs House requires payment in gold specie which the bank won't provide.
- The buildings on the right are the sheriff's office and the law firm of Peter Pillage.

---

1. According to Clay, what were the causes of the 1837 depression?
2. How did Clay convey the disastrous impact of the depression in New York City?
3. How did the bursting hot air balloon labeled "safety fund," the exploding Old Glory sun, the inverted flags and the July 4th parade give the depression a national context?
4. Why was the contrast between the city and the countryside significant?

THE TIMES.

UNIT 3-4. CITY BUILDING: JOHN JACOB ASTOR, THE LANDLORD OF NEW YORK

John Jacob Astor personified the wealth that is so identified with New York City. His life story demonstrated how many opportunities for profit existed in the burgeoning early-nineteenth-century city. At the same time, Astor's success raised questions about the meaning of wealth, about the relationship between rich and poor and about the obligations, if any, of the rich to the larger society. Astor represented the best and worst aspects of capitalism.

Astor was a master of the moment who saw and took advantage of every opportunity for profit. He was imaginative and innovative, patient and persistent, determined and demanding. His success was no accident. It all began in 1784 when the fifth son of a butcher from the German town of Waldorf migrated to America at age 20 with $25 and seven flutes. While getting himself established in the musical instrument business, Astor worked briefly for a baker and then for a fur merchant who sent him upstate to buy animal pelts. Trips to Albany and Montreal taught him about the new business and motivated him to shift from flutes to furs.[13]

Envisioning a national economy long before America had conquered the West and perceiving the possibilities of trade with China, Astor convinced President Thomas Jefferson to grant him a monopoly over the fur trade. Consequently, Astor became America's first monopolist. In addition, he got the exclusive right to have his ship, appropriately called the Beaver, trade with China during the 1808 trade embargo. For this purpose he established a trading post in Oregon called Astoria, which was also the name of his 13-acre seat in today's Queens, New York.[14]

Clearly, he was ahead of himself because the nation did not acquire Oregon for another 50 years and because the British who owned Oregon at the time confiscated all his goods. Nonetheless, Astor's agents made plenty of money for him by selling liquor to Native Americans. He had to abandon Astoria, but he bought up western lands that he would later sell at a profit. In addition, Astor made so much money in the China trade, including shipping opium, that by 1808, he became America's first millionaire.[15]

Anticipating New York City's expansion before anyone else and always alert to opportunity, in 1834 Astor decided to focus on investing in Manhattan real estate. For decades he already had been using profits from the fur and tea trades to buy properties considered worthless because they were so far out of town at the time, such as today's Greenwich Village, Astor Place, and 42nd Street. He was willing to invest in the future and wait for the city to catch up to him.

In one instance, he sold a house on Wall Street to a man who thought he had gotten a real bargain out of Astor and predicted that the value of the house would increase by at least fifty percent in a matter of years. Astor agreed, but observed that, after using the money from selling that one house to buy a lot of cheap land above Canal Street, he would make a profit of at least six hundred percent in the same time span. Of course, he was right; no one ever outmaneuvered Astor.[16]

At the same time, Astor aggressively promoted development of his existing interests. For example, as early as 1820, he purchased former Vice President Aaron Burr's mansion and moved it to Greenwich Village. Turning it into an attractive destination for socializing enhanced his other real estate investments in the area. Meanwhile, Astor flattened the hill on which Burr's house formerly stood and had it developed into a new community from which he soon reaped reams of rents.[17]

By 1835, Astor had spent $832,000 on Manhattan real estate from which annual rents earned him $1,265,000. His profit margin marked a shift in New York City's land-use patterns. Land that had previously been considered public property available to poor squatters was rapidly being converted into private property from which the poor were displaced. Land riots reflected the pain of eviction.[18]

Disaster benefited him too. During the depression of 1837, Astor purchased scores of sites in the already settled areas of Manhattan at bargain prices and foreclosed hundreds of homes when mortgages could no longer be met. Because he owned so much property, Astor was called the "Landlord of New York," much despised for extracting high rents from poor people without improving his buildings. He became notorious for demanding rent regardless of the circumstances of the renter, and demanding it on time. Moreover, his leases for vacant land required renters to build and maintain substantial houses on the land. These structures would revert to Astor when the lease expired, before which time renters could be evicted for not maintaining them properly.

By 1840, Astor was supposedly worth $25 million dollars, making him America's richest man. Cornelius Vanderbilt was second with a mere $1.2 million. By contrast, the average American earned only one dollar a week. Understandably, Astor expressed only one regret on his deathbed. "Could I begin life again, knowing what I now know, and had money to invest, I would buy every foot of land on the Island of Manhattan."[19]

Major philanthropic contributions were not expected in early-nineteenth-century New York because there were so few people with huge fortunes. That said, many well-to-do people supported charities on a modest scale. Astor was not among them. His primary motive was to acquire wealth for himself and bequeath it to his heirs. Nonetheless, he cared enough about the city and his image to leave some money to aid the poor, the aged, the blind and German immigrants. Astor also decided to create a public library. Although he delayed its actual establishment for many years while he toyed with the architectural plans, he left funds for its construction in his will. Finally erected on Lafayette Street in 1854, the Astor library planted the seed for the famous New York Public Library system, which was later expanded by another multimillionaire, Andrew Carnegie. [20]

Although Astor always dressed simply and never put on airs (nor acquired proper manners), he built America's most elegant hotel in 1836. Located on lower Broadway between Barclay and Vesey Streets, the Astor House was a sumptuous six-story affair with 300 rooms, a first-rate restaurant and an exceptional wine cellar. There were an astonishing 17 bathrooms per floor in an era when indoor bathrooms were rare and only for the very rich. From carpets to chandeliers, no cost was spared, and no person of prominence could afford not to be seen there. However, none of them wanted to be seen with prostitutes like Helen Jewett who frequented the third tier of Astor's Park Theater, located across the street from Astor House. [21]

The contrasts between the theater and the hotel, the wealthy realtor and his tenants, reflected the economic realities of New York in the early nineteenth century when opportunities were great but class divisions were getting greater. John Jacob Astor's life exemplified the tensions of his times and made people wonder about the ramifications of the wealth everyone sought. The 1849 riots at the elegant Astor Place

Opera House (see Unit 4-3), which was built with his money and named in his honor, heightened public awareness of rising economic inequality and showed how frayed the social contract had become. On the one hand, Astor's life was a testimony to the American dream based on hard work, foresight and skillful business practices. He was the ultimate capitalist. On the other hand, Astor was the first exemplar of a negative quality also associated with the American dream, and especially with New York City — its "soulless acquisitiveness.[22]

1. What were the keys to Astor's success?
2. How did Astor help New York City?
3. How did Astor hurt New York City?
4. Which of Astor's accomplishments embodied the best and worst aspects of capitalism?

3-4-1. ASSESSING ASTOR: PHILIP HONE, DIARIST, 1840s

Astor is an icon of New York City history because of his business acumen and astounding wealth. Yet, even his friends wondered whether his wealth was a panacea. Former mayor Philip Hone was long associated with Astor as in the roles of friend, business associate and author of a book about Astor's western enterprises. As in his report of the Robinson trial, Hone's ability to be both a participant and an observer enriched his diary.

Source: Allan Nevins (ed.), *The Diary of Philip Hone, 1828–1851* vol. I. (New York: Dodd Mead, 1927), 716–717, 847–848.

Wednesday, October 9, 1844. *Dinner and Reflections.*

I went out yesterday to dine at Mr. Blatchford's, at Hell's Gate ... Mr. Astor, one of our dinner companions yesterday, presented a painful example of the insufficiency of wealth to prolong the life of man. This old gentleman with his fifteen millions of dollars would give it all to have my strength and physical ability ... His life has been spent amassing money, and he loves it as much as ever. He sat at the dinner table with his head down upon his breast, saying very little, and in a voice almost unintelligible; the saliva dropping from his mouth, and a servant behind him to guide the victuals which he was eating, and to watch him as an infant is watched. His mind is good, his observation acute, and he seems to know everything that is going on. But the machinery is all broken up, and there are some people, no doubt, who think he has lived long enough.

Wednesday, March 29, 1848. *Death of Mr. Astor.*

John Jacob Astor died this morning at eight o'clock, in the eighty-fifth year of his age; sensible to the last, but the material of life is worn out, the lamp extinguished for want of oil. Bowed down with bodily infirmity for a long time, he has gone at last, and left reluctantly his unbounded wealth. His property is estimated at $20,000,000, some judicious persons say $30,000,000; but, at any rate, he was the richest man in the United States in productive and available property; and this immense, gigantic fortune was the fruit of his own labor, unerring sagacity, and far-seeing penetration.

He came to this country at twenty years of age; penniless, friendless, without inheritance, without education, and having no example before him of the art of money-making, but with a determination to be rich, and ability to carry it into effect. His capital consisted of a few trifling musical instruments, which he got from his brother, George Astor, in London, a dealer in music. He sold his flutes, and set up a small retail shop of German toys, but soon emerged from obscurity, and became a great and successful merchant.

The fur trade was the philosopher's stone of this modern Croesus; beaver skins and musk-rats furnished the oil for the supply of Aladdin's lamp. His traffic was the shipment of furs to China, where they brought immense prices, for he monopolized the business; and the return cargoes of teas, silks, and rich productions of China brought further large profits; for here, too, he had very little competition at the time of which I am speaking. My brother and I found Mr. Astor a valuable customer. We sold many of his cargoes, and had no reason to complain of a want of liberality or confidence. All he touched turned to gold, and it seemed as if fortune delighted in erecting him a monument of her unerring potency.

---

1. Why did Hone admire Astor?
2. How did Hone explain the limits of Astor's otherwise limitless wealth?
3. According to Hone, how did Astor embody the American dream?
4. Why are Hone's comments on the Helen Jewett case and on Astor's life so valuable to historians?

3-4-2. CRITICIZING ASTOR: JAMES GORDON BENNETT, NEWSPAPER EDITOR, 1848

James Gordon Bennett weighed in on Astor's death with a typically strong statement in *The New York Herald.*

Source: *New York Herald*, April 5, 1848.

If we had been an associate of John Jacob Astor … we should have given him some instruction in political economy, at least, of a very different character from what it appears he has imbibed from those whom he lived among. The first idea we should have put into his head, would have been that *one-half of his immense property—ten millions at least—belonged to the people of the city of New York.* During the last fifty years of the life of John Jacob Astor, his property has been augmented and increased in value by the aggregate intelligence, industry, enterprise and commerce of New York, fully to the amount of one-half its value. The farms and lots of ground which he bought forty, twenty, ten and five years ago, have all increased in value entirely by the industry of the citizens of New York. Of course, it is as plain as that two and two make four, that half of his immense estate, in its actual value, has accrued to him by the industry of the community.

Having established this principle, we would have counseled John Jacob Astor to leave at least half of his property for the benefit of the city of New York, in beautifying the public buildings, in making stone warves on both sides of the river, in paving the streets...and in ornamenting the city in every possible manner, leaving ten millions to be given to his relations—a sum quite enough for any reasonable persons of any rank of life in this country. But instead of this, he has only left less than half a million for a public library. What a poor, mean, and beggarly result from associating with such distinguished literary men, philosophers, and poets!

We cannot, therefore, pronounce the highest species of eulogy upon the character of the late John Jacob Astor. He has exhibited, at best, but the ingenious powers of a self-invented money-making machine; and his associates, advisers, and counselors, of his later years, seem to have looked no further than to the different pins, cranks, and buttons of this machine, without turning it to any permanent benefit to that community from whose industry he obtained half the amount of his fortune, in the indirect values added to his estates in the course of years.

---

1. According to Bennett, who really made Astor wealthy?
2. Was the *Herald*'s position reasonable or ridiculous?
3. How did Bennett's assessment of Astor's success differ from Hone's?
4. In what ways did Bennett understand or misunderstand the meaning of capitalism and the American dream?

3-4-3. RECONSIDERING RAGS TO RICHES: EDWARD PESSEN, HISTORIAN, 1973

The historian Edward Pessen challenged the "rags to riches" concept that it was easy to become wealthy in America, particularly in the Jacksonian era and particularly in New York City. Using tax assessment lists, he proved that most of the rich started out well off, not poor. Consequently, John Jacob Astor's story was the exception, not the rule. Pessen's evidence is important for our understanding of the American dream and New York City's place in that dream.

Source: Edward Pessen, *Riches, Class and Power in America Before the Civil War* (New Brunswick, NJ: Transaction, 1973/1990), 31, 33–35, 84, 86, 140, 148.

From [Alexis de] Tocqueville's time to our own, antebellum America has enjoyed the reputation of being a society marked by an unprecedented economic equality. No one, not even the most inveterate yeasayer, believed that material goods and services were distributed perfectly equally. Blacks and Indians, and the masses of new Irish immigrants obviously were not in the feast. But it has been widely believed the cornucopia was almost equally available to all others. ...

A contemporary yeasayer wrote that in Jacksonian New York City "wealth was universally diffused." Even the normally optimistic Philip Hone disagreed, noting disconsolately that his beloved New York City late in the era had "arrived at the [unhappy] state of society to be found in the large cities of Europe." In which "the two extremes of costly luxury in living, expensive establishments and improvident waste are present in daily and hourly contrast with squalid misery and hopeless destitution."

The evidence bears out Hone's gloomy assessment. In the year of Andrew Jackson's first election to the presidency [1828], the wealthiest 4 per cent of the population, in owning almost half the wealth, possessed a larger proportion of New York City's wealth than the richest 10 per cent had ... owned in the urban northeast as a whole half a century earlier [1778]. By 1845 the disparities had sharply increased. ...

Hypothesizing that the personal property of the rich equaled the worth of their real estate and that the wealthiest 4 per cent owned about 90 per cent of New York City's unassessed personal property in 1828, the upper 1 per cent would have owned about 35 per cent; and the next wealthiest 3 per cent about 22 per cent of all non-corporate wealth. In 1845, by this reckoning, the richest 1 per cent would have owned about 47 per cent, while the next wealthiest 3 per cent would have held an additional 32 per cent of the city's wealth. ...

Some of the best known among the wealthy citizens did, in fact, have the kind of background ascribed to them by the egalitarian thesis. Although John Jacob Astor's story is ... described as "rags to riches," there is some question as to the precise wealth or status of his father. Whether the latter was a "very worthy" minor office-holder, as some described him, or a poor man devoted more to tippling than to industry, as others saw him (and it is not clear that the two judgments are mutually exclusive), it seems fairly certain that the great merchant was indeed a self-made man of humble origins. ... The most interesting feature of such evidence, however, is its uncommonness. ...

Vastly rich or fairly rich, celebrated or obscure, it mattered not: the upper 1 per cent of wealth holders of the great cities—the rich of their time—almost universally were born to families of substance and standing. ...

In New York City, as in Boston, the relative worth of persons at the beginning of the period appeared to be the most significant factor in determining their chances of belonging to the rich by the mid-1840s. New York City's more dynamic economic growth was reflected by the greater ease with which individuals from each of the five categories [of wealth] were able to remain in or move slightly upward within the rich class. The great disparity between the two cities in this respect was the rate of increase in absolute wealth made by New York City's lower-wealth categories.

Nonetheless, in New York City as in Boston, the few persons who rose from the "upper middle" level at the beginning of the period to the rich of the 1840s were more often than not from families of great wealth. New York City's supremely rich suffered no sudden loss of fortune during the era. Not one of the dozen families that contained individuals worth $200,000 or more in 1828 dropped below $100,000 by 1845. Only William Jauncey, of the almost fifty persons valued between $100,000 and $200,000 in 1828, fell from the class of the rich by 1845; and even he barely failed to qualify. ...

The pursuit of wealth in the antebellum decades was marked not by fluidity but by stability.

---

1. According to Pessen, was the distribution of wealth in New York City widening or narrowing from 1778 to 1828 to 1848?
2. Which of Pessen's statistics on the distribution of wealth in New York City is most surprising? Why?
3. According to Pessen how was wealth acquired in mid-nineteenth-century New York City?
4. Why did Astor represent the exception rather than the rule for getting rich in New York City?
5. Why was it easier for the rich to get richer in New York City than in Boston?
6. What was Pessen's message about equal opportunity and social mobility in mid-nineteenth-century America and especially in New York City?

3-4-4. FRAMING BROADWAY: AUGUSTUS KÖLLNER, ARTIST, 1850

From the founding of New Amsterdam to the present day, Broadway has been New York City's most famous street. It is also New York's longest street—stretching from the Battery in the harbor all the way up Manhattan, through the Bronx and upstate. Originally an Indian path, it became the place to be for fancy homes, stores and restaurants, churches, theaters, and prominent businesses, including the Astor House Hotel, which is the large building in the right foreground of the following drawing. The church with the pillars next to the hotel is St. Paul's Anglican Chapel built in 1766 and used by George Washington as well as by the 9-11 mourners.

Barnum's Museum was across Broadway at Ann Street with the flag and snake sign on top. Phineas T. Barnum was an impresario who so skillfully displayed and advertised his collection of freaks and fantasies that his dime museum became the nation's first and foremost entertainment emporium. The building next to Barnum's with the striped awning was the substantial business of a merchant. Further to the left, but omitted from the drawing, was Astor's Park Theater.

Broadway has been memorialized in poems, novels, songs, and paintings, such as this 1850 lithograph by a German immigrant whose images of America were and still are widely admired.

Source: Augustus Köllner, "Broadway." *Views of American Cities* (New York: Goupil, Vibert and Co., 1848-1851).

1. According to this drawing, how busy and prosperous was lower Broadway during the 1840s?
2. How did the Astor House Hotel compare with the other buildings on Broadway? Why does it matter?
3. How did the buildings across from the Astor House and St. Paul's Chapel reflect the integration of social and economic functions in mid-nineteenth century New York City?
4. How did this drawing reflect the diversity and vitality of mid-19th New York City?
5. How is this drawing similar to but different from the drawing of New York City in Document 3-3-4 above? Were there two New York's?

SELECTED RESOURCES

Gilfoyle, Timothy J. *City of Eros: New York City, Prostitution, and the Commercialization of Sex, 1790–1920.* New York: W. W. Norton, 1992.

Gilje, Paul A. *The Road to Mobocracy: Popular Disorder in New York City, 1763–1834.* Chapel Hill, NC: University of North Carolina Press, 1987.

Headley, Joel Tyler. *The Great Riots of New York, 1712–1873.* New York: Dover, 1873/1971.

Hill, Marilynn Wood. *Their Sisters' Keepers: Prostitution in New York City, 1830–1870.* Berkeley, CA: University of California Press, 1993.

Rock, Howard B. *Artisans of the New Republic: The Tradesmen of New York City in the Age of Jefferson.* New York: New York University Press, 1984.

Stansell, Christine. *City of Women: Sex and Class in New York, 1789–1860.* New York: Alfred A. Knopf, 1986.

Weinbaum, Paul O. *Mobs and Demagogues: The New York Response to Collective Violence in the Early Nineteenth Century.* Ann Arbor, MI: University of Michigan Press, 1977.

Wilentz, Sean. *Chants Democratic: New York City and the Rise of the American Working Class, 1788–1850.* New York: Oxford University Press, 1984.

www.lost museum.cuny.edu: P. T. Barnum

www.merchantshouse.org: an 1832 merchant's house

www.nydivided.org: the riots of 1834 and 1863

www.vny.cuny.edu: the 1835 fire and the cholera epidemics of 1834 and 1849

CHAPTER 4

1840–1865

Mid-nineteenth-century New York City was explosive in many ways. Riots in 1849, throughout the 1850s and in 1863 exposed the stresses of a city confronting change. The economic growth stimulated by the Erie Canal and extensive immigration was offset by two major fires, several devastating epidemics and the depression of 1857. Intense political conflict within New York City as well as between the city and the state kept Gotham in turmoil.

Being a major port, a railroad hub, a marketing and financial center could bring wealth and opportunity, but could also breed exploitation and social stratification. Indeed, the sufferings of the poor became strikingly apparent when the city spawned the nation's first slum, called the Five Points, where density, disease, filth and crime revealed the underside of progress. It evoked the poverty of European cities and embodied what America did not want to be.

The material in this chapter looks at the implications and complications of mid-nineteenth-century urban growth. First, it examines the debate over Central Park and its national significance for urban development. Second is the tension that emerged between native-born Americans and Irish Catholic immigrants. Third is the debate over the role of the police set within the context of persistent riots. Fourth is an exploration of African American activism through material about a school teacher and others struggling for equality in mid-nineteenth-century Gotham.

Together these topics provide perspective on the challenges faced by the city as it grew economically, geographically and demographically. As poet Walt Whitman explained in 1860, New York was bubbling over with diverse economic activities and engaging, spirited people (see Document 1-3). Because Whitman cherished its uniqueness, he urged Gotham to "submit to no models but your own, O city"[1]

UNIT 4-1. CITY BUILDING: CENTRAL PARK

Central Park was a response to urban growth and a model for cities all over the nation. New York City already had three small parks downtown (Bowling Green, Battery Park, and City Hall Park) plus five further uptown (Washington Square, Tompkins Square, Union Square, Madison Square, and Reservoir Square, later called Bryant Park). These parks marked the city's movement up the island and, as squares, they simply punctuated the city's grid, which had been laid out in 1811. The decision to build a much bigger park in a yet unsettled area as a counterpoint to the grid posed provocative questions about economic development and social organization.

By 1850, New York had expanded to 42nd Street where the monumental Croton Reservoir, completed in 1842, provided the city's first decent water supply. It signaled the city's relentless movement uptown and its growing need for public services. Accordingly, William Cullen Bryant, editor of the New York Evening Post, introduced the idea of a major park in 1844. Bryant believed that a booming city like New York needed a gracious public space in order to compare favorably with great European cities like London and Paris, where parks were valued not only as sources of civic pride but also as "lungs for the city."

Bryant's campaign for a park was reinforced by Andrew Jackson Downing, a prominent New York State landscape architect. Downing championed the democratic virtues of a "People's Park" in the center of Manhattan to be shared by rich and poor alike. In his view, the park would complement "the common school and the ballot-box" by breaking down the distance between classes. Downing hoped that exposure to the upper classes and to the soothing effects of nature would transform workingmen into gentlemen, thereby uplifting the uncouth inhabitants of the unruly city.

Gradually, support for the park grew, but it remained mired in controversy for the next twelve years. Much of the argument was about whether to locate the park on the existing 150 acres of Jones Wood stretching from 68th to 77th Streets between Third Avenue and the East River. In 1851, the city and state legislatures approved of the Jones Wood site, but, soon thereafter, support emerged for a bigger park situated on 750 less lovely acres in the center of the island. Not discussed was the fact that those acres were home to communities of working-class whites and blacks who would have to be evicted.

The debate over location reflected competing agendas. Businessmen wanted land by the East River to remain available for commercial purposes, not parks. Real-estate speculators and property owners supported whichever site best suited their pocketbooks. Politicians savored the park's vast potential for patronage in construction work. The elite wanted a safe, serene place to promenade and ride in their fancy carriages. Reformers concerned about slums downtown opposed wasting precious fiscal resources uptown. Some people complained that the park would only benefit the rich and would be too far away for the poor to get there; others feared the opposite and warned that a park would bring the poor uptown along with beer, noise and crime. The controversy over the park captured the different priorities of different people in a diversified city.[2]

4-1-1. OPPOSING CENTRAL PARK: DR. JOHN GRISCOM, HEALTH REFORMER, 1853

Writing to the New York Times on June 30, 1853, health reformer, Dr. John H. Griscom, explained his reasons for opposing a large central park. Public health was a major concern in nineteenth-century New York because of the frequency of major epidemics including yellow fever, typhoid and cholera. With over 5,000 people dying from cholera in 1849 and much of the blame being placed on slum conditions in the Five Points, the call for a park seemed frivolous.

Source: *New York Times,* June 30, 1853.

To the Editor of the New York Daily Times:
... My objections to additional large parks in New York are:

1. That they are not needed for sanitary purposes, there being an abundance of other resources for recreation and fresh air;

2. That they would directly and indirectly augment the evils of crowded tenements and high rents, which now press upon this City with the most direful results; and

3. Because other measures are imperatively needed for the ventilation and purification of the city, which public parks cannot accomplish. ...

Our great difficulty is not a defective supply of good air. No city in the world is more blest than this, with an exuberance of that important article at our very doors. No number of parks, of any dimensions, would increase the supply one grain. The noble rivers, ... the adjacent illimitable country, ... our proximity to the ocean ... all these are sources of pure air, which no other city can boast. No, it is because we shut it out from our dwellings, our schools, our workshops and our public assemblies; because we permit our citizens to be crowded into cellars, alleys and rear courts; because by filthy streets and yards we allow the air to become poisoned, so that what little does get into our dwellings is unfit to breathe. It is for these reasons that we suffer in health, and fill premature graves. ...

If we would, therefore, ventilate the City, we must begin by enlarging and ventilating the dwellings; by prohibiting the erection and occupation of the thousands of rooms no larger than prison cells, and by prohibiting the occupation as residences, of hundreds of cellars, in which the poor are now compelled to crowd themselves. ...

Unlike most other large cities, New York can extend itself only in one direction. The space for it is limited, and... its population must necessarily continue concentrated, and land and rents maintain a high value. I hold this proposition to be self-evident, that the greater the amount of space on this island, rendered unavailable for dwellings, the higher in price, and more densely crowded with tenements and people, will be the remainder. ...

If, however, our Legislature will compel us to reserve so large a portion of our restricted area from more useful purposes, we beg them to give it in divided doses, and, instead of one plot of 800 acres... give eight parks of 100 acres each or sixteen of 50 acres, and disperse them over the island, that the air, the trees, the flowers, the fountains and the walks, may be brought more within the reach of all. This would certainly be less aristocratic; more democratic, and far more conducive to public health.

---

1. Why did Griscom believe that the park was unnecessary and would not make New York more healthful?
2. What did he identify as the real reasons for New York's health problems?
3. What public policies would he have preferred to solve those problems?
4. Which of his arguments made most sense? Why were they not widely supported?

4-1-2. PROMOTING CENTRAL PARK: FERNANDO WOOD, MAYOR, 1855

Real-estate interests were upset that so many potentially marketable lots would be lost to the park. Allied with city legislators, they got a bill passed to start the park further uptown, thereby freeing up more blocks for commercial and residential development. Their scheme to shrink the park was foiled by Fernando Wood, a long-time park booster who was mayor from 1855–1858 and 1860–1862. Despite questions about his personal integrity and despite evidence that he had financial interests in real estate near the park, most observers then and since considered this veto message of March 23, 1855 his finest moment in office. To be sure, Wood knew that the park would mean a lot of construction jobs for his political supporters, but perhaps he also saw beyond self-interest. Certainly he deserves some credit for urging that Central Park construction jobs be provided for the destitute during the 1857 Depression, a suggestion that was widely rejected. Even if politically motivated, Wood's concept of government's social responsibility was well ahead of its times.[3]

Source: *New York Times*, March 24, 1855.

In my opinion, future generations who are to pay the expense, will have good reasons for reflecting upon us, if we permitted the entire island to be taken possession of by population, without some spot like this, devoted to rural beauty, healthful recreation, and pure atmosphere. ...

We will be derelict, if by any narrow or selfish feeling of present saving, we deprive the teeming millions yet to inhabit and toil upon this island, of one place not given up to mammon, where they can, even if but one day in the year, observe and worship nature, untarnished by art. To admit the necessity of a great park, and to assert that this will be too large, is, in my opinion, an exceedingly limited view of the question, and entirely unworthy of even the present position of this metropolis, to say nothing of a destiny now opening so brilliantly before us.

Let us not follow our Dutch ancestors in their views of municipal prudence, who considered cow-paths as proper sites for streets and avenues, inasmuch as they saved the necessary expenses of surveys, etc. ...

But [even if] admitting the park too large, and that it should be diminished, this resolution proposes to do it in an improper manner, inasmuch as it asks that the only portion of it that can be accessible to the foot-passenger now shall be lopped off, and, in fact, remove it nearly a mile further off from the present densely populated part of the city.

---

1. What were Wood's main reasons for supporting a large central park?
2. In opposing shrinking the park, whose interests did Wood have in mind? Why?
3. Did his Central Park veto suggest that Wood was a visionary, a realist, a bold leader and/or just a clever politician?

4-1-3. EXPLAINING CENTRAL PARK: FREDERICK LAW OLMSTED, LANDSCAPE DESIGNER, 1871

It was amazing that any consensus emerged from so much controversy and so many contending interests. However, it did, and, finally the central site was adopted by the city and approved by the state in 1856. The next step was to design the park, a challenge that was ably met by Frederick Law Olmsted and Calvert Vaux, Olmsted was the newly appointed park superintendent with a background in scientific agriculture and landscape design who had written articles for Downing's horticulture magazine. Vaux was an architect who worked for Downing. Their shared faith in the benign influence of the natural environment on human behavior defined their proposal for Central Park, which they called the Greensward Plan.[4] In 1871, Olmsted explained the concepts behind the park.

Source: Frederick Law Olmsted, "Public Parks and the Enlargement of Towns," *Journal of Social Science* (1871), 18, 21, 22, 34.

Consider that the New York Park and the Brooklyn Park are the only places in those associated cities where…you will find a body of Christians coming together, and with an evident glee in the prospect of coming together, all classes largely represented, with a common purpose, not at all intellectual, competitive with none, disposing to jealousy and spiritual or intellectual pride toward none, each individual adding by his mere presence to the pleasure of all others, all helping to the greater happiness of each. You may thus often see vast numbers of persons brought together, poor and rich, young and old, Jew and Gentile. …

If the great city to arise here is to be laid out little by little, and chiefly to suit the views of the landowners, acting only individually, and thinking only of how what they do is to affect the value in the next week or the next year of the few lots that each my hold at the time, the opportunities …to give the lungs a bath of pure sunny air, to give the mind a suggestion of rest from the devouring eagerness and intellectual strife of town life, will always be few to any [and] to many will amount to nothing. …

We want a ground to which people may easily go after their day's work is done, and where they may stroll for an hour, seeing, hearing, and feeling nothing of the bustle and jar of the streets, where they shall, in effect, find the city put far away from them. We want the greatest possible contrast with the streets and the shops and the rooms of the town which will be consistent with convenience and the preservation of good order and neatness. We want, especially, the greatest possible contrast with the restraining and confining conditions of the town, those conditions which compel us to walk circumspectly, watchfully, jealously, which compel us to look closely upon others without sympathy. Practically, what we most want is a simple, broad, open space of greensward, with sufficient play of surface, and a sufficient number of trees about it to supply a variety of light and shade. This we want as a central feature. We want depth of wood enough about it not only for comfort in hot weather, but to completely shut out the city from our landscapes. …

No one who has closely observed the conduct of the people who visit the Park, can doubt that it exercises a distinctly harmonizing and refining influence upon the most unfortunate and most lawless classes of the city—an influence favorable to courtesy, self-control and temperance. ...

1. What functions did Olmsted want parks to perform?
2. How did his design for parks promote those functions?
3. Was Olmsted anti-city?
4. Was Olmsted an elitist?

4-1-4. ENVISIONING CENTRAL PARK: CALVERT VAUX, ARCHITECT, 1860

Calvert Vaux was an English architect who came to the United States in 1850 to work with landscape designer, Andrew Jackson Downing. In 1856 Vaux invited Frederick Law Olmsted to join him in the competition for planning Central Park, which they won. The pair also designed Prospect Park and Fort Greene Park, both in Brooklyn. Vaux later worked on the Metropolitan Museum of Art and the American Museum of Natural History. Over time, however, his style seemed old-fashioned and his personality abrasive. Perhaps disappointment led to his drowning in Brooklyn's Gravesend Bay at the age of 73. The following drawing reflects Vaux's vision of Central Park.[5]

Source: Board of Commissioners of the Central Park, *Third Annual Report, January 1860* (New York: William C. Bryant Co., 1860), 40.

1. What words best describe Vaux's vision of Central Park?
2. What aspects of the drawing best promote that vision?
3. How well did Vaux's drawing reflect Olmstead's concept of the park as expressed above?
4. Did Vaux's drawing suggest that the park would complement and/or compensate for the realities of urban life? Was Vaux anti-city?

4-1-5. QUESTIONING CENTRAL PARK: EDWARD K. SPANN, HISTORIAN, 1981

The historian Edward K. Spann questioned the long-term legacy of the park and the urban priorities it reflected.

Source: Edward K. Spann, *The New Metropolis, New York City, 1840–1857.* (New York: Columbia University Press, 1981), 172–3.

Rather than weaving humane and humanizing space into its changing fabric, New York chose to set one great park against its city self, a magnificent exception to its rampant commercialism, disorderliness and congestion, but an exception nonetheless. Olmsted's noble design would ameliorate some of the problems of a troubled city. It could not, however, eliminate the effects of the prevailing mismanagement of space. As a refuge for the wealthy and the influential from those effects, it complemented the principle that Manhattan Island be developed chiefly in the interests of commerce rather than as an urban society of civilized men. Great triumph of metropolitan design though it was, Central Park was the product of a flawed metropolis and metropolitan way of life, of a society which served to encourage many of its citizens to dream of escape to better places beyond the limits of the city.

1. From Spann's perspective, what were the advantages and disadvantages of Central Park?
2. From Spann's perspective, how did the park reflect a fundamentally "flawed metropolis"?
3. Which of the preceding documents support or refute Spann's analysis?
4. In the light of Spann's criticisms, should New Yorkers still treat Central Park as "sacred ground"?

UNIT 4-2. CHANGE AND CHALLENGE: IRISH IMMIGRANTS

William R. Grace and Winifred O'Reilly had one thing in common. They both defied the stereotype of Irish Catholic immigrants as shiftless, unskilled, improvident, impoverished criminals and alcoholics who were tools of Tammany Hall, the political machine of the Democratic Party. Grace was a wealthy shipper and anti-Tammany reformer who became the city's first Irish-born Catholic mayor serving two terms during the 1880s. O'Reilly was a poor immigrant from Ireland who started working at age seven. At eleven, she acquired the sewing skills that enabled her to help her mother survive, to later supplement her husband's grocery store, and, after his death, to support herself and her daughter, Leonora. That daughter also worked as a child in the needle trades and became an important labor leader. Although Grace and O'Reilly represented opposite ends of the economic spectrum, they reflected similar patterns of hard work, success and social activism so associated with New York, but rarely associated with Irish Catholic immigrants.[6]

In the mid-nineteenth century, Irish Catholics composed the largest and poorest migration of people to the United States since its founding. They faced formidable obstacles. Economically devastated by the potato famine and the enclosure of land in Ireland, they traveled to America in so-called 'coffin ships' because the conditions onboard were awful. Upon arrival, they were subject to cultural prejudice, job discrimination and housing exploitation. Yet, they survived by a combination of resistance and resilience.

4-2-1. TOURING THE FIVE POINTS: JAMES D. McCABE, WRITER, 1872

Poor as they were, most of New York City's mid-nineteenth-century Irish immigrants settled in the Five Points, named for five intersecting streets that are now replaced by courts and a park next to Chinatown. Built over an old pond, the ground was unstable and fetid; the buildings were decrepit; the streets were filthy and unpaved. It was America's first slum. Although people condemned the Five Points, they found it fascinating. Escorted by two policemen, the English author Charles Dickens visited the site and vividly described its horrors in 1842. Images of crime, vice, alcohol, opium, prostitution, gambling, gangs, riots, disease and death shocked the nation. Representing the greatest dangers of immigration and urbanization, the Five Points became a metaphor for everything that was wrong with New York City.

America's ambivalence towards New York City was captured in several popular late-nineteenth-century books that claimed to explain New York to non-New Yorkers. The title and subtitle of James D. McCabe, Jr.'s 1872 guidebook played to the prevailing interest in and fear of the city. He promised to expose the *Lights and Shadows of New York Life; or the Sights and Sensations of the Great City. A Work Descriptive of the City of New York in all its Various Phases; with Full and Graphic Account of its Splendors and Wretchedness; its High and Low Life; its Marble Palaces and Dark Dens; its Attractions and Dangers; its Rings and Frauds; its Leading Men and Politicians; its Adventurers; its Charities; its Mysteries, and its Crimes*. McCabe's discussion of the Five Points served his purposes well.

Source: James D. McCabe, Jr., *Lights and Shadows of New York Life; or the Sights and Sensations of the Great City* (Philadelphia, PA: National Publishing Company, 1872), 398–403.

Just back of the City Hall, towards the East River, and within full sight of Broadway, is the terrible and wretched district known as the Five Points. You may stand in the open space at the intersection of Park and Worth streets, the true Five Points, in the midst of a wide sea of sin and suffering, and gaze right into Broadway with its marble palaces of trade, its busy, well-dressed throng, and its roar and bustle so indicative of wealth and prosperity. It is almost within pistol shot, but what a wide gulf lies between the two thoroughfares, a gulf that the wretched, shabby, dirty creatures who go slouching by you may never cross.

There everything is bright and cheerful. Here every surrounding is dark and wretched. The streets are narrow and dirty, the dwellings are foul and gloomy, and the very air seems heavy with misery and crime. For many a block the scene is the same. This is the realm of Poverty. Here want and suffering, and vice hold their courts. It is a strange land to you who have known nothing but the upper and better quarters of the great city. It is a very terrible place to those who are forced to dwell in it. For many blocks to the north and south of where we stand in Worth street, and from Elm street back to the East River, the Five Points presents a succession of similar scenes of wretchedness. ...

Twenty years ago there stood in Park street, near Worth, a large dilapidated building known as the "Old Brewery." It was almost in ruins, but it was the most densely populated building in the city. It is said to have contained at one time as many as 1200 people. Its passages were long and dark, and it abounded in rooms of all sizes and descriptions, many of which were secure hiding places for men and stolen goods. The occupants were chiefly the most desperate characters in New York, and the "Old Brewery" was everywhere recognized as the headquarters of crime in the metropolis. The narrow thoroughfare extending around it was known as "Murderers' Alley" and "The Den of Thieves." No respectable person ever ventured near it, and even the officers of the law avoided it except when their duty compelled them to enter it. It was a terrible place. ...

The locality is better now. In 1852, the Old Brewery was purchased by the Ladies' Home Missionary Society of the Methodist Episcopal Church, and was pulled down. Its site is now occupied by the neat and comfortable buildings of the Five Points Mission. Just across Worth street is the Five Points House of Industry, and business is creeping in slowly to change the character of this immediate locality forever. ...

From Franklin to Chatham street there is scarcely a house without a bucket shop or "distillery," as the signs over the door read, on the ground floor. Here the vilest and most poisonous compounds are sold as whiskey, gin, rum, and brandy. Their effects are visible on every hand. Some of these houses are brothels of the lowest description, and, ah, such terrible faces as look out upon you as you pass them by! Surely no more hopeless, crime-stained visages are to be seen on this side of the home of the damned. The filth that is thrown into the street lies there and decays until the kindly heavens pour down a drenching shower and wash it away. As a natural consequence, the neighborhood is sickly, and sometimes the infection amounts almost to a plague.

Between Fourteenth street and the Bowery, half a million of people are crowded into about one-fifth of the island of Manhattan. Within this section there are about 13,000 tenement houses, fully one-half of which are in bad condition, dirty and unhealthy. One small block in the Five Points district is said to contain 382 families. The most wretched tenement houses are to be found in the Five Points. ... Every room is crowded with people. Sometimes as many as a dozen are packed into a single apartment. Decency and morality fade away here. Drunkenness is the general rule.

1. According to McCabe, what were the biggest problems of the Five Points?
2. What were the five most negative terms that McCabe used to describe the Five Pointers?
3. How did McCabe think that the problems of the Five Points could be solved?
4. What image of New York did McCabe convey to non-New Yorkers?

4-2-2. ILLUSTRATING THE FIVE POINTS

This famous lithograph of the Five Points on the facing page is really a commentary on the people in the neighborhood and their social behavior. Like all documents, it has a point of view. At the same time, it provides a window on the physical city in terms of density, housing, business, transportation, lighting, water supply and sanitation (see the pig). Note that groceries were also liquor stores.

Source: "Five Points, 1827, Intersection of Cross, Anthony and Orange Streets," from *Valentine's Manual,* 1885, page 112, same as #35910; negative no. 44668. Collection of the New York Historical Society.

1. What aspects of life in the Five Points were emphasized in this drawing by the types of people, activities and buildings?
2. In what ways did this drawing confirm McCabe's description above?
3. What are the rich people in the drawing doing in the Five Points?
4. How would this drawing have been interpreted by Griscom, Wood, Olmsted and Spann from unit 4-1 or by Hughes, Stone, Stott and Diner from this unit? In what ways would they agree and disagree?
5. In terms of the streets, buildings and people, what were the major differences between the Five Points and Broadway? (see Document 3-4-4) What conclusions about mid-nineteenth-century New York City can be drawn from the comparison?

4-2-3. EXPANDING RELIGIOUS FREEDOM: BISHOP JOHN HUGHES, 1844

Bishop John Hughes was one of the most controversial figures of the era. He was nicknamed "Dagger John" for two reasons. One was the cross that he always drew next to his signature; the other was his combative personality. In his quest to strengthen the Irish Catholic community in New York City, Hughes waged a war against anti-Catholicism in the public schools, expanded the Catholic educational system and mobilized Irish Catholic voters. By increasing the number of parishes, priests and nuns, he was able to develop social services for the poor. In order to protect Irish workers from dishonest financial schemers, Hughes played a key role in the 1851 creation of the Emigrant Savings Bank, a successful financial institution that survives today. By promoting Irish Catholic interests, he was resisting assimilation to the dominant Anglo-Saxon Protestant culture.

Indeed, Hughes was best known for his opposition to nativism, the anti-Catholic movement mounted by American-born (and therefore called native) Protestants during the 1840s and 1850s. The more Hughes challenged the status quo by advocating aggressively for a despised group, the more bitterly he was assailed by politicians and the press. The public school controversy of the 1840s was particularly intense because, thanks to reformer Horace Mann, public schools

were increasingly considered central to assimilation in a heterogeneous society and to community building in a democracy.

From the perspective of a Protestant-dominated society, Hughes seemed audacious, obnoxious, and dangerous when he accused the Protestant-dominated public schools of being prejudiced and when he advocated public support for Catholic schools. In a series of open letters published in various New York City newspapers, Hughes defended his opposition to the use of overtly anti-Catholic texts and teachers in the Protestant-controlled public schools. As he attacked the newspaper editors who attacked him, the argument became nasty and personal. However, at its core lay two issues that remain central to the history of New York and the nation—the role of public schools and the meaning of freedom of religion in a complex, pluralistic country.

Source: *New York Tribune*, May 22, 1844.

[I]ntolerance was a barrier to every hope in my native land, and there was but one other country in which I was led to believe that the rights and privileges of citizens rendered all men equal. I can even now remember my reflections, on first beholding the American Flag. It never crossed my mind that a time might come when that flag, the emblem of the freedom just alluded to, would be divided by apportioning its *stars* to the citizens of native birth, and its *stripes* only to the portion of the naturalized foreigner. I was of course but young and inexperienced; and yet, even recent events have not diminished my confidence in that ensign of civil and religious liberty. It is possible that I was mistaken, but I still clung to the delusion, if it be one, and as I trusted to that flag, or a Nation's faith, I think it more likely that its stripes will disappear altogether, and that before it shall be employed as an instrument of bad faith towards the foreigners of every land, the white portion will *blush i*nto crimson, and then the glorious stars alone will remain.

---

1. Why did Hughes come to the United States? What did the American flag symbolize to him?
2. What was the double meaning of the words "stars" and "stripes" in Hughes' metaphor?
3. Did Hughes advocate assimilation or pluralism?
4. Would Hughes have supported the Flushing Remonstrance and/or King's college (see Unit 2-2)?

4-2-4. LIMITING RELIGIOUS FREEDOM: WILLIAM LEETE STONE, NEWSPAPER EDITOR, 1844

Responding to Hughes, William Leete Stone, the controversial editor of the *New York Commercial Advertiser*, clarified the nativist position.

Source: *New York Commercial Advertiser,* June 6, 1844.

We have, or ought to have, a predominant national lineage, a predominant national character, and (as that without which no nation ever yet has existed, and I think never can exist, any more than a body without a soul), a *predominant national* religion, although God forbid we should ever have an established national Church. Last, though not least in importance, and as a necessary consequence of the preceding, should we have our national *sacred book*, our old, long established, well beloved, *faithfully translated, English, Protestant Bible*. ...

Proceeding on the ground that, as *matter of fact*, we were a Christian and a Protestant nation, [the New York City public schools] adopted the English Bible as a standard book, notwithstanding the objection of the infidel, who rejected its authority, and of Popish priests who treated it with still greater contumely, by refusing to have it taught to the people. This was the best compromise between sectarianism and infidelity that could be made. It represented the *soul of the nation*. It was carried to the extreme of liberality.

The foreigner who came seeking protection among us, be he Mohametan, Pagan or Papist, was expected to conform to the spirit of this plan or yield its benefits. The first had as good a right to demand the exclusion of *any* Bible, because the Koran was not also used, as the latter to raise this clamor about the infringement of rights which were never vested. It was not an infringement of your rights, as you deceptively represent it, but a determination to preserve our own national character, our own national religion, our own national Bible, against the attacks of those who thus repaid the liberality and protection which our laws, beyond those of any nation on earth, held out to them.

---

1. According to Stone, what was the "national character" and how did it relate to religion in the United States?
2. What is the difference between a "predominant national religion" and "an established national Church"? Should the United States have either one?
3. How did Stone justify using the Protestant Bible in public schools?
4. Who did Stone consider infidels? Did Stone believe that infidels could become good Americans?
5. Did Stone advocate assimilation or pluralism?
6. Would Stone have supported the Flushing Remonstrance and/or King's college (see Unit 2-2)?

4-2-5. CHARTING JOBS IN 1855: RICHARD B. STOTT, HISTORIAN, 1990

Employment patterns are a fascinating mirror of socio-economic structure and, therefore, provide windows on both social mobility and socio-economic conflict. The historian Richard B. Stott based this chart on four charts that came from the 1855 New York State Census. Stott's chart illuminates the opportunities for and limitations of social mobility in the mid-nineteenth-century city.

Source: Richard B. Stott, *Workers in the Metropolis: Class, Ethnicity and Youth in Antebellum New York City* (Ithaca, NY: Cornell University Press, 1990), 92.

Ethnic division of labor, New York City, 1855

Occupation	No.	% Foreign-born	% Native-born	% Irish	% German	% English & Scot	% Black
Manual							
Servant	31,749	93	7	74	14	3	3
Laborer	20,238	98	2	86	9	2	3
Tailor	12,609	96	4	33	53	5	0
Seamstress	9,819	67	33	46	10	7	1
Carpenter	7,531	64	35	30	22	9	0
Shoemaker	6,745	96	4	31	55	5	0
Carter	5,498	58	41	46	7	4	1
Baker	3,692	90	10	23	54	8	0
Bricklayer	3,634	79	21	61	9	9	0
Cabinetmaker	3,517	83	17	12	61	4	0
Painter	3,485	77	23	31	26	15	0
Porter	3,052	64	36	48	11	3	6
Blacksmith	2,642	82	18	51	20	9	0
Laundress	2,563	79	21	69	6	2	14
Shipbuilder	2,287	57	43	29	7	13	0
Printer	2,077	55	45	25	11	14	0
Cigarmaker	1,996	77	23	5	61	4	0
Peddler	1,915	98	2	39	49	3	1
Stonecutter	1,914	96	4	65	11	17	0
Driver	1,741	56	44	46	3	5	6
Machinist	1,714	72	28	23	21	22	0
Manufacturing jeweler	1,705	61	39	10	28	10	0
Hatter	1,422	63	37	20	30	5	0
Leatherworker	1,386	71	29	30	28	9	0
Total, manual occupations	156,610	84	16	51	23	7	2

Percentage of all workers in manual occupations = 77

Total, in manufacturing = 75,248
Percentage of all workers in manufacturing = 37

Occupation	No.	% Foreign-born	% Native-born	% Irish	% German	% English & Scot	% Black
Nonmanual							
Clerk	13,929	43	56	15	16	7	0
Food dealer	8,300	63	37	22	37	3	0
Merchant	6,299	27	72	4	10	7	0
Shopkeeper	2,641	69	31	35	17	12	0
Boardinghouse keeper	1,723	44	56	17	14	7	1
Physician	1,469	38	62	8	16	8	0
Total, nonmanual occupations	44,734	49	51	17	20	7	1

Percentage of all workers in nonmanual occupations = 23

TOTAL, All	204,344	76	24	43	23	7	2

1. In which occupations were the foreign-born concentrated?
2. Which white ethnic groups dominated which occupations?
3. What was the biggest difference between black and white job patterns?
4. Which occupations were most desirable and had the most status in 1855? Who held them?
5. How can this chart help explain class, ethnic and racial conflict in mid-nineteenth-century New York City?

4-2-6. DESCRIBING THE IRISH STRUGGLE: HASIA DINER, HISTORIAN, 1996

The historian Hasia R. Diner described the challenges faced by the Irish Catholics who came to America during the Great Migration, when almost 850,000 people left Ireland for an uncertain future. By 1850, over a quarter of New York City's population was Irish-born, making them the largest ethnic group in the city and redefining New York accordingly.

Source: Hasia R. Diner, "The Most Irish City in the Union: The Era of the Great Migration, 1844–1877," in Ronald H. Bayor and Timothy J. Meagher (eds), *The New York Irish* (Baltimore, MD: Johns Hopkins University Press, 1996), 99–105.

Life was not easy for the rural Irish struggling to adjust to urban America. Statistics on Irish housing find them living in New York's most overcrowded neighborhoods. Figures on income put them more often among the city's paupers than anyone else. Arrest records put them either among the criminals or victims of the police in regard to police brutality and false arrests. ... The Irish entered lunatic asylums, charity hospitals, prisons, and almshouses more than any other group. They had the city's highest rates of typhus, typhoid fever, cholera, and all other diseases that accompany hunger, poverty, and congestion. ...

But not all of Irish life in New York in the nineteenth century could be described under the heading of "social pathology." Many Irish moved from poverty to small business. It was not unheard of to capitalize on Old World skills in the New York setting. Unmarried women who could take advantage of opportunities in domestic service found New York a treasure trove of unimagined possibilities. ...

The New York setting and the thick clustering of the Irish in massive numbers made it possible for the Irish to create institutions to ease the difficulties of migration and to help sustain the movement of some, slowly for sure, out of poverty. The political machine and the machinery of urban government, the Roman Catholic Church, the social and cultural organizations of the community, and the nationalist movements all helped define Irish ethnicity and a New York urban life that transcended the pathos of poverty. ... They bridged the chasm between being immigrants from Ireland to being Irish Americans. ...

The Irish began their political career in New York as the pawns of the urban Democratic machine. They exchanged their votes for unskilled jobs, petty licenses, and other relatively low-cost benefits. These "crumbs" represented the absolutely highest these impoverished rural newcomers expected. But as they grew in number, they became more American and experienced a modest degree of economic mobility, their demands increased, their appetites were whetted, and the Democratic factions responded. The crumbs grew into substantial slices, and by the 1860's, the time of Tweed's hegemony, the Irish garnered the most jobs, the best patronage, and increasingly significant positions, even key leadership roles. ...

Where the political system was inherited from someone else's and over time manipulated by the Irish, the Catholic Church represented their own key institution, which they made, sustained, and dominated. ... On the eve of the Famine immigration, in 1842 John Hughes became the bishop of New York. Until his death in 1864 Hughes staked out a Catholic and Irish position within the church and without. He aggressively called on New York's Catholics to defend themselves, symbolically and physically, against attacks from Protestant nativists. He called for the creation of separate Catholic institutions, including schools, hospitals, orphanages, banks, and benevolent associations to incubate an Irish American culture, blending Catholic piety, love of the Irish homeland, and American patriotism. Internally, he made the Catholic Church more responsive to the needs of the poor Irish masses. He vigorously increased the number of parishes to make the church more accessible to the masses. ...

By the end of the 1870's although the Irish were still clustering in low-paying jobs, they had begun to dominate the city's political apparatus and command the resources of a mighty church structure. The leadership of the increasingly respectable trade union movement rested primarily in their hands, and some highly visible jobs, including teaching, police work, and firefighting, had become almost synonymous with being Irish. The Irish had a political cause they could offer as a litmus test to non-Irish politicians and developed a hybrid culture that organically blended Irish and American motifs. This was true all over America, but more so in New York, because it was New York.

---

1. According to Diner, what obstacles did Irish immigrants confront?
2. According to Diner, how were Irish immigrants transformed into Irish Americans?
3. According to Diner, how important was Bishop Hughes?
4. According to Diner, how did Irish Americans provide a model for other immigrant groups?
5. Which of the documents in this unit best support Diner's analysis?

UNIT 4-3. LAW AND ORDER: THE RIOTS OF 1849 AND 1863

Life in mid-nineteenth-century New York City was complicated by a tremendous population increase fueled by domestic migrants and foreign immigrants. The bigger the city got, the harder it was to control. Consequently, the period was marked by gang fights, riots and strikes. As the city prospered, the distance between the upper and lower classes grew and bonds of common interest shrank, particularly as the nature of work became more impersonal and less secure. The result was conflict between workers and employers, immigrants and the native-born, Democrats and Republicans.

The chaos caused by the gang fights, riots and labor strikes of the 1830s and 1840s convinced the city's leaders to establish a formal police department in 1845. Until this time, New York City had preferred a small police force in order to avoid creating a military state reminiscent of the Old World. All it had and felt it needed was a citizen's watch comprised of untrained, poorly paid volunteers. Although still limited and not fully professional, the new police force represented a turning point in New York's history. Its creation inaugurated a long debate over how to balance diversity and unity, order and disorder, freedom and social control in a democracy.[7]

4-3-1. PROTESTING THE 1849 RIOTS: CITIZENS, 1849

The 1849 Astor Place Riots made the problem of disorder very real. They emerged from the competition between a British actor favored by New York's elite and an American actor favored by the masses. Class conflict was inflamed by patriotism. The result was rioting inside and outside the newly constructed, elegant Astor Place Opera House, funded by and named for America's richest man, John Jacob Astor (see Unit 3-4). Twenty-two people were killed and over 150 were injured when the military, supplementing the police, fired on the crowd. The city was so shocked that on the next day perhaps as many as 25,000 people convened at City Hall Park and passed the following resolutions.[8]

Source: *New York Tribune*, May 12, 1849.

Resolved, That we love the peace, are law abiding citizens, and devoted to the welfare of this, the first city of the Union, but, above all, we cannot sanction the murder of innocent men by them whose sworn duty is to protect them in all the rights of American citizens.

Resolved, That we believe it to be the duty of our city authorities, if a riot takes place, or if they have good reason to believe that a riot, involving the destruction of life or property, will take place, to exhaust the civil power of the county before resorting to the military, which is, in fact the right arm of despotism, and ought to be the last resort of Americans. And here we must condemn the Mayor of our city, for not causing the Astor Place Opera House to be closed, when he knew (as he says) that a riot would ensue if it were opened.

Resolved, That we look upon the sacrifice of human lives in the vicinity of the Astor Place Opera House, last night, as the most wanton, unprovoked, and murderous outrage ever perpetrated in the civilized world; that the aiders, abettors and instigators of that unparalleled crime, deserve and shall receive the lasting censure and condemnation of this community.

Resolved, That, in our opinion, it is the imperative duty of the Grand Jury of this county to indict the Mayor, Recorder, and the Sheriff of this city, for ordering the military to fire on the citizens, during the disastrous and bloody tragedy of last night. ...

Resolved, That while we are opposed to all violence, in the theaters or elsewhere, we still insist that our citizens have a perfect and indisputable right to express their approbation or disapprobation in all places of public amusement; and we regard the arrest and imprisonment of persons last night, for merely expressing their opinion in the Opera House, as only surpassed in atrocity by the outrage perpetrated outside amongst the people.

---

1. What was the public's primary complaint?
2. How did they think the tragedy could have been avoided?
3. How did they define the roles of the mayor and the police?
4. Why did they reaffirm the right to protest?
5. How did they try to balance freedom and order?

4-3-2. DEFENDING THE 1863 RIOTS: A RIOTER, 1863

At least 100 people died in the Draft Riots which ravaged the city over four days in mid-July of 1863. What started out as a protest against the military draft, developed into an attack against Republicans (such as *New York Tribune* editor Horace Greeley) who supported the Civil War and against African Americans who symbolized Abraham Lincoln's recent Emancipation Proclamation. The Colored Orphan Asylum at 43rd Street and Fifth Avenue was destroyed. Blacks were attacked in the streets and their homes were burned down. Eleven were killed and many fled to Brooklyn, Long Island and New Jersey. As in 1834, white workers feared that emancipated slaves would gravitate to the city and compete with them for jobs. As in 1849, class conflict was involved because the rich could avoid the draft by paying $300 for a substitute to replace them in the army. The working classes were also angry because salaries for the soldiers and provisions for their families were minimal.[9] A letter in the *New York Tiimes* explained the rioters' perspective. Note that John A. Kennedy was a Republican and Superintendent of the Metropolitan Police who barely survived a brutal attacked by the mob on the first day of the riot.

Source: *New York Times*, July 15, 1863.

You will no doubt be hard on us rioters tomorrow morning, but that 300 dollar law has made us nobodies, vagabonds and cast-outs of society for whom nobody cares when we must go to war and be shot down. We are the poor rabble, and the rich rabble is our enemy by this law. Therefore we will give our enemy battle right here, and ask no quarter. Although we got hard fists and dirty without, we have soft hearts and have clean consciences within, and that's the reason we love our wives and children more than the rich, because we got not much besides them; and we will not go and leave them at home for to starve. Until that draft law is repealed, I for one am willing to knock down more such rum-hole politicians as Kennedy.* Why don't they let the nigger kill the slave-driving race and take possession of the South as it belongs to them.

A Poor Man, but a Man for all that.

---

1. What were the writer's primary concerns?
2. How did the writer's concerns reflect class conflict?
3. Was his last sentence serious or sarcastic?
4. What was the significance of the way he signed the letter?
5. How was this 1863 letter similar to and/or different from the 1849 protest above?

4-3-3. DEFENDING THE POLICE: GEORGE WASHINGTON WALLING, CHIEF OF POLICE, 1887

George Washington Walling, the Metropolitan Police Chief, saw the Draft Riots differently. In his *Recollections of a New York Chief of Police* (1887), he described the rioters, the difficulties the police faced and the strategies they pursued under the circumstances. With people being attacked and fires being set all over the city, the police could not control the situation and, as in 1849, the military had to come to the rescue on the third day of the riots. To Walling, the riot proved how badly New York City needed a strong police force.

Source: George W. Walling, *Recollections of a New York Chief of Police* (New York: Caxton Book Concern, 1887), 80, 83–85.

We marched up Forty-fifth Street, and through it to Fifth Avenue. We were confronted by a howling mob of men and women, numbering over 2000. A large number were armed with bludgeons. There was but one thing to do, and that was done quickly. I shouted at the top of my voice, so that the rioters could hear me: "Kill every man who has a club. Double quick. Charge!" And at them we went with our clubs. The rioters dropped their bludgeons, tumbling over each other, and took to their heels. We took no prisoners, but left the rioters where they fell. The number of broken heads was large. The mob dispersed in all directions, despite the frenzied cries of the women for the men to "stand up and give the police ____." ...

At night, word was brought that the mob had attacked a church at Twenty-seventh Street belonging to a colored congregation, and that we must disperse the rioters. No time was lost in getting to the scene of the action, but the rioters were well prepared to give us a warm reception. They had thrown out a line of pickets to warn them of our approach. It happened that several fire engines were passing through the street at the time, and mixing with the party of firemen we approached close to the church without attracting much attention. The building was occupied by the rioters, and no sooner was our presence made known than we were greeted with a sharp fusillade from pistols, muskets, shotguns, etc. My men returned the fire with their revolvers, and this was the first time during the day that the police under my command had recourse to fire-arms. But now they did use them they proved most effective, as the following incident will show:

One of the rioters had straddled the ridge-pole of the church and was hacking away at the timbers with an axe. The outline of his form stood out boldly against the sky, and he was in full view of the crowd. His actions were watched with great interest, and I kept my eye on him, as did everybody else. Presently the arm of one of my men was slowly raised to the proper level, there was a flash and a report, and the man on the roof disappeared from sight. Next day his body was found at the rear of the church. The bullet had lodged in his skull, and death must have been instantaneous.

That shot was followed by a howl of rage from the rioters, who attacked us in a savage and determined manner. We also set to work with a will, clubbing our opponents unmercifully. The neighborhood was cleared in short order.

I am entirely aware that resistance to the draft was the first incentive to these disturbances; but in New York, as in all large centres of population, where any set of men makes a demonstration to ventilate its grievances, there will always be grouped around this party of malcontents the very worst elements of society. Aside from the strictly criminal classes—always ready to take advantage of any local troubles in order to carry on their peculiar vocations—there is a large body of idle persons, with no interests at stake, who amalgamate with the thieves for the purpose of sharing in the plunder. ...

For more than a year after the draft riots, various articles, stolen during the disturbances from the houses of well-to-do citizens, were discovered by the police in different parts of the city. Furniture, carpets, china and other articles of a domestic character...were found decorating some of the most squalid and poverty-stricken shanties on Manhattan Island.

---

1. According to Walling, how formidable were the rioters?
2. How did Walling depict the role of women in the riots?
3. How did Walling justify clubbing and shooting the rioters?
4. Whom did Walling blame for the Draft Riots?
5. How could Walling's account be used by both the supporters and the critics of a strong police force?

4-3-4. BATTLING THE BARRICADES IN 1863: J. F. J. TRESCH, ILLUSTRATOR, 1887

The following drawing documented the challenge of quelling the 1863 riots.

Source: George W. Walling, *Recollections of a New York Chief of Police* (New York: Caxton Book Concern, 1887), 81.

1. Using numbers, dress and equipment, how did the artist contrast the class, character and tactics of the police versus the rioters?
2. Which side seemed to be winning the battle?
3. How did this drawing support or contradict Walling's testimony above?
4. How did this drawing clarify the possibilities for and dangers of riot in a city?

UNIT 4-4. BREAKING BARRIERS: ELIZABETH JENNINGS, TEACHER

For some people, the historical record is plentiful; for others, it is skimpy. One such person is Elizabeth Jennings whose story was painstakingly recreated in 1990 by the historian John H. Hewitt in order to more fully document the African American resistance to racism in mid-nineteeth-century New York City. The title of his article, "The Search for Elizabeth Jennings, Heroine of a Sunday Afternoon in New York City," urges us to think about human agency in history.[10] What is heroism? Can ordinary people change history? Should minorities agitate for equality? What strategies of protest are most or least effective? Is principle worth the risk of harm? These questions suffuse the Elizabeth Jennings story and the larger conflict over equality throughout the history of New York and the nation. It is a story of individual, family and community, of anger, courage and action, of perseverance, professionalism and social commitment. It encompasses all the dilemmas of social reform in a democracy, complicated by the dynamics of race and gender.

Elizabeth Jennings was born into dignity and defiance. Her parents, who had never been slaves, were middle class; all of her siblings pursued skilled professions. One brother was a businessman, another was a dentist and her sister was a dressmaker. Her father, Thomas L. Jennings, ran a boarding house and was a merchant tailor. Most importantly, he was a leader in New York's mid-nineteenth-century African American community. He helped form and took an active role in a variety of organizations designed to improve life for African Americans and to assert their rights. This involved belonging to benevolent societies, abolitionist groups, black suffrage organizations and the National Colored Convention Movement. In addition, he was a founder of the Abyssinian Baptist Church and the Legal Rights Association of New York. In other words, Thomas L. Jennings was model of bold, conscientious activism in an era when African American equality was severely limited.[11]

Therefore, it was not surprising that his daughter, Elizabeth, was equally forthright. Born in 1830, she began teaching at Colored Public School #2 in 1848 and soon shifted to a school run by the New York Society for the Promotion of Education among Colored Children. There she worked with Charles L. Reason, one of the leading African American educators of the period. In mid-nineteenth-century New York, it was a struggle to provide education for African American children, especially since school attendance was not mandatory and poor children had to work to survive. New York City's public schools mainly served white middle-class students with only a few schools designated for blacks. There were hardly high schools for anyone and none for blacks. Determined to overcome these obstacles, Elizabeth Jennings dedicated her life to educating African American children.[12]

The crusading spirit that imbued her choice of profession spilled over into her private life, propelling Jennings onto the public stage and into the historical record. A hundred years before Rosa Parks refused to give up her seat to a white man on a public bus in Montgomery, Alabama, Jennings fought against segregation on a New York City horse-drawn trolley car. An accomplished musician, Jennings played the organ for the First Colored American Congregational Church located on Sixth Street near the Bowery. Trying to get there from her parents' home further downtown on Church Street, she and a friend boarded a Third Avenue trolley car on Sunday, July 16, 1854. However, the conductor refused to let them ride because he claimed that his car was designated for whites only despite the fact that there was no such sign. An argument ensued during which Jennings and her companion were violently ejected from the trolley.[13]

On Monday, Jennings' church pastor convened a protest meeting at which a committee was created to pursue legal action. Ignored by the mainstream press, except for Horace Greeley's *New York Tribune,* but covered by abolitionist papers such as the *National Anti-Slavery Standard,* and *Frederick Douglass' Paper,* word of the incident spread across the country. A New York law firm with abolitionist leanings agreed to handle the case for which Thomas Jennings tried to raise funds. Chester A. Arthur, young lawyer and future president of the United States, guided the case through trial in 1855 and won. Most of the jury wanted to grant the $500 for which Jennings had sued, but some felt that African Americans should not get such a large settlement, so they compromised at $225. Nonetheless, the principle seemed to be established that private companies providing public transportation were obliged to serve all persons as long as they were "sober, well-behaved and free from disease." Segregation in the city suffered a severe blow.[14]

Unfortunately, the victory was incomplete because it was not enforced and trolley conductors continued to refuse to carry African American riders. Consequently, Jennings' father organized and became president of the Legal Rights Association for the purpose of bringing more suits to challenge New York City's segregated transportation policies. In this effort Jennings was joined by the Reverend James W. C. Pennington, an outstanding man who had escaped from slavery in Maryland and had risen from blacksmith to teacher and community leader in Newtown, Long Island. After studying unofficially at the officially segregated Yale Divinity School, Pennington went to Germany to earn his doctorate of divinity. He then became pastor of the Shiloh Presbyterian Church on Prince Street, author of the first African American history book, and a prominent abolitionist. [15]

Shortly after the Jennings' case was resolved, Pennington was thrown off a Sixth Avenue trolley car and sued for damages. In this instance, however, the rights of the trolley company to control its business by setting "reasonable rules" was upheld. Finally, a similar case on the Eighth Avenue trolley line seemed to resolve the issue when the company agreed to desegregate its trolley cars in 1859. Except for the Sixth Avenue line, other trolley companies followed suit within the year, but segregation was reinstated after the Draft Riots of 1863 (see Unit 4-3). The struggle for equality took three steps forward and two steps backward. Not until 1873 was segregation in public transportation finally outlawed in New York State.[16]

Meanwhile, Elizabeth continued her teaching career and, after attending a segregated school for teacher training, successfully obtained special certification from the New York City Board of Education in 1859. She married in 1860, but lost a year old son in 1863 and her husband in 1876. After leaving full-time teaching in 1865, she worked (probably part-time) as a private teacher or tutor, became treasurer of St. Philip's Church Sunday school and of the Dorcas Society, a women's organization that gave clothing to poor children. In 1890, she supported T. Thomas Fortune, African American editor of the New York Age, in his suit against a hotel that refused to serve him a beer.[17]

Five years later, at age sixty-five, she was still pursuing equality in education by establishing a kindergarten in her home staffed by two teachers. This was doubly bold because the kindergarten movement was new at the time and because hers was the first kindergarten for African American children. In addition, there were sewing classes for older girls on Saturdays and a small lending library. All of these services were free of charge, supported by herself and her circle of middle-class African American women. They attested to the importance of education, mutual aid and activism for African Americans in general and to the constructive, often courageous roles played by African American women in particular. Throughout her life, Elizabeth Jennings was committed to causes greater than herself. She died on June 5, 1901 after a full life of public service that repeatedly defied the odds.[18]

---

1. How did Elizabeth Jennings' family background shape her personality and her profession?
2. Why was the trolley incident significant?
3. How did Elizabeth Jennings' life contradict stereotypes of African Americans and of women?
4. What did Elizabeth Jennings' life reveal about racial equality in mid-nineteenth-century New York?

4-4-1. ASSERTING EQUALITY: ELIZABETH JENNINGS, TEACHER, 1854

Elizabeth Jennings wrote the following account of her July 16, 1854 altercation with a horse car conductor. Because she was too "sore and stiff" to attend, the statement was read on her behalf at a July 17 public protest meeting.

Source: *Frederick Douglass' Paper*, July 28, 1854.

Elizabeth and a companion were on their way to church when they were refused admission to a horse-drawn trolley car because it was not specifically designated for "colored people." When the conductor told them to wait for the next car,

"I told him that I could not wait, as I was in a hurry to go to church (the other car was about a block off); he then told me that the other car had my people in it, that it was appropriated for that purpose. I then told him that I had no people; it was no particular occasion; I wished to go to church, as I had been going for the last six months, and I did not wish to be detained.

He insisted upon my getting off the car. I told him I would wait on the car until the other car came up. He again insisted on my waiting in the street, but I did not get off the car.

By this time, the other car came up, and I asked the driver if there was any room in his car. He told me very distinctly "no," that there was more room in my car than there was in his. Yet this did not satisfy the conductor. He still kept driving me out or off his car, said he had as much time as I had and could wait just as long. I replied, "Very well, we'll see."

He waited some few minutes, when the driver becoming impatient, he said to me, "Well, you may go in, but remember, if the passengers raise any objections you shall go out, whether or no, or I'll put you out."

I answered again and told him I was a respectable person, born and raised in New York, did not know where he was born, that I had never been insulted before while going to church, and that he was a good for nothing impudent fellow for insulting decent persons while on their way to church."

He then said I should come out or he would put me out. I told him not to lay his hands on me. He took hold of me, and I took hold of the window sash and held on. He pulled me until he broke my grasp from that (but previously he had dragged my companion out, she all the while screaming for him to let go). He then ordered the driver to fasten his horses, which he did, and come out and help him put me out of the car. Then they both seized hold of me by the arms and pulled and dragged me flat down on the bottom of the platform, so that my feet hung one way and my head the other, nearly on the ground.

I screamed murder with all my voice, and my companion screamed out, "You'll kill her. Don't kill her."

The driver then let go of me and went to his horses. I went again in the car, and the conductor said you shall sweat for this. Then [he] told the driver to drive as fast as he could and not to take another passenger in the car, to drive until he saw an officer or a Station House.

They got an officer at the corner of Walker and Bowery, whom the conductor told that his orders from the agent were to admit colored persons if the passengers did not object, but if they did, not to let them ride.

When the officer took me, there were some eight or ten persons in the car. When the officer, without listening to anything I had to say, thrust me out, and then pushed and tauntingly told me to get redress if I could. This the conductor also told me and gave me some name and number of his car. He wrote his name Moss and the car No. 7, but I looked and saw No. 6 on the back of the car.

After dragging me off the car, he drove me away like a dog, saying, not to be talking there and raising a mob or fight.

I came home down to Walker St. and a German gentleman followed, who told me he saw the whole transaction in the street as he was passing. His address is Latour, No. 148 Pearl St—bookseller.

When I told the conductor I did not know where he was born, he answered, "I was born in Ireland" I made answer (that) it made no difference where a man was born, that he was none the worse or better for that, provided he behaved himself and did not insult genteel persons.[19]

---

1. In the context of the 1850s, how reasonable or unreasonable was the behavior of Jennings, the conductor and the policeman?
2. What class, racial and ethnic tensions were revealed by this incident?
3. Based on this account, how difficult was it to fight discrimination in mid-nineteenth-century New York City? What were the major obstacles?
4. Based on this account, what three words would best describe Jennings' personality?
5. Explain whether and why you agree or disagree with Hewitt that Jennings was a heroine.

4-4-2. SUBVERTING SLAVERY: HORACE GREELEY, NEWSPAPER EDITOR, 1850

In 1841, Horace Greeley founded the *New York Tribune,* through which he became one of the nation's most influential figures and most important reformers. He consistently supported abolition, workers' rights and women's rights (but not the radical feminist Fanny Wright). He advocated aid to New York City's poor and famously recommended that they "Go West." Greeley was also active in politics and ran for president as a Liberal Republican in 1872. By that time, however, his prominence had dimmed. Beset by financial woes complicated by psychological depression, he died a few weeks after the election. Nonetheless, there is no denying the positive contributions he made in his prime, especially in the fight against slavery.[20]

Although slavery was illegal in New York State by 1827, it remained legal in the United States and was still divisive in New York City. On the one hand, New York City was a center for abolitionism and an important station on the underground railroad. On the other hand, many New York City merchants who traded in plantation products had strong ties to the slaveholding South. Moreover, many urban workers feared that freed slaves would flood the job market as cheap labor. (see Unit 3-1) Tension was exacerbated in 1850 when a federal Fugitive Slave Act reaffirmed the right of slave owners to retrieve runaway slaves from the free states.

The first New York City resident seized under this act was James Hamlet, a porter. Immediately, 1,500 people attended a church rally to protest his capture. Funds were raised to purchase him from his owner with one African American man subscribing $100, a huge sum at the time. Five thousand people greeted Hamlet upon his return.[21] In recounting these events, Greeley criticized not just the Fugitive Slave Act, but the entire institution of slavery.

Source: *New York Daily Tribune*, October 1 and 7, 1850.

October 1, 1850

Let us take the case of James Hamlet to illustrate the beauties of Slave Catching and Slavery, assuming that he has been properly returned into bondage. He was born a slave, and served his legal master or mistress till twenty-six years old. He seems to have been a good servant, or the owner would not have sent so far to get him back again. While he remained in Baltimore, he received a slave's bread and clothing for his work; but no education, no mental culture, and the law allowed him no human rights. He became tired of this, and quit. He has since lived here, where he has married a wife by whom he has two children. There is no intimation that he failed to discharge faithfully all his duties as a husband, a father, and a member of society. Yet, as he is quietly earning his livelihood, he is suddenly seized, handcuffed, taken before a Commissioner, his liberty sworn away, and he hurried off into slavery—probably to wear out his life quickly in severe and unrequited labor on a cotton or sugar plantation. He was not permitted to exchange a parting word with his wife and children, nor even to apprise them of his sudden calamity; and it is not probable that he will ever lay eyes upon either of them again. All this is of course according to law and we see no present help for it; but if there really is no 'higher law' than this which has remanded James Hamlet into Slavery, then the Devil has more power in the Universe than honestly belongs to him.

October 7, 1850

Several thousand people, white and black, attended a meeting in the [City Hall] Park at noon on Saturday at which James Hamlet, the first New York victim of the man-stealers was exhibited. The greatest enthusiasm prevailed and the meeting was addressed by Misters W. P. Powel, Rev. John P. Raymond, Robert Hamilton, and Rev. Charles B. Ray, all colored. Resolutions of thanks were offered to the gentlemen who had assisted in the liberation of Hamlet, and a strong spirit of resistance manifested to the Fugitive Slave Law, and the persons who sustained and secured its passage. ... The meeting adjourned at 1 o'clock. A great rush was made by spectators to see Hamlet, and he was borne in triumph to the east side of the Park on the shoulders of his sympathizing friends, and chased down Spruce st. by a large number of men who were anxious to catch a glimpse of him.

It was stated that since the passage of the Fugitive Slave Reclamation Bill more slaves had run away than ever was known before, six women reaching the City on Sunday, Sept. 29, who had fled from Baltimore.

Mayor Woodhull has announced that none of his Police would aid or abet in the capture of runaways, and cheers were given when this was stated. Hamlet was loudly cheered several times, and a fugitive song was given at the close of the meeting, in which a great portion of the audience joined. ...

Man-thieving is at a discount in the vicinity of New York.

---

1. How did Greeley's description of Hamlet humanize the man while dehumanizing slavery?
2. How did Greeley address the legal and moral issues surrounding the Fugitive Slave Act?
3 What did Greeley's account reveal about the status of African Americans in mid-nineteeth-century New York City?
4. What did Greeley's account reveal about inter-racial support for abolitionism?
5. What did Greeley's last sentence mean?

4-4-3. PETITIONING FOR THE VOTE: JAMES McCUNE SMITH, JAMES P. MILLER AND JOHN J. ZUILLE, REFORMERS, 1860

New York City's abolitionists may have saved James Hamlet, but they could not secure equal voting rights for African Americans. In 1821, New York State legislators eliminated the requirement that white men pay property taxes in order to vote. At the same time, they increased the property tax requirement for black men, assuming that few would ever own enough land to qualify. (Of course, neither white nor black women could vote at all until 1920.) Eliminating this inequity was a priority for abolitionists. However, when it was discussed in the New York State Assembly and Senate, the strongest opposition came from New York City and Brooklyn. In 1860, a state referendum to eliminate the property requirement for black men was defeated by 140,000 votes, many of them from those cities. Despite valiant African American service during the Civil War, a similar referendum was defeated in 1869. In fact, New York State's black males did not obtain equal voting rights until the Fifteenth Amendment was added to the U. S. Constitution in 1870. The situation revealed the limitations of Northern urban liberalism.[22]

In support of the 1860 referendum on equal voting rights, the New York City and County Suffrage Committee of Colored Citizens issued a poignant assertion of the right to vote. Note that the leader of the convention was James McCune Smith, New York City's first black doctor. Unable to attend American medical schools because of his race, McCune Smith earned his degree in Scotland whereupon he returned to New York City to open a medical practice and a pharmacy serving whites and blacks alike. In addition, he became a tireless, influential activist in New York's African American community.[23]

Source: James McCune Smith, James P. Miller, and John J. Zuille, "The Suffrage Question in Relation to Colored Voters in the State of New York," Respectfully submitted by the New York City and County Suffrage Committee of Colored Citizens, September, 1860.

Fellow Citizens: We have had, and still have, great wrongs of which to complain. A heavy and cruel hand has been laid upon us. As a people, we feel ourselves to be not only deeply injured, but grossly misunderstood. Our white countrymen do not know us. They are strangers to our character, ignorant of our capacity, oblivious to our history and progress, and are misinformed as to the principles and ideas that control and guide us, as a people. The great mass of American citizens estimate us as being a characterless and purposelessness people; and hence we hold up our heads, if at all, against the withering influence of a nation's scorn and contempt.

It will not be surprising that we are so misunderstood and misused, when the motives for misrepresenting us and for degrading us are duly considered. Indeed, it will seem strange... that we have not fallen even lower in public estimation than we have done; for, with the exception of the Jews, under the whole heavens there is not to be found a people pursued with a more relentless prejudice and persecution, than are the free colored people of the United States.

What stone has been left unturned to degrade us? What hand has refused to fan the flame of popular prejudice against us? What American artist has not caricatured us? What wit has not laughed at us in our wretchedness? What songster has not made merry over our depressed spirits? What press has not ridiculed and condemned us? Few, few, very few; and that we have borne up with it all—that we have tried to be wise, though pronounced by all to be fools—that we have tried to be upright, when all around us have been teaching its impossibility—that we have remained here, when all our neighbors have advised us to leave, proves that we possess qualities of head and heart, such as cannot but be commended by impartial men.

It is believed that no other nation on the globe could have made more progress in the midst of such an universal and stringent disparagement. It would humble the proudest, crush the energies of the strongest, and retard the progress of the swiftest.

In view of our circumstances, we can, without boasting, thank God and take courage, having placed ourselves where we may fairly challenge comparison with more highly favored men. ... In 1856, ... twenty five per cent more colored than white children, in proportion to the relative population, attended Common Schools. ...

The colored people have not only taken good care of themselves in this State, notwithstanding the prejudice of color which limits their sphere of occupation, by amassing real and personal estate of large amount, but they are no greater, if so great a burden to the State in almshouses and prisons than other classes of citizens. ... And it should be taken into consideration that, from their lack of political influence, colored persons committing any, even the slightest misdemeanors, are arrested; while it is notorious that the whites, who all vote, enjoy a comparative immunity from arrest and even from punishment for crime. ...

Principles of justice to the individuals who compose the State, and thereby of justice to the State itself, require that the basis of voting should be equal to all. No one class can be depressed and made unequal without injury to the other classes, and to the whole State. And are not these patriotic, industrious, provident, exemplary citizens deserving equal right at the ballot-box?

1. Why was this appeal addressed to "fellow citizens"?
2. How did the appeal explain the discriminatory voting policy?
3. How did this appeal justify giving black men the right to vote?
4. How did the style and tone of this appeal counter stereotypes of African Americans?

4-4-4. CHERISHING WEEKSVILLE: JUDITH WELLMAN, HISTORIAN, 2005

Like their neighbors in New Amsterdam, Brooklyn's Dutch settlers imported slaves from the 1640s on. In fact, slavery played a major role in the development of Brooklyn. As a farming community, Brooklyn relied so heavily on African labor that by 1700 over forty percent of its families owned at least one slave and many others hired slaves for seasonal work. By 1738, Brooklyn had proportionately the largest number of slaves in New York State. Moreover, because smugglers avoided Manhattan customs officials by unloading slaves in Brooklyn, that city played a significant role in the illegal slave trade well into the nineteenth century.

As in Manhattan, slaves often ran away, and some earned or were granted their freedom, especially as New York State emancipation approached in 1827. Yet, African American lives remained difficult because prejudice persistently narrowed their economic, political and social opportunities. It is not surprising, then, that Brooklyn's African Americans sought a place where they could live in peace and dignity. Weeksville was the result. It soon became a solid African American neighborhood, scorned by whites but cherished by blacks as a measure of African American economic independence, political activism and cultural vitality. Another settlement of free blacks was established in Sandy Hook, Staten Island in the 1840s. By their very being, Weeksville and Sandy Hook declared defiance against the status quo. [25]

Source: Judith Wellman, "Weeksville," in Ira Berlin and Leslie M. Harris (eds), *Slavery in New York* (New York: The New Press, 2005), 255.

In the 1830s, African American land investors organized the community of Weekswille to promote economic, social, and political rights for African Americans. Located four miles east of downtown Brooklyn, Weeksville grew rapidly. In 1855, with a black population of 521, Weekswille had become the second largest independent African American community in the United States, and the only one with urban rather than rural roots. Its residents originated in various parts of the United States and the Caribbean. Two came from Africa.

With a high rate of property ownership, Weeksville became a highly politicized black community, with two newspapers—*Freedom's Torchlight* and the *National Monitor*—and a host of African American institutions, including several churches, an orphan asylum, and a home for the aged. Its residents participated in movements against slavery and for equal rights. Weeksville became a major station on the Underground Railroad, and following the Draft Riots, it became a shelter for refugees from the vicious pogrom in Manhattan. Weeksville's was also the first New York City public school to fully integrate its teaching staff.

As the thicket of community institutions grew, so did Weeksville's national importance. Weeksville became the national headquarters for the African

Civilization Society. Junius C. Morel, who settled in Weeksville following his escape from slavery in South Carolina, became a nationally known convention organizer., journalist, and educator. Susan McKinney Steward, another Weeksville resident, was one of America's first African American women doctors. T. McCants Stewart—lawyer, school board member, and African Methodist Episcopal pastor in Weeksville—promoted the integration of Weeksville's school system and later emigrated to Liberia.

Today, four frame houses on Hunterfly Road, maintained by the Society for the Preservation of Weeksville and Bedford Stuyvesant History, represent the historic Weeksville community.

1. How many different functions did Weeksville fulfill?
2. What did those functions reveal about the socio-economic status, political leanings and civic commitments of Weeksville's residents?
3. Based on this account, why might whites have resented Weeksville?
4. How did Weeksville document patterns of racial equality and inequality in the Northern city?

SELECTED RESOURCES

Anbinder, Tyler. *Five Points: The 19th Century New York City Neighborhood That Invented Tap Dance, Stole Elections, and Became the World's Most Notorious Slum.* New York: The Free Press, 2001.

Berlin, Ira, and Leslie M. Harris (eds). *Slavery in New York.* New York: The New Press, 2005.

Bernstein, Iver. *The New York City Draft Riots: Their Significance for American Society and Politics in the Age of the Civil War.* New York: Oxford University Press, 1990.

Foner, Philip S. *Business and Slavery: New York Merchants and the Irrepressible Conflict.* Chapel Hill, NC: University of North Carolina Press, 1941.

Headley, Joel Tyler. *The Great Riots of New York, 1712–1863.* New York: Dover, 1873/1971.

Hodges, Graham Russell. *Root and Branch: African Americans in New York and East Jersey, 1613–1863.* Chapel Hill, NC: University of North Carolina Press, 1999.

Homberger, Eric. *Scenes in the Life of a City: Corruption and Conscience in Old New York.* New Haven, CT: Yale University Press, 1994.

McKay, Ernest A. *The Civil War and New York City.* Syracuse, NY: Syracuse University Press, 1990.

Miller, Stuart Creighton. *The Unwelcome Immigrant: The American Image of the Chinese, 1785–1882.* Berkeley, CA: University of California Press, 1969.

Moody, Richard. *The Astor Place Riot.* Bloomington, IN: Indiana University Press, 1958.

Mushkat, Jerome. *Fernando Wood, A Political Biography.* Kent, OH: Kent State University Press, 1990.

Ravitch, Diane. *The Great School Wars, New York City 1805–1973: A History of Public Schools as Battlefields of Change.* New York: Basic Books, 1974.

Richardson, James F. *The New York Police, Colonial Times to 1901.* New York: Oxford University Press, 1970.

Rosenzweig, Roy, and Elizabeth Blackmar. *The Park and the People: A History of Central Park.* Ithaca, NY: Cornell University Press, 1992.

Ryan, Mary P. *Civic Wars: Democracy and Public Life in the American City during the Nineteenth Century.* Berkeley, CA: University of California Press, 1997.

Spann, Edward K. *The New Metropolis, New York City, 1840–1857.* New York: Columbia University Press, 1981.

Stott, Richard B. *Workers in the Metropolis: Class, Ethnicity and Youth in Antebellum New York City.* Ithaca, NY: Cornell University Press, 1990.

Wilder, Craig Steven. *A Covenant with Color: Race and Social Power in Brooklyn.* New York: Columbia University Press, 2000.

www.ashp.cuny.edu/5ps: Five Points

www.projects.ilt.columbia.edu/Seneca: pre-Central Park African American settlement

www.weeksvillesociety.org: African American community in Brooklyn

www.vny.cuny.edu: the 1863 draft riots and the 1866 cholera epidemic

CHAPTER 5

1865–1900

As the home of the Stock Exchange and the trusts, the major port of entry for new immigrants, the center of communications and trade, it seemed so exceptional that one English woman quipped, "New York is New York and nothing else."[1] In this era, above all others, Gotham earned its reputation for bold innovation, technological progress, economic opportunity, ruthless competition and, of course, exorbitant wealth. Wall Street, Fifth Avenue, the Brooklyn Bridge and the Statue of Liberty all testified to New York's importance.

When the five boroughs were consolidated into one metropolitan unit in 1898, New York's population exploded from 2 to 3.4 million. Instantly, New York doubled Chicago and became a world-class city, second only to London. New York, said the writer Mark Twain, was characterized by a "ceaseless buzz, and hurry, and bustle that keeps a stranger in a state of unwholesome excitement all the time, and makes him restless and uneasy."[2]

Although New York City was associated with wealth on a hitherto unprecedented scale, it was also known for its poverty, labor strife and political corruption. As Twain suggested when he coined the term, the Gilded Age, the shiny surface of the era camouflaged its tarnished reality. The depressions of 1873–1879 and 1893–1897 made the precarious nature of progress very real to farmers, bankers and businessmen, not to mention thousands of workers rendered jobless in an era before unemployment insurance and welfare.

In other words, the economic developments that brought great promise also created serious problems that New Yorkers and Americans tried to understand and address. This chapter looks at those dilemmas by examining key markers of urban growth in the Gilded Age, the crusade against corruption, and changing attitudes towards poverty. Lastly, it reviews the career of the nation's most despised robber baron, Jay Gould, who symbolized the complexity of New York's late-nineteenth-century dynamism.

UNIT 5-1. CITY BUILDING: THE BROOKLYN BRIDGE, THE STATUE OF LIBERTY AND CONSOLIDATION

During the Gilded Age, New York City's wealth and prominence generated changes that heralded the modern city and the modern nation. Technology revolutionized the physical city. In keeping with the exploding industrial economy, elevators and steel pushed buildings higher and higher. Horse cars and cable cars were supplemented by elevated trains. Telegraph and telephone wires, so essential to commercial enterprise, hung over the streets like spiders' webs. Electricity redefined the appearance and function of the city at night.

Wealth also reshaped the city. The new department stores on Broadway created a Ladies Mile that proclaimed New York's centrality to the nation's retail trade and its new consumerism. Fifth Avenue sprouted enough mansions to be called Millionaire's Row. Elegant restaurants like Delmonico's and fancy hotels like the Plaza flourished. The City Beautiful movement spawned the Metropolitan Museum of Art (1870), the Metropolitan Opera House (1883), the American Museum of Natural History (begun in the 1870s), and the New York Public Library (formed in 1895). Imposing in every way, New York seemed to embody the best of American ambition. It was truly an Empire City that, said a foreign observer, pulsed with a "new, seething, urgent modernity."[3]

5-1-1. PRAISING THE BROOKLYN BRIDGE: SETH LOW, MAYOR OF BROOKLYN, 1883

The Brooklyn Bridge was often called the Eighth Wonder of the World. It instantly became a national icon in 1883 after 14 years of construction costing 20 lives. America's longest suspension bridge, it was praised for fusing art with technology, old with new. It testified to the soaring spirit of both New York and the nation in the Gilded Age. Perhaps no other bridge has been so frequently and so lovingly celebrated in photographs, paintings, poems, essays and novels, not to mention architectural and historical studies. Hardly just a matter of transportation, the Brooklyn Bridge symbolized America's faith in progress. The speeches given at the bridge's opening ceremonies, such as that by Seth Low, Brooklyn's mayor from 1881–1884, reveal that people at the time fully appreciated both the beauty and the utility of the bridge. No wonder that the historian Alan Trachtenberg considered the Brooklyn Bridge to be "the cardinal emblem of the age." [4]

Source: *Opening Ceremonies of the New York and Brooklyn Bridge*, May 24, 1883 (Brooklyn, NY: Eagle Job Printing Dept., 1883), 31–37.

Fourteen years ago a city of 400,000 people on this side of the river heard of a projected suspension bridge with incredulity. The span was so long, the height was so great, and the enterprise likely to be so costly, that few thought of it as something begun in earnest. The irresistible demands of commerce enforced these hard conditions. But Science said, "It is possible," and Courage said, "It shall be!" To-day a city of 600,000 people welcomes with enthusiasm the wonderful creation of genius. Graceful, and yet majestic, it clings to the land like a thing that has taken root. Beautiful as a vision of fairyland, it salutes our sight. The impression it makes upon a visitor is one of astonishment, an astonishment that grows with every visit. No one who has been upon it can ever forget it. The great structure cannot be confined to the limits of local pride. The glory of it belongs to the race. Not one shall see it and not feel prouder to be a man. ...

The importance of this Bridge in its far-reaching effects at once entices and baffles the imagination. ... Brooklyn becomes available, henceforth as a place of residence to thousands, to whom the ability to reach their places of business without interruption from fog and ice is of paramount importance.

To all Brooklyn's present citizens a distinct boon is given. The certainty of communication with New York afforded by the Bridge is the fundamental benefit it confers. Incident to this is the opportunity it gives for rapid communication.

As the waters of the lakes found the sea salt when the Erie Canal was opened, so surely will quick communication seek and find this noble Bridge, and as ships have carried hither and thither the products of the mighty West, so shall diverging railroads transport the people swiftly to their homes in the hospitable city of Brooklyn. The Erie Canal is a waterway through the land connecting the great West with the older East. This Bridge is a landway over the water, connecting two cities bearing to each other relations in some respect similar. It is the function of such works to bless "both him that gives and him that takes. The development of the West has not belittled, but has enlarged New York, and Brooklyn will grow by reason of this Bridge, not at New York's expense, but to her permanent advantage.

The Brooklyn of 1900 can hardly be guessed at from the city of to-day. The hand of Time is a mighty hand. To those who are privileged to live in sight of this noble structure, every line of it should be eloquent with inspiration. Courage, enterprise, skill, faith, endurance— these are the qualities which have made the great Bridge, and these are the qualities which will make our city great and our people great.

---

1. Which of Low's phrases best convey the beauty and symbolic significance of the bridge?
2. In what practical ways did Low expect the bridge to benefit both Manhattan and Brooklyn?
3. Why did Low emphasize the bridge as an extension of the Erie Canal?
3. How did the bridge reflect the spirit of Gotham in the Gilded Age?
4. How did the Brooklyn Bridge pave the way for the Consolidation of New York in 1898?

5-1-2. HONORING THE STATUE OF LIBERTY: EMMA LAZARUS, POET, 1883

In 1886, just three years after the Brooklyn Bridge was completed, New York City acquired another iconic structure. On the opposite side of Manhattan, in the magnificent harbor leading to the Hudson River, the Statue of Liberty beckoned to the world. A gift from the people (not the government) of France to the people (not the government) of the United States, the statue celebrated the spirit of freedom embodied in the American Revolution.

Although it was not completed in time for the centennial in 1876, it was finally installed a decade later. The statue itself was financed by contributions made by the citizens of France. So too, its base was paid for by pennies, nickels and dimes raised from ordinary Americans in a campaign organized by publisher Joseph Pulitzer's *New York World*.

The statue's practical and symbolic significance was captured by Emma Lazarus, daughter of a wealthy Portugese-Jewish merchant, whose sonnet was read at a fund-raising event in 1883 and later was inscribed on the base of the statue. Like the statue itself, the poem is world-renowned, a fitting tribute to a cherished human ideal. Standing 305 feet tall and weighing 225 tons, the Statue of Liberty was monumental in every sense of the word.

Source: Emma Lazarus, "The New Colossus," *Catalogue of the Pedestal Fund Art Loan Exhibition.* (New York: De Vinne, 1883).

Here at our sea washed sunset gates shall stand
A mighty woman with a torch, whose flame
Is the imprisoned lightning, and her name
Mother of Exiles. From her beacon hand
Glows world wide welcome; her mild eyes command
The air bridged harbor that twin cities frame,
"Keep ancient lands your storied pomp!" cries she
With silent lips. "Give me your tired, your poor,
Your huddled masses yearning to breathe free,
The wretched refuse of your teeming shore.
Send the homeless, tempest tossed to me,
I lift my hand beside the golden door!

1. What was the "air bridged harbor that twin cities frame"?
2. Why did Lazarus use the words "imprisoned lightning," "beacon," and "golden door"?
3. How did Lazarus criticize old Europe and explain immigration?
4. Which phrases in the poem best reflected America as a nation of immigrants and New York as America's Gateway City?

5-1-3. FEARING FOR LIBERTY: THOMAS NAST, 1889

Because the Statue of Liberty is such a powerful positive symbol, cartoonists ever since have used it for negative purposes, especially to warn America of threats to its ideals. An excellent example is the image overleaf drawn in 1889 by Thomas Nast, the father of American cartooning. He fully appreciated the visual significance of the statue and of New York. Commenting on the role of trusts and the concentration of wealth in the Gilded Age, Nast called this drawing "The Rise of the Usurpers, and the Sinking of the Liberties of the People."

Source: Thomas Nast, "The Rise of the Usurpers, and the Sinking of the Liberties of the People."

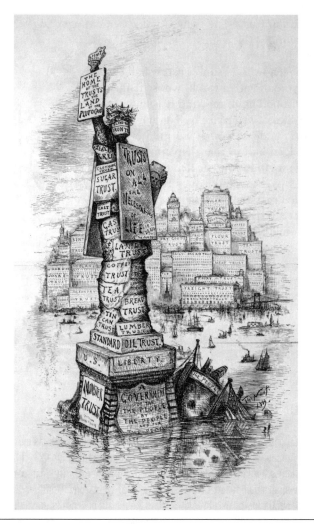

1. How did Nast cleverly invert standard American slogans and assumptions?
2. What was the symbolism of the boat and its reflection in the lower right corner?
3. What was Nast's message about the relationship between the city and the trusts?
4. Was Nast concerned about economic freedom or political freedom or both?

5-1-4. OPPOSING CONSOLIDATION: THE REVEREND R. S. STORRS, 1894

The most dramatic political example of city building in Gilded Age America was the consolidation of 40 communities into the five boroughs of New York City in 1898. From the beginning, the city had expanded by moving up Manhattan Island. It reached beyond Manhattan by annexing sections of the lower Bronx in 1874 and building the Brooklyn Bridge in 1883.

The concept of consolidation was first advanced by Andrew Haswell Green in 1868, but languished for two decades. Finally inspired by the consolidation of Greater London in 1888 and worried that Chicago might soon outpace New York, a cross-section of business interests decided that the city needed to redefine itself. Led by Green, a long-time public servant, the campaign for consolidation was waged from 1890 to 1894.

Support for consolidation was strong in Manhattan, Bronx, Staten Island and most of Queens. However, Brooklyn was evenly divided. An opposition group called the League of Loyal Citizens feared being overwhelmed, overtaxed and overrun by Manhattan's greedy land speculators, corrupt politicians and poor immigrants. Across the city, the Democratic party and its working class supporters worried that the merger would undermine their political power.

Ultimately, the issue was resolved in 1897 when the Republican-dominated New York State legislature approved the creation of a Greater New York City starting January 1, 1898. For the victors, it was confirmation of New York's "municipal grandeur." For the losers, it was the Great Mistake of 1898.[5] The Reverend R. S. Storrs spoke for Brooklyn's opponents of consolidation.

Source: Brooklyn League of Loyal Citizens, *Letters Worth Reading*. Pamphlet #4 (New York, 1894), 3–7.

[Brooklyn has] a comparatively homogeneous population, more than two-thirds of it having been born on American soil and trained from childhood in American traditions. It is very largely a home-loving population, valuing and maintaining social order, honoring schools, churches, charities, respecting law and putting a high estimate on industry, while capable of being widely and energetically moved ... by a common purpose to make its government honest, economical, and worthy of respect. ...

[Manhattan] has far greater splendor and wealth than we possess, or can ever rival; and it annually draws to itself greater numbers of the rich, the famous, the influential, from all parts of the land. Its hotels, theaters, libraries, galleries, clubs, churches, museums are magnificent; its whole material equipment is opulent and impressive.

But much greater multitudes of its people live in tenement houses than among us. It includes a larger proportion of those foreign born—nearly three-sevenths, according to the last census, of its aggregate number, against our proportion of less than one-third. It absorbs far more numerous elements brought to this country by recent immigration, and profoundly ignorant of our customs and laws, or profoundly opposed to both. The extremes of wealth and poverty face each other in it more sharply and widely than here. Its population is heterogeneous, to a proverb; and the administration of its public affairs has been for many years in the hands of crafty and mercenary leaders of the ignorant or unscrupulous rabble. According to irresistible testimony, its city government has for years been absolutely honey-combed with corruption. ...

[We do not want Brooklyn] to become a mere district in an enormous metropolis.

1. In Storrs' opinion, what characteristics made Brooklyn a solid American city?
2. In Storrs' opinion, what were Manhattan's strengths and weaknesses?
3. What was Storrs' attitude towards immigrants?
4. According to Storrs, what was the best reason to oppose consolidation?

5-1-5. SUPPORTING CONSOLIDATION: ALBERT E. HENSHEL, PUBLIC SERVANT, 1895

Albert E. Henschel was Andrew Green's associate and former assistant to the lawyer and politician, Samuel J. Tilden. Henschel coordinated the campaign for consolidation on behalf of Green by soliciting support from businesses, civic groups and the press. Pamphlets making the following arguments were distributed widely.

Source: Albert E. Henschel, *Municipal Consolidation. Historical Sketch of the Greater New York.* (New York: Stettiner, Lambert and Co., 1895), 54–56.

The Greater New York affords a rare opportunity for improving the condition of our city affairs. ... By gathering the fragments of what should be a political unit and administering them as a municipal whole, the common interests of every section of the Greater New York will be subserved and promoted, without jar or discord, and with the greatest good to all.

The interests of the Greater City will be large, surpassing those of many States of the Union, as will necessarily bring forth a comprehensive and dignified local government with ample administrative and legislative powers.

The care and control of the Greater City will inevitably lead to the realization of home rule; representative government will be revived, and with it our best hopes for the city's welfare.

Consolidation will bring about a harmonious system of development; it will give us bridges, tunnels, canals, and other means of approach and communication, rendering accessible all parts of the Greater New York by an adequate system of rapid transit; it will effect a tremendous saving in time and energies, and add largely to the wealth and comfort of the community.

Consolidation will cause a more natural distribution of population and will give more breathing space to the people; there will be less crowding, less vice, less crime; more and better and cheaper homes; the tenement house as the home of the laborer will gradually disappear. Consolidation means health, happiness, sunlight, better and happier men, women, and children. It will give the touch of nature to city life and provide city comforts for suburban homes.

It will combine the forces for good against the contending forces for evil; it will generate civic pride and elevate the standards of private and official morality; it will tend to greater economy in public expenses and lighten taxes. It will enhance our importance, preserve our prestige, increase our commerce, give to labor a more steady and lucrative employment, and keep us at the head of American cities, and in time make us the Metropolis of the World.

---

1. According to Henschel, what were the advantages of consolidation?
2. How were Henschel's concerns similar to and/or different from Storrs' concerns?
3. How did Henschel try to respond to the Brooklyn opposition?
4. According to Henschel, what was the best reason to support consolidation?
5. How was consolidation an outgrowth of the Brooklyn Bridge?

UNIT 5–2. POLITICS AND THE PUBLIC INTEREST: BOSSISM

Bossism was a product of the Gilded Age. As cities grew geometrically, traditional municipal governments fell out of date and out of touch. The solution was to create a new system of politics that organized the city by block and by neighborhood. Providing services to the new immigrants created a base of political power controlled by one man, a boss. Although bossism emerged in several late-nineteenth-century American cities, New York's Tweed Ring was the most infamous of all. Its master was William M. Tweed, leader of Tammany Hall, which was synonymous with New York City's Democratic Party.

Tweed was never mayor himself, but he held a variety of positions that gave him access to patronage jobs and money. His henchmen became the governor (John T. Hoffman), the mayor (A. Oakey Hall), the city comptroller (Richard B. Connolly), plus the county treasurer and parks commissioner (Peter B. Sweeney). Tweed controlled New York City and New York state as no one had before or has since. In the process, he and his friends became rich, defrauding the city from between 20 and 200 million dollars.

The New York Times began its campaign against the Tweed Ring in 1869, but an investigating committee chaired by John Jacob Astor III concluded in 1870 that the city's account books were "faithfully kept." It took two more years to get the hard evidence needed to prove how extensively the city was being robbed. After a Tweed bookkeeper died, he was replaced by a Tweed opponent, who copied the records and gave them to the *Times* in 1871. When Andrew H. Green (see Unit 5–1) replaced Connolly as City Comptroller later in 1871, he further documented the corruption.[6]

Under the Ring, the city was grossly overcharged in kickback schemes epitomized by the Tweed Courthouse, which is located behind City Hall. Contractors hired by the city to build the courthouse had to give 65 per cent of their fees to the Tweed Ring. As a result, carpets, shades and curtains cost about $675,000; thermometers cost $7,500; every window cost $8,000. Although Tweed died in prison in 1878, he remains the consummate symbol of what the journalist Lincoln Steffens called *The Shame of the Cities*.[7]

5-2-1. EXPLAINING BOSSISM: WILLIAM M. TWEED, BOSS OF TAMMANY HALL, 1878

Tweed understood that the key to political power was winning elections and used a variety of methods to fix the outcome. Immigrants were naturalized by Tammany-appointed judges at the rate of three a minute if they would vote for Tammany candidates. Gangs of Tammany supporters harassed or beat up opposition voters at the polls. Men, especially unemployed men, were given plenty of alcohol and promised (but not always given) payment if they would vote as asked. Many men were "repeaters," voting often by using fictitious names as they went from polling place to polling place. But, ultimately, it came down to the numbers, which Tweed carefully controlled. Brazenly daring anyone to challenge his political monopoly, he asked, "As long as I count the votes, what are you going to do about it?" He even admitted this malfeasance at one of his trials.[8]

Source: "Testimony of William M. Tweed, January 4, 1878," in Board of Aldermen, *Tweed Ring Investigation: Report of the Special Committee of the Board of Alderman Appointed to Investigate the "Ring" Frauds, Together with the Testimony Elicited During the Investigation*, Document No. 8, 208–209.

Q: Now, Mr. Tweed with regard to elections, ... did the Ring control the elections in this city at that time?

A. They did, sir; absolutely.

Q. Please tell me what the modus operandi of that was. How did you control the election?

A. Well, each ward had a representative man, who would control matters in his own ward, and whom the various members of the general committee were to look up to for advice how to control the elections. ...

Q. What were they to do, in case you wanted a particular man elected over another?

A. Count the ballots in bulk, or without counting them, announce the result in bulk, or change from one to another, as the case may have been.

Q. Then these really were no elections at all? The ballots were made to bring about any result that you determined upon beforehand?

A. The ballots made no result; the counters made the result. ... That was generally done in every ward by the gentleman who had charge of the ward. ...

Q. Mr. Tweed, did you ever give any directions to any persons, to falsify or change the result of the actual bona fide ballots cast in any election?

A. More in the nature of a request than a direction.

---

1. Based on Tweed's election machinery, how efficient was bossism?
2. What did Tweed's distinction between making a request and a direction reveal about his power?
3. Which of Tweed's answers is most important for understanding bossism?
4. Which of the Tweed Ring's strategies was most brazen and/or most dangerous for democracy?

5-2-2. ATTACKING BOSSISM: THOMAS NAST, CARTOONIST, 1871

The cartoonist Thomas Nast played a central role in the battle against the Tweed Ring. His drawings dramatized Tammany's corruption and aroused enough public anger to inspire the reform movement that eventually destroyed the ring, even though it did not eliminate Tammany. Nast depicted Tweed as a corpulent figure with a money bag for his head. Perhaps his most famous cartoon had the members of the ring standing in a circle, each one pointing to the next one in answer to the question "Who Stole the People's Money?" The power of Nast's images was so great that Tweed himself declared, "I don't care a straw for your newspaper articles. My constituents don't know how to read, but they can't help seeing those damned pictures."[9] A good example of the power of Nast's images is "The City Treasury," published in *Harper's Weekly* in 1871.

Source: Thomas Nast, "The City Treasury," *Harper's Weekly,* October 14, 1871.

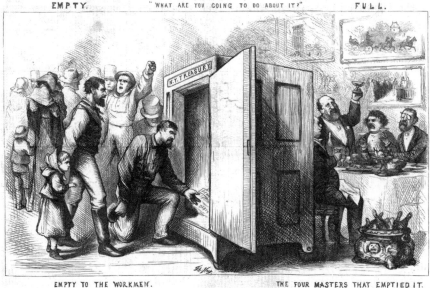

EMPTY. " WHAT ARE YOU GOING TO DO ABOUT IT?" FULL.

N.Y. TREASURY.

EMPTY TO THE WORKMEN. THE FOUR MASTERS THAT EMPTIED IT.

THE CITY TREASURY.

1. Describe the setting, clothing and attitude of the people on the left.
2. Describe the setting, clothing and attitude of the people on the right. They are Tweed (standing center) and his cronies (seated left to right)—Tammany's Peter "Brains" Sweeney, Comptroller "Slippery Dick" Connolly, and Mayor A. Oakey Hall.
3. Explain the significance of the contrast between the two groups and the size of the safe.
4. How could the image and the words that surround it inspire political reform?
5. Was Tweed right to damn Nast's cartoons?

5-2-3. JUSTIFYING BOSSISM: GEORGE WASHINGTON PLUNKITT, TAMMANY WARD BOSS, 1905

George Washington Plunkitt was a Tammany ward boss whose base of operations was a shoeshine stand near Foley Square. He was born in Nanny Goat Hill, the disparaging name for an Irish squatter settlement that was eliminated when Central Park was created. While working his way up from cartman to butcher to construction contractor, Plunkitt also rose in Tammany politics from election district captain to assembly district leader, state senator, state assemblyman, police magistrate, county supervisor and city alderman. In the process, he became a millionaire. His plain talks on practical politics provide a priceless perspective on the philosophy of the Tammany politician.

The Tweed Ring remains controversial. Without denying their corruption, some historians have pointed out that urban bosses were the first politicians to address the struggles of the new immigrants at a time when municipal governments did not provide aid. To be sure, the bosses were not motivated by compassion or idealism. They took full advantage of the power they gained without improving the living conditions of the slums. Yet, as Plunkitt demonstrates, they served the immigrants' immediate needs and helped them adjust to their new life in America.[10]

Source: William L. Riordon, *Plunkitt of Tammany Hall: A Series of Very Plain Talks on Very Practical Politics*. (New York: McClure, Phillips and Company, 1905), 3, 107–173.

Honest Graft

Everybody is talkin' these days about Tammany men growin' rich on graft, but nobody thinks of drawin' the distinction between honest graft and dishonest graft. There's all the difference in the world between the two. Yes, many of our men have grown rich in politics. I have myself. I've made a big fortune out of the game, and I'm getting richer every day, but I've not gone in for dishonest graft—blackmailin' gamblers, saloonkeepers, disorderly people, etc.—and neither has any of the men who have made big fortunes in politics.

There's an honest graft, and I'm an example of how it works. I might sum up the whole thing by sayin': "I seen my opportunities and I took 'em."

Just let me explain by examples. My party's in power in the city, and its going to undertake a lot of public improvements. Well, I'm tipped off, say, that they're going to lay out a new park at a certain place.

I see my opportunity and I take it. I go to that place and I buy up all the land I can in the neighborhood. Then the board of this or that makes its plan public, and there is a rush to get my land, which nobody cared particular for before.

Ain't it perfectly honest to charge a good price and make a profit on my investment and foresight? Of course, it is. Well, that's honest graft."

Strenuous Life of the Tammany Leader:

2 a.m.: Aroused from sleep by the ringing of his doorbell; went to the door and found a bartender, who asked him to go to the police station and bail out a saloonkeeper who had been arrested for violating the excise [liquor] law. Furnished bail and returned to bed at 3 o'clock.

6 a.m.: Awakened by fire engines passing his house. Hastened to the scene of the fire, according to the custom of the Tammany district leaders, to give assistance to the fire sufferers, if needed. Met several of his election district captains who are always under orders to look out for fires, which are considered great vote-getters. Found several tenants who had been burned out, took them to a hotel, supplied them with clothes, fed them, and arranged temporary quarters for them until they could rent and furnish new apartments.

8:30 a.m.: Appeared in the Municipal District Court. Directed one of his district captains to act as counsel for a widow against whom dispossess proceedings had been instituted and obtained an extension of time. Paid the rent of a poor family about to be dispossessed and gave them a dollar for food.

11 a.m.: At home again. Found four men waiting for him. One had been discharged by the Metropolitan Railway Company for neglect of duty, and wanted the district leader to fix things. Another wanted a job on the road. The third sought a place on the Subway and the fourth, a plumber, was looking for work with the Consolidated Gas Company. The district leader spent nearly three hours fixing things for the four men, and succeeded in each case.

3 p.m.: Attended the funeral of an Italian as far as the ferry. Hurried back to make his appearance at the funeral of a Hebrew constituent. Went conspicuously to the front both in the Catholic church and the synagogue, and later attended the Hebrew confirmation ceremonies in the synagogue.

7 p.m.: Went to district headquarters and presided over a meeting of election district captains. Each captain submitted a list of all the voters in his district, reported on their attitude toward Tammany, suggested who might be won over and how they could be won, told who were in need, and who were in trouble of any kind, and the best way to reach them. District leader took notes and gave orders.

8 p.m.: Went to a church fair. Took chances on everything, bought ice cream for the young girls and the children. Kissed the little ones, flattered their mothers and took their fathers out for something at the corner.

9 p.m.: At the clubhouse again. Spent $10 on tickets for a church excursion and promised a subscription for a new church bell. Bought tickets for a baseball game to be played by two nines from his district. Listened to the complaints of a dozen pushcart peddlers who said they were persecuted by the police and assured them he would go to police headquarters in the morning and see about it.

10:30 p.m.: Attended a Hebrew wedding reception and dance. Had previously sent a handsome wedding present to the bride.

12 p.m.: In bed.

---

1. How convincing was Plunkitt's distinction between honest and dishonest graft?
2. Did Plunkitt work hard? How extensive was his influence?
3. Was Plunkitt's approach to politics humane and/or exploitative?
4. How did bossism promote and pervert democracy?

5-2-4. ASSESSING BOSSISM: THEODORE ROOSEVELT, POLITICIAN, 1914

As a member of New York's elite, Theodore Roosevelt did not have to choose a life of public service. Nonetheless, after graduating from Harvard, he became a New York State assemblyman. Despite losing a bid for mayor in 1886, he served as U.S. civil service commissioner and New York City's police commissioner. He befriended journalists Lincoln Steffens and Jacob Riis with whom saw the slums at first hand. Roosevelt went on to become assistant secretary of the Navy, governor of New York State, vice president and president, the only one born in New York City. A man of immense energy and strong conviction, Roosevelt made his mark on the national and international stage. But much of his education about the challenges of his era came from the streets of New York.

Source: Theodore Roosevelt, *An Autobiography* (New York: Macmillan, 1914), 152–154.

One of the reasons why the boss so often keeps his hold ... is ... because so many of the men who claim to be reformers have been blind to the need of working in human fashion for social and industrial betterment. ... If the bosses were responsible for nothing but pure wickedness, they would probably last but a short time in the community. ... The trouble is that the boss does understand human nature. ...

There is often much good in the type of boss, who fulfills towards the people of his district in rough and ready fashion the position of friend and protector. He uses his influence to get jobs for young men who need them. He goes into court for a wild young fellow who has gotten into trouble. He helps out with cash or credit the widow who is in straits, or the breadwinner who is crippled or for some other cause temporarily out of work. He organizes clambakes and chowder parties and picnics and is consulted by the local labor leaders when a cut in wages is threatened. For some of his constituents he does proper favors, and for others wholly improper favors; but he preserves human relations with all. He may be a very bad and very corrupt man. ... But these constituents are for the most part men and women who struggle hard against poverty and with whom the problem of living is very real and very close. They would prefer clean and honest government, if this clean and honest government is accompanied by human sympathy, human understanding. ...

By the time I was ending my career as Civil Service Commissioner, I was already growing to understand that mere improvement in political conditions by itself was not enough. I dimly realized that an even greater fight must be waged to improve economic conditions, and to secure social and industrial justice, justice as between individuals and justice as between classes.

---

1. According to Roosevelt, how was bossism both good and bad?
2. According to Roosevelt, what lesson should all politicians learn from bossism?
3. What would Roosevelt have thought of Tweed and Plunkitt?
4. Why did Roosevelt put these words in a chapter of his autobiography called "Applied Idealism"?

UNIT 5-3. CHANGE AND CHALLENGE: THE CLASSES AND THE MASSES

During the Gilded Age, the extremes of wealth and poverty were magnified as the new industrial economy stimulated the concentration of wealth by the few while the vast majority toiled at meager wages. The gap between rich and poor in America had never been so great. At one end of the economic spectrum were New York robber barons like John D. Rockefeller, J. P. Morgan, Cornelius Vanderbilt and Jay Gould whose wealth reached unprecedented dimensions. Ostentation was the rule of the day as seen in the huge mansions along Fifth Avenue, soon known as Millionaire's Row.

At the other end of the economic spectrum were countless native-born and immigrant workers whose lives were defined by sweatshops and slums. Tenement housing tested the limits of survival through crowding, disease, filth and stench. The contrast upset reformers like Henry George who ran for mayor in 1886 in order to represent "not a class but the mass." His goal was to expose "the shocking contrast between monstrous wealth and debasing want."[11]

5-3-1. COMPARING RICH AND POOR: FIFTH AVENUE AND THE POVERTY GAP

The home of A. T. Stewart reflected the new dimensions of wealth in the Gilded Age. In the 1860s, he replaced John Jacob Astor as New York's richest merchant. An Irish immigrant, Stewart became the father of the American department store when he expanded his dry goods business into a large store carrying a variety of items at fixed, reasonable prices. It was called the Marble Palace for the stone used on the front and its lavish interior.

Worth $50,000,000 at his death in 1876, Stewart spent $5,000,000 building a mansion at 34th Street and Fifth Avenue that, like his extravagant department store, was really a marble palace. Its reception rooms, hallway, stairway, breakfast room, dining room and ballroom were all adorned in marble and the dinner service was made of gold. The art gallery measured 72 feet long by 36 feet wide with ceilings 18 feet high. The mansion aptly reflected the Gilded Age and proved that Stewart "thinks money, makes money, lives money."[12]

By comparison, there is a typical slum dwelling located on West 28th Street, near the Hudson River. The photograph by Jacob Riis was published in his famous book *How the Other Half Lives: Studies Among the Tenements of New York* (1890). Significantly, the street was called Poverty Gap. The family lived in this one room with the pile of rags in the left foreground serving as their only bed. In the seasons when he could get work, the father earned $5.00 a week shoveling coal. Riis reported that the girls were "bright and pretty" and the mother was "cheerful, even light-hearted" despite "the utter wretchedness of the place."[13]

Sources: "A. T. Stewart Mansion," in Henry Collins Brown (ed.), *Valentine's Manual of Old New York* (New York City: Chauncey Holt, 1924), 315.

Jacob Riis, "Poverty Gap," 1889 in *How the Other Half Lives: Studies Among the Tenements of New York* (New York: Charles Scribner's Sons, 1890), 169.

---

1. Based on the photographs, explain the major differences between the homes of the classes and the homes of the masses.
2. What elements of each photograph are most surprising and/or shocking?
3. How do these photographs help explain the double meaning of the term Gilded Age?
4. How do these photographs help explain the rise of reform movements in the late nineteenth and early twentieth centuries?

5-3-2. SATIRIZING WEALTH: TONY PASTOR, ENTERTAINER, 1863

In May 1883, the Metropolitan Opera House opened its doors with a lavish auditorium for 3000 surrounded by 122 exclusive private boxes, each decorated with gold leaf. The boxes were more important than the acoustics because the new opera house was all about status, not music. New York did not really need a new opera house; the existing Academy of Music served the city well. However, the boxes in the Academy were taken by families of old wealth and none were available to families of new wealth, like the Vanderbilts, the Morgans and the Goulds. Consequently, the people who had made their money during the industrial era decided to build their own bigger opera house, properly equipped with boxes for them all. The result was a fitting monument to the concentration of wealth in the Gilded Age and the widening gap between rich and poor.[14]

By contrast, Tony Pastor's Opera House catered to the masses, not the classes. A child entertainer, Pastor could sing, play musical instruments, ride horses, do acrobatics, and serve as clown or ring master. He was a one-man circus who used his talents to develop a new form of entertainment called vaudeville. Like the old variety show, it presented a dazzling array of acts, but Pastor made the raunchy more respectable by banning alcohol, smoking and rowdy behavior. Like Phineas T. Barnum before him and Coney Island after him, Pastor legitimized and democratized amusement. (see Document 3-3-4 and Unit 6- 2)

Paralleling the growth of the city, Pastor moved his Opera House from the Bowery in 1865 to Union Square in 1881 to Times Square in 1900. For 10 to 25 cents, different types of people could enjoy themselves together bridging class, ethnic and gender barriers. With the important exception of its racist stereotypes and segregated seating, vaudeville was democratic because it offered, as Pastor put it, "something for everybody."[15]

Throughout his life, Pastor acted in his own performances and wrote his own songs, many of which became popular. As the following lyrics indicate, Pastor also was a social critic.

Source: "The Upper and Lower Ten Thousand," Tony Pastor, *New Comic Irish Songster* (New York: Dick and Fitzgerald, 1863), 10–11.

> The Upper Ten Thousand in mansions reside,
> With fronts of brown stone, and with stoops high and wide
> While the lower Ten Thousand in poverty deep,
> In cellars and garrets, are huddled like sheep.
> The Upper Ten Thousand have turkey and wine,
> On turtle and ven'son and pastry they dine.
> While the Lower Ten Thousand, whose meals are so small,
> They've often to go without dinner at all.
>
> If an Upper-Ten fellow a swindler should be,
> And with thousands of dollars of others make free
> Should he get into court, why, without any doubt,
> The matter's hushed up and they let him step out.
> If a Lower-Ten Thousand chap happens to steal,
> For to keep him from starving, the price of a meal,
> Why the law will declare it's a different thing—
> For they call him a thief, and he's sent to Sing Sing.

---

1. What social problems did Pastor identify?
2. Which of Pastor's points were most sarcastic?
3. Which of Pastor's points were most powerful?
4. Who would have been amused and who would have been offended by Pastor's song?

5-3-3. PREACHING SOCIAL DARWINISM: HORATIO ALGER, NOVELIST, 1867

The growing gap between rich and poor in the Gilded Age was closely identified with urbanization and industrialization, both of which seemed to be undermining the American Dream, even as they promoted America's wealth. Horatio Alger's dime novels were the first books to incorporate the city into the American Dream. While acknowledging poverty and other negative aspects of urban life,

Alger also examined the excitement of the city and the opportunities it offered for the ambitious, hard working, virtuous person. He popularized the city as a place of possibility. By reassuring Americans that individual effort and self-reliance were still the keys to success, Alger reinforced the social Darwinism of the era, replete with its faith in survival of the fittest. Alger's first and most famous story was about *Ragged Dick*, a poor orphan boy who, with luck, street smarts and perseverance rose from the gutter to respectability. Note that Frank was a rich boy whom Dick met by accident when Frank was in New York with his uncle staying at the Astor House Hotel.

Source: Horatio Alger, *Ragged Dick: Street Life in New York with the Bootblacks* (Boston, MA: Loring, 1868), 84–92.

"Have you always lived in New York, Dick?" asked Frank, after a pause.

"Ever since I can remember."

"I wish you'd tell me a little about yourself. Have you got any father or mother?"

"I ain't got no mother. She died when I wasn't but three years old. My father went to sea; but he went off before mother died, and nothing was ever heard of him. I expect he got wrecked, or died at sea."

"And what became of you when your mother died?"

"The folks she boarded with took care of me, but they was poor, and they couldn't do much. When I was seven the woman died, and her husband went out West, and then I had to scratch for myself."

"At seven years old!" exclaimed Frank, in amazement.

"Yes," said Dick, "I was a little feller to take care of myself, but," he continued with pardonable pride, "I did it."

"What could you do?"

"Sometimes one thing, and sometimes another," said Dick. "I changed my business accordin' as I had to. Sometimes I was a newsboy, and diffused intelligence among the masses, as I heard somebody say once in a big speech he made in the Park. Them was the times when Horace Greeley and James Gordon Bennett made money."

"Through your enterprise?" suggested Frank.

"Yes," said Dick; "but I gave it up after a while."

"What for?"

"Well, they didn't always put news enough in their papers, and people wouldn't buy 'em as fast as I wanted 'em to. So one morning I was stuck on a lot of *Heralds*, and I thought I'd make a sensation. So I called out 'Great News! Queen Victoria Assassinated!' All my *Heralds* went off like hot cakes, and I went off too, but one of the gentlemen what got sold remembered me, and said he'd have me took up, and that's what made me change my business."

"That wasn't right, Dick," said Frank.

"I know it," said Dick; "but lots of boys does it."

"That don't make it any better."

"No," said Dick, "I was sort of ashamed at the time, 'specially about one poor old gentleman,— a Englishman he was. He couldn't help cryin' to think the queen was dead, and his hands shook when he handed me the money for the paper."

"What did you do next?"

"I went into the match business," said Dick; "but it was small sales and small profits. Most of the people I called on had just laid in a stock, and didn't want to buy. So one cold night, when I hadn't money enough to pay for a lodgin', I burned the last of my matches to keep me from freezin'. But it cost too much to get warm that way, and I couldn't keep it up."

"You've seen hard times, Dick," said Frank, compassionately.

"Yes," said Dick, "I've knowed what it was to be hungry and cold, with nothin' to eat or to warm me; but there's one thing I never could do," he added, proudly.

"What's that?"

"I never stole," said Dick. "It's mean and I wouldn't do it."

"Were you ever tempted to?"

"Lots of times. Once I had been goin' round all day, and hadn't sold any matches, except three cents' worth early in the mornin'. With that I bought an apple, thinkin' I should get some more bimeby. When evenin' come I was awful hungry. I went into a baker's just to look at the bread. It made me feel kind o' good just to look at the bread and cakes, and I thought maybe they would give me some. I asked 'em wouldn't they give me a loaf, and take their pay in matches. But they said they'd got enough matches to last three months; so there wasn't any chance for a trade. While I was standin' at the stove warmin' me, the baker went into the back room, and I felt so hungry I thought I would take just one loaf, and go off with it. There was such a big pile. I don't think he'd have known it."

"But you didn't do it?"

"No, I didn't, and I was glad of it, for when the man came in ag'in, he said he wanted someone to carry some cake to a lad in St. Mark's Place. His boy was sick, and he hadn't no one to send; so he told me he would give me ten cents if I would go. My business wasn't very pressin' just then, so I went, and when I come back, I took my pay in bread and cakes. Didn't they taste good, though?"

"So you didn't stay long in the match business, Dick?"

"No, I couldn't sell enough to make it pay. Then there was some folks that wanted me to sell cheaper to them; so I couldn't make any profit. There was one old lady—she was rich, too, for she lived in a big brick house—beat me down so, that I didn't make no profit at all; but she wouldn't buy without, and I had sold none that day; so I let her have them. I don't see why rich folks should be so hard upon a poor boy that wants to make a livin'."

"There's a good deal of meanness in the world, I'm afraid, Dick."

"If everybody was like you and your uncle," said Dick, "there would be some chance for poor people. If I was rich I'd try to help 'em along."

"Perhaps you will be rich sometime, Dick."

Dick shook his head.

"I'm afraid all my wallets will be like this," said Dick, indicating the one he had received from the dropper, "and will be full of papers what ain't of no use to anybody except the owner."

"That depends very much on yourself, Dick," said Frank. "[A. T.] Stewart wasn't always rich, you know."

"Wasn't he?"

"When he first came to New York as a young man he was a teacher, and teachers are not generally very rich. At last he went into business, starting in a small way, and worked his way up by degrees. But there was one thing he determined in the beginning: that he would be strictly honorable in all his dealings, and never overreach any one for the sake of making money. If there was a chance for him, Dick, there is a chance for you."

"He knowed enough to be a teacher, and I'm awful ignorant," said Dick.

"But you needn't stay so."

" How can I help it?"

"Can't you learn at school?"

"I can't go to school 'cause I've got my livin' to earn. It wouldn't do me much good if I learned to read and write, and just as I'd got learned I starved to death."

"But are there no night schools?"

"Yes."

"Why don't you go? I suppose you don't work in the evenings."

"I never cared much about it," said Dick, "and that's the truth. But since I've got to talkin' with you, I think more about it. I guess I'll begin to go."

"I wish you would, Dick. You'll make a smart man if you only get a little education."

"Do you think so? Asked Dick, doubtfully.

"I know so. A boy who earned his own living ever since he was seven years old must have something in him. I feel very much interested in you, Dick. You've had a hard time of it so far in life, but I think better times are in store. I want you to do well, and I feel sure you can if you only try."

"You're a good fellow," said Dick, gratefully. "I'm afraid I'm a pretty rough customer, but I ain't as bad as some. I mean to turn over a new leaf, and try to grow up 'spectable."

"There've been a great many boys begin as low down as you, Dick, that have grown up respectable and honored. But they had to work pretty hard for it."

"I'm willing to work hard," said Dick.

"And you must not only work hard, but work in the right way."

"What's the right way?"

"You began in the right way when you determined never to steal, or do anything mean or dishonorable, however strongly tempted to do so. That will make people have confidence in you when they come to know you. But, in order to succeed well, you must manage to get as good an education as you can. Until you do, you cannot get a position in an office or counting-room, even to run errands."

"That's so," said Dick, soberly. "I never thought how awful ignorant I was till now."

"That can be remedied with perseverance," said Frank. "A year will do a great deal for you."

"I'll go to work and see what I can do," said Dick, energetically.

---

1. What positive qualities did Dick possess from the start?
2. What strategies did Alger advocate for individual self-improvement and social mobility?
3. Did Alger support any social policies for improving the plight of the poor?
4. How did Alger advocate social Darwinism?

5-3-4. PREACHING SOCIAL REFORM: JACOB RIIS, JOURNALIST, 1890

Horatio Alger's optimism was countered by realism. In 1890, the journalist and reformer Jacob A. Riis published his account of *How the Other Half Lives.* Through riveting descriptions and poignant photographs, Riis documented the suffering in the slums. (see Document 5-3-1 above.) His objective was not only to record reality, but also to awaken social conscience and spur social reform. Riis was part of a larger group of reformers who were reassessing social Darwinism. Seeing the slums and factories convinced them that personal virtues were often not enough to conquer the obstacles to success. Instead, they concluded that negative behavior was influenced by negative conditions such as too much crowding, too many saloons, too few schools and hardly any parks. Consequently, the reformers developed new attitudes towards poverty and new efforts to address it.[16]

In New York and other cities, people marshaled public and private resources to establish settlement houses, provide medical services, and build model tenements. Local governments were pressured to build schools, public baths and parks, pass housing and factory legislation, improve sanitation and restrict alcohol consumption. Religious groups reached out to the poor through the social gospel movement. Philanthropic groups sponsored schools, kindergartens, hospitals and visiting nurse services. Organizations were formed to protect women and children from exploitation by employers. In other words, the traditional American emphasis on individual self-reliance was being supplemented (not replaced) by a new emphasis on social responsibility.[17]

Source: Jacob A. Riis, *How the Other Half Lives: Studies Among the Tenements of New York.* (New York: C. Scribner's Sons, 1903), 64–65, 192–193, 268–269, 296–297.

Bottle Alley is around the corner on Baxter Street, but it is a fair specimen of its kind wherever found. Look into any of these houses, everywhere the same piles of rags, of malodorous bones and musty paper. ... Here is a "flat" of "parlor" and two pitch-dark coops called bedrooms. Truly, the bed is all there is room for. ... One, two three beds are there, if the old boxes and heaps of foul straw can be called by that name. [See] a broken stove with crazy pipe from which the smoke leaks at every joint, a table of rough boards propped up on boxes, piles of rubbish in the corner. The closeness and smell are appalling. How many people sleep here? The woman with the red bandanna shakes her head, sullenly, but the bare-legged girl with the bright face counts on her fingers—five, six! ...

It is with a sense of glad relief that one turns from this misery to the brighter page of the helping hands stretched forth on every side to save the young and the helpless ... The Day Nurseries, the numberless Kindergartens and charitable schools in the poor quarters, the Fresh Air Funds, the thousand and one charities that in one way or another reach the homes and lives of the poor with sweetening touch. ...

Tenements quite as bad as the worst are too numerous yet; but one tremendous factor for evil in the lives of the poor has been taken by the throat, and something unquestionably has been done, where that was possible, to lift lives out of the rut where they were equally beyond the reach of hope and of ambition. It is no longer lawful to construct barracks to cover the whole of a lot. Air and sunlight have a legal claim, and the day of rear tenements is past. ... The dark, unventilated bedroom is going with them, and the open sewer ...

The sea of a mighty population, held in galling fetters, heaves uneasily in the tenements. ... The gap between the classes in which it surges, unseen, unsuspected by the thoughtless, is widening day by day. ... I know of but one bridge that will carry us over safe, a bridge founded upon justice and built of human hearts.

---

1. According to Riis, what caused the problems of the slum?
2. Who and what did Riis suggest could solve the problems of the slum?
3. Why was Riis considered a social reformer?
4. If Stewart, Pastor, Riis and Alger met for lunch, where would each man suggest that they eat? In what ways would they agree and disagree about the causes of and solutions to poverty in the nineteenth-century city? Would they be able to change each other's opinions? Who would pay the bill?

UNIT 5-4. ECONOMICS AND THE PUBLIC INTEREST: JAY GOULD, ROBBER BARON

Jay Gould loved his family, his books and his orchids and his money. Like George Washington Plunkitt, Gould "saw his opportunities and he took 'em." His skillful financial maneuverings made him the most feared man on Wall Street and the most hated 'robber baron' in America. Depicted as the devil in countless cartoons, Jay Gould was the evil of New York incarnate. In some ways a classic Horatio Alger figure, Gould began life as the son of a struggling upstate New York farmer and rose to become one of America's wealthiest men, worth somewhere between $75,000,000 and $125,000,000. However, his real assets were determination, discipline and deception.

Born in 1836, Gould was a shy, studious child, who rose at 3 am to read before performing his duties of the day. Although Gould was physically frail and small, he was mentally agile and extremely smart. After his father sold the farm and bought a tin shop, Gould helped with the accounts, but in 1851 at age 15, he taught himself the skills of surveying and obtained his first paid job. By age 17, he had raised enough money to become self-employed as a surveyor of two upstate New York counties, about one of which he wrote a still respected book. At 18, Gould confronted typhoid fever, a serious infection, and pneumonia; for the rest of his life he fought fatigue. In addition, he coughed—a dark omen of the tuberculosis that would kill him, which, although not hereditary, had already killed many of his relatives. Haunted by this reality and driven by intellectual restlessness, Gould determined to maximize the time he had.[18]

Ever ambitious, Gould spent the next few years building business acumen and acquiring assets in two growing industries—leather tanning and railroads. Working as a surveyor in 1856, he met 66-year-old Zadoch Pratt, one of upper New York State's richest and most respected older men. Only 20 himself, Gould convinced Pratt to expand his lucrative tanning business to Pennsylvania with Gould as an equal partner in the venture. Gould personally supervised the creation of the tannery and a town that he named Gouldsboro in the Pocono mountains. In short order, Gould bought out Pratt.

In 1860 he moved to New York City and began studying Wall Street while conducting his tanning business from Spruce Street. In 1863 he bought control of a railroad that ran from Vermont to upper New York State and two years later connected it with another line for access to the Hudson River. Not content to be an armchair entrepreneur, Gould cemented his understanding of the industry by becoming directly involved in the management, finance, upkeep, and marketing of his railroads. Characteristically industrious, meticulous and efficient, Gould made the lines profitable.[19]

In 1867, Gould got into a financial war with Cornelius Vanderbilt over controlling the Erie Railroad, a line that was supposed to link Manhattan to Buffalo. At age 70, Vanderbilt was using a fortune made from steamboats to build a new fortune in railroads. He already controlled the New York Central, the Harlem Railroad and the Hudson Railroad. Now he wanted to turn his partial control of the Erie into full control so that he could dominate the nation's railroad system all the way to Chicago.

Gould tricked Vanderbilt into buying Erie stock at artificially inflated prices. When the scheme was exposed, Gould and his allies grabbed $7,000,000 in Erie money and fled by boat to New Jersey. Vanderbilt got a court injunction against Gould and Gould got a counter-injunction against Vanderbilt. Then Gould engineered an Erie Bill through the New York State legislature by bribing the legislators. Vanderbilt's men did likewise and the legislators shuffled between the two camps looking for the best payoff. Among them was State Senator William M. Tweed, a Vanderbilt ally who readily switched to the highest bidder and joined Gould's Erie Ring.

The month-long Erie War resulted in an agreement between Vanderbilt and Gould whereby Vanderbilt withdrew after being largely compensated for his loss and Gould became the Erie's new president and treasurer. But it was a hapless victory because the railroad was a losing proposition doomed by debt and entangled by lawsuits. Gould tried to extend the line by buying adjacent lines. When one line represented by a young banker named J. P. Morgan resisted, there was an actual battle between thugs recruited for each side— 800 of them from the Five Points. Finally, Gould resigned and settled the legal case against him in 1872. The whole affair made him a major player on Wall Street, but earned him as much contempt as profit.[20]

Meanwhile, another episode had already rendered Gould the nation's most despised robber baron. He wanted to corner, or get control over, the nation's gold supply, which was traded in New York City. Gold formed the basis of America's currency and was always in great demand for domestic and foreign business. If Gould could control the supply, he could bid up the price and rake in the profits.

The only problem was that the federal government held considerable gold in reserve and Gould needed to keep it from being released onto the market, thus increasing the supply and decreasing the price. He planned to shape public policy for his personal profit. Towards this end, he bribed President Ulysses Grant's brother-in-law to arrange for Gould to meet the President in order to convince him that the government should hold onto its gold and trust the gold market to benefit the nation's economy. Confident that all was in order, Gould's agents began buying gold in the summer of 1869. Slowly, the price rose until Friday, September 24, 1869 when it got so high that it caused a panic.

Paying higher prices was bankrupting the businessmen and merchants who needed gold to function. The hysteria was so great that a riot was feared. Even worse, Gould was actually selling gold while instructing his agents to buy it and profiting from the confusion. When the Secretary of the Treasury finally recognized the crisis, he got Grant to release 4,000,000 dollars worth of gold onto the market causing prices to fall and the scheme to collapse.[21]

Black Friday was truly a disaster. Banks faced collapse; scores of merchants and brokerage firms failed; one businessman committed suicide. The New York City gold market was paralyzed and, because the city was so central to finance, the ripple effect reached across America and over to Europe. But the blackest blot befell Jay Gould personally. From then on, he was branded an unparalleled scoundrel—a "skunk," a "serpent," a "despicable worm," a "spider," a "pitiless human carnivore," and, most lasting, "the Mephistopheles of Wall Street."[22]

Despite being Protestant, Gould was often labeled Jewish and condemned as a devious, money hungry, cheating Shylock. These stereotypes prevailed throughout Gould's lifetime, even in his obituaries. Gould later claimed that "No man can control Wall Street," but his role in the gold corner and his subsequent speculations suggested otherwise. He was so widely demonized and despised that he received death threats and was physically attacked twice in public, forcing him to hire bodyguards for himself and his family.[23]

The collapse of the gold market hurt Gould financially, but he got friendly judges to protect his interests and he soon recouped. After leaving the Erie, Gould pursued an even more ambitious railroad vision—controlling a transcontinental line. Taking advantage of the Panic of 1873, Gould purchased enough stock in the struggling Union Pacific railroad to be elected to its board of directors in 1874. He fixed its finances, acquired adjacent lines and bought resources like coal mines along the route. As in upper New York State, he mastered all the practical details of management and traveled the railroad himself twice yearly.[24]

Gould understood the crucial role that railroads played in fueling and nationalizing the new industrial economy. So too, he saw that new methods of communication were essential for economic efficiency. Convinced that the railroad and the telegraph were partners in progress, he wrestled control over the Western Union telegraph system from Vanderbilt's son in 1881. Gould also appreciated the power of the press and often used reporters for his own purposes. Not surprisingly, he influenced the New York Tribune after giving a loan to its editor in 1872. He owned the New York World outright from 1879 to 1883 and rumor suggested that he also influenced the Associated Press whose reports had to pass through his Western Union cable service.[25]

An extension of Gould's interest in railroads was his desire to control New York City's elevated train system, a crucial component of the growing urban economy. From his perch at the New York World in 1879, he began a campaign to undermine confidence in the Manhattan Elevated Company, which coordinated the Metropolitan Elevated and the New York Elevated systems. The object was to drive down the Manhattan's stock so that Gould and his allies could buy it up. It worked. By 1881, Gould was president of the Manhattan company and held significant shares of the Metropolitan and the New York lines too. He used these positions to merge the three companies, thereby creating a monopoly for which he was widely condemned, especially as the trains became increasingly crowded, noisy and dirty.[26]

The relentless attacks hurt, but Gould took solace from his family—the wife he adored and the six children he cherished. In addition, he was the surrogate father and financial supporter of his sister's nine children after her husband committed suicide. Gould was retiring, but his wife wanted to participate in New York's social scene. However, the Goulds were scorned by the old-money elite and were banned from prominent social clubs. In response, Gould joined the benefactors of the new Metropolitan Opera House where he had a box. (see Unit 5-3)

Gould owned a large brownstone on Fifth Avenue and a Gothic mansion called Lyndhurst in Tarrytown, New York, which is now part of the National Historic Trust. After a fire (perhaps arson) ruined his huge greenhouse, he built America's first steel frame greenhouse where he nurtured 8,000 orchids. Because of the infamy attached to his every move, Gould insisted on anonymity when contributing to charities like the Five Points Mission or funding the uptown campus of New York University (now occupied by Bronx Community College). He died of tuberculosis in 1892 at age 56, mourned by his family but despised by everyone else. In final farewell, Gould's stocks sold higher upon word of his passing. To this day, Jay Gould is remembered as the most calculating capitalist in the most cutthroat city.[27]

---

1. Which of Gould's personal attributes and professional activities were most contemptible?
2. Which of Gould's personal attributes and professional activities were most admirable?
3. How was Gould both a pioneer and a product of his times?
4. Does Gould deserve to be the most despised 'robber baron'?

5-4-1. SCORNING STRIKES: JAY GOULD, CAPITALIST, 1883

One of the most significant aspects of the Gilded Age was a revolution in the relationship between management and labor. As factories displaced workshops and trusts swallowed small businesses, individual workers became less important. This development confirmed a shift begun earlier in the century. (see Unit 3-3) Now workers were merely cogs in the machine, easily replaced by numerous new immigrants desperate for jobs. While employers justified low wages and long hours as part of a social Darwinian survival of the fittest, workers responded by organizing to improve labor conditions. The result was conflict.

Even if Gould was exceptionally devious, he was probably fairly typical in reflecting capitalists' attitudes towards workers and labor organizations. He fought back bitterly when workers struck for higher wages in the various businesses he controlled. He fired strikers, reneged on wage agreements, brought in scabs, used police and hired goons to attack strikers. His frank testimony in 1883 before a U.S. Senate Committee investigating labor-management relations provides a useful perspective on economic conflict in the Gilded Age.

Source: "Testimony of Jay Gould," U.S. Senate, Committee on Education and Labor Report on the Relations Between Capital and Labor. Senate Hearing: 41st Congress. (Washington, DC: U.S. Government Printing Office, 1885.)

Q. What is your observation and opinion in regard to strikes, their causes and their results?

A. Strikes, of course, come from various causes, but they generally come from a class of dissatisfied men—the poorest part of your labor generally are at the bottom of a strike. Your best men do not care how many hours they work, or anything of the kind; they are looking to get higher up; either to own a business of their own and control it, or to get higher up in the ranks. ...

Q. ... Do you not think that their dissatisfaction may oftentimes be based on the fact that they do not receive compensation enough to keep them from suffering?

A. Is it not true that they get better pay here than in any other country? That is why they come here, I believe. ... And is it not true also that capital, if it gets better remunerations in some other country than it gets here, will go there? You cannot transfer your house, but you can transfer your money; and if labor is put up too high here, all the manufacturing will be done abroad, because the capitalists will go where they can get cheaper labor. So that when you sit down and try to get a panacea for a particular evil, you run against a great many obstacles that come in the way of putting it into practice, and my observation has been that capital and labor, let alone, generally come together and mutually regulate their relationship to each other. There are some of these people who think they can regulate the whole of mankind, but they generally get wrong ideas into the minds of the public. ...

Q. Do you think that the labor unions of the country are an injury or a benefit to the laborers and the country generally?

A. Well, I cannot say about that. I have not paid much attention to those unions. I think that anything that tends to elevate the working classes or to educate them, or that provides for those who are in want, provides a fund for the widows and orphans in any particular business, I think anything of that kind is the legitimate object of such societies. But when they get beyond that I think they get into a broad sea that they cannot control, because labor, like everything else, is regulated by the law of supply and demand. "You can lead a horse to water, but you cannot make him drink."

---

1. What did Gould think of labor leaders?
2. Why did Gould consider strikes unnecessary, unreasonable and unwise?
3. How did Gould think wage disputes should be resolved?
4. What positive role did Gould think workers' organizations could play?
5. Would Gould have considered organizations of manufacturers more legitimate than organizations of workers? Why?

5-4-2. DEFENDING STRIKES: SAMUEL GOMPERS, LABOR LEADER, 1883

Samuel Gompers (1850–1924) was president of the American Federation of Labor (AFL) from its founding in 1886 until 1923. Working in cigar-making factories since he was 10 and being involved in several strikes taught him how necessary but difficult it was for labor to organize and protest.

Unlike the Knights of Labor, which advocated cooperation between labor and management, the AFL believed that employers would never improve working conditions unless pressured to do so through strikes. At the same U. S. Senate hearings where Gould testified, Gompers explained the importance of this strategy.

Gompers referred to a strike against Gould by Western Union telegraphers which lasted for a month in the summer of 1883 but was defeated by hunger, bad press, some violence, and a totally immovable management. In 1874, Gould had undermined the organizing efforts of Scandinavian mine workers by replacing them with cheaper Chinese laborers. However, during the great railroad strike of 1877, he reversed a pay cut after deciding that it was not worth the potential damage that the strikers could inflict on his railroads. In return, Gould's workers kept his lines safe and he took advantage of the situation by purchasing the depressed stock of competing lines that were still fighting the strike.[28]

Source: "Testimony of Samuel Gompers," U.S. Senate, Committeeon Education and Labor Report on the Relations Between Capital and Labor. Senate Hearing: 41st Congress. (Washington, DC: U.S. Government Printing Office, 1885.)

Strikes ought to be, and in well-organized trades unions they are, the last means which workingmen resort to [in order] to protect themselves against the almost never satisfied greed of the employers. Besides this, the strike is, in many instances, the only remedy within our reach as long as legislation is entirely indifferent to the interests of labor. ...

Q. You understand that this recent strike of the telegraphers has failed.
A. Yes, sir. I understand that the strike is finally at an end.
Q. Do you know the cause of its failure, or have you a well-considered opinion as to the cause?
A. I have an opinion as to the cause of the failure of that strike.
Q. What is your opinion?
A. My opinion is that the first few strikes that workingmen generally indulge in are lost, from the fact that their employers are unable to comprehend the idea that labor has certain rights which they ought to respect; second, because they are really unaware that the laborers who are on strike are capable of inflicting an injury upon them; and third, that when they are once in a strike and hold out for a considerable period they do not like to weaken and accede to the terms of their employees, but prefer to make large sacrifices from their wealth or capital rather than to accede to those demands.

This being the second telegraph strike ... the company, that is, Jay Gould, was unable to comprehend at first, what he was forced to comprehend in the case of the locomotive engineers and firemen last year, that the workingmen were in a position to inflict considerable damage upon the company. This strike has another instructive feature. It will teach the telegraphers this, that if they are desirous of holding out for a long period and fighting a concern of the magnitude of the Western Union Telegraph Company, they will have in time of peace to prepare for war.

Q. They will have to have a treasury, you mean?

A. They will have to have a treasury. Further the accumulation of such a treasury, the payment of benefits to members, and the demonstration to members that the organizations are fully capable of keeping their promises ... will insure the confidence of the members in their organization, and they will find that when they next indulge in or threaten a strike, Mr. Jay Gould will be more willing to lend an ear to their complaints and grievances. ...

When we strike as organized workingmen, we generally win, and that is the reason of the trouble that our employers go to when they try to show that strikes are failures, but you will notice that they generally or always point to unorganized workers. That is one reason also why when the employers know that the workingmen are organized and have got a good treasury, strikes are very frequently avoided. ... .

The trades unions are not what too many men have been led to believe they are, importations from Europe; if they are imported, then, as has been said, they were landed at Plymouth Rock from the Mayflower. Modern industry evolves these organizations out of the existing conditions where there are two classes of society, one incessantly striving to obtain that largest amount or number of hours of labor; and the members of the other class being, as individuals, utterly helpless in a contest with their employers, naturally resort to combinations to improve their conditions, and, in fact, are forced by the conditions which surround them to organize for self-protection. Hence trade unions.

1. How did Gompers justify strikes and trade unions?
2. Why did he link trade unions to the *Mayflower*?
3. How and why did Gompers recommend careful preparation before a strike?
4. Which of Gompers' arguments would Gould have found most objectionable?
5. Was Gompers being realistic or idealistic in thinking that strikes could change Gould?
6. Compared to 1836 (see Unit 3-3), how had the situation of labor improved or not improved by the 1880s?

5-4-3. CASTIGATING JAY GOULD, *THE NEW YORK TIMES*, 1892

The New York Times was a consistent critic of Jay Gould starting with the Gould's cornering of the gold market in 1869, which coincided with its attacks on Boss Tweed. *The Times* considered these two men equally unethical, equally eager to sacrifice the public interest for their own private interests. *The Times* contributed to a larger press campaign against Gould and the ways in which he manipulated the new industrial economy for profit throughout his career. The newspapers helped fashion the negative image of Gould that prevailed from his day to ours and which historian Maury Klein tried to revise in 1986. As the following obituary demonstrates, *The Times* minced no words in death as in life.

Source: *The New York Times*, December 3, 1892.

A career in the least comparable with that of Jay Gould not only has never been run, but has never been possible before our time. It is in our time that the "operator" has been born, and Jay Gould was an operator pure and simple, although in a general way of speaking, he was as far as possible from pure and as far as possible from simple. What we mean to say is that he was nothing else but an operator, a trader in the values of the Stock Exchange. There were, of course, men of the same ambitions and pretensions in Wall Street before him, there will be such men after him. But nobody has been so prodigiously successful in the same line. No man has ever grasped the leadership of Wall Street anything like so long. Nobody has ever escaped from it, or been withdrawn from it by death, with anything like the same amount of booty to his credit. The total of his gains is currently estimated at something like seventy millions. This is one of the greatest fortunes of America, and there is no other great fortune comparable to it in the amount that has been attained by the same means.

The Astor fortune, originally acquired in adventurous mercantile enterprise, has been increased in two generations by a safe and far-sighted calculation of the probable growth of the City of New York. The Vanderbilt fortune was built by a similarly safe and far-sighted calculation of the future increase of the traffic of the country and by the sagacious taking of measures adapted to confirm and secure its proper share of this increase to the route that commanded the greatest natural advantage for this traffic. The Gould fortune has not been acquired by such means. It is simply the measure of the success that has attended to the skill of its founder in intercepting the earnings of other people and diverting them from their natural destination. ...

The common term of reproach against an "operator" is that he is a gambler, but it would be very unjust to apply this term to Gould. It is not properly applicable to a player who stacks the cards or loads the dice beforehand. The effort of Gould throughout his whole career was to eliminate the element of chance from his operations. Of course, it entered more or less, and from time to time, but in so far as it was allowed to enter at all, it was a disappointment and a grievance to him. What he aimed at, and what he often attained, was as great a certainty in the operations of the Wall Street game as is attainable in the most legitimate lines of business. Of course, it is difficult to attain this degree of certitude, and the difficulty is enhanced by the restrictions of the criminal law. These restrictions he evaded with remarkable success. Throughout his entire career he remained at large, and this fact, considering the nature of his operations, is a high tribute to his skill. ...

He seems to have relied upon the American worship of money, however got, as sufficient to secure his "position," and, at any rate, he never gave himself the trouble of making any false pretenses. Accordingly, any remarks upon him, now that he is dead, which do not sharply distinguish him from men who have acquired wealth in the pursuit of useful ends by honorable means, must have a corrupting and demoralizing effect upon the young men of the United States.

1. What were the most negative and the most positive terms used by *The Times* to describe Gould?
2. How convincing and significant was *The Times'* distinction between being an "operator" and a "gambler"?
3. How convincing and significant was *The Times'* comparison of Gould to Astor and Vanderbilt?
4. How does this obituary clarify the term 'robber baron'?

5-4-4.   REHABILITATING JAY GOULD: MAURY KLEIN, HISTORIAN, 1986

In 1986, historian Maury Klein published *The Life and Legend of Jay Gould* in order to reassess Gould's negative image. In Klein's opinion, the Gould legend was at least partly the result of Americans' need to make sense out of the confusing world of the Gilded Age and the new concentration of wealth in the hands of a few men. Americans wanted to know that the old pre-industrial emphasis on individual success through hard work and personal virtue, as extolled by Horatio Alger, was still valid. Gould became the antithesis of those values—the exception that proved the rule. *The New York Times* obituary provides evidence of this approach; Klein offers a different interpretation.

Source: Maury Klein, *The Life and Legend of Jay Gould* (Baltimore, MD: Johns Hopkins University Press, 1986), 490–497.

The Gould legend was firmly in place years before his death and has remained intact for nearly a century. Two questions posed at the beginning still demand answers. Why did the legend arise, and why has it endured?

Clearly the legend has its origins in the two sensational episodes that first brought Gould's name to the public eye, the Erie War and the Gold Corner. The press accounts of these events ... fixed Gould's reputation for decades to come. Later exploits on the Street enhanced it to the point of coloring the interpretation of everything else Gould did. Part of the reason lay in Gould's habit of secrecy and his stubborn refusal to cater to public opinion. The fact that he often took pains to defend his actions suggests that he cared deeply about his image, especially in the last decade of his life, but he would not bend a policy to improve it or concede an inch to its polishing. In the end he accepted his reputation reluctantly, even bitterly, as the price of his determination to go his own way. ...

As I have noted elsewhere, the one event that separates American history into two distinct eras is not the Civil War but the Industrial Revolution. ... Gould was not only part of this revolution but one of its prime movers. His role as an instrument of change, an author of upheaval, was too conspicuous not to attract attention. He emerged as the foremost villain of the age not merely by piling up a fortune; that was acceptable, even desirable, so long as one did it in the proper way with appropriate gestures toward convention. His rise to success followed the classic pattern of the rags-to-riches myth except in the crucial area of method. He did not display the probity and purity of conscience so prominent in the Horatio Alger heroes, but neither did the vast majority of businessmen. Elsewhere, however, Gould snubbed convention at every turn. In business he was ruthless and devious, clever and unpredictable, secretive and evasive. Above all he was imaginative, not only brilliant but thoroughly original. In an age that relished flourish, he possessed a stunning economy of motion. Few men matched the cold realism by which Gould conducted his affairs. ...

Therein lay one of the cruelest ironies about Gould. Critics condemned him for his deceit and treachery. Yet the impression lingers that many of them actually loathed Gould because he was too honest for minds used to dealing with reality under wraps. Gould knew what he wanted, went after it, and did not mouth pieties to justify his course. Nor did he ever try to disguise himself in airs of respectability. Religion interested but never absorbed him. Never a strong sectarian, he made no pretense of piety and never coated his activities with a glaze of Christian virtue. By shunning polite society, he cut himself off from the surest and safest road to cleansing a tarnished reputation. By keeping his numerous acts of charity behind the scenes, he deprived himself of the standard act of atonement expected from man of vast wealth. ...

Here then were all the ingredients for an ideal villain of the new industrial society. Gould was a man of dubious past who had amassed immense wealth and power in secretive fashion by unscrupulous means. He respected no values or conventions, held no loyalties, had no friends, honored no trust. No one could understand or identify with him. He marched to the beat of a drummer whose rhythms baffled and disturbed others for reasons they could not grasp. In an age unsettled by vast, impersonal forces he seemed to personify the evils gnawing at the bosom of society. He was the perfect foil for an age that liked to interpret its nature in moral parables. That is why editorial writers rushed to protest the influence of his example on young men before his body was scarcely cold in its bed. He was the embodiment of the darker side of the American Dream, a reflection of the forces that tainted the gospel of success. There could be no remorse at his passing; one might as well mourn the lifting of a plague. ...

By any reckoning Gould must be counted among the two or three most important figures in the development of the American industrial economy. Contrary to legend, he was not a meteor flashing across a turbulent sky before vanishing without a trace. He was not the king of speculators content to amass riches but the prime mover in two industries vital to the Industrial Revolution, transportation and communication. No man did more to make the railway map what it is—through his own work and through the influence he exerted on others responding to his moves. He was that rarest of geniuses, the man of vision who possessed the talent and the tools to realize his vision.

---

1. According to Klein, how did Gould help create his negative image?
2. According to Klein, how unique was Gould?
3. According to Klein, what were Gould's positive qualities and contributions to America's economic growth in the Gilded Age?
4. Explain Klein's statement that Gould reflected "the darker side of the American dream."
5. In what ways do Klein and *The Times* agree or disagree? Which is most convincing?

5-4-5. CARICATURING JAY GOULD: FREDERICK OPPER, CARTOONIST, 1882

During his lifetime, Jay Gould was the subject of numerous cartoons, all of which reinforced his negative image. Frederick Opper was one of the most important cartoonists of the late nineteenth century. From 1880 to 1898, he drew for *Puck,* which was the nation's first cartoon-dominated political magazine. It was so successful that the cartoon medium quickly spread to more magazines and newspapers, including *Judge*, *Life*, the *New York Daily Graphic* and William Randolph Hearst's *New York World*, where Opper worked after leaving *Puck*. The power of a cartoon to distill issues and influence opinion is evident in the image that Opper called "Jay Gould's Private Bowling Alley."

Source: Frederick Opper, "Jay Gould's Private Bowling Alley," *Puck*, March 29, 1882.

JAY GOULD'S PRIVATE BOWLING ALLEY.

1. How did Opper depict Gould's appearance and attire in order to reinforce Gould's negative image?
2. How did Opper use the bowling balls and the pins to criticize Gould's impact on Wall Street?
3. Why did Opper include the American flag and Trinity Church?
4. Why did Opper list Gould's holdings on the blackboard in the foreground?
5. How was this cartoon similar to the *New York Times* obituary in Document 5-4-3?
6. How was Opper's cartoon similar to and/or different from Nast's cartoon of Tweed in Document 5-2-2?

SELECTED RESOURCES

Allen, Oliver E. *The Tiger: The Rise and Fall of Tammany Hall.* Reading, MA: Addison-Wesley, 1993.
Callow, Alexander B., Jr. *The Tweed Ring.* New York: Oxford University Press, 1965.
Hammack, David C. *Power and Society: Greater New York at the Turn of the Century* New York: Columbia University Press, 1987.
Homberger, Eric. *Scenes from the Life of a City: Corruption and Conscience in Old New York.* New Haven, CT: Yale University Press, 1994.
Kessner, Thomas. *Capital City: New York City and the Men Behind America's Rise to Economic Dominance, 1860–1900.* New York: Simon and Schuster, 2003.
Lieberman, Richard K. *Steinway and Sons.* New Haven, CT: Yale University Press, 1995.
Nasaw, David. *Children of the City at Work and at Play.* New York: Oxford University Press, 1985.
Scobey, David. *Empire City: The Making and Meaning of the New York City Landscape.* Philadelphia, PA: Temple University Press, 2002.
Trachtenberg, Alan. *Brooklyn Bridge: Fact and Symbol.* Chicago, IL: University of Chicago Press, 1970.
www.eagle.brooklynpubliclibrary.org: consolidation, Ellis Island, immigrants
www.ellisisland.org and www.nps_gov/ellis: Ellis Island
www.museumofnyc.doetech.net/voyager.cfm: Byron Company photos
www.tenement.org: tour of Lower East Side tenement
www.thehistorybox.com; section on The World of Society in the Gilded Age
www.vny.cuny.edu; the blizzard of 1888

CHAPTER 6

1900–1920

Early-twentieth-century New York City was "a city of giants" because it was "a city of ambition." The undisputed center of the modern economy, Wall Street defined America's wealth and power. And Wall Street was epitomized by J. P. Morgan—the mastermind of finance capitalism, architect of the world's first billion-dollar trust and twice (1895 and 1907) the savior of the American economy. In his orbit revolved the nation's biggest corporations, many of which were headquartered in the metropolitan area. Perhaps the city could be forgiven for harboring the "delusions of grandeur" that a contemporary doctor diagnosed as "New Yorkitis."[1]

The self-confidence that came with prosperity fueled optimism. Consequently, the Progressive reformers believed that the problems created by industrialism could be solved through private charity and public policy. They called for trust-busting, food and drug laws, housing standards, better sanitation, labor legislation, conservation and suffrage. In Washington their champion was a New Yorker, President Theodore Roosevelt. Locally, the work was promoted by countless individuals—male and female, white and black, native born and immigrant. Across society there was a new commitment to the social good accompanied by a sense that change was not only necessary but achievable.

This chapter focuses on different aspects of change in early-twentieth-century Gotham. Starting with physical change, the first unit investigates issues surrounding the subway and the skyscraper. The second unit examines the social and cultural changes represented by Coney Island. The third unit shows how the tragic Triangle Fire ignited changes in attitudes toward labor.

The last unit highlights the spirit of Progressivism through a profile of Mary White Ovington, a social worker and a founder of the National Association for the Advancement of Colored People (NAACP). In addition, it presents W. E. B. Du Bois' appeal for African American activism along with women's struggles to promote birth control, secure the right to vote, and feed their families. All of these efforts reflected the optimism of the age and involved many different types of people. Progress seemed possible.

UNIT 6-1. CITY BUILDING: THE SUBWAY AND THE SKYSCRAPER

In the early twentieth century, the congested city's need for space and desire for speed stimulated innovation both above and below ground. The subway and the skyscraper embraced technological progress and transformed the physical city. Constructed simultaneously, they matched the city's commitment to limitless growth in a boundless future. Together, they embodied the spirit of the city of ambition and its emergence as *the* model modern city in America, if not the world.

6-1-1. PRAISING THE SUBWAY: GEORGE McCLELLAN, MAYOR, 1904

As the most ambitious, most complicated, most expensive public works project yet attempted by an American city, the subway confirmed New York's coming of age. The novelty and scale of the undertaking posed technical, financial and political challenges. It also raised fundamental questions about urban life, monopoly, the relationship of Manhattan to the boroughs as well as the partnership between private and public interests. In other words, it tested New York's social contract in the Progressive era.

Ever since London opened its underground in 1863, New Yorkers had talked about building a subway. The streets were crowded with horse-drawn carriages, streetcars, trolleys, carts and cable cars, not to mention pedestrians. The elevated railroads partly solved the problem by being overhead and moving faster than horse-drawn conveyances. However, their steam engines spewed hot coals and ashes onto the streets and, being outside, they were often hampered by bad weather. The blizzard of 1888, which paralyzed the city for three days, drove this point home and strengthened Mayor Abram Hewitt's belief that New York needed a subway.[2]

The problem was how to finance, build and maintain it. Hewitt suggested that the city pay for and own the subway, but that it be run by private business. Despite public support for a subway, it was blocked by men like Jay Gould's son who controlled the surface and elevated railroads and feared competition from a subway. Finally, in 1900 the city signed a contract with the banker August Belmont who formed the Interborough Rapid Transit Company (IRT). Although the city financed construction, Belmont operated the system and paid for equipment, promising not to charge more than five cents a ride. At first, this public–private partnership seemed to work.[3]

In order to build it quickly and to make it convenient to use, the subway was constructed as close to the surface as possible, unlike London's, which was deep underground. In some areas, the Irish, Italian and African American laborers built bridges; in others they bored through rock, but most often they dug tunnels, keeping the city streets in chaos for four years. After the tracks were laid and the holes were covered again, the stations were adorned with elegant entrance kiosks, oak ticket booths, colorful ceramic station signs, and decorative tiles.

When first leg of the system (from City Hall to 145th Street and Lenox Avenue) opened on October 27, 1904, it was the fastest electric railway in the world with the first all-steel cars plus the most extensive use of express and local tracks. Everyone considered it as significant as the Erie Canal, the Croton Reservoir and the Brooklyn Bridge. At the opening-day ceremony, George McClellan, mayor from 1904–1909, expressed the city's pride in its newest accomplishment.[4]

Source: *The New York Times*, October 28, 1904.

Without rapid transit Greater New York would be little more than a geographical expression. It is no exaggeration to say that without inter-borough communication Greater New York would never have come into being.

The present boundaries of our city included ten years ago a multitude of independent and heterogeneous communities which would have continued in all human probability to work out their own destinies independently had not modern genius and modern enterprise afforded their population the possibility of movement.

When the Brooklyn Bridge was opened, Greater New York was born. Every addition to transit facilities has stimulated her growth, which can only reach its full development when a complete system of rapid transit shall be rapid in fact as well as in name.

Every step in the direction of inter-borough communication has tended to improve conditions, not only the borough immediately affected, but benefits the city as a whole. The constant shifting of population among the boroughs, acting and reacting upon them, results in the increase of the population of all of them.

We have met here to-day for the purpose of turning over a page in the history of our city; for the purpose of marking the advent of a new epoch in her development. If this new underground railroad which we are about to open proves as popular and as successful as I confidently expect it to be, it will be only the first of many more which must ultimately result in giving us an almost perfect system of inter-borough communication.

When that day arrives borough boundaries will be remembered only for administrative purposes, and New Yorkers, forgetting from what part of the city they come and only conscious of the fact that they are the sons of the mightiest metropolis the world has ever seen, will be actuated by a common hope and united in a common destiny.

1. How did McClellan think the subway would help New York City?
2. Why did McClellan see the subway as an extension of the Brooklyn Bridge and the consolidation of New York?
3. Which of McClellan's predictions were correct and which were incorrect?

6-1-2. CRITICIZING THE SUBWAY: RAY STANNARD BAKER, JOURNALIST, 1905

The subway was a great success and real estate values rose wherever subway stations were built. In fact, the subway was so popular that the system was always over-crowded, dirty and hot. The IRT added more cars to each train, but the city cried for expansion. Reformers hoped that extending the subway into the boroughs would enable people to move out of the slums. From Belmont's perspective, however, more crowding meant more cash and he refused to build more lines himself because they would be costly; nor did he want anyone else to build them. Accordingly, in 1905 he bought out his major competitor, the Metropolitan Street Railway Company, thereby acquiring a monopoly of Manhattan's transit system—its elevateds, streetcars, and subway. Reaction was swift and condemnation was loud. The publisher William Randolph Hearst led the attack on

Belmont and his "Traction Trust" by calling for full municipal ownership and control of the subways. Likewise, the journalist Ray Stannard Baker criticized Belmont and the concept of public–private ownership.[5]

Source: Ray Stannard Baker, "The Subway Deal: How New York City Built Its New Underground Railroad," *McClure's Magazine* (March 1905), 451–469.

The Subway is not more wonderful than the skyscraper. It came to us not as a heaven-born miracle, but as the next step in the evolution of a Modern City. It was as inevitable as the course of nature; it was not due to the work of any one man or men, however large personalities may seem at the conclusion of the task. ...

The people do not realize what this Belmont monopoly has already come to be. It is not only the greatest combination of streetcar interests New York ever had, but it promises to be the most piratical. The aim of Belmont—and the European Rothschilds behind him—is *complete* monopoly. Already he controls the Subway and all the elevated roads in Manhattan, he owns the surface car lines in Long Island City, and he has just acquired the old *perpetual* franchise of the Steinway Tunnel Company, which enables him to build another tunnel to Brooklyn; and he is on the way to obtain other important rights. Through his associates, also, he is interested in the new Hudson River tunnel which recently obtained a franchise up Sixth Avenue, thereby giving him a grasp of the passage traffic of Jersey City.

And now he is trying to get hold of the financially distressed Metropolitan Railway Company, which controls the surface-car lines of Manhattan. When he gets that he can rest with smiling content, having captured the city. ...

All these transactions have their solemnly humorous side. To the simple mind it appears that the Belmont syndicate has made a very good bargain. No outsider probably knows definitely, but it is commonly reported that McDonald and Belmont made a profit of $6,000,000 to $8,000,000 on the actual building of the Subway. ... Out of all of this the city will get not one cent—though the city has no right now to begrudge Belmont his earnings *on the original enterprise*. He ventured and he won. ...

Here is the plain truth: if the history of the Subway shows anything at all, it shows that capital all the way through has not only been greedy, not only pursued a dog-in-the-manger policy, but it has been wholly unoriginal, non-progressive. Capital wants no changes; capital stands pat. Nothing could show more clearly the utter failure of private monopolies in furnishing the public—promptly—with new conveniences.

The public suggested the Subway, the public through its engineers made the plans and proved the feasibility of the enterprise, the public forced the building of the Subway through a threat of municipal construction (the worst bogy of capital), and finally furnished all the money for the work—and then deliberately gave Mr. Belmont all of the property and afterwards tied itself up for fifty years by a contract which prevents city control! Oh, the financiers might well present a cup to Mr. Belmont! Surely he is unmatched, unequaled in all this country! Talk about financial genius! Is not this its supreme manifestation?"

1. How did Baker simultaneously praise and criticize Belmont?
2. According to Baker, who really built the subway?
3. According to Baker, why was there a conflict between private interests and the public interest? How did he think that conflict should have been resolved?
4. In 1906, President Theodore Roosevelt said that journalists like Baker were merely "muckrakers" digging up the bad and ignoring the good. How well did Baker fit this description? Did Baker expect anything positive to result from his negative reporting?
5. What conclusions can be drawn from the similarities between Baker's criticism of Belmont, Bennett's criticism of Astor and the *New York Times'* criticism of Gould? (see Units 3-4 and 5-4)

6-1-3. OBSERVING THE SUBWAY: REGINALD MARSH, ARTIST, 1923

Reginald Marsh was an illustrator and painter best known for his depictions of crowds at Coney Island and the Bowery, in dance halls and on the streets. Having studied with John Sloan, an artist who documented urban realities, Marsh focused on the city's entertainers, bums, beaches and bread lines.

From 1922 to 1923, he completed a series of 111 small drawings about city life including the subway and the skyscraper. Significantly, he called the series "Subway Sunbeams" and this particular drawing was labeled "The Melting Pot."

Source: Reginald Marsh, "The Melting Pot," *New York Daily News*, June 26, 1923.

1. Explain how Marsh suggested at least four different threats posed by subway crowding.
2. Explain at least three different reasons why Marsh called this drawing "The Melting Pot."
3. Explain two reasons why Marsh called this series "Subway Sunbeams."

6-1-4. PRAISING THE SKYSCRAPER: WILLIAM GEORGE FITZGERALD, BRITISH WRITER, 1919

While, the subway was heralding progress underground, skyscrapers were proclaiming the city's pre-eminence above ground. Steel, electricity and the elevator made it possible to construct sleek, vertical towers so high that buildings seemed to scrape the sky. Ever anxious to outdo Chicago, which built the first skyscrapers, New York welcomed the Flatiron Building in 1902 with its 20 stories rising 285 feet tall at 23rd Street and Broadway. In 1913 the Woolworth Building on lower Broadway became the tallest building in the world with 60 stories at 792 feet tall. In 1930 it was displaced by the Chrysler Building on 42nd Street and Lexington Avenue at 1046 feet tall only to be topped by the Empire State Building on 34th Street and Fifth Avenue at 1250 feet tall in 1931. And that was just the beginning. Sensing the spirit of change, in 1919, the British author William George Fitzgerald captured the ways in which the skyscraper reflected the many meanings of modern New York.

Source: William George Fitzgerald, *America's Day: Studies in Light and Shade* (New York: Dodd, Mead, 1919), 68, 69, 73, 75, 80, 85.

A glance at Lower Manhattan from this height [47 stories atop the Singer building] shows the difficult building problem of New York, and how the skyscraper has solved it with characteristic daring. Business interests of enormous range are here squeezed into an area less than two square miles.... The only outlet was gained by the steady pushing of non-business dwellings to the north end—and by going up in the air. Hence the skyscraper, a cage of steel beams carried on sixty or eighty legs which are thrust down to bedrock, ninety feet or so below New York's famous Broadway. These legs are the wind-anchors of a land-lighthouse which is without any peer in any nation ... It is these tremendous buildings which make New York unique, and turn the streets into profound chasms, with dizzy troglodyte walls that blaze at night with dim and weird effects. ...

The note of New York is impermanence; it never is, but always to be blest with civic and architectural perfection. Last season's hotel, with an amusement annex that cost a fortune, is this year already under a cloud. For another is projected—one of fifteen hundred rooms and the soaring splendor of eclipse. It will cost fifteen million dollars. Before it opens, a still more attractive palace is planned and talked of—not necessarily larger—but with novelties that take the town and are flashed for thousands of miles to maintain the siren fame which has been New York's since Revolutionary times.

It is a city of noise, of course, with electric railways borne upon iron pillars over tram-laid streets paved with granite blocks. The passion for altering is everywhere seen. Great pits yawn here and there—perhaps for the leg-rests of yet another skyscraper. Or the hole may be part of a city tube. Bombs explode; there is quarrying in the building lots—erection, demolition, carting away of debris, and the dumping of new and costly materials. ...

It is for her invaders that New York displays electric signs so glaring that the native citizen cultivates blindness, hoping to save his soul alive and keep his limbs from the mercy of Broadway joy-riders. For here night shineth as the day. There is a blazing publicity for all manner of wares. Ebullient rainbows leap and race, flicker and flash, as for a Fourth of July that never ends. ... "More light" is the city's motto; the blaze of it is another form of idealism which dispels the gloom of life. ... .

The Athenian appetite for "something new" is a keen American trait, and keenest of all in New York, which is the most inquisitive and acquisitive of cities ... Twenty years ago, the social axis of New York was at Fifth Avenue and Thirty-Seventh Street. It is now in the Sixties and beyond. Even Newspaper Row is dissolving and dispersing. "Nothing stays put" is the good-humored plaint of this restless city."

1. According to Fitzgerald, how did skyscrapers reflect the spirit of New York City?
2. Why did Fitzgerald focus on so many different aspects of light?
3. According to Fitzgerald, what were the positive and negative implications of New York's bigness and restlessness?

6-1-5. CRITICIZING THE SKYSCRAPER: CLEMENT WOOD, POET, 1916

The Woolworth Building was called the "Cathedral of Commerce" because of its architecture and its owner. Much like A. T. Stewart (see Unit 5-3), F. W. Woolworth started with a small store in 1879 and revolutionized retailing. Woolworth's contribution was selling a wide variety of goods for five and ten cents. "He won a fortune," wrote the *New York Sun*, "not in showing how little could be sold for much, but how much could be sold for little." Indeed, by the time he died in 1919, his chain of stores numbered over 1,000 and was worth over $65 million.[6]

Woolworth paid $13.5 million in cash for architect Cass Gilbert to design a grand office building on Broadway across from City Hall Park between Park Place and Barclay Street, a block north of the Astor House (see Unit 3-4). By camouflaging its steel frame with stone and terracotta, it combined new technology with old Gothic designs, as had the Brooklyn Bridge (see Unit 5-1). Completed in 1913, just as the Astor House was coming down, the Woolworth Building's entrance was arched like a church, but surrounded with sculptures of workers. Also like a church, the lobby was constructed as a cross lavishly embellished with marble, mosaics, gilding and wood carvings. Among the sculptures in the lobby were "Commerce," "Labor," and Woolworth himself holding a bag of nickels and dimes. The building was an architectural masterpiece, a homage to the American dream.

However, as skyscrapers multiplied, they threatened to smother the city and block out the sun. The issue was dramatized in 1915 by the construction of the 36-story Equitable Building consuming an entire block on lower Broadway between Cedar and Pine streets. It cast a shadow over the surrounding seven and a half acres, plunging even 20-story buildings into darkness. A year later, the city established standards for skyscraper construction that would not only limit their height, but also require the upper stories to be set back allowing light to reach the street. The 1916 zoning law became a model for the nation and a hallmark of urban planning.[7]

As the following poem suggests, the skyscraper could also be criticized as an emblem of the economic inequality and exploitation that accompanied prosperity in the Gilded Age and Progressive era. Clement Wood was an early-twentieth-century writer of novels, biographies, literary guides and social analysis. Some of his articles and poems were published in *The Crisis,* from which he won an award in 1927. Although he was white, Wood's 1922 novel, *Nigger,* about the black struggle for freedom, was widely acclaimed. According to the historian David Levering Lewis, it may even have "helped launch" the Harlem Renaissance[8] (see Unit 7-1). Wood's poem about the Woolworth Building was a searing criticism of progress.

Source: Clement Wood, "Woolworth Cathedral," *The Masses* (April, 1916), 20.

Lost in a climbing forest of sky-scrapers
Trinity sulks, a deserted shrine;
Her few worshippers walk tremblingly,
Sniffing the musty air from her buried dead,
Senselessly mumbling over and over
The ritual of a dead god.

Towering aloft into the conquered sky
The Woolworth Temple soars above its neighbors—
A triumphant monument of the millions of worshippers
Of the true God of today …
Raised by blood-soaked and vice-stained pennies
Squeezed out of weak and pitiful girls,
Robbed of life and beauty,
That it might first kiss the morning sunshine;
Raised by trickling nickels and dimes
Levied on needy families,
That it might be a glory and a dream
In the soft gray shine of dusk,
And a pillar of white splendor at night,
Outsparkling the other lights of the city,
And the poor imitations passing slowly above it,
Night after night.

O Shrine of the God of Gold,
O Temple to the true God of Today.
Who will reign until we have made a new god, Man,
To rule in earth and heaven,
I pause for a moment,
To lay a worshipper's tribute before you!

1. According to Wood, how did Woolworth make his millions?
2. Why did Wood contrast Trinity Church with the Woolworth Building? According to Wood, what god did Americans worship?
3. Explain why Wood emphasized life and death, light and dark, day and night.

4. How were the perspectives of Wood and Baker similar or different?
5. Subways and skyscrapers were intrinsically linked in terms of both time and space. In fact, skyscrapers tended to rise near subway stops. Based on the above material, explain how both the subway and the skyscraper reflected the hopes and fears of the "city of ambition."

UNIT 6-2. CHANGE AND CHALLENGE: CONEY ISLAND

In addition to physical change, Progressive-era New York City experienced social and cultural change. In Times Square, Greenwich Village and Coney Island, old concepts of social behavior, gender roles and leisure were reassessed, and sometimes rejected. Formalism was replaced by innovation, exclusion by inclusion, restraint by freedom.

A case in point was Times Square. Originally called Longacre Square, its name was changed in 1904 when the *New York Times* bought land from August Belmont at 42nd Street and Broadway to build a tall, thin skyscraper right above the new subway station. By illuminating its tower and inviting New Yorkers to take the subway to a communal New Year's Eve party, the *Times* celebrated modernity and the democratization of public life. Previously an exclusive residential neighborhood built by the Astors in the mid-nineteenth century, by 1900 the area already had both legitimate theaters and illegitimate brothels. Electricity, the subway and the skyscraper made Times Square the city's center for drama, vaudeville, music, dance halls, cabarets and nightclubs.[9]

The spirit of challenging convention also flourished in Greenwich Village where mainly white, middle-class poets, dancers, playwrights, artists, musicians, novelists and reformers shared common cause. The cultural ferment they created was significant enough to earn Greenwich Village the label of Bohemia, a term associated with gypsies and artists—both considered outside of mainstream society. Accordingly, the early-twentieth-century rejection of Victorian culture was called the Bohemian Rebellion.[10]

Coney Island joined Times Square and Greenwich Village in expanding the definition of urban life and the quest for individual freedom. In the late nineteenth century, Coney Island was a resort for the well-to-do traveling to the far reaches of Brooklyn by costly steamboat or railway and staying in fancy hotels. Another section, however, harbored saloons, gambling and prostitution, all of which earned Coney Island the epithet "Sodom by the Sea." But Coney Island became more than its seamy side. Developers quickly saw its commercial potential as an entertainment center. They transformed the industrial technology of electricity, trains, elevators, and tall buildings into thrilling rides and dazzling, illuminated structures. When the trolley, elevated train, railroad and subway made travel faster and cheaper, Coney Island became accessible to the middle and working classes seeking a new form of urban fun and an alternative to Victorian constraints.[11]

6-2-1. SEEING CONEY ISLAND: GUIDEBOOK, 1904

Coney Island combined thrilling entertainment with fantastic spectacle for the urban masses. It was the nation's first big mechanized amusement park. Because it offered an exciting, inexpensive escape from the dirty, crowded city and the drudgery of work, going there was an event worth sharing with friends and family. Consequently, a market emerged for pictures and postcards of the various hotels, rides, towers, restaurants, beaches and fanciful buildings. Spreading the word around America, these images publicized the rise of popular entertainment tailored to the urban industrial age. A 1904 guidebook promoted the spirit of Coney Island.

Source: "Seeing Coney Island: An Official Guide." Original repository, Brooklyn Historical Society.

1. How did this image suggest the variety of amusements at Coney Island?
2. How did this image make Coney Island seem exciting and inviting?
3. How did this image make Coney Island seem safe and respectable?
4. How did the four different depictions of women in this image reflect their complex (and changing) social roles?

6-2-2. CELEBRATING CONEY ISLAND: LINDSAY DENISON, JOURNALIST, 1905

The wonder and novelty of Coney Island was described in a 1905 magazine article.

Source: Lindsay Denison, "The Biggest Playground in the World," *Munsey's Magazine* 33 (August, 1905), 557–566.

Coney Island is a unique illustration of the fact that men and women are but children of a larger growth. It is the vast summer playhouse of a great city—a playground in which boys and girls of all ages and all classes may find such amusement as they choose. ...

Now, where the waste was and where the catchpenny hovels were, there rise to the sky a thousand glittering towers and minarets, graceful and stately and imposing. The morning sun looks down upon them as it might upon the magically realized dream of a poet or a painter. At night, the radiance of the millions of electric lights, which glow at every point and line and curve of the great play city's outlines, lights up the sky and welcomes the home-coming mariner thirty miles from shore. To this playhouse, every day of the summer, come from ten thousand to three hundred thousand merry makers from the American metropolis. ...

It is essentially a place of merriment. There is no reason for going to Coney Island except to have fun. Over its railway termini might well be written, "Leave Care Behind All Ye Who Enter Here." ... The fun-loving spirit cannot but get into the very atmosphere. There are hundreds who come only with their return carfare in their pockets, merely for the joy of mixing with the crowds on the public streets and catching the live sense of humanity and of good humor that is everywhere. ...

There is a constant braying of bands on the main thoroughfare and its branches. The frankfurter kitchen, the miniature barbeque for the manufacture of beef sandwiches, the mechanized taffy-pullers, the swishing popcorn roasters, countless exhibitions of marksmanship with rifle and hand-thrown ball at a hundred booths—these entertainments and countless others are free for those who want them. For him who has ten cents of good and lawful money and a willingness to spend it, the enclosures are open with further opportunities to laugh. Here one may watch those who ride on camels or miniature trains, who "shoot the chutes" or "slide the slides"—exploits that sometimes prove more amusing to the spectator than to the performer. ...

The appetite of the American people for rapid motion has produced innumerable gravity railways and chutes and whirling air-ship swings. ... All the enclosures, too, have dancing pavilions, where public dancing is free. ...

The playhouse will become the permanent temple of fun for the people.

Already, in other populous centers from the Atlantic to the Pacific, other amusement cities are building. It has been established as a fact, and as a safe basis for investment, that the American people will pay freely and eagerly for fun that is clean and honest.

1. According to Denison, how did Coney Island promote freedom, fun and fantasy?
2. According to Denison, how did light reflect the spirit of Coney Island?
3. According to Denison, how were class barriers crossed at Coney Island?
4. According to Denison, how did Coney Island promote key American values?

6-2-3. CONDEMNING CONEY ISLAND: MAXIM GORKY, RUSSIAN WRITER, 1907

Not everyone approved of Coney Island. In 1907, the Russian writer Maxim Gorky criticized Coney Island from a Marxist perspective. To him, the very lights that heralded modernity and made Coney Island possible were just a garish symbol of capitalism run amok, another tool for controlling and oppressing the masses.

Source: Maxim Gorky, "Boredom," *The Independent* (August 8, 1907), 309–317.

With the advent of night a fantastic city all of fire suddenly rises from the ocean into the sky. ... Fabulous and beyond conceiving, ineffably beautiful, is this fiery scintillation. ... But the sun of day brings man nearer to the truth of life. Then the fiery magic castles are tall white buildings.

The blue mist of the ocean vapors mingles with the drab smoke of the metropolis across the harbor. Its flimsy white structures are enveloped in a transparent sheet, in which they quiver like a mirage. They seem to beckon alluringly, and offer quiet and beauty. ...

The city hums with its constant, insatiate, hungry roar. ... And the people go forth to the shore of the sea, where the beautiful white buildings stand and promise respite and tranquility. ...

First a long ride by trolley through Brooklyn and Long Island amid the dust and noise of the streets. Then the gaze is met by the sight of dazzling, magnificent Coney Island. From the very first moment of arrival at this city of fire, the eye is blinded. It is assailed by thousands of cold, white sparks, and for a long time can distinguish nothing in the scintillating dust round about. Everything whirls and dazzles, and blends into a tempestuous ferment of fiery foam. The visitor is stunned; his consciousness is withered by the intense gleam; his thoughts are routed from his mind; he becomes a particle in the crowd. People wander about in the flashing, blinding fire, intoxicated and devoid of will. A dull-white mist penetrates their brains, greedy expectation envelopes their souls. Dazed by the brilliancy the throngs wind about like dark bands in the surging sea of light, pressed upon all sides by the black bournes of night. ...

The soul is seized with a desire for a living, beautiful fire, a sublime fire, which should free the people from the slavery of a varied boredom. For this boredom deafens their ears and blinds their eyes. The soul would burn away all this allurement, all this mad frenzy, this dead magnificence and spiritual penury. It would have a merry dancing and shouting and singing; it would see a passionate play of the motley tongues of fire; it would have joyousness and life. ...

But it is necessary to make money, and in the commodious corners of the bright city, as everywhere in the world, depravity laughs disdainfully at hypocrisy and falsehood. Of course, the depravity is hidden, and, of course, it's a wearying, tiresome depravity, but it also is "for the people." It is organized as a paying business, as a means to extract their earnings from the pockets of the people. Fed by the passion for gold, it appears in a form vile and despicable indeed in this marsh of glittering boredom.

The people feed on it.

The people are always constrained. As yet they have never acted as free men. So they permit the enslavement of their bodies and their souls; for this alone are they to blame.

---

1. According to Gorky, why were city dwellers attracted to Coney Island?
2. Why did Gorky equate Coney Island's lights with fire and consider them blinding rather than illuminating?
3. Why did Gorky see Coney Island as a source of boredom rather than excitement?
4. Why did Gorky see Coney Island as an agent of oppression rather than freedom?

6-2-4. INTERPRETING CONEY ISLAND: JOHN F. KASSON, HISTORIAN, 1978

Unlike Maxim Gorky, the historian John F. Kasson saw Coney Island as a place of social change and individual liberation. After explaining the role of the postcard as a new kind of brief, informal communication well suited to a new era of leisure for the masses, Kasson suggested that having fun at Coney Island was not as simple as it seemed.

Source: John F. Kasson, *Amusing the Millions: Coney Island at the Turn of the Century* (New York: Hill and Wang, 1978), 41–42.

As such postcards suggest, an essential element of Coney Island's appeal for virtually all its visitors was the contrast it offered to conventional society, everyday routine, and dominant cultural authorities. Though traces of class and ethnic backgrounds still clung to Coney Island's amusement seekers, in arriving at the resort they crossed a critical threshold, entering a world apart from ordinary life, prevailing social structures and positions. Designers of both Central Park and the Columbian Exposition had sought to create environments that would ultimately reinforce existing social structures and discipline public life. Coney Island, by contrast, provided an area in which visitors were temporarily freed from normative demands. As they disembarked from ferryboats with fanciful names like Pegasus, or walked towards the amusement parks along Surf Avenue, they felt themselves passing into a special realm of exciting possibility, a distinctive milieu that encouraged types of behavior and social interaction that in other contexts would have been regarded askance. Commentators often observed, "Coney Island has a code of conduct which is all her own." The amusement center suspended conventional situational proprieties. It encouraged visitors to shed momentarily their accustomed roles and status. Coney offered a relatively "loose," unregulated social situation which contrasted markedly with the high degree of social attentiveness and decorum demanded in most other public activities. It broke down the sense of rigidity that dominated so much of the life of American cities at the turn of the century and lessened personal restraints. The kind of civil inattention prevalent in other public places was not nearly so strictly observed here. Coney's sense of conviviality was contagious. Visitors displayed open interest in one another's activities and fed upon their mutual hilarity. Strangers frequently fell into conversation. In what critics charged was an impersonal society, Coney Island provided a welcome institution for public fellowship.

The relaxation of conventional proprieties made Coney Island especially popular with young men and women. The middle-class ideal as described in etiquette books of the period placed severe restraints on the circumstances under which a man might presume even to tip his hat to a woman in public; and certainly such books would never approve a gentleman intruding himself upon a lady with whom he was unacquainted. The social codes of the working class were less formal, but many families observed a strict etiquette of courting, monitoring the activities of their daughters especially and insisting upon the presence of a chaperon, if need be a child, when male callers came to the home. In such circumstances, as one New Yorker from an immigrant working class family later recalled, for the young, ironically, "privacy could be had only in public." Sidewalks, public parks, dance halls, and amusement parks offered opportunities to meet and enjoy the company of the opposite sex away from familial scrutiny. At Coney Island in particular, unattached young men and women easily struck up acquaintanceships for the day or the evening. According to Coney Island folklore, some couples even married on the spot. The freedom of anonymity together with the holiday atmosphere of resort encouraged intimacy and an easing of inhibitions and permitted couples to display their affections in public."

---

1. According to Kasson, how did Coney Island differ from Central Park? (see Unit 4-1)
2. According to Kasson, in how many ways was Coney Island "a special realm of exciting possibility"?
3. According to Kasson, why did early-twentieth-century urbanites embrace "public fellowship"?
4. According to Kasson, how did Coney Island change gender relations? How does the pamphlet cover above reflect or reject his thesis?
5. Use the material in this unit to explain in what positive and negative ways Coney Island promoted the democratization and commercialization of leisure.

UNIT 6-3. ECONOMICS AND THE PUBLIC INTEREST: THE TRIANGLE FIRE

The Triangle Fire was one of the most tragic events of New York City's history. It occurred just before the 5 pm dismissal time on Saturday, March 25, 1911 in the factory of the Triangle Shirtwaist Company located at Waverly Place and Greene Street, a block from Washington Square Park. No one knows how the fire started, but it spread quickly among all the cloth, wooden tables and machine oil. In a half-hour it completely engulfed the factory's eighth, ninth and tenth floors where 700 people toiled, mainly young Italian and Jewish girls. With fire hoses and ladders unable to reach so high and the fire escapes melting from the heat, 146 young people died. They were overcome where they worked, or piled up behind locked exit doors, or splayed on the sidewalk after jumping from the windows. The burnt, mangled bodies shocked the city, the state and the nation.

The fire was the second act of a drama that began in 1909 when female garment workers mounted a daring strike for better working conditions. Not only were unions illegal at the time, but women were excluded from the labor organizations that did exist. As a result, they suffered from the worst working conditions, and the least job security, the longest hours and the lowest pay. For three months the workers picketed in defiance of hunger, the winter cold, arrests and beatings by the police and hired goons. Their courage earned them support from middle-class women and sympathy from the community at large.

After the fire, factory conditions were investigated throughout New York State and, within a few years, the state legislature passed factory reform laws that became a model for the nation. Change had emerged from the collective efforts of middle- and working-class women, the powerless and the powerful, Protestants, Jews and Catholics. Tragedy taught that people could make a difference and government could play a positive role in ameliorating the negative aspects of industrialism. Progressivism worked.[12]

6-3-1. WORKING: MIRIAM FINN SCOTT, WORKING GIRL, 1910

The Triangle strike and fire were the direct result of horrible working conditions in the garment industry, which was the major sector for female employment in late-nineteenth- and early-twentieth-century cities. Knowledge of these conditions became widespread when the Women's Trade Union League (WTUL) convened meetings at which workers told their tales. The league was a unique organization of upper-class and working-class women jointly dedicated to promoting unions in order to improve working conditions. The well-to-do raised money, walked the picket lines, got arrested and used political pressure to secure change. At great risk to their personal safety and livelihood, the working-class women organized in the factories, spoke out and struck.[13]

The dignity and resolve of the workers was evident in the following account of working conditions given by a 15-year-old girl who was arrested for striking, went to jail and promptly returned to the picket line. The clarity and poignancy of her words explain why she became a regular speaker at WTUL meetings and on the nation's labor circuit.

Source: Miriam Finn Scott, "The Spirit of the Girl Strikers," *The Outlook* 94 (February 19, 1910), 392–394.

Why do we strike? I will tell you where we work, how we work; from that perhaps you will understand. My shop is a long, narrow loft on the fifth floor of the building, with the ceiling almost on our heads. In it one hundred electric-power machines are so closely packed together that, unless I am always on the lookout, my clothes or hair or hand is likely to catch in one of the whizzing machines. In the shop it is always night. The windows are only on the narrow ends of the room, so even the few girls who sit near them sew by gaslight most of the time, for the panes are so dirty the weak daylight hardly goes through them. The shop is swept only once a week; the air is so close that sometimes you can hardly breathe. In this place I work from eight to six o'clock six days a week in the ordinary season; and in the busy season, when we are compelled to work nights and Sundays, I put in what equals eight work-days in the week. Thirty minutes is allowed for lunch, which I must eat in the dressing room four flights above the shop, on the ninth floor. These stairs I must always climb; the elevator, the boss says, is not for the shopgirls.

I began as a shirt-waist maker in this shop five years ago. For the first three weeks I got nothing, though I had already worked on a machine in Russia. Then the boss paid me three dollars a week. Now, after five years' experience, and I am considered a good worker, I am paid nine. But I never get the nine dollars. There are always 'charges' against me. If I laugh, or cry, or speak to a girl during working hours, I am fined ten cents for each 'crime.' Five cents is taken from my pay every week to pay for benzine, which is used to clean waists that have been soiled in the making; and even if I have not soiled a waist in a year, I must pay the five cents just the same. If I lose a little piece of lining, that possibly is worth two cents, I am charged ten cents for the goods and five cents for losing it. If I am one minute late, I am fined one cent, though I get only fifteen cents an hour; and if I am five minutes late, I lose half a day's pay. Each of these things seem small, I know, but when you only earn ninety dimes a week, and are fined for this and that, why, a lot of them are missing when pay day comes, and you know what it means when your money is the only regular money that comes in a family of eight. …

Now and then in the past there have been attempts made by the workers to fight the conditions, but the individual uprisings had no effect. The spirit of discontent among the workers grew, and continued to grow deeper and wider; it set the girls thinking, and finally they realized that the only possible remedy for these conditions was for all of them to stand together and make common demands—to organize a strong union and gain recognition for it.

---

1. What were the most negative, most shocking conditions of Scott's workplace?
2. What were the most negative, most unfair aspects of Scott's payment?
3. What was the nature of the relationship between worker and employer in the sweatshop?
4. Did this account justify striking?
5. How did the situation of labor in the early twentieth century compare to that of labor in the early and late nineteenth century? (see Units 3-3 and 5-4)

6-3-2. DYING: *THE NEW YORK TIMES*, 1911

The horror of the fire was in the details, which dominated all the newspapers for days. The more you knew about the fire, the worse it seemed. Even the coroner broke down in tears over the endless stream of burnt and mangled young bodies that arrived at the morgue.

Source: *The New York Times*, March 26, 1911.

On the ninth story, which like the eighth was filled with sewing machines and was used for cutting and sewing shirtwaists, the girls fared worse than those on the floor below. They crowded about the elevator shaft, but no cars responded to their frantic ringing of the bell. Time after time they saw the cars approach, only to be filled at the eighth floor and go down again.

Girls who rushed to the staircase were met with flames, which bore them down before they could retreat. Those who reached the windows and waited there for firemen saw the ladders swing in against the building two stories below them.

The one little iron fire escape, leading from a rear window was pitiably inadequate and it was from this floor that most of those came who fell like paper dolls, end over end, to the pavement. ...

A thirteen-year-old girl hung for three minutes by her finger tips to the sill of a tenth floor window. A tongue of flame licked at her fingers, and she dropped to death.

A girl threw her pocketbook, then her hat, then her furs from a tenth floor window. A moment later her body came whirling after them to death.

At a ninth-floor window a man and a woman appeared. The man embraced the woman and kissed her. Then he hurled her to the street and jumped. Both were killed. Five girls smashed a pane of glass, dropped in a struggling tangle, and were crushed into a shapeless mass.

A girl on the eighth floor leaped for a fireman's ladder, which reached only to the sixth floor. She missed, struck the edge of a life net, and was picked up with her back broken.

---

1. What aspects of this account would have most upset the public?
2. What specific reforms should this account have inspired?

6-3-3. FALLING: BOARDMAN ROBINSON, ARTIST, 1911

Boardman Robinson participated in the Bohemian rebellion and drew cartoons for the radical journal, *The Masses*.

Source: Boardman Robinson, "In Compliance with Law?" *New York Daily Tribune*, March 28, 1911.

IN COMPLIANCE WITH LAW?
The fire-escape that ends in midair must be abolished.

1. How did Robinson dramatize both the cause and the result of the fire?
2. How did Robinson reinforce 6-3-1 and 6-3-2 above?
3. How did Robinson's drawing and caption reflect the spirit of Progressivism and muckraking?

6-3-4. MOURNING: ROSE SCHNEIDERMAN, LABOR ORGANIZER, 1911

After the fire, the city was in mourning. Thousands gathered in front of the factory building or went to view the bodies—some to identify lost loved ones, others to show solidarity with the bereaved. Protest meetings called for better fire safety laws and factory regulations, for aid to the victims' families, for the legalization of unions, and even for social revolution. On April 5, 120,000 marchers wearing black armbands, accompanied by 300,000 spectators, commemorated the fire by parading in the rain from the Lower East Side to the factory near Washington Square and up Fifth Avenue to 34th street. It was the largest workers' demonstration that the city had yet seen.

The most important protest meeting was held two days earlier, on April 3, at the Metropolitan Opera House, which was rented for the occasion by J. P. Morgan's daughter. While the rich entered through a separate door and sat in reserved boxes or tiers, the working classes were admitted free of charge to the orchestra and the galleries. The overflow crowd supported resolutions to improve factory conditions through legislation. The highlight of the meeting was a famous speech by strike leader, union organizer and WTUL member, Rose Schneiderman.

Source: *The New York Times*, March 3, 1911.

I would be a traitor to these poor burned bodies if I came here to talk good fellowship. We have tried you good people of the public and we have found you wanting. The old Inquisition had its rack and its thumbscrews and its instruments of torture with iron teeth. We know what these things are to-day; the iron teeth are our necessities, the thumbscrews the high-powered and swift machinery close to which we must work, and the rack is here in the firetrap structures that will destroy us the minute they catch on fire.

This is not the first time girls have been burned alive in the city. Every week I must learn of the untimely death of one of my sister workers. Every year thousands of us are maimed. The life of men and women is so cheap and property is so sacred. There are so many of us for one job it matters little if 143 of us are burned to death.

We have tried you citizens; we are trying you now, and you have a couple of dollars for the sorrowing mothers and brothers and sisters by way of a charity gift. But every time the workers come out in the only way they know how to protest against conditions which are unbearable the strong hand of the law is allowed to press down heavily upon us.

Public officials have only words of warning to us—warning that we must be intensely peaceable, and they have the workhouse just back of all their warnings. The strong hand of the law beats us back when we rise into the conditions that make life unbearable.

I can't talk of fellowship to you who are gathered here. Too much blood has been spilled. I know from my experience it is up to the working people to save themselves. The only was they can save themselves is by a strong working-class movement.

---

1. How convincing was Schneiderman's comparison of contemporary working conditions to the Inquisition?
2. In Schneiderman's opinion, what was the problem with "good fellowship"?
3. Why did Schneiderman conclude that the working classes must save themselves?
4. How did Schneiderman challenge conventional assumptions about class and gender?

6-3-5. EVALUATING: FRANCES PERKINS, PUBLIC SERVANT, 1946

Schneiderman's skepticism seemed validated in late December 1911 when the Triangle factory owners were acquitted of responsibility for the fire and went right back into business. Three years later, their insurance company finally granted $75 compensation for each victim, a paltry sum for the lives lost. Meanwhile, the New York State legislature held hearings and ultimately passed 54 truly progressive laws. Led by state senator Robert Wagner, Sr. and state assemblyman Al Smith, who were supported by reform groups, labor organizations and Tammany Hall, New York State established factory standards for fire safety, sanitation, lighting and crowding as well as regulations for child labor and female labor.

One of the leaders in these efforts was Frances Perkins (1880–1965), a Mount Holyoke graduate and social worker who was active in the Consumers' League, an organization that boycotted retailers and lobbied the New York State legislature to improve women's working conditions. She witnessed the fire, served on the State commission investigating the fire, and held important positions under governors Al Smith and Franklin Delano Roosevelt. When President Roosevelt appointed Perkins as Secretary of Labor in 1933, she became the first woman cabinet officer in U. S. history. Perkins believed that the labor legislation resulting from the Triangle Fire marked a "turning point" in the nation's history and set the stage for the New Deal.

Source: Frances Perkins, *The Roosevelt I Knew* (New York: Viking, 1946), 22–24.

I was an investigator for the Factory Investigation Commission and we used to make it our business to take Al Smith, the East Side boy who later became New York's Governor and a presidential candidate, to see the women, thousands of them, coming off the ten-hour night-shift on the rope works in Auburn. We made sure that Robert Wagner personally crawled through the tiny hole in the wall that gave egress to a steep iron ladder covered with ice and ending twelve feet from the ground, which was euphemistically labeled "Fire Escape" in many factories. We saw to it that the austere legislative members of the Commission got up at dawn and drove with us for an unannounced visit to a Cattaraugus County cannery and that they saw with their own eyes the little children, not adolescents, but five-, six- and seven-year olds, snipping beans and shelling peas. We made sure that they saw the machinery that would scalp a girl or cut off a man's arm. Hours so long that both men and women were depleted and exhausted became realities for them through seeing for themselves the dirty little factories. These men realized something could be done about it from discussions with New York State employers who had succeeded in remedying adverse working conditions and standards of pay. ...

The extent to which this legislation in New York marked a change in American political attitudes and policies toward social responsibility can scarcely be overrated. It was, I am convinced, a turning point; it was not only successful in effecting practical remedies but, surprisingly, it proved to be successful also in vote getting.

New York was a great industrial state. It had within its borders one huge city, the largest in the United States, and a number of other large cities. This differentiated the influence of this program of labor legislation in New York from that, for example, in the State of Wisconsin. Wisconsin was a small, homogeneous community, more agricultural than industrial, with a few large industries and no large cities. The experimental development of legislation to remedy social adversity was of great value and was quoted in support of the New York legislation, even though in Wisconsin it was of lesser scope. But New York! If it could be done there, it could be done anywhere. The fact that the Democratic party became dominant in New York for many years largely on the basis of this program of legislation (combined with competent, sympathetic administration), riveted in American life the conception that it was the duty and opportunity of people elected to office to develop programs for the prevention of poverty and for improving the conditions of life and work of all people. ... Thousands of people became Democrats or voted that ticket when the Democrats espoused these ideas.

1. How did Perkins educate the legislators and why was it necessary to do so?
2. How did Perkins justify passing laws based on "social responsibility"?
3. Why did Perkins consider New York State's laws more important than Wisconsin's?
4. Explain which of her ideas and tactics suggest that Perkins was an idealist and/or a realist.
5. Overall, what were the messages of the Triangle Fire about working conditions, labor unions, female workers and labor legislation? Were any lessons learned?

UNIT 6-4. BREAKING BARRIERS:
MARY WHITE OVINGTON, REFORMER

As a white Anglo-Saxon middle-class Protestant woman with a social conscience, Mary White Ovington (1865–1951) was a prime example of urban progressivism. The daughter of a wealthy merchant, she grew up in exclusive Brooklyn Heights and attended prestigious private schools—graduating from the all-girls Packer Collegiate Institute and studying for two years at the Harvard Annex, later known as Radcliffe College. Upon returning to New York, she became active in the settlement house movement, through which middle class, college graduates tried to help working class people by providing kindergartens, health clinics, language classes and job skills training. For seven years, Ovington served the white, ethnic, working-class community of Greenpoint, Brooklyn by living and working in a settlement house in the Astral Apartments, built by Charles Pratt for his oil refinery workers. However, deciding to embrace the African American cause made her unique among white female progressives.[14]

A 1901 lecture by the African American education Booker T. Washington about the economic plight of urban blacks motivated Ovington to begin investigating the world around her that she had never really seen. For seven years, she collected data under the auspices of Greenwich House, the settlement run by her friend Mary Simkhovitch. Her findings appeared in several journal articles and *Half A Man: The Status of the Negro in New York* (1911), a study of the conditions of blacks in New York City. She also wrote articles about the condition of blacks, North and South, for Oswald Garrison Villard's *New York Evening Post*. By marshaling concrete evidence for the purposes of seeking change, Ovington pursued the Progressive's faith that reason and reform were partners. She optimistically believed that once people understood the problem, they would naturally want to solve it.[15]

At the same time, Ovington decided to do something more tangible. Having learned from her research about the lack of decent housing for blacks, she asked John E. Milholland (journalist, businessman, and founder of the Constitution League) to help her establish model tenements for blacks. He secured the financial support of wealthy steel magnate Henry Phipps, who had already built similar projects for immigrants. By 1907, the first four buildings of the Phipps houses were ready for occupancy, followed by four more in 1911. They were located in the heart of San Juan Hill, a crowded black neighborhood between 60th and 64th Streets from Tenth to Eleventh Avenues. In 1905, it had been the site of a riot during which whites attacked blacks with police support.

Getting the housing built was a major accomplishment, but Ovington went further. When the Tuskegee (named in honor of Booker T. Washington) was opened, she moved in herself and stayed for eight months, the only white person in residence. While collecting more data, she befriended her neighbors, especially the children to whom she read books and for whom she later wrote several black-oriented stories, an exceptional enterprise in those days. Together with an African American female doctor, she founded the Lincoln settlement house for blacks in Brooklyn, served as fund-raiser and chaired its board for 20 years. But she knew that racial problems went beyond Manhattan and Brooklyn.[16]

The national implications of segregation and lynching were highlighted by a horrific riot in Lincoln's hometown of Springfield, Illinois during August 1908. In response, William English Walling, a wealthy white socialist, wrote an article calling for action to renew the nation's commitment to equality. Ovington immediately contacted him and suggested strategizing to address the problem. She, Walling and Dr. Henry Moskowitz, a Jewish social worker, soon met in New York City and asked Villard to issue a call for a larger meeting to be held on the centennial of Lincoln's birth, February 12, 1909. At a second meeting in the following year, with many prominent black and white Progressives in attendance, the National Association for the Advancement of Colored People (NAACP) was created. It was a major turning point in American history.[17]

Ovington's initiatives did not emerge from a vacuum. When Walling called for renewing "the spirit of the abolitionist," he struck a sensitive nerve. Ovington, as well as several other whites in the NAACP, came from an abolitionist family. She learned about the Underground Railroad and anti-abolitionist riots from her grandmother, a friend of William Lloyd Garrison, the radical Boston abolitionist whom Ovington greatly admired. Her father was also an abolitionist. He even left Henry Ward Beecher's Plymouth Congregational Church because he considered that famous abolitionist preacher not abolitionist enough. The family then joined a Unitarian church with a long, solid abolitionist tradition. In this context, it was not surprising that Ovington hosted an inter-racial dinner of reformers in 1908. Nonetheless, she was quite surprised by the vulgar hate mail attacking her as a promoter of inter-racial sex. In terms reminiscent of the 1834 anti-abolitionist riot, Ovington was branded as an amalgamationist (see Unit 3-1).[18]

A second factor in the founding of the NAACP was the city itself. New York was already the national center for the black press and black self-help organizations. Under T. Thomas Fortune's tutelage, the *New York Age* had become the nation's most important black newspaper. There were negro YMCA's, negro trade schools, an organization to protect Southern black women migrating to New York, and an organization to improve employment opportunities for blacks (to which Ovington belonged). All of this activity reflected the existence of activist middle-class blacks affiliated with activist middle-class whites who were concerned about racial equality. To be sure, not all white Progressives fit this description, but, many who did were New Yorkers (including Ray Stannard Baker, John Milholland and suffragist Harriet Stanton Blatch).

A third factor behind the formation of the NAACP was the epic conflict between Booker T. Washington and the African American scholar W. E. B. Du Bois. The Committee for Improving the Industrial Condition of the Negro in New York (CIICN) embraced Washington's emphasis on work and was led by Dr. William Lewis Bulkley, New York's first black principal of a white school. CIICN members included a wide range of prominent progressives, some of whom also supported the NAACP, including Ovington. Yet, the tensions were real. When Du Bois formed the Niagara Movement to promote full civil and political liberties, Washington tried to sabotage it. So too with the NAACP. In the end, however, a balance was struck. Following Du Bois' agenda, the NAACP focused its efforts on civil rights issues and legal cases. The CIICN combined with other groups in 1911 to form the Urban League, which followed Washington's agenda by focusing on expanding economic opportunity for blacks in Northern cities. Despite being a solid supporter of Du Bois, Ovington remained active in the Urban League because she believed that the division of labor was practical and advanced the overall struggle against racial discrimination.[19]

Ovington served the NAACP in various capacities until 1947. She was treasurer for 15 years, a member of the board of directors for 37 years and its chairperson for 13 years. She played a critical role in getting her friend Du Bois appointed director of research and editor of the NAACP's journal *The Crisis*. Over the decades she repeatedly came to his defense, even when he offended other members of the organization. As she explained, "To me, the rest of us on the Board are able journeymen doing one day's work to be forgotten tomorrow. But Du Bois is the master builder, whose work will speak to men as long as there is an oppressed race on the earth."[20]

Concerns for racial justice naturally led Ovington to other reform movements, especially the women's movement. Like the female abolitionists, she linked rights for blacks with rights for women. She shared Du Bois' conviction that "Every argument for Negro suffrage is an argument for women's suffrage; every argument for woman suffrage is an argument for Negro suffrage; both are great moments in democracy." Accordingly, Ovington joined the suffrage movement where she tried to bridge the gap between white and black suffrage organizations. She brought the New York suffrage leader, Harriet Stanton Blatch, into the NAACP (see Document 6-4-2 below). While joining the fight against child labor, Ovington also supported the Manhattan Trade School for Girls and the Consumers' League, which pressured employers to improve women's working conditions.[21]

All of these causes reflected Ovington's deep commitment to social justice. True to Progressivism, she never abandoned her optimistic faith that society could be improved and that she was called upon to do so. Ovington held onto these beliefs throughout a long and distinguished career. Not until illness forced her to retire at age 82 did she leave the field of activism. To Walter White, the Secretary of the NAACP, Ovington was a "Fighting Saint." [22]

---

1. What factors influenced Ovington to focus on African American problems despite being a white woman of privilege?
2. Which of Ovington's activities were most daring for a white woman in the early twentieth century?
3. Which of Ovington's activities were most important?
4. Was Ovington a "Fighting Saint"?

6-4-1. ADVOCATING ACTIVISM: W. E. B. DU BOIS, SCHOLAR-ACTIVIST, 1910

W. E. B. Du Bois (1868–1963) was a brilliant, influential, controversial African American scholar and activist. Being born to free black parents and growing up in a small Massachusetts town, Du Bois did not fully confront racism and segregation until 1885 when he went South to study at Fisk University in Tennessee. As explained in his famous essays, *The Souls of Black Folk* (1903), Du Bois now understood the dilemma of blacks in America and the "double consciousness" that prejudice created.

Du Bois completed his bachelor's degree at Fisk in 1888 and then earned a second one in 1890 at Harvard which had originally rejected him and still forbade him to live in the dorms or join the glee club. After two years of graduate work in Berlin, he received a doctorate from Harvard in 1895, the first black to do so. Unable to get a job at white colleges, he taught at Atlanta University for 13 years. There he wrote books, edited a journal and, as part of his conflict with Booker T. Washington, organized the Niagara movement to promote full civil and political equality for blacks. After the NAACP was formed in 1909, he left Atlanta and moved to New York to become its director of research and propaganda. In that capacity, he edited *The Crisis: A Record of the Darker Races,* which became a powerful weapon in the struggle for equality.

Through *The Crisis*, Du Bois promoted his aggressive brand of activism designed to unsettle white America and awaken black America. His eloquence was powerful and his pen spared no one. Fiercely independent, often abrasive, Du Bois was controversial both inside and outside the NAACP. Ovington consistently negotiated temporary peace agreements, but eventually Du Bois left the integrated organization to form an all-black organization while Ovington remained with the NAACP.

Du Bois became an international celebrity, speaking so widely about pan-Africanism and so critically of the United States that his passport was revoked during the 1940s. In 1950, at age 81, he became the first African American to run for the United States Senate in New York State, albeit unsuccessfully. Finally, dispirited about the prospects for racial progress in America, he joined the Communist Party in 1961 and went to Ghana where he was revered until he died on the night before the 1963 March on Washington. His 95 years of struggle had been momentous; his impact on America and the world was immense. Throughout his life, Du Bois adhered to the fundamental ideas enunciated in his first issue of *The Crisis,* published in 1910.[23]

Source: W. E. B. Du Bois, Editorial, *The Crisis: Record of the Darker Races*, November 1910, 10–11.

The object of this publication is to set forth those facts and arguments which show the danger of race prejudice, particularly as manifested to-day toward colored people. It takes its name from the fact that the editors believe that this is a critical time in the history of the advancement of men. Catholicity and tolerance, reason and forbearance can to-day make the world-old dream of human brotherhood approach realization; while bigotry and prejudice, emphasized race consciousness and force can repeat the awful history of the contact of nations and groups in the past. We strive for this higher and broader vision of Peace and Good Will.

The policy of THE CRISIS will be simple and well defined:

It will first and foremost be a newspaper: it will record important happenings and movements in the world which bear on the great problem of inter-racial relations, and especially those which affect the Negro-American.

Secondly, it will be a review of opinion and literature, recording briefly books, articles and important expressions of opinion in the white and colored press on the race problem.

Thirdly, it will publish a few short articles.

Finally, its editorial page will stand for the rights of men, irrespective of color or race, for the highest ideals of American democracy, and for reasonable but earnest and persistent attempts to gain these rights and realize these ideals. The magazine will be the organ of no clique or party and will avoid personal rancor of all sorts. In the absence of proof to the contrary it will assume honesty of purpose on the part of all men, North and South, white and black.

Some good friends of the cause we represent fear agitation. They say: "Do not agitate—do not make a noise; work." They add, "Agitation is destructive or at best negative—what is wanted is positive constructive work.

Such honest critics mistake the function of agitation. A toothache is agitation. Is a toothache a good thing? No. Is it therefore useless? No. It is supremely useful, for it tells the body of decay, dyspepsia and death. Without it the body would suffer unknowingly. It would think: All is well, when lo! Danger lurks.

The same is true of the Social Body. Agitation is a necessary evil to tell of the ills of the Suffering. Without it many a nation has been lulled to false security and preened itself with virtues it did not possess.

The function of this Association is to tell this nation the crying evil of race prejudice. It is a hard duty but a necessary one—a divine one. It is Pain; Pain is not good but it is necessary. Pain does not aggravate disease—Disease causes Pain. Agitation does not mean Aggravation—Aggravation calls for Agitation in order that Remedy may be found.

---

1. What were Du Bois' objectives?
2. Were Du Bois' methods appropriate for his goals?
3. What were Du Bois' strongest and weakest arguments for agitation?
4. Was Du Bois angry, forthright, eloquent, aggressive and/or defensive?
5. Does this editorial help explain why Du Bois was considered a dangerous man?

6-4-2. MARCHING FOR THE VOTE: A SUFFRAGIST, 1908

One hundred and forty years after the first woman's rights convention was held at Seneca Falls, New York in 1848, women were still struggling for equality. Efforts to get the right to vote accelerated during the Progressive era, but were hampered by cultural assumptions that women were inferior and should neither organize nor speak in public. Moreover, in order to amend the U.S. Constitution, Congress had to pass a bill that required ratification by 34 states. Although some men, like Du Bois, supported women's suffrage, resistance was widespread. With men in control of the federal and state legislatures and not eager to share their powers with women, the prospect for success was slim.

New York City's suffrage movement was reorganized in 1906 by Harriet Stanton Blatch, daughter of pioneer suffragist Elizabeth Cady Stanton. Blatch decided to bring working-class women into what was a predominantly middle-class movement. (Significantly, she participated in the silent march commemorating the 1911 Triangle Fire.) Blatch also emphasized the use of parades to make the movement visible, even though public demonstrations violated the canons of female domesticity and were ridiculed by men.[24]

Nonetheless, the suffrage parades became increasingly large and the movement grew. Finally, by 1917 support for women's right to vote was strong enough in New York City, especially in its working class districts, to carry a New York State amendment that backed women's suffrage and paved the way for the ratification of a similar amendment to the U.S. Constitution in 1919. New York City played a pivotal role in securing the right to vote for all American women.[25] The following short poem was read at a suffrage parade in 1908.

Source: *The New York Times*, February 17, 1908.

For the long work day,
For the taxes we pay,
For the laws we obey,
We want something to say.

1. How did this poem link economic and political equality?
2. How did this poem challenge traditional assumptions about women?
3. In terms of both tone and content, why might men have found this poem threatening and/or surprising?
4. How was this poem a good example of Progressivism in New York City?

6-4-3. DEFENDING BIRTH CONTROL: EMMA GOLDMAN, FEMINIST-REFORMER, 1916

Emma Goldman (1869–1939) was an anarchist and radical feminist who was widely admired and even more widely reviled. Called "Red Emma," she was always lambasted by the mainstream press, frequently arrested and finally deported as an enemy of the state in 1919. Her crime was advocating for unpopular causes such as free speech, free love, homosexuality, and resistance to the draft. Goldman was proud to be a dissenter and a professional agitator capable of delivering eloquent lectures on drama as well as compelling condemnations of capitalism.

Goldman was a lifelong crusader for women's rights. She preceded Margaret Sanger in advocating birth control and supported Sanger's early efforts. However, Goldman considered Sanger too timid, while Sanger considered Goldman too radical. Although they went their separate ways, both women were equally committed to the cause and made substantial personal sacrifices for it at a time when birth control was not just illegal but unmentionable. In 1916, Goldman was arrested in New York City for giving a speech that violated the law by including information on contraception. She defended her position in court before being convicted and sent to the Queens County jail on Court Square in Long Island City.[26]

Source: *The Masses*, June 1916, 27.

I have been part of the great social struggle of this country for twenty-six years as nurse, as lecturer, as publisher. During this time I have gone up and down the land in the large industrial centers, in the mining region, in the slums of our large cities. I have seen conditions appalling and heart-rending, which no creative genius could adequately describe. I do not intend to take up the time of the court to go into many of these cases, but I must mention a few.

A woman, married to a consumptive husband has eight children; six are in a tuberculosis hospital. She is on the way with the ninth child.

A woman whose husband earns $12 per week has six children, on the way with the seventh child.

A woman with twelve children living in three squalid rooms, dies in confinement with the 13th child; the oldest, now the mainstay of the 12 orphans, is 14 years of age.

These are but a few of the victims of our economic grinding mill, which sets a premium upon poverty, and our puritanic law which maintains a conspiracy of silence. ...

After all, the question of birth control is largely a workingman's question, above all, a workingwoman's question. She it is who risks her health, her youth, her very life in giving out of herself the units of the race. She it is who ought to have the means and the knowledge to say how many children she shall give, and to what purpose she shall give them, and under what conditions she shall bring forth life.

Statesmen, politicians, men of the cloth, men who own the wealth of the world, need a large race, no matter how poor in quality. Who else would do their work, and fight their wars? But the people who toil and drudge and create, and receive a mere pittance in return, what reason have they to bring hapless children into the world? They are beginning to realize their debt to the children already in existence, and in order to make good on their obligations, they absolutely refuse to go on like cattle breeding more and more.

That which constitutes my crime, Your Honor, is therefore, enabling the mass of humanity to give to the world fewer and better children—birth control, which in the last two years has grown to such gigantic dimensions that no amount of laws can possibly stop the ever-increasing tide.

---

1. How did Goldman justify what is now called a woman's right to choose?
2. How effective was Goldman's speaking style? What was her most powerful argument?
3. In Goldman's opinion, what were the larger social, economic and political contexts of birth control?
4. Does this speech help explain why Goldman was considered a dangerous woman?

6-4-4. PLEADING FOR FOOD: WOMEN PROTESTORS, 1917

The Progressive spirit of activism spread across class and ethnicity as well as gender. Hunger motivated poor Jewish women on the Lower East Side to demonstrate against high food prices in 1902 and 1917. In order to feed their families, they organized boycotts, held meetings, canvassed the neighborhood, picketed stores, overturned vendors' carts, fought with the police and got arrested. As mothers and housewives they felt justified in abandoning their traditional stay-at-home roles during moments of crisis. Because they understood the national economic context of local prices, they formed a Ladies' Anti-Beef Trust Association that managed to get meat prices reduced temporarily.[27]

Mainstream New York was horrified by the 1902 food riots and depicted the women as violent, crazed savages who set fires, destroyed property and attacked policemen. They were deemed dangerous foreigners unfit for citizenship. In 1917, there were more food riots by poor Jewish women in Brooklyn coupled with a protest at City Hall. The event was captured by the following photograph which was originally published in the *Independent*, March 1917 and the *International Socialist Review*, April 1917. The protest was led by Mrs. Ida Harris, president of the Woman's Vigilance League, who said,

> We do not want to make any trouble. We are good Americans and we simply want the Mayor to make the prices go down. If there is a law fixing prices, we want him to enforce it, and if there isn't we appeal to him to get one. We are starving—our children are starving. But we don't want any riot. We want to soften the hearts of the millionaires who are getting richer because of the higher prices. We are not an organization. We haven't got any politics. We are just mothers and we want food for our children. Won't you give us food? [28]

Source: "Crowd of Women, 1917," Library of Congress, Prints and Photographs Division.

1. Did the women look dangerous, defiant, depressed and/or desperate?
2. Who were the men in the rear of the photograph and why were there so few of them?
3. How did Ida Harris' statement help explain why this photograph was published in journals called the *Independent* and the *International Socialist Review,* but not in the *New York Times*?
4. Explain whether or not Ida Harris' statement and the photograph justify concluding that the protest was un-American and the women were unfit for citizenship?
5. Explain how the material in this unit reflects the promise and the limits of Progressivism.

Selected Resources

Adickes, Sandra. *To Be Young Was Very Heaven: Women in New York Before the First World War.* New York: St. Martin's Griffin, 1997.
Hood, Clifton. *722 Miles: The Building of the Subways and How They Transformed New York.* Baltimore, MD: The Johns Hopkins University Press, 1993.
Kasson, John F. *Amusing the Million, Coney Island at the Turn of the Century.* New York: Hill and Wang, 1978.
McClymer, John F. *The Triangle Strike and Fire.* Orlando, FL: Harcourt Brace, 1998.
Peiss, Kathy. *Cheap Amusements: Working Women and Leisure in Turn-of-the-Century New York.* Philadelphia, PA: Temple University Press, 1986.
Stansell, Christine. *American Moderns: Bohemian New York and the Creation of a New Century.* New York: Henry Holt, 2000.
Taylor, William R., (ed.). *Inventing Times Square: Commerce and Culture at the Crossroads of the World.* Baltimore, MD: The Johns Hopkins University Press, 1991.
Traub, James. *The Devil's Playground, A Century of Pleasure and Profit in Times Square.* New York: Random House, 2004.
Von Drehle, David. *Triangle: The Fire That Changed America.* New York: Grove Press, 2003.
Wetzsteon, Ross. *Republic of Dreams, Greenwich Village: The American Bohemia, 1910–1960.* New York: Simon and Schuster, 2002.
www.ashp.cuny.edu/Heaven: women's working conditions and the 1909 strike
http://westland.net/coneyisland: Coney Island
www.ilr.cornell.edu/trianglefire: the 1909 strike and the 1911 fire
www.historyplace.com/unitedstates/childlabor: photographs by Lewis Hine
www.nycsubway.org: history of the subway

CHAPTER 7

1920–1945

The period from World War I through World War II was a study in contrasts. The Roaring Twenties were followed by the Threadbare Thirties compounded by major riots in 1935 and 1943. Mayor Jimmy Walker typified the Jazz Age with his elegant attire, flashy girl friends, frequent vacations and big spending. Four years into the Depression, however, the incompetence and corruption of his administration exposed the mirage of the good times and paved the way for Fiorello La Guardia to become mayor in 1933. His 12-year administration restored New York's hope and humanitarian traditions.

The contrast was also evident in architecture. Consider the lavish Roxy movie theater that opened at Seventh Avenue and 50th Street in 1926 with gold leaf decorative details, the world's largest circular rug, the world's largest organ, an orchestra pit for 100 musicians and seating for 2,500 patrons. It captured New York's role as the nation's center of entertainment and extravagance. Other evidence of New York's prominence and prosperity were the Chrysler Building, the Empire State Building and Rockefeller Center, all of which were constructed with private funds during the Great Depression.[1]

However, at the very same time, Hoovervilles were emerging in Central Park and along the riverbanks. Encampments of the homeless who made huts out of refuse, they exposed the social dislocation and human desperation created by economic disaster. Of course, it was the stock market that measured the rise and fall of the nation's economy. More than ever, Wall Street symbolized the best and the worst of the American dream, thereby fueling the nation's long love/hate relationship with Gotham.

The challenge of the inter-war decades was whether it was possible to bridge the gap between fun and famine; whether the city and the nation could simultaneously pursue both the private and the public good. Exploring that dilemma, this chapter first looks at the 1920s through the lenses of the Harlem Renaissance, Prohibition and the Flapper. Second, it documents how the Great Depression affected different urbanites. Third, it examines La Guardia's efforts to revive and redefine the city. Fourth, it shows how the Harlem Riots of 1943 mirrored the dreams and disappointments of the inter-war years.

UNIT 7-1. CHANGE AND CHALLENGE: THE ROARING TWENTIES

The Roaring Twenties was an appropriate name for a decade of exuberance. The city's economy was booming and its borders were bursting. After World War I, New York replaced London as the world's financial hub. Population doubled; commercialism and consumerism reigned supreme. The rich moved to Park Avenue and the Upper East Side while the middle classes left Manhattan for Brooklyn, Queens and the Bronx. New York spelled opportunity.

Nightclubs, movie palaces, theaters, the Great White Way and Yankee Stadium defined "the city of the good time." It was a truly cosmopolitan city, one in which cultures converged and boundaries dissolved. The result was new forms of art, drama, literature and music. The spirit of the city in this era was best captured by George Gershwin, the poor, Jewish, Lower East Side son of immigrants who became a famous composer for opera, jazz and the Broadway musical. As Gershwin explained, "New York is a meeting place, a rendezvous of the nations. I'd like to catch the rhythm of these interfusing peoples, to show them clashing and blending. I'd like to write of the melting pot, of New York City itself, with its blend of native and immigrant strains … its many kinds of music, black and white, Eastern and Western." For Gershwin and for so many others, New York in the 1920s was truly scintillating.[2]

7-1-1.   CONTEMPLATING HARLEM: EDWARD L. SILVERA, POET, 1928

The Harlem Renaissance was the cultural flowering of the self-assertive New Negro. African Americans moved to Harlem when the subway made uptown accessible in 1904 and a black realtor opened up the housing market. By the 1920s, Harlem was a mecca for black artists, intellectuals, dancers, musicians, actors and writers who together created a cultural movement of national and international significance. From the expensive, segregated Cotton Club to the inexpensive, integrated Savoy Ballroom, Harlem was the core of the Big Apple, the key note of the Jazz Age.

Many of the Harlem Renaissance artists evoked the ironies of African American life—the dream as well as the nightmare. By depicting that complexity and by giving voice to ordinary people, they spoke for African Americans and to mainstream society. Edward Silvera was a colleague of Langston Hughes (see Unit 8-3). They both attended Lincoln College in Pennsylvania during the 1920s, after which Silvera entered medical school at Howard. Although not as famous as Hughes, Silvera published his poetry in several magazines and won awards for his work.

Source: Edward L. Silvera, "Harlem," *The Crisis: A Record of the Darker Races*, December 1928, 408.

> Harlem
> They have bruised your body
> And nailed it to a cross—
> I saw a black Madonna
> Weeping for you
> On a tenement doorstep.

Midnight
You are a throbbing heart
Of stone—
The feet of lovers
Echo on your sidewalks
Like the ticking
Of a thousand clocks.

Skyscraper
It is easy to forget
In Harlem—
The skyscrapers are motherly fingers
Pointing to something
Afar off.

Street Corner
This is the rendezvous
Of dreamers—
What if the cop does tell them
To move along:
There is a joint up the street
Where coffee and buns sell for a dime,
And somewhere
There are soft dream beds
Waiting—

Stars
Heaven stoops down
To kiss the rooftops
Of Harlem—
Rent is cheaper
Up nearer the stars.

---

1. Explain how Silvera evoked the reality of struggle in each verse.
2. Explain how Silvera suggested hope and resilience in each verse.
3. Explain what elements in each verse made it distinctly a comment on New York.
4. Explain what elements in each verse made it universal.
5. Explain how this poem reflected the spirit of the Harlem Renaissance and the New
   Negro.

7-1-2. PARADING FOR PRIDE: THE UNIVERSAL NEGRO IMPROVEMENT ASSOCIATION, 1920

Marcus Garvey (1887–1940) translated the self-assertion of the New Negro into a movement of the masses. Arriving from Jamaica, West Indies in 1916, Garvey formed an American branch of the Universal Negro Improvement Association (UNIA). It mobilized blacks throughout the nation and the world to affirm racial pride and seek racial self-sufficiency. Accordingly, Garvey promoted the establishment of black-owned businesses in the United States and the restoration of black rule in Africa. However, Garvey's plans for a steamship line to take blacks back to Africa ran aground, causing him to be tried, convicted on a technicality, jailed and deported to Jamaica in 1927. The more Garvey was admired by the powerless, the more he was feared by the powerful; his success was his undoing.

Garvey's impact was evident at the international convention that he held in Harlem for the entire month of August, 1920. Among other activities, the delegates adopted a flag comprised of red for the blood spilled over the centuries, black for race pride, and green for a better future. A big parade on August 2, 1920 signaled the aggressive spirit of Garvey's movement.[3]

Source: Report of UNIA Parade in Negro World Convention Bulletin, August 3, 1920 in Robert A. Hill (ed.), *The Marcus Garvey and Universal Negro Improvement Association Papers*, vol. II (Berkeley, CA: University of California Press, 1983), 490–492.

Put all the minuses of his mistakes and omissions against all the pluses of his success, and by every known test, algebraically and otherwise, Marcus Garvey is great. To-day's parade has added one more feather to his already numerously feathered cap—one more chapter to the history of the New Negro in his strivings for self-determination and freedom; one more achievement to the credit of the race. ...

To-day's parade was the greatest ever staged anywhere in the world by negroes. It was a parade expressive, as it was intended to be, of the Negro's serious, his unswerving and unswervable determination to solve his own problems by a larger reliance on his own resources and powers, physically, economically, religiously and otherwise, than heretofore. From now on the Negro means to strike out for himself, or die in the attempt. For him it is not a case of "root hog or die," and he means to do oodles of rooting before he dies. He doesn't intend to say "die" either until he is dead, when he can't say it at all. So, there! That is the New Negro's perspective in a nut shell.

The procession lasted nearly three hours, and comprised not only the thousands of members of the New York Division of the [Universal Negro Improvement] Association, but the members of numerous branches scattered throughout the Union, as well as members from the established branches in the West Indies, South and Central America, and Africa. These members all came to the city as delegates to the great convention to be held here during the entire month of August for the purpose of framing a constitution—a bill of rights—for the negro peoples of the world.

1. According to this report, what were the key concepts of Garveyism?
2. How did the parade reflect Garvey's influence?
3. How did the parade reflect the spirit of the Harlem Renaissance and New Negro?
4. How does this description explain why Garvey was considered a dangerous man.

7-1-3. DEFYING PROHIBITION: ERNEST W. MANDEVILLE, JOURNALIST, 1925

Resistance to Prohibition was part of the larger rebelliousness that infused New York in the Roaring Twenties. The fast-living, high-flying city did not appreciate social controls. Passed in 1918, the Constitutional amendment prohibiting the sale and consumption of alcoholic beverages reflected a nation that was hostile to cities, afraid of modernity, contemptuous of the new immigrants and intent upon conformity. Not surprisingly, Gotham resisted. Liquor was smuggled into the city or made at home. Organized crime flourished and 32,000 illegal drinking establishments called speakeasies sprang up to serve rich and poor, male and female, native-born and immigrant. Journalists like Ernest W. Mandeville documented how the spirit of law breaking ruled until prohibition was repealed in 1933.

Source: Ernest W. Mandeville, "The Biggest City and Its Booze," *The Outlook*, March 4, 1925, 340–342.

As almost every one knows, New York City is wide open. Of course, liquor won't be served unless you ask for it, but that is about the only restriction.

I found high-powered drinks being sold in almost all of the fashionable and supposedly most respectable eating-places. In most cases it was brought to the table in teacups. In only one instance was it necessary to go through any further trouble than sitting down and ordering. In this restaurant, one of the finest lunch places in New York, the drinking patron must walk to the back room, and then downstairs, where he will be served openly without any deception.

Then, too, in the moderately priced eating-places, I found liquor obtainable either in teacups or in ginger ale bottles. ...

Drug stores, barber shops, and soliciting bootleggers help to take care of the other city demands. Only a few weeks ago a man set up a stand in the lobby of a prominent Times Square office building and peddled out half-pint flasks of what purported to be whisky at one dollar a bottle. They went like hotcakes until it was discovered that the contents were only cold tea. Ten minutes' selling, a sizable roll of bills in hand, and disappearance at the first sign of dissatisfaction on the part of customers. New York has her share of suckers.

Many of the large office buildings contain their own bars. These are hidden away by the following method. On one of the upper floors there will be a suite of offices run for this purpose. The lettering on the outer door resembles the legitimate offices. It will be, perhaps, "Stocks and Bonds" or "Insurance Broker." Upon entrance, one notices the usual business of an outer office. A man or woman at a typewriter, files and papers strewn about. If you are a stranger and do not mention someone who is known to them, you are politely told that they do not handle whatever business you mention. Otherwise you pass into the inner office marked president or some title, and there any drink that you crave is sold by the glass or by the bottle. ...

High-class bootleggers nowadays look like well-to-do brokers or bankers. They circularize through the mails and allow a customer to keep the shipment twenty-four hours in order to sample it. As they are carrying on an underhanded traffic, they are suspected of underhanded methods. In order to counteract this impression, those who are establishing regular trade operate by the best business methods. They offer money back or replacements for any of their goods which do not satisfy. They keep card indexes of prospective buyers with entries as to their favorite tastes. ...

The east side of Broadway between 41st and 42nd Streets is the Booze Curb Market for New York. There, on the sidewalk, the Westchester roadhouse man meets the rum-runner and arranges for delivery. The boatmen bargain with those who pick up the cases at the shore. Prices all over New York are set by the quotations of this market.

---

1. In how many ways did New Yorkers defy Prohibition? Which method was most brazen?
2. How did the defiance of Prohibition cut across class lines?
3. How was the resistance to Prohibition typically New York?

7-1-4. DEBATING THE FLAPPER: HELEN BULLITT LOWRY, JOURNALIST, 1921

Like the New Negro, the New Woman rejected limits and aggressively pursued equality. During Prohibition, going to speakeasies and drinking in public was one way of challenging conventional notions of women's narrowly domestic, dependent role. By the 1920's, "the flapper" defined the modern woman who wore make-up and short straight skirts, discarded the corset, bobbed her hair and smoked cigarettes. She was educated, worked outside the home and most often lived in cities. Everything about her represented change and horrified the older generation. The conflict between old and new was explored in several articles by Helen Bullitt Lowry, a female reporter for the *New York Times*, a job that showed how women's roles were expanding in the new century.

Source: Helen Bullitt Lowry, "Mrs. Grundy and Miss 1921," *New York Times*, January 23, 1921.

Whenever two or three elders were gathered together in the last year, there was somebody to whisper about the outrageous new customs of the outrageous new generation. Now for the benefit of those of the "older generation" who have been imperfectly informed, who have been forced until now to exclaim in abstract terms of those "awful children" without knowing exactly what it is that those awful children do, the truth is that the awful children do some awful things, according to the standards of ten years ago. ...

A physician with many patients in the fashionable "sets" discussed the matter frankly with me. "This younger generation," said he, "is throwing off the old tradition of one rule for the men and another for the girls."

"Are men of the better class distressed and bewildered by this development?" I asked him.

"Perhaps. But have they a right to be? Men made the rule that they could do things not permissible for the womenfolk, and now the women have decided to apply the rule to themselves. Suffrage is only one small item, remember, in the restless struggle of the last century, which has been for equality of the sexes. The younger generation—in New York and I presume everywhere—is modeling itself after women of a type which defies old conventions, a type which was not common in polite society until recently. The debutante is rouging and painting her lips with frank abandon today. Groups of very young girls and men go to the Broadway jazz restaurants without any chaperone to give them the background of experience. ... "

Not only in the restricted limits of New York society or the wealthy circles of other cities is the older generation bemoaning new manners and morals. A few days ago, dear old Wellesley fairly shivered from the shock of a lecture given by Mrs. Augustus Trowbridge, wife of a Princeton professor.

To Mrs. Trowbridge belongs the credit for giving circulation to a new colloquialism—"petting parties." She did not explain what a "petting party" was. Apparently, she didn't need to. But observers of recent New York social changes infer that she referred to the not uncommon scenes of fondling such as are witnessed at many public places and private houses where propriety formerly reigned. "It was like a Coney Island boat," remarked the physician above quoted in describing to me the behavior of young men and women at a party in a supposedly elegant circle. ...

In Mrs. Trowbridge's Wellesley lecture, other menaces besides "petting parties" were held up before the college flappers. Included among the evils to be avoided were lip-sticks, jazz dances, "cut-ins" at dances and chaperoneless entertainments.

The war is what most of the commentators, at least here in New York, hold responsible for the exit of the chaperones. Motor Corps girls and the other war "causes" emancipated the "sub-deb." For example, when a TNT explosion in New Jersey occurred, two younger girls of families of "formal society" were dispatched from New York with an ambulance absolutely alone. They played up as true sports, rescued and gave first aid. To put them back under chaperones would be to squeeze the chicken back into the shell.

---

1. Identify at least five ways in which the flapper rebelled against conventional norms of social behavior for women.
2. Which of those behavioral changes would have been most shocking in 1921 and/or today?
3. What were the major explanations for and/or justifications of those changes?
4. Why was it significant that this article focused on upper-class women?
5. Explain the connection between Coney Island and the flapper.

7-1-5. DEPICTING THE FLAPPER, 1921

The article cited above was accompanied by the following drawing.

Source: Source: Illustration accompanying Helen Bullitt Lowry, "Mrs. Grundy and Miss 1921," *New York Times*, January 23, 1921.

1. Identify the major differences between the appearance of the old and young women.
2. Identify the major difference in the generational relationship between the sexes.
3. What about the young woman would have most horrified the older women?
4. Based on the article and the drawing, how revolutionary was the flapper?

UNIT 7-2. ECONOMICS AND THE PUBLIC INTEREST: THE GREAT DEPRESSION

The Great Depression hit New York City hard. As the capital of capital and the home of the Stock Exchange, its symbolic and real identification with the nation's financial health was profound. After the October 1929 crash, banks failed, businesses closed and unemployment soared. Churches and charities tried but could not meet the ever-growing demand for food. Without salaries, people lost their homes and were forced to roam the streets, sleep in subways or build shacks in parks. The federal government did not believe in providing aid and, under Mayor Jimmy Walker, the local government was too incompetent and debt-ridden to do so.

F. Scott Fitzgerald was the literary light of the Jazz Age. Upon migrating from Minnesota to Manhattan in 1919, he began chronicling the shallow life of the materialistic elite in novels and short stories. Fitzgerald experienced "the restlessness of New York" in the 1920s when "the parties were bigger, ... the shows were broader, the buildings were higher, the morals were looser and the liquor was cheaper." He was, therefore, struck by the contrast between the city before and during the Great Depression. Finally forced to admit "that New York was a city after all and not a universe, the whole shining edifice that he had reared in his imagination came crashing to the ground." For Fitzgerald, the Depression had sapped the life out of New York transforming his "incalculable city" into his "lost city." His pain was widely shared.[4]

7-2-1. CRASHING: JAMES N. ROSENBERG, ARTIST, 1929

James N. Rosenberg was particularly well suited to capture the shock of the stock market crash not only because he was a trained printmaker, but also because he was a bankruptcy lawyer. The title of his lithograph, Dies Irae, is Latin for Day of Wrath; October 29, 1929 was the day that the stock market crashed. Rosenberg recorded the punishing effect of an economic system that collapsed under its own weight due to over-speculation, over-consumption, under-regulation and the uneven distribution of wealth. Perhaps because the economic crisis was structural, Rosenberg's image was dominated by buildings. Note that the word curb in the drawing refers to the Curb Exchange, a name derived from stockbrokers who traded on the street after the formal Stock Exchange closed for the day. The Curb Exchange acquired indoor facilities in 1921 and became the American Stock Exchange in 1953.

Source: James N. Rosenberg, "October 29, Dies Irae," 1929.

1. At first glance, what three words best describe the overall mood of this drawing?
2. Upon closer inspection, how was that mood conveyed by the details of the drawing?
3. Why are the buildings falling on each other and on the people?
4. Why did the artist choose to depict the Stock Exchange, the Curb Exchange, Trinity Church, and the Empire State building?
5. How is this image similar to and/or different from the Jay Gould cartoon in Unit 5-4?

7-2-2. STRUGGLING: MICHAEL GOLD, JOURNALIST AND NOVELIST, 1930

Michael Gold depicted the Depression from the vantage point of the poor. A radical journalist, he wrote for the *Masses* and edited its two offshoots. Gold also contributed to the *Daily Worker*, the paper of the American Communist Party, which appealed to many struggling New Yorkers during the Depression. In his 1930 novel, *Jews Without Money*, Gold captured the impact of the Depression on the Lower East Side.

Source: Michael Gold, *Jews Without Money* (New York: Carroll & Graf, 1985), 241–244.

On the East Side people buy their groceries a pinch at a time: three cents worth of sugar, five cents worth of butter, everything in penny fractions. The good Jewish black bread that smells of harvest-time, is sliced into a dozen parts and sold for pennies. But that winter even pennies were scarce.

There was a panic on Wall Street. Multitudes were without work; there were strikes, suicides, and food riots. The prostitutes roamed our street like wolves; never was there so much competition among them.

Life froze. The sun vanished from the deadly gray sky. The streets reeked with snow and slush. There were hundreds of evictions. I walked down a street between dripping tenement walls. The rotten slush ate through my shoes. The wind beat on my face. I saw a stack of furniture before a tenement: tables, chairs, a washtub packed with crockery and bed-clothes, a broom, a dresser, a lamp.

The snow covered them. The snow fell, too, on a little Jew and his wife and three children. They huddled in a mournful group by their possessions. They had placed a saucer on one of the tables. An old woman with a market bag mumbled a prayer in passing. She dropped a penny in the saucer. Other people did the same. Each time the evicted family lowered its eyes in shame. They were not beggars, but "respectable" people. But if enough pennies fell in the saucer, they might have rent for a new home. This was the one hope left to them. ...

Mrs. Rosenbaum owned a grocery store on our street. She was a widow with four children, and lived in two rooms back of the store. She slaved from dawn until midnight; a big, clumsy woman with a chapped face and masses of untidy hair; always grumbling, groaning, gossiping about her ailments. Sometimes she was nervous and screamed at her children, and beat them.

But, she was a kind-hearted woman, and that winter suffered a great deal. Every one was very poor, and she was too good not to give them groceries on credit.

"I'm crazy to do it!" she grumbled in her icy store. "I'm a fool! But when a child comes for a loaf of bread, and I know her family is starving, how can I refuse her? Yet I have my own children to think of! I am being ruined! The store is being emptied! I can't meet my bills!"

She was kind. Kindness is a form of suicide in a world based on the law of competition.

One day we watched the rewards of her kindness. The sheriff's men arrived to seize Mrs. Rosenbaum's grocery. They tore down the shelves and fixtures, they carted off tubs of butter, drums of kerosene, sacks of rice, flour and potatoes.

Mrs. Rosenbaum stood by watching her own funeral. Her fat kind face was swollen with crying as with toothache. Her eyes blinked in bewilderment. Her children clung to her skirts and cried. Snow fell from the sky, a crowd muttered its sympathy, a policeman twirled his club.

What happened to her after that I don't know. Maybe the Organized Charities helped her; or maybe she died. O golden dyspeptic God of America, you were in a bad mood that winter. We were poor, and you punished us harshly for this worst of sins.

---

1. According to Gold, was government the friend or the foe of the poor during the Depression?
2. How did the title of Gold's book and this excerpt challenge stereotypes of Jews, the poor and women?
3. What were Gold's messages in the sentence about kindness and the last two sentences?
4. Did Gold's description explain and/or justify his criticism of capitalism?

7-2-3. SURVIVING: NEW YORKERS IN THE GREAT DEPRESSION

The 1929 stock market crash caused massive unemployment. Before unemployment insurance, welfare and food stamps, people who lost their jobs could not pay their rent and became homeless. Shanty towns called Hoovervilles sprung up in the parks and the lines at soup kitchens were so long that the food supply often ran out. As the following testimonials indicate, surviving the Depression was a struggle that tested the character of the city.

Elton Fax (1909–1993) was a prolific African American illustrator and writer during and after the Depression (also see Note 3 to this chapter). Augusta Savage (1892–1962) was a famous sculptor who produced acclaimed images of W. E. B. Du Bois and Marcus Garvey. Her sculpture, the Harp, was a highlight of the 1939 World's Fair, after which it was unfortunately destroyed. Savage taught art in Harlem during the Depression and was a supervisor in the New Deal's Works Progress Administration. She influenced a whole generation of black artists including Jacob Lawrence and Romare Beardon. Throughout her life, Savage experienced and fought against racial discrimination.[5]

Source: Jeff Kisseloff, *You Must Remember This: An Oral History of Manhattan from the 1890s to World War II* (San Diego, CA: Houghton Mifflin, 1989), 72, 140, 239, 327, 329.

LARRY SCHNEIDER: The Depression was terrible. People were livin' in cardboard boxes under the Williamsburg Bridge. I seen people on the street beggin' for pennies, sellin' whatever they could find—apples, a fountain pen, somethin' they picked up or stole—to get a coupla pennies. People that didn't wanna steal had to steal. Basically, they were honest people, but they stole to survive. They'd steal clothin' off a rack on Orchard Street, pants, shirts, shoes.

FRANCES LOEB: I had an Aunt Settie, who was living at what was then the Savoy Hotel at Fifth Avenue and 59th Street. There were a lot of apple sellers on the street then, and for a while Aunt Settie would leave her apartment at noon every day and go to Madison Avenue. She would then send the apple seller at that corner off to lunch with a dollar while Settie tended her stand.

MARY DEVLIN: My husband was a policeman and in the '30s, the policemen, the firemen, and sanitation all took two big cuts in salary in order not to lose their jobs. Nobody did, but along the river they had tents set up for others, who had no place to go, and if you had leftover vegetables or leftover bread, you'd bring it down to them.

ELTON FAX: I was teaching down south when one day a letter came saying that there was a job for me in Harlem. The job was a WPA [Works Progress Administration] job. Augusta Savage had at that time established art classes under government sponsorship on 136th Street, and she had classes there in weaving, drawing, painting, and sculpture, which she conducted ... My salary for the WPA was $23.86 a week. Rent was $35 a month. Through being frugal, I was able to save money. Man, I was eating hard rolls for my supper. I was kind of tough. This is the thing I take a little pride in. I was able to make it without stepping on anybody—without being a bastard.

STRETCH JOHNSON: We saw people starving, people raggedy. We saw people being evicted for nonpayment of rent, put out on the street. We also saw groups like the Communists and other militants putting furniture back after the city marshal would evict people. The Unemployed Councils were very active. After I was unemployed, I got very active in these movements.

1. In how many different ways did people respond to the hardships of the Depression?
2. What common thread in these accounts cuts across class, race, ethnicity and gender?
3. Did suffering bring out the best and/or the worst of human nature?
4. Which of these statements is the most poignant, inspiring and/or surprising?
5. How are these statements similar to and/or different from the Michael Gold excerpt above?

7-2-4. ORGANIZING: PETER KWONG, SOCIOLOGIST, 2000

The Depression presented special challenges for people whose economic situation was already precarious before the Depression. One such group was the Chinese who were socially isolated from mainstream America, prohibited from participating in American politics and banned from working in numerous fields, including most blue-collar and all white-collar jobs. Consequently, many became hand laundrymen, a job that few white men wanted, not only because it was considered women's work, but also because it meant hard work, long hours, six day weeks and very low wages. After World War I, however, when steam presses and washing machines were introduced, whites began opening large-scale, mechanized laundries. Because Chinese laundrymen did not have the money to buy such machines, they increased their free services (like mending and delivery) and decreased their prices. It was a struggle for economic survival.

To further complicate matters, the Chinese laundrymen in New York City were not supported by Chinatown's dominant organization, the Chinese Consolidated Benevolent Association (CCBA) which charged high membership fees, but provided few services. Peter Kwong, who qualified as a sociologist, a political scientist and a historian, analyzed the laundrymen's dilemma. He discovered that, in confronting their plight, the laundrymen not only challenged the status quo, but also forged a new path for Chinese American identity and activism.[6]

Source: Peter Kwong, *Chinatown, New York Labor and Politics, 1930–1950*, (New York: The New Press, 2000), 61, 63–67.

The hand laundry trade was hit hard by the Great Depression; there was sharp competition for whatever business remained, and the Chinese—as had happened so often in past economic crises—became the targets of increasing hostility. A series of incidents finally precipitated a crisis that threatened the very survival of all Chinese hand laundries in New York City, and the Chinese laundrymen, who had never before been political, organized in order to survive. In the process, they formed an association that was to remain the largest and most independent in Chinatown for years to come. ...

As competition intensified, New York's non-Chinese laundries formed a city-wide trade organization and requested the Chinese laundrymen to abide by the industry-wide minimum prices it had established. When the Chinese refused, claiming they could not raise prices without losing customers, the trade organization retaliated with a massive boycott of the Chinese laundries. Once again, as in California during the late nineteenth century, the Chinese were made the scapegoats for all the ills of an economic depression. And, as before, this was a highly "racial" attack: a scurrilous cartoon poster appeared in store windows throughout the city, showing a Chinese laundryman with a queue and buckteeth using his spit to wet the clothing before ironing. The poster campaign was effective and the Chinese laundry business began to suffer. Only when the Chinese consul-general enlisted the cooperation of the New York City Police Department were storeowners convinced to take down the posters.

But this was only the first round of the attack. Early in 1933, New York's non-Chinese laundries convinced the Board of Aldermen to pass a laundry ordinance establishing a $25 yearly registration fee and requiring one-person laundries applying for a license to post a $1,000 bond, supposedly to cover the possible loss of customers' property. The bond (which represented a substantial outlay even for the larger, mechanized laundries) seemed specifically designed to drive the Chinese out of business, for there was no way a small "family"-run hand laundry (which averaged only $400 to $500 a year in profits) could raise that much money.

How were the laundrymen to stop this ruling, divided and unorganized as they were? Neither the CCBA, the nominal representative of the community, nor any of the other traditional associations showed any interest in fighting the new ordinance. ... A few of the more active laundrymen decided to establish an independent laundry association. ... On April 26, 1933 the first public meeting of the laundrymen was to be held at a Catholic church on Mott Street. The CCBA and the other traditional associations, recognizing the threat to their hegemony, tried to sabotage the meeting. ... These efforts were to no avail, however: several thousand people showed up, representing two thousand Chinese laundries throughout the city. At last they had realized that their problems could not be dealt with individually, that a united effort of all Chinese laundrymen was required. Under the slogan "Laundry Alliance for the Laundrymen," it was decided to form the Chinese Hand Laundry Alliance (CHLA), an organization to be set up along trade lines, thus avoiding family, clan, and geographic divisions.

The creators of the CHLA attempted to ensure that it would not reproduce the corrupt and autocratic structure of the traditional associations. Its leaders were to be democratically elected by the membership from among all laundrymen. Greater New York was to be divided into three hundred districts (approximately ten laundries in each), and every district was to send one delegate to a representative body. There was to be a supervisory committee made up of fifteen of these delegates, including a president, a Chinese secretary, and an English secretary. The CHLA thus became the first democratic mass organization in the history of New York's Chinatown.

The CHLA, with the help of two lawyers, proceeded to challenge the proposed "bond" ordinance, arguing that it discriminated against small laundries. The Board of Aldermen agreed to modify the ordinance by reducing the registration fee from $25 to $10, and the bond to $100. The CHLA thus won its first battle, and the victory greatly boosted its popularity and prestige. Little more than a month after its formation, it claimed a membership of over 2,400.

The leadership emphasized repeatedly that the organization was not only to be independent of traditional controls, but was to be the standard bearer of new values and practices in the community. In its constitution, the CHLA promoted the principles of democracy, austerity, and scrupulous honesty; it also urged cooperation and mutual aid among its members. ...

The growth of the CHLA not only drew members and financial resources away from the CCBA and the other traditional organizations, but posed a major challenge to the established community structure. It began a confrontation between "old" and "new" that was to polarize the Chinese community for years to come.

1. What different obstacles did the Chinese laundrymen face?
2. How courageous and/or clever was their solution?
3. How did the laundrymen's new organization reflect a coming-of-age within their own community as well as within the larger American community?
4. How did the new organization both embrace and resist assimilation?

UNIT 7-3. CITY BUILDING: FIORELLO H. LA GUARDIA, MAYOR

Most people think that Fiorello H. La Guardia (1882–1945) was New York City's best mayor. From 1934 to 1945, he governed economically, efficiently and humanely. Born to Jewish and Catholic parents, but raised as an Episcopalian, La Guardia was always many in one, a bridge between groups. According to the historian Arthur Mann, La Guardia was "the most remarkable hybrid in the history of New York City." During the Depression, he not only rescued the city's finances, but also restored its pride. Whether defying Tammany or defending labor, assaulting corruption and vice or building schools and health stations, he worked hard and loved every minute of it. La Guardia's energy was as boundless as his ambition. Never before or since did American cities have such a dedicated, dramatic, dynamic defender.[7]

By his own account, La Guardia's lifelong reform agenda evolved from his experiences growing up on an Arizona army base where his immigrant father was a bandleader. La Guardia's positive association with the West was evident in his later concern for farmers and in his big, black stetson hat. However, Arizona also taught him some sober lessons, including anti-Italian prejudice. He was horrified when political appointees diverted government food rations from Indians, lobbyists swindled servicemen with false promises of promotions, bookies deceived the poor and railroad companies exploited their workers. Newspaper accounts of corrupt New York City politics shocked him into such a deep hatred of Tammany that, he admitted, it later became "almost an obsession." La Guardia's contempt for corruption in any form was confirmed when his father died after eating bad meat sold to the Army by dishonest companies during the War of 1898.[8]

La Guardia's early career prepared him for his later career. In 1900, at age 18, he began working for the American Consulate in Hungary where he learned six languages and improved the medical inspection system for immigrants. Leaving Europe for New York in 1906, he became an interpreter at Ellis Island and in night court, but, he said, "I never managed … to become callous to the mental anguish, the disappointment and the despair I witnessed almost daily." In fact, both experiences confirmed his compassion for the powerless and motivated him to obtain a law degree from New York University, attending at night while working during the day.[9]

Not surprisingly, La Guardia dedicated his legal practice to helping immigrants who valued him as a true "people's attorney." Working with immigrants exposed La Guardia to labor issues, involved him in labor struggles, and made him an ardent labor advocate for the rest of his life. Soon he decided that he "wanted to make law and not merely to construe it." However, getting started in politics proved difficult for an anti-Tammany Republican in a Tammany-run Democratic town. Not even the Republicans took him seriously until he started cutting into the Democrats' vote tallies. Although not yet a winner, La Guardia developed his campaigning skills by canvassing his lower Manhattan district in a secondhand Ford, speaking Italian and Yiddish to whoever would listen, ringing doorbells, attending weddings and funerals.[10]

His reward was being appointed deputy attorney general of New York State and getting the Republican nomination for Congress in 1914 and 1916. After losing the first election, La Guardia won the second only because he and his supporters carefully monitored the ballot counting to prevent fraud. Much to the dismay of both Republican and Democratic regulars, he carried his district by 357 votes. Having to struggle against the entrenched party system made him, as he put it, "an incurable insurgent."[11]

La Guardia took that spirit to Congress where he immediately defended immigrants by speaking against the literacy test and the Espionage Act while calling for aid to poor people suffering from high food prices and low wages during wartime. In 1917, he took a one-year leave from Congress to serve in the armed forces as a pilot and interpreter attaining the rank of major. Upon his return, La Guardia was re-elected to Congress in 1918, but left again in 1919 to serve as president of the New York City Board of Aldermen. In 1921, he faced personal and professional disaster when he not only lost his wife and infant daughter to tuberculosis but also failed to get the mayoral nomination.[12]

Within a year, he bounced back and was re-elected to Congress, this time from East Harlem, a working-class Italian and Jewish neighborhood that he represented from 1922 to 1932. The prosperous Roaring Twenties were difficult years for a politician with a social justice agenda. As a result, most of his proposals were rejected, but his voice was heard nationwide as he fought for minimum wages, maximum hours, workmen's compensation, old-age pensions, rent control, free speech, the right to strike and higher taxes on the rich. He opposed child labor, prohibition, national origin immigration quotas and income taxes on the poor. His greatest congressional accomplishment was the 1932 Norris–La Guardia Act, which protected workers' rights to unionize and strike. La Guardia's tenure in Congress, wrote the historian Howard Zinn, made him "the conscience of the twenties."[13]

Good and bad luck combined to make La Guardia New York City's mayor from 1934 to 1945. Having lost his mayoral bid in 1929 and his congressional seat in 1932, La Guardia's political future looked dim. However, his concern for the causes of the poor became increasingly relevant as the Great Depression became increasingly severe. Moreover, his long time opposition to Tammany proved politically prescient when Judge Samuel Seabury, a prominent upper-class reformer, uncovered extensive governmental corruption under Jimmy Walker, New York's charming but irresponsible Tammany mayor. The scandals were so egregious that Walker was forced to resign and the stage was set for La Guardia to re-enter politics.[14]

The only problem was getting the mayoral nomination. Tammany Democrats viewed him as the enemy and the Republicans thought he was too unpredictable, too abrasive, too rumpled, too Italian. Consequently, Seabury had to pressure the Republicans and the weak Fusion party to consider La Guardia. They resisted. In fact, they offered the nomination to anyone else they could think of including Seabury himself and a rising politician named Robert Moses (see Unit 8-4), who was politically independent but worked for Tammany Governor Al Smith. Finally, by a process of elimination, both the Fusion and the Republican parties reluctantly nominated La Guardia.[15]

The 1933 mayoral campaign was so intense that it spurred exceptionally high voter registration. Two Democrats ran against La Guardia—one a solid Tammany man, the other a quasi-independent Democratic reformer. Undaunted, La Guardia used ethnicity to further his cause by campaigning in Yiddish and Italian, fielding New York's first ethnically balanced ticket and attacking one of his opponents as anti-Semitic. Vito Marcantonio, La Guardia's protégé and a future congressman, organized grassroots Italian-American support, including poll watchers. Along with upper-class reformers and middle-class Jews, Italian Americans were essential to La Guardia's victory when they abandoned Tammany to vote for one of their own. Although the Democrats still held the citywide majority, their vote was split between two candidates, thereby enabling La Guardia to win. Accompanied by his second wife, La Guardia took the oath of office in Seabury's library without fanfare, It was a modest beginning to a momentous mayoralty which, said Robert Moses, "set [the city] to shuddering, heaving and quivering for twelve eventful years."[16]

As a candidate, La Guardia envisioned "a great big beautiful, kind New York." As mayor, he pursued an efficient, non-partisan government, famously declaring that "there is no Democratic or Republican way of cleaning the streets." Perhaps that is why he called his program the New Broom. However, first he had to get New York City out of the debt bequeathed to him by Mayor Walker. Cutting his own salary in half set the tone for reducing the city payroll, reorganizing the city bureaucracy, levying various business taxes plus overcoming his personal opposition to a sales tax. The result was a balanced budget by 1934, which enabled him to apply for federal funds and to begin, as he put it, "the greatest and most daring experiment in social and political democracy."[17]

Cultivating a special relationship with President Franklin Delano Roosevelt, whom he had known as governor of New York, and with Secretary of the Interior, Harold Ickes, who ran key New Deal programs, La Guardia managed to get a lot of federal money for capital improvements in New York City. At a time when a quarter of the city's men were unemployed, the jobs provided by these projects were literally lifesavers. In addition, they significantly improved the city with sewage treatment plants, an extended subway, enclosed retail markets, new docks, bridges, parks, playgrounds, parkways, public housing, schools, hospitals and health stations. Orchestrated by Robert Moses, this was the most extensive construction program any American city had ever undertaken. Not only did this program modernize New York, explains the historian Thomas Kessner, but it also redefined relationships between the city and its citizens as well as between cities and the federal government.[18]

La Guardia's leadership style was hands-on, personal, temperamental and abrasive. He supervised everything and cared about everybody, perhaps to a fault. When he wasn't rushing to fires, conducting orchestras, giving advice over the radio or writing letters to children, he was berating his commissioners, firing lax city workers, taking over court cases, smashing slot machines, and chastising reporters. His explosive, dramatic persona revealed a sense of self-righteousness and an insatiable need for attention. Yet, it also reflected a desire to inspire public interest in and support for his fight against crime, corruption and the callous disregard for human suffering. Both La Guardia's strengths and weaknesses derived from his ambition to give New York "government with a soul."[19]

La Guardia was the first reform mayor to be re-elected to office, not once but twice for a total of three terms. Although he may have aspired to higher office, his dreams for New York never diminished. Under his tutelage, New York hosted the 1939 World's Fair and acquired the nation's most modern airport, the largest consolidated mass transit system and the first health insurance plan (HIP) for public service workers. He never conquered crime, but he did establish the High School of Music and Art, free concerts and the City Center, all of which made culture more available to more people. True to his nickname, the city bloomed under the Little Flower's bold leadership and innovative urban vision.

After failing to get a commission to serve in World War II, La Guardia agreed to run the federal Office of Civil Defense in 1941 while still mayor. Distracted, he failed to fully address the issues that led to the Harlem Riots of 1943. Upon leaving the mayoralty in 1945, La Guardia became director-general of the United Nations Relief and Rehabilitation Administration in 1946, through which he hoped to alleviate suffering in the post-World War II world. However, in 1947 La Guardia's generous spirit was snuffed out by pancreatic cancer. At age 64, the complicated little man with the big hat was gone. But his legacy lived on.

---

1. What aspects of La Guardia's early life and career best prepared him to be New York City's mayor?
2. Why and how was La Guardia a successful mayor?
3. Why and how was La Guardia a controversial mayor?
4. In terms of ideas and actions, policy and practice, what were La Guardia's most important contributions to the city?

7-3-1. CHAMPIONING CHANGE: FIORELLO H. LA GUARDIA, MAYOR, 1945

In 1945, La Guardia delivered his final report to the city. Among his many accomplishments, he particularly valued the beginning of public housing because he believed that governments were as obligated to promote decent living conditions as to provide public safety and schools. This claim was controversial then and remains so now.

Source: "Mayor's Final Report," in Rebecca B. Rankin (ed.), *New York Advancing: Victory Edition* (New York: Municipal Reference Library, 1945), xxviii-xxix.

When I was but 21 years of age back in 1904, I was laid up once with influenza, way out in a little port in the Adriatic, where I was serving in the American Consulate. While sick I read a book called "How the Other Half Lives" by Jacob Riis [see Unit 5-3]. I did not believe such conditions could possibly exist in an American City. I had been raised way out West and I had never really lived in New York City. When I came back in 1906, to my horror, I found the conditions even worse than that described by Jacob Riis for the buildings were just that many years older.

Everybody was talking housing. I really have never been able to count all of the organizations, associations, committees and groups actually interested in public housing. Resistance to the enactment of the first Tenement House Law was powerful. The first law was indeed mild. But it was a great step forward. How weak, and limited, and ineffective it is in comparison to what we now have and are doing in housing today.

When I became President of the Board of Aldermen in 1920, there still had been very little done in housing and nothing at all in public low-rent housing by that time. Fire traps were still occupied. The fire retarding provisions of the Multiple Dwelling Law were a dead letter, ignored. It was not pleasant to live through the nights of those early years of my administration when a fire call would come in. Every winter scores of lives were needlessly lost in tenement fires. I did not go to fires for fun. It was my job. It was also a liberal education. It produced results in many ways.

No one can talk about low-rent housing in this country without giving credit to President Franklin D. Roosevelt. For the first time in the history of our country, the Federal Government recognized that the preservation of health, and the protection of life, were functions of government. All constitutional arguments of 150 years were brushed aside when President Roosevelt sent his message to Congress on housing. The Federal Government for the first time in the history of our country appropriated money to subsidize low-rent housing which provided sanitary, safe, cheerful dwellings for the lowest income groups. Our city followed and then the State. ...

At the laying of the cornerstone of the Williamsburg Houses, I placed in the box a copy of Jacob Riis' book "How the Other Half Lives." Just about thirty years after I had been inspired by that book!

Since then the Legislature has enacted laws facilitating public housing and has generously provided funds. So we stopped talking about it and started building. The Williamsburg was followed by the Harlem River Houses and then Red Hook until we have 14 projects accommodating 17,039 families built at a cost of 90 millions of dollars. ...

Can you recall the pictures of the old railroad flat tenement house? Compare it with the modern low-rent beautifully landscaped public housing projects. The change is most impressive. But the change that I cannot adequately describe is the transformation of the tenant. From the dismal, cheerless, dark, crowded old law flat to the light—window in every room— sunshine in every window—apartment with bath—the change is shown in a smile on mother, cleanliness of the children, cheerfulness in the family. The change and happiness in family life is something that cannot be recorded with the lens.

---

1. How did La Guardia's attitude toward housing reflect his larger social agenda?
2. Why was the role of the federal government so important to La Guardia? Why does it remain so controversial today?
3. Was La Guardia a dreamer and/or a doer?
4. Jacob Riis never advocated public housing. Explain whether and why he would have been surprised and/or supportive of public housing in 1945. Which of La Guardia's points would Riis have found most compelling and/or most disturbing?

7-3-2. OPPOSING LA GUARDIA: CARTOON, 1941

La Guardia represented and reached out to a broad cross-section of New Yorkers. In fact, he was the city's first Fusion candidate when he ran for mayor in 1933 and all of his subsequent campaigns harnessed a broad coalition of interests that he consistently contrasted to the narrow self-interest of Tammany. Accordingly, it was appropriate that La Guardia's 1937 campaign was run by an All Partisan Committee for La Guardia. However, his Tammany opponents tried to turn that label against him by suggesting that he was too friendly to too many interests and would align with anyone in order to win. As they put it:

"All Partisan" is right. The La Guardia administration has been all things to all people. You know what a chameleon is. You put the little animal on a red handkerchief and it very obligingly turns red. The Mayor has been a chameleon all his life. Red to the Communists to get the Communist vote. Pink to the Socialists to get the Socialist vote and he has worn the white tie and tails on Park Avenoo (don't laugh, he has!) to enlist the Republican carriage trade.[20]

In 1941, the Tammany candidate ran a cartoon that made the same point.

Source: "There are Two Kinds of Dishonesty," The Citizens' Committee for O'Dwyer, Church and Fertig (October 21, 1941).

1. How did the cartoonist use size, clothing and attitude to ridicule La Guardia?
2. What was the irony of the argument between the communist and the banker?
3. How did the cartoonist suggest that La Guardia's coalition was a weakness, not a strength?
4. How did the cartoonist suggest that La Guardia was more interested in himself than in the city?

7-3-3. WORKING WITH LA GUARDIA: NEWBOLD MORRIS,
PUBLIC SERVANT, 1955

Newbold Morris (1902–1966) descended from the colonial family that settled Morrisania, the Bronx. A Yale-educated lawyer, Morris was a dedicated liberal reformer who was a member of New York City's Board of Aldermen from 1935–1937 and chairman of its successor, the City Council, from 1937 to 1945. He lost two bids for mayor in 1945 and 1949, but served on the City Planning Commission in the 1940s and succeeded Robert Moses as New York City Parks Commissioner from 1960 until shortly before his death. Morris actively promoted the arts and chaired Lincoln Center's board of directors. His autobiography provided rich insights into La Guardia's style and substance.

Source: Newbold Morris, *Let the Chips Fall: My Battles Against Corruption* (New York: Appleton-Century-Crofts, 1955), 95, 110–111, 113–117, 137.

Shortly after La Guardia took office, he asked me to come and work in his administration. I was thirty-one years old, and only just starting to make a place for myself in a law office. It was quite a decision to make, but the restlessness of the times gave me a spirit of restlessness. ...

I was to know the mayor in his later years as well as any other political associate of his, but the man became a legend long before I undertook to write about him. He was, in fact, a legend while he lived. The people of New York called him the "Little Flower" and "The Hat." Whenever the aggressive little figure under the big-brimmed Stetson trudged across the newsreel screens of the nation, audiences were engulfed with laughter. The high-pitched voice declaiming in righteous wrath was well worth the price of a ticket to any movie house. But, as mayor, he had a certain majesty that added cubits to his stature. ...

Yes, La Guardia was a funny man. He was an unsparing, opinionated man. And he was a man of political genius. Taking over the helm of the largest city in the world, in the throes of the depression, La Guardia restored it to financial health ... One out of every three jobholders was out of work and the state relief funds available for the unemployed were woefully inadequate. ... He believed that mass unemployment was a concern of all the people of the country. And he did not consider relief charity. He had to match the federal expenditures by raising additional millions on his own. Furthermore, at a time when too many other communities were flagrantly sponging on federal relief and getting little or no results with the money, La Guardia put thousands of men to work on a job program that transformed the physical aspect of the city.

Under his regime New York blossomed into a community of beauty. Old parks were restored; new ones were built. Plans for arterial highways that had gathered dust in the files for years were put into operation. In addition to his works program, the mayor put an end to the land condemnation racket that had been bleeding the city treasury for the profit of landowners, lawyers and politicians. He established in each borough a small claims court where the man in the street could get speedy justice without having to resort to lawyers. He helped to push through the reorganization of county governments, wiping out old sinecures and putting the remainder on a civil service basis. La Guardia appointed Lewis Valentine, a career policeman, as his police commissioner, and New York mobsters had a very bad time of it. ...

The mayor displayed the passion of the bon vivant, exhibiting the idiosyncrasies of some of his Bohemian forebears. He rushed to fires in a fireman's helmet; he stood before symphony orchestras and conducted them with the bravura of a professional. He read the Sunday comics over the radio to the children during a strike of newspapers. He was so popular a broadcaster that whenever he spoke, there was a marked falling off of water consumption. Taps were turned off throughout the city. People sat glued to their radio sets.

Historically, La Guardia was a phenomenon. He was the only New York mayor ever to serve three consecutive terms. Even more significant, he was the only reform mayor to be re-elected to office. This had profound consequences. As Eddie Flynn, the Democratic boss of the Bronx, has pointed out, Tammany had always operated on the assumption that reform movements would expend themselves in a single term. The Tammany machine had been capable in the past of withstanding four years of a reform administration because of its carry-over appointees. However, before the twelve years of La Guardia's administration were over, there was not a single official outside of the state and county courts and the Board of Elections who owed his position to Tammany. Starved from a prolonged lack of patronage, the machine had come apart at the joints. ...

There never was a more autocratic democrat. Like old Frederick the Great, he swooped down suddenly, unexpectedly, on various parts of his domain, meting out awards and penalties with equal promptness. Every appearance was dutifully reported in the press; each was meant to dramatize a point, to function as a tableau in a morality play. Only weeks after his inauguration, the mayor, calling attention to the fact that under the law he was entitled to sit as a judge, suddenly appeared in the West 100th Street Police Station and presided as magistrate, sentencing a slot-machine operator to jail. A week later, he sat on the bench in Brooklyn, sentencing a second gambler—and then, to make sure that the point was not missed by the public, the mayor personally presided over the smashing of "one-armed bandits" throughout the city and posed with a sledgehammer for a photographer before they were dumped into the East River. ...

More than once as he was in the very act of sending a blundering commissioner to hell, I would see La Guardia suddenly change into a mood of tenderness and a smile would annihilate his frown. I would follow his eye to a window and observe, pressed above the rail of an iron fence, the face of a kid who had sneaked across the driveway to get a glimpse of him through the window. Someone once declared that if children could vote, La Guardia would have been elected President of the United States. No other politician has ever been so greatly worshipped by the small fry. To thousands of children the mayor was a magnificent, fun-loving imp straight from the Sunday comic strip. And to grown-ups as well he was an irrepressible imp—with a giant's heart.

---

1. According to Morris, what were La Guardia's objectives?
2. What methods did La Guardia use to accomplish his goals?
3. How did La Guardia's policies and personality make Tammany obsolete?
4. Explain whether being an "autocratic democrat" was La Guardia's strength or weakness.

7-3-4. ASSESSING LA GUARDIA: THOMAS KESSNER, HISTORIAN, 1989

In his definitive biography, the historian Thomas Kessner analyzed La Guardia's long-term legacy.

Source: Thomas Kessner, *Fiorello H. La Guardia and the Making of Modern New York* (New York: McGraw-Hill, 1989), 590.

Before La Guardia, the metropolis was a congeries of antiquated boroughs; a city haphazardly administered with parsimonious social and health services, no public housing, decaying parks, and inadequate bridges; a city in which it was said every department had its price and its contact person for graft. Under La Guardia the city built itself anew, throwing bridges over the waters and digging tunnels under them, erecting new reservoirs, sewer systems, parks, highways, schools, hospitals, health centers, swimming pools, and super air terminals. For the first time New York offered its poor public housing, its working class a unified transit system, and its artists and musicians special training and subsidies. The outdated charter of 1898 was replaced by a fresh compact that centralized municipal powers.

La Guardia came into office with an idea, and to an extent few would have dared imagine, he achieved it. He made New York a modern city, an honest city, a humane city, a city that got out from under the thumb of the state to develop its own relationship with Washington. He wanted New Yorkers to be happy (though sometimes he seemed more involved with making them good), to live with a sense of ease and security, to be rid of debt, to inhabit decent quarters and raise healthy children. Walter Lippmann once said that La Guardia took the human sympathy, which had been the abiding strength of Tammany, and infused it into the tradition of good government.

La Guardia led not only New York City, but all other cities in the country in forging a new relationship with the federal government. As president of the United States Conference of Mayors from 1935 to 1945, he fashioned the lineaments of this new partnership. As mayor of New York, in great favor with the New Deal, he won for his city a richly disproportionate share of federal funds, while insisting on as much local autonomy as possible.

So comprehensively did he reform the city that his successors still address the agenda he defined for them and continue to insist in their campaigns that they are the true heirs of a man who died [decades] ago.

---

1. According to Kessner, how did La Guardia unify and modernize New York City?
2. According to Kessner, how did La Guardia humanize New York City?
3. According to Kessner, how did La Guardia change the relationships between the federal, state and city governments? Why does it matter?
4. How does the material in this unit support a positive or negative interpretation of La Guardia's goals, methods and legacies? Was La Guardia a great mayor?

UNIT 7-4. LAW AND ORDER: THE 1943 HARLEM RIOTS

Riots are extreme events reflecting major unresolved tensions that acquire explosive proportions. The fact that there were two Harlem riots (in 1935 and 1943) during this period doubles their significance as barometers of both long-standing and immediate problems. Their location was not an accident. In Harlem, the dreams and disappointments of the era were particularly acute. The Harlem Renaissance was infused with optimism, pride and the hope for equality. The Depression replaced hope with despair and reinforced historic patterns of inequality. The hungry were hungrier; the underemployed were unemployed. Responses to the crisis were noble, but inadequate. Organized protests against discriminatory hiring at Harlem Hospital and in white-owned businesses raised the temperature of the community. As a result, simple sparks could easily ignite a fire.

Both riots occurred while La Guardia was mayor. The 1935 riot began after reports that a non-white child was beaten in a white-owned store; the 1943 riot started after a black soldier was wounded, but was rumored to have been killed, by a white policeman. These incidents were volatile because they echoed widely felt, long-term grievances against racism and police brutality. The 1935 riot lasted one day with three black deaths; the 1943 riot lasted three days with six black deaths. In addition, both caused many injuries and much property damage. Because they were confined to Harlem and focused on attacking property, not people, they are called Harlem riots or commodity riots, rather than race riots when whites attacked blacks, as in 1712, 1834, 1863, 1900, 1905 and 1910.

There were many causes of the riots. A report on the 1935 riot pointed to crowding, unemployment, low wages, high rents, high prices, inferior schools, poor health care, and police brutality. La Guardia suppressed the report but addressed some of its concerns, particularly regarding housing, schools and health services. The same causes fueled the 1943 riot, but were exacerbated by local and national incidents of discrimination. World War II complicated matters because of segregation in the military and abuse (even murder) of black soldiers in the South. Accordingly, African Americans mounted a Double V campaign for democracy both at home and abroad. Black labor leader A. Phillip Randolph planned a March on Washington in 1943 to protest discrimination in defense industry employment. Race riots in five states during the summer of 1943 increased tensions, especially after 34 deaths in Detroit during June.

In 1943, these national issues echoed locally when Mayor La Guardia allowed segregated military units to be trained in public facilities. He also condoned the closing of the Savoy Ballroom, an integrated Harlem nightclub. Moreover, he allowed a segregated semi-public housing complex called Stuyvesant Town to be built in lower Manhattan by the Metropolitan Life Insurance Company. These policies contrasted sharply with La Guardia's efforts to open up municipal jobs to blacks and improve public services in Harlem. To many African Americans, the inconsistency was profoundly disappointing. It compounded the misery of the Depression and set the stage for riot.[21]

7-4-1. DEFINING THE SAVOY: ANDY RAZAF, LYRICIST, 1943

The Savoy Ballroom was an icon of the Harlem Renaissance and the Jazz Age. A huge block-long facility in Harlem capable of holding 4,000 patrons, it was renowned for its inexpensive entrance fees and outstanding jazz bands. Innovative dances like the Lindy Hop and the Charleston earned the club the nickname, "Home of the Happy Feet." Most daring, the Savoy was integrated, unlike the Cotton Club where blacks could only be performers and waiters, not patrons. In 1943, the club was accused of fostering prostitution and was closed while other much less reputable (but not integrated) clubs were allowed to remain open.[22]

Harlem residents were furious and expressed their anger through rallies and the press. They pointed out that many prominent whites patronized the Savoy, which was also the site of war bond benefits. Even if La Guardia believed the salacious allegations about the Savoy, it was odd that he rejected all efforts to resolve the issue made by Walter White, executive secretary of the NAACP, who was also La Guardia's advisor on African American affairs. Significantly, La Guardia claimed that he was unable to reverse the decision before the riots, but promptly re-opened the Savoy after the riots.[23]

The inconsistency of the situation was captured by Andy Razaf who was an important lyricist during and beyond the Harlem Renaissance. He collaborated with several of the era's composers, most notably Fats Waller, with whom he created such famous songs as *The Joint is Jumpin'*, *Ain't Misbehavin'*, *Honeysuckle Rose* and *Black and Blue*. In addition, Razaf was an editor and writer for Marcus Garvey's paper, the *Negro World*, and was known as an astute critic of racial issues. He was inducted into the Songwriters Hall of Fame in 1972 and died in 1973. As the lyricist for the famous song, "Stompin' at the Savoy," Razaf was well-suited to write the following poem about the closing of the Savoy in 1943.[24]

Source: Andy Razaf "Guilty Savoy," *The People's Voice*, May 22, 1943.

Yes, the Savoy is guilty
Its crime are now exposed,
Therefore by "special orders"
Those famous doors are closed.
Yes, the Savoy is guilty
Of things most indiscreet.
Here's what they were guilty of
At "THE HOME OF THE HAPPY FEET."
Guilty of impartiality
Of healthy geniality,
Guilty of hospitality,
Of showing good will to all,
Guilty of syncopation
Of joy and animation,
Of decent recreation
For everyone, great and small.
Guilty of national unity,
Of practicing real Democracy,
By allowing the races, openly
To dance and mingle in harmony.
Guilty of its location—
By now, you can guess where the place is:
Guilty of being in HARLEM
And that's where the core of the case is!

1. What words did Razaf use to make the Savoy seem moral, not immoral?
2. What words did Razaf use to link the Savoy to basic American ideals?
3. How effectively did Razaf expose the hypocrisy of closing the Savoy?
4. How did Razaf reflect the spirit of the Harlem Renaissance and the New Negro?
5. How did the poem help explain the anger that lay behind the 1943 riots?

7-4-2. DEPLORING STUYVESANT TOWN: ADAM CLAYTON POWELL JR., POLITICIAN, 1943

Mayor La Guardia supported the Stuyvesant Town housing development because he wanted to promote private investment in public projects. However, he also declared his support for a law making it illegal to discriminate in housing and urged Metropolitan Life Insurance Company to build another project in Harlem. Of course, that housing would be for blacks only, so African Americans saw it as just another form of segregation. Even worse, Frederick Ecker, the chairman of Metropolitan Life, justified the discrimination by declaring that "Negroes and whites don't mix; perhaps in a hundred years they will."[25]

The Stuyvesant Town controversy heightened the tension between La Guardia and Adam Clayton Powell, Jr. (1908–1972). After graduating from Colgate, Powell returned to Harlem, becoming minister at the Abyssinian Baptist Church and organizer of boycotts against businesses that refused to hire African Americans. The success of his "Don't Buy Where You Can't Work" campaigns made Powell New York City's most prominent African American politician. He became the first African American member of the New York City Council in 1942 and served as New York's first African American congressman from 1944 to 1967. Powell was a charismatic, outspoken and controversial figure. He was so angered by Stuyvesant Town that he called for La Guardia's impeachment and wrote the following scathing editorial for his newspaper, *The People's Voice*.[26]

Note that the Board of Estimate was a legislative body comprised of the mayor, the city council president, the city comptroller and the five borough presidents. It set the city budget and was powerful until abolished in 1990 for giving equal representation to boroughs of very different population densities, thereby violating the one-man-one-vote principle.

Source: *The People's Voice*, June 12, 1943.

Hitler won a victory in New York City last week. Democracy was raped by all but two of the members of the Board of Estimate.

The Negro and fair-minded whites of this city were shown conclusively that dollars and not democracy run this city! The arch jim-crocorporation [sic] of America—the Metropolitan Life Insurance Company—was granted permission to transfer all the wretchedness—misery—discrimination—and racial hatred of a European Ghetto into the heart of New York City.

It was told it could build a housing project to accommodate 25,000 select people. Letters were introduced at the hearing in which representatives of the Metropolitan Life Insurance Company stated that Negroes would be barred from the project. Therefore, it will be an "all white" community. This company was told it could drive the present inhabitants of the houses in the location where the proposed project will be erected from their homes by the power of eminent domain without providing new dwellings for these outcast people. It was assured that it could close the existing churches in this area and drive the worshippers from before the face of their God.

It was also told that the Metropolitan Life Insurance Company and not the people, black and white, rule New York City. Democracy and civic pride were sold in whoredom by our Board of Estimate.

A wall over 12 feet in height will surround the city of seclusion, and signs will forbid passers-by to stop or enter.

The rooms will rent for over $14 each. The people in that area now pay far less. When they are forced from their homes, they will not be able to pay this exorbitant rent and will have to move on to create slums elsewhere.

Is this "slum clearance" or the vicious transplanting of poverty?

Negroes who go from New York City to the armed forces have one more straw added to the camel's back of their loyalty. Black lads across the seas, working and fighting for democracy, will be glad to hear that their city welcomes a community where they will not be able to live when they return?

Newbold Morris and Edgar Nathan are the only two men on the Board [of Estimate] worthy of any man's respect. Park Commissioner [Robert] Moses is a traitor to the public generally, and [Frederick] Ecker is as we expect, a member of "democracy's black market."

The fight has just begun. We will not take this lying down. We are Americans. New York is our city too. We will be heard! Every Negro and patriotic white must rally now to prevent this infiltration of fascism.

Remember, you who voted in favor of this project and betrayed us—white and black—that we will meet you at the polls in a near day, and we will show you than that you cannot wantonly sell our trust! We are going to defeat you and all Hitler-minded anti-victory agents who are sabotaging all that America stands for and is fighting to preserve. It is far better to have slums inhabited by free people than a magnificent Ghetto of slaves to prejudice and fascism.

---

1. Identify at least three ways in which Powell tried to arouse black anger.
2. Identify at least three ways in which Powell tried to make the issue relevant to whites.
3. Based on this editorial, what were the strengths and weaknesses of Powell's leadership style?
4. How did the Stuyvesant Town issue help explain the anger that lay behind the 1943 riots?

7-4-3. RESPONDING TO THE RIOTS: FIORELLO H. LA GUARDIA, MAYOR, 1943

After the disastrous Detroit riots in June 1943, Mayor La Guardia pleaded with New Yorkers to remain calm and reaffirmed his commitment "to extend equal protection of the law to all." Acknowledging "that in New York City we still have the aftermath of prejudice, racial hatred and exploitation that has existed in many parts of the country," he asked for "cooperation" in order "to cope with any situation" that might arise.[27] However, he still refused to form the inter-racial committee recommended by the report on the 1935 riots and reinforced by a variety of leaders, black and white, after the Detroit riots. In general, he failed to see and, therefore to defuse, the signs of the gathering storm.

Nonetheless, when riot struck, La Guardia immediately took charge. He brought policemen and police reinforcements up to Harlem and ordered them to act with restraint, a policy that was widely praised by blacks and whites alike, including Powell. Trying to contain the violence, La Guardia quarantined Harlem, imposed a curfew, recruited citizens to help patrol the area and asked prominent blacks to call for calm. In addition, he had medical personnel ready to handle injuries. True to his hands-on style, La Guardia walked the streets of Harlem himself, giving orders and asking people to go home. He also used the radio to communicate with the people of Harlem, delivering several messages like this one from City Hall.[28]

Source: Broadcast made by Mayor F. H. La Guardia from his desk at City Hall, August 2, 1943.

Shame has come to our city and sorrow to the large number of our fellow citizens, decent, law-abiding citizens, who live in the Harlem section. After an unfortunate incident at the Braddock Hotel, and some of you will remember that the Police have had trouble with the Braddock Hotel before, there was disturbance all through the night in west Harlem. Stores on 125th Street, 7th Avenue, 8th Avenue and Lenox Avenue had their windows broken and there was considerable looting.

The situation is under control. I want to make clear that this was not a race riot, for the thoughtless hoodlums had no one to fight with and gave vent to their activity by breaking windows of stores, looting many of these stores belonging to the people who live in Harlem. There were some 310 arrests made. About 150 people were injured by their own neighbors throwing missiles and bottles from rooftops.

The Police were most efficient and exercised a great deal of restraint. Commissioner Valentine arrived early and assumed command.

Now I want to tell the people of Harlem that I expect full and complete cooperation today and tonight and until order is completely restored. Traffic will be limited, and with all these stores with broken windows to guard, we do not want people from other sections of the city going there. Pedestrian traffic must keep moving. We cannot permit crowds to gather at any points or on street corners.

We expect full and complete cooperation with the Police and anyone attempting to loot will be arrested, brought to court and prosecuted for burglary and unlawful entry—a very serious offense. There was no need for all of this. It was just hoodlums—men, people with criminal intent—doing violence and stealing from their own group and injuring their own people. We have mobilized Police reserves who are charged with maintaining order. I know I can depend upon the law-abiding citizens of Harlem and I am addressing this to those who might be tempted to do anything today, tonight or at any other time.

I am now conferring with Commissioner Woolley of the Department of Markets who is in my office, trying to get food to the stores up in that section, but many of you will realize that perhaps some of these storekeepers, your own neighbors, your own people, may hesitate to reopen their stores after what happened to them last night. And I can assure you that we will get food up there, particularly milk for the children and, of course, it will take several days to obtain again the normal flow of supplies to retail stores.

Now, it was only the quick action of the Police that saved many lives there last night. I know that the decent law-abiding citizens appreciate this service for their protection and for the protection of their families. Law-abiding citizens can rest assured that they will get this protection but nothing can be expected by the hoodlums and those bent on committing crimes.

I have asked a group of distinguished citizens in whom I have confidence to speak direct to the people today, this afternoon and this evening. Give them heed, take their advice and give us cooperation so that we may properly protect all of you in Harlem as I intend to do all over the City.

Law and Order must and will be maintained in this city.

---

1. Whom did La Guardia blame for the riots? To whom was he appealing by contrast? Why?
2. What four strategies did La Guardia adopt in response to the riots?
3. How did these strategies and the tone of the message reflect his priorities and leadership style?
4. What was La Guardia's attitude towards Harlem and its citizens?
5. In what ways was La Guardia's message an adequate and/or inadequate response to the riots?

7-4-4. CLARIFYING THE RIOTS: THE NATIONAL COUNCIL OF NEGRO WOMEN, 1943

The National Council of Negro Women (NCNW) was formed in 1935 in order to coordinate and amplify the voice of women on African American issues. Under the leadership of activist and educator Mary McLeod Bethune, it brought together a variety of pre-existing black women's groups and played an important national role in the quest for equality. The New York City chapter of the NCNW assessed the riots through this strong letter.

Source: Letter from the Metropolitan Chapter of the National Council of Negro Women to Mayor Fiorello H. La Guardia, August 6, 1943.

Dear Mayor La Guardia:

The organizations listed below deplore and condemn the lawless and irresponsible manifestations indulged in by the citizens of this community on Sunday and Monday, August 1st and 2nd, resulting in the death and injury of numerous persons, destruction of property and cessation of normal activities. Such outbursts have far-reaching affects and were the acts of impetuous and reckless persons.

This violent disregard of law and order stems, however, from roots which intertwine deep into the lives of Negroes and into every phase of community and civic life. The unrestrained and spontaneous action of the crowds who ran from avenue to avenue, from street to street, destroying and stealing, was the vendetta of the ignorant, the forgotten, the undisciplined and the unwanted. The origin of race riots and community explosions such as this most recent one springs out of a long, long history of accumulated wrongs, uncorrected. Bold, brazen and humiliating discriminations within the Federal Government itself and filtering down through every state and locality, the endless exploitation which makes the Negro the victim of all that is undesirable, weakening and self-destructive, the general attitude of apathy and indifference to the most elemental rights of the Negro, and the hypocrisies of white America in their preachments on democracy have borne bitter fruit.

There are immediate causes which provoked this unfortunate tragedy. The unexplainable silence of the President of the United States when asked by organizations representing thousands of persons to make a radio or public address following the riots in Mobile, Alabama, Beaumont , Texas and Detroit, Michigan; the disgraceful and contemptible treatment of Negro soldiers, the general confinement of Negroes to the upper section of New York City, the very name of which, thanks to our metropolitan press, is synonymous with murder, "mugging," ignorance and prostitution, and the general feeling that Negroes can be mistreated with impunity, are conditions, the impact of which has aroused most Negroes in one way or another.

The irresponsible and less patient individual expresses his feelings in lawlessness and defiance. The thoughtful, rational, intelligent portion of Negro population attempt to secure relief from these conditions through every acceptable and recognized technique. The latter have used the device of inter-racial conferences, publicized studies, factual newspaper and magazine articles, radio addresses, conducted forums, petitions, delegations to government officials, the theatre and all other means available to create an understanding, enlightened and articulate public opinion. Through these techniques, remedies, sound as well as lasting, eventually evolve, but the remedies are so slow in materializing that many of the general populace become discouraged—lose confidence in their leaders—repudiate the orthodox methods of race development—and finally, in despair, take matters into their own hands.

There must be no retreat from orderly processes, but those processes must be speeded up, they must not wait for a crisis to precipitate action. To delay, to propitiate and to lull oneself into the belief that because there is no open rebellion, all is well and under control is a fatal assumption. There are remedies which must be adopted forthwith and without delay:

1. That apartments and living space be made available to Negroes in every section of the city, throughout the five boroughs,
2. That arbitrary rent levels be adopted through a program of rent control so that Harlem and similar sections have the same the rent level,
3. Sufficient and acceptable accommodations be provided on a city-wide basis for Negro members of the armed forces and their families visiting in New York City, and immediate abolition of discrimination in the armed forces,
4. Provisions be made whereby draftees of teen age rejected by the army be rehabilitated through proper medical care and trained in useful work under the auspices of the military,
5. Supervised recreational facilities for teen age boys and girls,
6. Official recognition of, and action by, on all governmental levels, of citizens' committees consisting of men and women of all races and creeds

who are following a program designed to correct injustices and help secure the development and inclusion into full citizenship of the Negro and other minority groups.

---

1. How did the NCNW explain the long- and short-range causes of the 1943 Harlem Riots?
2. How did the NCNW explain the national and local contexts of the 1943 Harlem Riots?
3. How did the NCNW condemn the rioters, but also express sympathy for them?
4. Which of the NCNW's recommendations were most and least surprising, compelling, reasonable or radical?
5. What were the major differences between the NCNW letter and La Guardia's broadcast?
6. What kind of letter should/would La Guardia have written in response?

SELECTED RESOURCES

Anderson, Jervis. *This Was Harlem, A Cultural Portrait, 1900–1950*. New York: Farrar Straus Giroux, 1981.

Bayor, Ronald H. *Fiorello La Guardia: Ethnicity and Reform*. Wheeling, IL: Harlan Davidson, 1993.

Capeci, Dominic J., Jr. *The Harlem Riot of 1943*. Philadelphia, PA: Temple University Press, 1977.

Cronon, E. David. *Black Moses: The Story of Marcus Garvey and the Universal Negro Improvement Association*. Madison, WI: University of Wisconsin Press, 1964.

Douglas, Ann. *Terrible Honesty: Mongrel Manhattan in the 1920s*. New York: Noonday Press, 1995.

Greenberg, Cheryl Lynn. *"Or Does It Explode?": Black Harlem in the Great Depression*. New York: Oxford University Press, 1991.

Kessner, Thomas. *Fiorello La Guardia and the Making of Modern New York*. New York: McGraw Hill, 1989.

Kwong, Peter. *Chinatown, New York Labor and Politics, 1930–1950*. New York: The New Press, 2000.

Lerner, Michael A. *Dry Manhattan: Prohibition in New York City*. Cambridge, MA: Harvard University Press, 2007.

Lewis, David Levering. *When Harlem Was In Vogue*. New York: Oxford University Press, 1979.

www.international.ucla.edu/Africa/mgpp: Marcus Garvey
www.laguardiawagnerarchive.lagcc.cuny.edu: Fiorello La Guardia
www.satchmo.net: Louis Armstrong
www.thirtrrn.org/harlem: walking tour of Harlem
www.si.umich.edu/CHICO/Harlem: Harlem

CHAPTER 8

1945–1970

World War II propelled New York City onto the center of the world's stage as the richest city in the richest country, a shining beacon to other cities devastated by six years of destruction and death. The United Nations proclaimed New York's leadership role in the international community, thereby complementing similar prominence in finance, industry, communications and the arts. Moreover, America's post-war standard of living was the envy of the world confirmed by the rise of suburbia, single-family home ownership and the car culture. A massive building program for roads, schools, parks, hospitals, bridges and swimming pools made New York City a national and international model for urban development.

The downside of progress was growing polarization within the city across class, racial and ethnic lines. The rise of suburbia meant the flight of the white middle classes out of the city just as blacks and Puerto Ricans were arriving in large numbers. The remaining whites often felt isolated and ignored, especially when the civil rights movement spread to the North. All of these factors made the city increasingly volatile, as seen in the 1964 Harlem Riots. Other conflicts erupted over public services as well as over the impact of new construction on old neighborhoods.

This chapter examines some of the most provocative issues that confronted mid-twentieth-century New York City. The first unit covers efforts to promote equality for blacks, Puerto Ricans, homosexuals and women. The second unit discusses the 1964 Harlem Riots. The third unit chronicles the controversy over the Civilian Review Board. The last unit evaluates Robert Moses' impact on the city. Running through the chapter are questions that plague Gotham to this day: Can a city built on diversity survive? How should urban progress be defined?

UNIT 8-1. BREAKING BARRIERS

The war against fascism and Nazism abroad heightened American appreciation of democracy at home. One reaction was defensive. It resulted not only in punishing domestic critics like the activist W. E. B. Du Bois and the actor-singer Paul Robeson, but also led to broader persecutions of dissenters, labor unions and radicals during the

McCarthy era. Another, more positive thrust was to expand democracy by challenging discrimination in New York City.

8-1-1. DESEGREGATING BASEBALL: JACKIE ROBINSON, ATHLETE, 1972

On April 15, 1947, about a century after baseball was born in Manhattan, America's favorite sport became more American. When Branch Rickey, the manager of the Brooklyn Dodgers, took the bold and risky step of signing Jackie Robinson (1919–1972) as the first African American in major league baseball, history was changed. Facing vicious opposition from the team, the sports world and the nation, Rickey and Robinson stuck to their principles and defied the odds. Dignified, articulate, gracious and strong-willed, Robinson proved to be the perfect choice for the role of pioneer.

Robinson's father was a Georgia sharecropper and his mother was a domestic worker. He grew up in California where he attended Pasadena Junior College and UCLA, excelling academically and in four sports. Drafted in 1942 before graduating, Robinson protested against discrimination in the army, an act for which he was court marshaled and received a medical discharge in 1944. He then played baseball in the Negro Leagues before moving to the Montreal Royals and finally to the Brooklyn Dodgers.

Like Hank Greenberg, the Jewish home run hitter from the Bronx who desegregated baseball along ethnic lines in the 1930s, Robinson served as a model for other minorities wanting to break barriers in baseball and beyond. He became a national hero. However, it was a hard role to play requiring great self control under difficult circumstances. The constant pressure took such a toll on Robinson's health that, at age 53, he died of complications from diabetes and heart disease. A year later, his wife established the Jackie Robinson Foundation, which still provides college scholarships and leadership training for minority youth.[1]

Source: Jackie Robinson, *I Never Had It Made: Autobiography* (New York: HarperCollins, 1972/1995), xxi–xxiv.

"I guess if I could choose one of the most important moments in my life, I would go back to 1947, in the Yankee Stadium in New York City. It was the opening day of the world series and I was for the first time playing in the series as a member of the Brooklyn Dodgers team. It was a history-making day. It would be the first time that a black man would be allowed to participate in a world series. I had become the first black player in the major leagues.

I was proud of that and yet I was uneasy. I was proud to be in the hurricane eye of a significant breakthrough and to be used to prove that a sport can't be called national if blacks are barred from it. Branch Rickey, the president of the Brooklyn Dodgers, had rudely awakened America. He was a man with high ideals, and he was also a shrewd businessman. Mr. Rickey had shocked some of his fellow baseball tycoons and angered others by deciding to smash the unwritten law that kept blacks out of the big leagues. He had chosen me as the person to lead the way.

It hadn't been easy. Some of my own teammates refused to accept me because I was black. I had been forced to live with snubs and rebuffs and rejections. Within the club, Mr. Rickey had put down rebellion by letting my teammates know that anyone who didn't want to accept me could leave. But the problems within the Dodgers club had been minor compared to the opposition outside. It hadn't been easy to fight the resentment expressed by players on other teams, by the team owners, or by bigoted fans screaming "nigger." The hate mail piled up. There were threats against me and my family and even out-and-out attempts at physical harm to me.

Some things counterbalanced this ugliness. Black people supported me with total loyalty. They supported me morally; they came to sit in a hostile audience in unprecedented numbers to make the turnstiles hum as they never had at ball parks all over the nation. Money is America's God, and business people can dig black power if it coincides with green power, so these fans were important to the success of Mr. Rickey's "Noble Experiment."

Some of the Dodgers who swore they would never play with a black man had a change of mind, when they realized I was a good ballplayer who could be helpful in their earning a few thousand more dollars in world series money. After the initial resistance to me had been crushed, my teammates started to give me tips on how to improve my game. They hadn't changed because they liked me better; they had changed because I could help fill their wallets.

My fellow Dodgers were not decent out of self-interest alone. There were heartwarming experiences with some teammates; there was Southern-born Pee Wee Reese, who turned into a staunch friend. And there were others.

Mr. Rickey stands out as the man who inspired me the most. He will always have my admiration and respect. Critics had said, "Don't you know that your precious Mr. Rickey didn't bring you up out of the black leagues because he loved you? Are you stupid enough not to understand that the Brooklyn club profited hugely because of what your Mr. Rickey did?"

Yes, I know that. But I also know what a big gamble he took. A bond developed between us that lasted long after I had left the game. In a way I feel I was the son he had lost and he was the father I had lost.

There was more than just making money at stake in Mr. Rickey's decision. I learned that his family was afraid that his health was being undermined by the resulting pressures and that they pleaded with him to abandon the plan. His peers and fellow baseball moguls exerted all kinds of influence to get him to change his mind. Some of the press condemned him as a fool and a demagogue. But he didn't give in.

In a very real sense, black people helped make the experiment succeed. Many who came to the ball park had not been baseball fans before I began to play in the big leagues. Suppressed and repressed for so many years, they needed a victorious black man as a symbol. It would help them believe in themselves. But black support of the first black man in the majors was a complicated matter. The breakthrough created as much danger as it did hope.

It was one thing for me out there on the playing field to be able to keep my cool in the face of insults. But it was another for all those black people sitting in the stands to keep from overreacting when they sensed a racial slur or an unjust decision. They could have blown the whole bit to hell by acting belligerently or touching off a race riot. That would have been all the bigots needed to set back the cause of progress of black men in sports another hundred years. I knew this. Mr. Rickey knew this. But this never happened. I learned from [my wife]

Rachel, who had spent hours in the stands, that clergymen and laymen had held meetings in the black community to spread the word. We all knew about the help of the black press. Mr. Rickey and I owed them a great deal.

Children from all races came to the stands. The very young seemed to have no hang-up at all about my being black. They just wanted me to be good, to deliver, to win. The inspiration of their innocence is amazing. I don't think I'll ever forget the small, shrill voice of a tiny white kid who, in the midst of a racially tense atmosphere during an early game in a Dixie town, cried out, "Attaboy, Jackie." It broke the tension and it made me feel I had to succeed. The black and the young were my cheering squads. But also there were people—neither black nor young—people of all races and faiths and in all parts of the country, people who couldn't care less about my race.

Rachel was even more important to my success. I know that every successful man is supposed to say that without his wife he would never have accomplished success. It is gospel in my case. Rachel shared those difficult years that led to this moment and helped me through all the days thereafter. She has been strong, loving, gentle and brave, never afraid to either criticize or comfort me.

1. What challenges did Robinson face in desegregating baseball?
2. What factors changed the minds of his teammates and the fans?
3. From whom did he get the most support? Why?
4. How many barriers did Robinson break?

8-1-2. CROSSING THIRD AVENUE: HUMBERTO CINTRON, WRITER, 1974

Many Puerto Ricans migrated to New York City during the post-World War II period. Although they were already American citizens, they faced discrimination. On the Lower East Side and in East Harlem, they met resistance from other more established groups. Like those groups, however, Puerto Ricans struggled to conquer the obstacles to social mobility. Humberto Cintron was a case in point because, despite the trials of growing up in the 1950s and 1960s, he became a significant figure in the Latino art world as a writer, television producer, and museum director.

Source: Humberto Cintron, "Across Third Avenue: Freedom" in Edward Mapp (ed.), *Puerto Rican Perspectives*, (Metuchen, NJ: The Scarecrow Press, 1974), 158–162.

Third Avenue. As far as the eye could see, the cobblestone street was saddled by a great black, spider-like iron monster called the "Third Avenue El." It cast a checkerboard shadow, alternating with shafts of sunlight like a huge web draped across the boulevard waiting for unsuspecting victims. I remember sitting on the curb, staring across to the east side of the street, the ominous, foreboding presence of the "El" weighing on my 8-year-old mind and giving more substance to the taboo that Third Avenue was for the Puerto Rican kid in East Harlem.

Across the no-man's land was an unknown world filled with exotic delights and adventures not accessible to me except through hearsay. Somewhere beyond was Jefferson park and an Olympic-sized swimming pool; the Italian festival of Our Lady of Mt. Carmel, complete with ferris wheel, merry-go-round, pizza pies, cotton candy, multi-flavored ices, and fireworks; there were a live market, fishing piers that extended into the East River, and the Boys Club. That I knew of for certain. The things I didn't know about were endless. My imagination soared as I sat watching the red and gold trolleys rattle along on the shiny silver tracks embedded in the cobblestones and listened to the roar and clatter of the iron horse overhead, spattering sparks into the air.

The traffic wasn't so heavy, and the traffic light was no different from any other. Red meant stop, green meant go. There wasn't any barbed wire or solid wall or alligator-filled moat or any other physical obstacle to keep me sitting on the curb day-dreaming. ... None of that. The fact is, with my [sneakers] I could probably beat nearly anyone across and back.

No, the barrier wasn't one my wiry body couldn't run under, over or through. The barrier was inside my head. Not that it wasn't real. It was real. But it had gotten inside my head the same way the knowledge of Jefferson pool and the Boys club had gotten there—through hearsay; stories, rumors and countless tales that fill the ether, the "stuff" of which tradition is made, transmitted from one person to another over time and distance. It was accepted fact without having been experienced. It was self-fulfilling.

Puerto Ricans were not to cross Third Avenue; that was Italian territory. Period. ...

Beyond Third Avenue you risked your life. It was a challenge I grew up with. Over the years the Third Avenue "barrier" appears to have crumbled under the steady flow of Puerto Ricans into "El Barrio" and Italians out of East Harlem. Not without a good measure of violence and heartache and bloodshed. Yet although the "Third Avenue El" and the trolleys no longer run on Third Avenue, and although the movement of Puerto Ricans in and around New York seems, on the surface, to have overcome the "barrier," no such thing has ever happened.

The wall of "unwelcome" flourishes. As always it is invisible. It came to us through tradition, through institutional behavior—it is the life-style of America. It can be traced back through the various ebbs and flows of waves and waves of immigrants who were nursed on an institutional inferiority syndrome which required them to cast away their cultural values in order to assume the American identity.

Nor am I suggesting that this behavior was peculiar to Italians in East Harlem. No such luck—had it been that way it would be easy to deal with. No, they learned it here, as a result of their experience as newcomers. And others had learned it before them, and they in turn learned it from their predecessors. That's what tradition is. That's how social institutions are built.

In those days I never questioned the pennies dropped into the church basket or the coins for the poor box that mom gave us ritually on Sunday, though our table seldom saw a chicken or pork chop. That too was tradition. ...

"Third Avenue" has been with me all my life and I suspect it will be with all Puerto Ricans all of their lives, in one form or another. And it affected and will continue to affect every experience of any significance in my lifetime.

It was there in the military when, after four years as an instructor and "Guided Missiles Expert," I was discharged A/2S.

It was there in college, which required seven years and three dropouts to complete.

It was there in Mississippi when we started 'freedom schools" to achieve "equal" education.

It was still there in "El Barrio" during the rent strike and community action days when the anti-poverty program raised hopes and generated dreams of self-help, only to be ground into the dust of yesterday's rhetoric.

And it lived on with the experimental school districts and the struggles for "community control" and the vain attempts to wrest control in a neighborhood shared politically by legislators from other communities but served by none.

It was there when the publishers sent rejection slip after rejection slip and I finally had to raise the bucks to publish my book myself.

It's still there now when every instrument of mass communications—print or electronic—chooses to ignore the Puerto Rican editorially, or carefully selects the images it presents, thus helping to perpetuate stereotypical negativism or promote a token Puerto Rican personality while systematically denying employment and opportunities to Puerto Ricans exclusive of the mailroom. In New York City today you can count on the fingers of your hands the number of Puerto Ricans employed in a professional capacity in all the major television, radio and print media combined.

I suppose I'll always sit on the curb somewhere, staring at the Third Avenues of the world, wanting to belong. And I suppose too that I'll venture forth into that unknown, seeking and probing and discovering. And I expect too that I'll always have my pennies for the poor box, eager to serve and be "good" in what is likely to be a quixotic adventure. But one thing you can count on as absolutely certain:

"Third Avenue" was not and will not be a deterrent to joining the struggle and doing the things that need to be done—or better said, trying to do what needs to be done. It certainly can not deter me from choosing to put on my [sneakers] and running under, over or through it.

---

1. What kind of barriers did Cintron confront? Why was the "El" good metaphor for barriers?
2. What caused the barriers? How embedded were they in the history of New York and America?
3. How did Cintron try to overcome the barriers? Did he succeed?
4. How similar and/or different were the struggles of Robinson and Cintron?

8-1-3. ANALYZING STONEWALL: DAVID EISENBACH, MEDIA HISTORIAN, 2006

The gay rights movement started when federal liquor agents raided a bar called the Stonewall Inn on June 27, 1969. The resulting violence spilled out into the streets of Greenwich Village for three nights and, suggests the historian David Eisenbach, attracted media attention largely because it occurred in Gotham. Soon the spirit of resistance spread beyond New York inspiring grass-roots organization across the nation to fight discrimination against gays in political, economic and social life. In the process, says Eisenbach, rights were expanded for everyone, thereby justifying the subtitle of his book, which calls the gay rights movement an American revolution.

Source: David Eisenbach, *Gay Power: An American Revolution* (New York: Carroll and Graff, 2006), 98–101.

In comparison to the scale of damage caused by other riots in New York City during the 1960s, the Stonewall riot was mild. One night in 1967, rioters in East Harlem looted an estimated twenty-five stores while snipers on rooftops shot at police and firefighters. The next year, after Martin Luther King was assassinated, hundreds of Harlem stores were sacked or vandalized, 77 people injured, 373 arrested. The Stonewall riot did not become a legendary event because of the amount of physical damage, one smashed up storefront, or because of the number of arrests, less than two dozen. It quickly became legend because the gay and straight press seized on the surprising fact that the rioters were homosexuals. ...

A week after the disturbances, both the *Daily News* and the *Post* ran follow-up articles that reflected their political leanings. Under the headline "Homo Nest Raided, Queen Bees Are Stinging Mad," the conservative *Daily News* recounted how "queens" had "turned commandos and stood bra strap to bra strap against an invasion of the helmeted Tactical Patrol Force." The liberal *New York Post* tried to explain the "gay anger behind the riots" by quoting twenty-two-year-old Dick Kannon on how important the Stonewall was to gays. "It was the best place we ever had. Most gay people were extravagantly paranoid. If there was ever a place that cured that, it was the Stonewall. You felt safe among your own. You could come down around here without fear of being beaten up by some punk out to prove his masculinity to himself. Around here, we outnumber the punks...."

More than any other "straight" publication, the *Village Voice* emphasized the social significance of what [*Voice* reporter] Howard Smith called the "gay power riots...." [Freelance reporter] Lucian Truscott IV called the Stonewall upheaval an "unprecedented protest...to assert presence, possibility and pride...." Truscott summed up his account of the riots by admonishing his readers to "Watch out. The liberation is under way." The *Voice*'s presentation of the riot as a historical turning point was so powerful that the first chronicler of the gay militants of the 1970s, Don Teal, speculated that Truscott's article "may have inadvertently initiated the gay liberation movement."

Truscott's piece contained an anecdote that would become an essential part of the Stonewall lore. On the Sunday after the riot, the reporter bumped into [the poet] Allen Ginsberg surveying the scene outside the Stonewall. After hearing everything that had happened on the two previous nights, Ginsberg exclaimed, "Gay power! Isn't that great! We're one of the largest minorities in the country—10 percent, you know. It's about time we did something to assert ourselves. ..."

The eruption of the Stonewall riot on the streets of the "media capital of the world" was key to the event's transformation into legend. The most detailed and influential accounts of the riots were written by *Voice* reporters who happened to be in the Village on the first night of the upheaval. Local coverage of the events in the city's dailies was followed by national media reports in *Time* and *Newsweek*. Had the first gay riot taken place in any other city, it would not have achieved legendary status so quickly.

---

1. In what ways were the Stonewall riots similar to, but different from, other 1960s riots?
2. How did the significance of the Stonewall bar among gays explain the riot?
3. How were the Stonewall riots "a historical turning point'?
4. How did being in New York City increase the impact of the Stonewall riots?

8-1-4. ASSERTING THE NEW FEMINISM: THE WOMEN'S LIBERATION MOVEMENT, 1970

Like the many other groups inspired by the 1960s civil rights movement, women wanted more equality and opportunity. Now that the old struggle for suffrage was won, the New Feminists focused on equality in economic and social relations. By drawing attention to sexism, they hoped to improve the condition of women across society. However, traditional gender roles were difficult to discuss and even more difficult to change because they were so deeply embedded in the culture. Consequently, the New Feminists were dismissed and demeaned as unfeminine.

In response, the women staged several spectacular demonstrations, including a nationwide day of parades, rallies and sit-ins on August 26, 1970. The parade in New York City was so large (35,000 to 50,000 strong) that the women took over Fifth Avenue, forcing the police to stand aside. Another successful event was invading the offices of the *Ladies Home Journal* for an 11-hour sit-in, akin to the sit-ins of the civil rights movement. Considered shockingly brazen at the time, it drew a lot of attention and, therefore, raised awareness of gender discrimination.

Source: "The New Feminism: A Special Section Prepared for the *Ladies Home Journal* by the Women's Liberation Movement," *Ladies Home Journal*, August, 1970, 63, 64.

On Wednesday morning, March 18, 1970, two hundred of us walked in—unannounced—to the offices of the *Ladies Home Journal*. As it turned out, we stayed for 11 hours because we had many things to say. We "occupied" the *Journal's* office because we wanted to articulate our dissatisfaction with the editorial content of the *Journal*—and all other women's magazines. We also brought to the *Journal* some of our ideas for structural change at the magazine.

It occurred to us, for example, that the *Journal*, a magazine for wives and mothers, would do well to take the lead in child care by establishing on its premises a day-care center for the pre-school age children of its employees. We raised the idea that a women's magazine ought to be run entirely by women, and that the magazine seek out nonwhite women for its staff in proportion to the population. We called for a minimum wage of $125 a week and a new plan for job classifications so that all employees would have a chance to participate in meaningful editorial discussions and work.

In response to our demands, the *Journal* agreed to give us this eight-page supplement. (They have also agreed to have further discussions with us on the subject of day care.) The work on this supplement was done collectively by a small group of women in our movement. As you read the next few pages, you will be able to explore our ideas on marriage, housekeeping, sex, work, education and other subjects.

Because our movement, though less than three years old, has already attracted women from a broad spectrum of society, you will find that our ideas, far from being uniform, are varied. We feel this is all to the good. We do not seek to impose a "line"; we seek to raise questions, to analyze the condition of womankind, to search for new answers. Consider this a woman's liberation sampler. Dip into it and extract what is relevant to you. And when you have finished, write to us and tell us what you think.

---

1. Why didn't the New Feminists use less aggressive tactics than an 11-hour sit-in?
2. Which of the New Feminists' ideas would have seemed most and least reasonable in 1970 as compared to today?
3. What did their collective authorship and the material in the last paragraph reveal about the objectives and methods of the New Feminist movement?
4. Explain the similarities and differences between the early- and late-twentieth century women's movements (see Units 6-3 and 6-4 and Unit 7-1).

UNIT 8-2. LAW AND ORDER: THE 1964 HARLEM RIOTS

The 1964 Harlem Riots marked a critical moment in the history of the city and the nation. Ignited when a policeman shot and killed a 15-year old boy, the riots quickly spread from Harlem across the river to Brooklyn, upstate to Rochester, over to New Jersey, down to Philadelphia and out to Chicago. Riots engulfed city after city across the nation during the next four years, creating both the reality and the mentality of crisis. The optimism of earlier peaceful civil rights demonstrations literally went up in flames.

The Harlem riots were important, not just because they initiatied this extended crisis, but also because they were in Harlem, the country's acknowledged center of African American life. The anger embodied by the riots exposed the limits of the civil rights movement and the desperation of African Americans living in Northern slums. The riots shocked America into admitting that discrimination existed outside the South. For many whites, the riots also bred anger and created a backlash against change. In all of these ways, they were a historical turning point.

8-2-1. CONTEMPLATING THE RIOTS: LANGSTON HUGHES, POET, 1964

Poet Langston Hughes (1902–1967) came to New York City in 1921 to study at Columbia College, by which time he was already published in W. E. B. DuBois' *The Crisis*. Hughes was an icon of the Harlem Renaissance and was considered the poet laureate of Harlem. As the following essay indicates, Hughes was always an acute and eloquent observer of human behavior.

Source: Langston Hughes, "Harlem," *The New York Post,* July 23, 1964.

The placing of blame for the current riot goes, of course, far beyond the simple shooting in front of a public school of little Jimmy Powell by Police Lt. Gilligan. Knife or no knife, Jimmy was a little boy. I saw him lying in his coffin looking very small and dead. And I heard people wondering in front of the funeral parlor why a very big man with a pistol—who had received medals for disarming grown criminals without shooting them—felt the need to shoot and kill this kid who looked in his coffin, small even for the age of 15.

The crowd in front of the funeral parlor felt that it was because Jimmy Powell was colored. Well, there have been billions of words written on the warp and woof of race relations in America. By now not only the cloth but the words describing its condition are moth-eaten. Do we think more mere words will do any good? ...

Opinion in Harlem is divided as to whether or not riots do any good. Some say *yes*, they achieve concrete results in community improvements. Others say *no*, they set the Negro race back 50 years. Those who disagree say, in effect, "But Negroes are always set back 50 years by something or another, so what difference does a riot make?"

Old-timers who remember former riots in Harlem say, "White folks respect us more when they find out we mean business. When they only listen to our speeches or read our writing—if they ever do—they think we are just blowing off steam. But when rioters smash the plate glass windows of their stores, they know the steam has some force behind it. Then they say, "Those negroes are mad! What do they want?" And for a little while, they will try to give you a little of what you want.

"After every riot in Harlem, the whites respect you more. After that big riot in 1935, the white-owned shops all along 125th Street that would not hire Negro clerks, began to hire at least one. We got a great many jobs out of that riot that we couldn't get before in our own community because the clerks, cashiers and everything were all white."

The big riot in 1943, which grew out of a white policeman shooting a black soldier at 126th Street and 8th Avenue during a period of much police brutality in the area, produced remarkable changes in police attitudes in Harlem, and resulted in a number of additional Negro officers being added to the force.

Chocolate and vanilla teams of policemen appeared on uptown streets walking together. Squad cars became integrated. And a white policeman would often grant his Negro colleague the courtesy of making the arrest, if an arrest had to be made. And for a long time after the '43 riots, seldom did Negro or white cops beat a culprit's head in public—as they frequently did before the riots. Mop-mop! Be-bop! Mop! Is where the musical term be-bop came from, so say jazz musicians—the sound of Harlem police clubs on Negro heads. ...

For me personally, the best thing that so far has come out of our current Harlem riots is that on Tuesday night I saw a Chinese cop in Harlem. Had it not been for the riots, I can hardly believe this surprising example of integration would ever have happened. I never saw a Chinese policeman in our neighborhood before. But there he was right on 125th Street in the block between the Theresa Hotel and Lenox Avenue with the 95 other cops I counted in that block from one corner to the other. Ninety-three of the cops were white, one was colored, and the other one, Chinese. In my heart I welcomed him to Harlem. I hope they let him stay here after the riots are over.

To me the Chinese have always seemed a delightful people with a warm sense of humor, quiet and friendly and courteous. I am sure that this Chinese cop would not wield a nightstick so violently, or shoot off his pistol so recklessly as other policemen have done in Harlem this week. In that long block between Seventh and Lenox Avenues, his was a face that looked decent and friendly.

---

1. According to Hughes, what were the long- and short-range causes of the riots?
2. According to Hughes, how were the 1964 riots a product of previous activism in Harlem?
3. According to Hughes, was police brutality a real problem in Harlem?
4. According to Hughes, why did some Harlemites support riots? Did the means justify the ends?
5. Explain why Hughes was both pessimistic and optimistic about the future of race relations in New York City.

8-2-2. RESPONDING TO THE RIOTS: ROBERT F. WAGNER, JR., MAYOR, 1964

Robert F. Wagner, Jr. (1910–1991) was mayor of New York City from 1954 to 1965. Like his father, the renowned New Deal senator, Wagner also was a liberal Democrat. After being elected Manhattan borough president in 1950, he became mayor in 1954 and was reelected in 1957 and 1961. Although he did not run for a fourth consecutive term in 1965, he tried to get nominated in 1969, but failed. Nonetheless, Wagner played a major role New York City politics for almost two decades. He supported public housing, city workers' unions, more city jobs for minorities and laws against housing discrimination. Although not a dynamic, inspiring leader like La Guardia, Wagner's low-key style enabled him to negotiate the complexities of New York City politics. His response to the 1964 riots reflected his ability to speak in different voices to different audiences simultaneously. Note that he was also concerned about the effect of the riots on attendance at the 1964 World's Fair.

Source: Remarks by Mayor Robert F. Wagner on CBS-TV, July 22, 1964.

The mandate to maintain law and order is absolute, unconditional and unqualified. It is the primary obligation of local government, under constitutional and statutory law. In fact, of all the groups in America, Negroes have the most to gain from law and order. ... The opposite of law and order is mob rule, and that is the way of the Ku Klux Klan, the night riders, and the lynch mobs. Let me also state, in very plain language, that illegal acts, including defiance of, or attacks upon the police, whose mission it is to enforce law and order, will not be condoned or tolerated by me, at any time.

Now I want to address some remarks directly to the people of Harlem, Bedford-Stuyvesant, South Jamaica, East Harlem, and all the other areas of our City, marked by congestion, unemployment, slum housing, and other adverse social conditions. ... I say to you, my fellow citizens, in all the affected areas of our City, that I think I am aware of most of your needs and problems in regard to housing, jobs, discrimination, and the education of your children, in regard to the training and retraining of the unskilled, and in regard to the sick and the handicapped ... and the wayward, too.

We must go all out to remedy injustice, to reduce inequality, and to resolve all conditions and practices which are a source of resentment and recrimination among these fellow citizens of ours. We are no richer than our poorest citizens, no stronger than the weakest among us.

Having said all this, I must now address myself to the rest of our citizens. We all want safety on the streets, and we shall have it to the maximum extent that it is possible, to the full extent that police and other security measures can assure it. ...

Now, I want to address myself to the people outside our city. We have had some troubles in New York in recent days and there have been over-sensationalized reports of crime in our city. It is a fact that some people, hearing these reports of riots, have cancelled hotel reservations and plans to visit New York. ... Within the last three months, 4½ million visitors have come here, and not one case of major physical assault against a visitor has been recorded. Our City depends upon its visitors for a part of our income and for the general level of economic activity. I say to all our citizens that we must repair the repute of our City by all the measures that are necessary. ...

There is, within the Police Department, a Civilian Review Board, composed of Deputy Commissioners of the Department. There has been instituted by my authority an arrangement whereby a careful review will be made in my office ... of every case in which charges involving alleged police brutality are brought before the Police Review Board. ...

[In addition, we plan] to station more Negro policemen in Harlem, and to institute on the part of the City government, a program to recruit and provide pre-training for more qualified young men and women belonging to minority groups for the Police force and to help prepare them for the entrance examinations. ...

Now, I want to emphasize that, in taking any of the steps we are taking, we are not bowing or surrendering to pressure. We will not be brow-beaten by prophets of despair, or by peddlers of hate, or by those who thrive on continued frustration. ...

I cannot possibly exaggerate what is at stake here for the minority communities, for the public at large, for the City as a whole, for the cause of justice and human rights, and for the sake of our country, in the eyes of the world.

The nation and the world have their eyes on New York. The racists, in the South and the North, certainly do. Minority groups everywhere do. Africa and Asia do. Indeed, all the world is watching us. We carry the deepest responsibility in these hours and days of our troubles. ...

Let us turn anger into reason. Let us turn despair into hope. By moving in the right direction, we move toward a high new ground of order, safety, progress, justice and brotherhood. By moving in the wrong direction, we steer straight into the pit of chaos.

---

1. According to Wagner, what were the long- and short-range causes of the 1964 riots?
2. What remedies to riot did Wagner propose? To what degree would they have alleviated and/or solved the problems that led to riot?
3. How many audiences did Wagner address? Which ones did he seem most anxious to reach?
4. What was Wagner's major message? How did it resemble or differ from Hughes' message?
5. How did Mayor Wagner's response to the 1964 riots resemble or differ from Mayor La Guardia's response to the 1943 riots? (see Unit 7-4)

8-2-3 AND 8-2-4. ASSESSING THE RIOTS: ARTHUR POINIER AND AL LIEDERMAN, CARTOONISTS, 1964

Political cartoons are useful primary sources because they capture contemporary concerns and provide perspective on reality. The following cartoons, both published in July 1964, depicted the riots from different angles. One dealt with cause; the other dealt with effect. Both emphasized the larger significance of the event. Al Liederman was a cartoonist for several papers and cartoon syndicates including Fawcett and Marvel. Although he drew sports and editorial cartoons, he was best known for his comic book characters, especially Captain Kid. Arthur B. Poinier was an editorial cartoonist for the *Cleveland Press*, the *Des Moines Register Tribune*, the *Detroit Free Press* and, for 25 years, *The Detroit News*. He was president of the American Association of Editorial Cartoonists and won many awards for his work.

Sources: "What Do I Have to Lose?" Arthur Poinier, *The Detroit News*, 1964. Al Liederman, "Grist For The Mill," *The Long Island Daily Press*, 1964.

"What do I have to lose"   "Grist for the mill"

---

1. How did each cartoonist explain the causes and/or the consequences of the 1964 riots?
2. Whose voice did each cartoon represent?
3. In what ways did these cartoonists agree or disagree with Hughes and/or with Wagner?
4. Was one cartoon more accurate than the other or did they complement each other?
5. What were the similarities and differences, the constructive and destructive aspects of riots in New York City over time? Consider the riots of 1765, 1834, 1849, 1863, 1943, 1964 and 1969.

UNIT 8-3. POLITICS AND THE PUBLIC INTEREST: THE CIVILIAN REVIEW BOARD

The ferment of the 1960s spilled over into debates about public policy in New York City. Increasingly, it pitted whites against minorities and the middle classes against the poor. Set against the backdrop of the civil rights movement and the 1964 Harlem Riots, debates over public priorities became intense. One of the most emotional, most divisive confrontations occurred over whether or not there should be any civilian review over police conduct. This was a sensitive issue in a nation that wanted internal security but feared the development of a police state. Nonetheless, the urban riots, rising crime and social unrest of the 1960s clouded the issue and seemed to pit safety against liberty.

The role of the police in New York City was always controversial. The 1849 Astor Place Riots (see Unit 4-3) highlighted the dangers of using force in the pursuit of law and order. In the late nineteenth century, protests mounted against police brutality in general. Since the Race Riots of 1900, African Americans had been calling attention to police brutality against minorities and requesting some system for redress. Skeptical that the police would censor themselves, citizens wanted the review process to include civilian input. Hence the name, Civilian Review Board (CRB).

The 1964 riots exacerbated these concerns. On the one hand, said the *Amsterdam News*, they reinforced "the strong public feeling that no matter what a policemen does to a Harlemite ... any charge against that policeman will be whitewashed by a board of review on which there sits no one else but a policeman." Instead, they called for a board comprised of "citizens who will weigh a brutal policeman on the same scale on which it weighs a Negro hoodlum—citizens who will judge the rights of a man on the receiving end of a nightstick by the same yardstick it judges the policeman who wields it."[2]

The police objected on the grounds that outside review would threaten their professional integrity and cripple their effectiveness on the job. Nonetheless, Mayor John V. Lindsay supported the concept of an independent review board and in 1966 appointed a police commissioner who shared his opinions. When four civilians were added to the existing three-man police-controlled review board, the civilians became more powerful than the police. Crisis followed. The Policeman's Benevolent Association (PBA) challenged the mayor by turning the issue into a ballot referendum. After easily raising $1,500,000 (a huge sum at the time), the PBA mounted an aggressive campaign against the new CRB. The ensuing public policy debate polarized the city and permanently altered New York City politics.[3]

8-3-1.   OPPOSING THE CIVILIAN REVIEW BOARD:
THE POLICE, 1966

An Independent Citizens Committee Against Civilian Review Boards was formed to present the police perspective. It ran several ads in local newspapers during the month preceding the referendum. One showed a cop in handcuffs and asked, "Do you want your police handcuffed?" The answer was "yes" if you wanted to "subvert his integrity, his courage, his dedication." The answer was "no" if you wanted "respect for law, order, decency." Another ad explained that "a police officer must not feel that his every action is being judged by non-professionals on the Lindsay Civilian Review Board. He must not feel that his job, pension or reputation can be jeopardized. He must feel free to take swift and direct action when danger strikes." Politics, said the ads, should not interfere with policing. The ads worked and the Civilian Review Board was resoundingly defeated at the polls. The following ad was particularly controversial. [4]

Source: Independent Citizens Committee Against Civilian Review Boards, "The Civilian Review Board Must Be Stopped," *New York Times*, September 26, 1966.

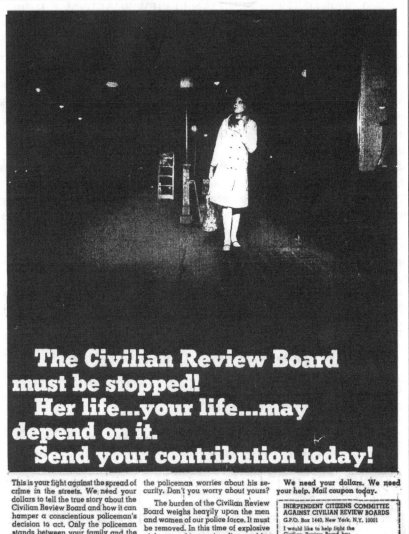

The Civilian Review Board
must be stopped!
Her life...your life...may
depend on it.
Send your contribution today!

This is your fight against the spread of crime in the streets. We need your dollars to tell the true story about the Civilian Review Board and how it can hamper a conscientious policeman's decision to act. Only the policeman stands between your family and the continuous threat of the hooligan, the addict and the criminal. Without your total support and confidence, he cannot be completely effective. A police officer constantly puts his life on the line for you. He must not hesitate. If he does, because he fears the possibility of unjust censure; or, if he feels his job, pension or reputation is threatened, the security and safety of your family may be jeopardized. Sure

the policeman worries about his security. Don't you worry about yours?

The burden of the Civilian Review Board weighs heavily upon the men and women of our police force. It must be removed. In this time of explosive violence and increasing disregard for law and order, our Police Department must be given the authority to act effectively to safeguard the entire community. With a Civilian Review Board, it may be the police officer who hesitates, not the criminal.

Enlist in the fight to end the Civilian Review Board in our city. In order to take this story to all the people, we need your dollars...and your help.

We need your dollars. We need your help. Mail coupon today.

INDEPENDENT CITIZENS COMMITTEE
AGAINST CIVILIAN REVIEW BOARDS
G.P.O. Box 1440, New York, N.Y. 10001

I would like to help fight the
Civilian Review Board by:

☐ Distributing   ☐ Making phone calls
   material
☐ Working at   ☐ Doing anything
   headquarters
           ☐ DONATION ENCLOSED*

*Make checks payable to Independent Citizens
Committee

NAME _____
ADDRESS _____
CITY _____ STATE _____
ZIP _____ PHONE _____

THIS IS YOUR FIGHT! WE NEED YOUR DOLLARS!
WE NEED YOUR VOTE. VOTE "YES" TO END THE CIVILIAN REVIEW BOARD ON NOVEMBER 8TH

---

1. What emotions are triggered by this image of a girl exiting the subway at night? Why?
2. What were the policemen's major concerns about the impact of the CRB on their jobs?
3. What kind of appeal did the policemen use to win popular support?
4. What were the policemen's strongest and weakest arguments against civilian review?

8-3-2. SUPPORTING THE CIVILIAN REVIEW BOARD: M. F. DUBIN, CITIZEN, 1966

Response to the ad was strong. Many African Americans thought it implied that the white girl was going to be attacked by a black man unless protected by the predominantly white police force. This subtext seemed confirmed when the PBA president said, "I'm sick and tired of giving in to minority groups" and when other opponents of the CRB repeatedly linked minorities with crime. For Roy Wilkins, the NAACP's Executive Director, the ad was part of the white backlash against the civil rights movement. "It spreads fear," he wrote. "It spreads racial suspicion and hate. It arouses passions. It splits the city."

Supporters of the CRB argued that civilian review would benefit everyone, not just minorities. In fact, they noted that whites registered more complaints against the police than blacks. Furthermore, the board was just advisory. It could only recommended which complaints the police department should review for possible discipline by the department, not the board. Yet, even such a limited role was considered valuable by people who wanted some avenue of redress against abusive policemen. While he insisted that "the people must have a say," Wilkins also acknowledged that most policemen were "not persecutors of Negroes" and were "doing their duty fairly. These good officers," he said, "need a civilian review board in order to set them apart from the bad policemen."[5]

Reason notwithstanding, the anti-CRB campaign touched a sensitive nerve within New York's African American community. Their feelings were expressed by a Brooklynite named M. F. Dubin in a poem called "Backlash Serenade," which included these lines.

Source: *The New York Amsterdam News*, October 22, 1966.

> Civilian Review Board cannot hurt a flea.
> But you'll vote against it emotionally.
> Elect into office a brute in white sheets.
> He'll promise to keep all the blacks off your streets.
> What has become of America's Dream?
> I don't know whether to laugh—or scream.

---

1. In Dubin's opinion, what was the CRB debate really about?
2. In Dubin's opinion, what was the historical context of the CRB debate? Why was the debate more than a New York City squabble?
3. What about the CRB fight would make Dubin laugh? What would make him scream?
4. If there was a televised debate between the CRB's supporters and opponents, which arguments on each side would be most convincing? Who would win?

8-3-3. EVALUATING THE CIVILIAN REVIEW BOARD: EDWARD T. ROGOWSKY, LOUIS H. GOLD, AND DAVID W. ABBOTT, POLITICAL SCIENTISTS, 1971

The following article suggested that conflict over the Civilian Review Board marked a significant realignment of New York City's ethnic, class and racial politics. Like the Harlem riots, it represented a turning point in the psychology of the city when the spirit of "practical toleration" seemed to have exhausted itself (see Unit 2-2).

Source: Edward T. Rogowsky, Louis H. Gold, and David W. Abbott, "Police: The Civilian Review Board Controversy," in Jewel Bellush and Stephen M. David (eds), *Race and Politics in New York City: Five Studies in Policy-Making* (New York: Praeger, 1971), 92–95.

The CRB (Civilian Review Board) referendum proved to be a rout for civil rights forces. For the first time in years, New York City's electorate rejected a liberal position on the ballot. The referendum appeared to intensify basic intergroup cleavages. ... Blacks voted overwhelmingly for the board. Irish and Italian Catholics, apparently because of their group identification with the police force and their large representation in the working and lower-middle classes, opposed the board by a huge majority. Jews were divided roughly according to their attitudes toward the direction of the civil rights movement. ...

The CRB referendum was something of a critical election in the overall pattern of New York City's politics. The concept of a critical election has usually meant a fundamental change in basic party loyalties signaling the emergence of a new electoral majority. The critical element in the CRB election did not have to do with basic party loyalties, since the referendum campaign was conducted without the involvement of party labels. Instead, it can be argued that the CRB referendum was a critical election in that it provided a *legitimate* means for the direct expression by voters of race-related attitudes on a matter of public policy. ... .

In addition, the critical nature of the CRB election included the emergence of new symbols or power aggregations that have the capacity of enlisting voter support or opposition. The interesting thing is that these new symbols are the bureaucracies that have come to dominate life in New York—organizations such as the school system, the police, the teachers' union, the welfare agencies, the sanitation men—around which so much of the urban crisis revolves. ...

Analysis of the CRB referendum and subsequent elections suggests a decline of political parties as the major expressive institutions in urban politics. In fact, attitudinal and group differences cut within and across party lines to rearrange the usual liberal and conservative coalitions. ...

A decade ago, the sanguine view of the pluralists held that the openness of New York City's political system, with its overlapping and fragmented decision-making structures, permitted a high capacity of responsiveness. In the face of growing militancy for social change, it appears that this very same quality of openness is now what prevents the system as a whole from responding with sufficient effectiveness to create meaningful change while maintaining the social order.

With the decline of traditional party politics, the "new machine" in city politics consists of the constellation of organized bureaucracies and their supportive constituencies, which dominate in separate aspects of the city's life. While demands for change are focused on these separate systems—demands for police review, decentralization or community control in the school system, and so on—the city as a whole is without the capacity to coordinate change in several sectors at once or to respond with over-all effectiveness.

At best, this means the continuation of a crisis climate wherein those who seek change can achieve only partial satisfaction. At the same time, the expression of demands has itself engendered a departure on the part of many voters from the liberal values that were formerly taken for granted by a majority of the electorate. Many of the progressive values that underlie the call for urban reform and aid to blacks and other minority groups still hold the allegiance of city voters. Nonetheless, a more narrowly defined "politics of interest" has come to have an influence greater than the traditional politics of liberal values.

---

1. How did the CRB controversy divide the city by race, class and ethnicity?
2. Why was the CRB referendum considered a critical election?
3. How did the CRB controversy reflect the decline of political parties in New York City?
4. What are the advantages and/or disadvantages of a "politics of interest?"
5. What was the impact of the CRB controversy on New York City's liberal, pluralistic traditions?

UNIT 8-4. CITY BUILDING: ROBERT MOSES, PUBLIC SERVANT

Who was the real Robert Moses (1888–1981)? On the one hand, there was the autocrat who tore down the slums, ran highways through the center of neighborhoods, and supported housing discrimination. On the other hand, there was the democrat who believed that urban development must benefit everyone, not just the rich. In addition, there was the city booster who insisted that public works be beautiful, not merely useful. Could the ruthless, power-hungry realist be the same well-intentioned idealist who claimed that his primary objective was "making the city livable"?[6]

The son of wealthy German Jews, Moses graduated from Yale College, Oxford University and Columbia University where he got a doctorate in political science. His thesis criticized the inferior quality of America's politically appointed civil servants and praised England's exam-driven system dominated by the educated upper and middle classes. According to Moses' main critic, Robert A. Caro, this was an early expression of the arrogance and elitism that would define Moses' career.[7]

Certainly, there is plenty of evidence for Moses' arrogance. The more power he got, the more flagrantly he attacked his critics. For example, he assailed the highly respected New York State Governor Herbert H. Lehman as "weak," "stupid," "sniveling" and "contemptible." To Moses, Mayor John V. Lindsay was a "goddamned whippersnapper," and lesser people were treated with even greater scorn. Considering himself superior to all others, Moses was infuriated by dissent and criticism. Everyone who worked for him agreed with him or risked withering insults and rapid dismissal. No wonder Moses was called "the great intimidator." [8]

By the same token, Moses was a great builder; he was the man who "gets things done." At his peak he held 12 state and city jobs which gave him control over transportation, housing, recreational facilities, and other construction projects. From 1924 to 1968, he dominated development not just in New York City, but also in Long Island and upstate. He created thousands of miles of highways, thousands of public housing units, thousands of acres of parks. He was responsible for the United Nations Building, the Coliseum, Lincoln Center, and La Guardia Airport. His seven bridges united the city and his 16 expressways made it navigable. Scores of playgrounds, golf courses, swimming pools, baseball diamonds, zoos, beaches and skating rinks enlivened New York.[9]

There is no controversy over the scope of Moses' contributions, but there is controversy over Moses' intentions and impact. Caro emphasized Moses' obsession with building itself, his disinterest in and disregard for the human toll of his projects and the imperious way in which he pursued his goals. By consolidating so much power in his own hands, wrote Caro, Moses was able to control politicians and ignore public protest, thereby putting himself above the law. His policies were as undemocratic as his methods. Facilities in rich neighborhoods were nicer than in poor neighborhoods. Razing slums and building roads meant displacing hundreds of thousands of working class people. From Moses' perspective, however, the ends justified the means because, he said, "You can't make an omelet without breaking eggs."[10]

Moses was accused of being racist. He seemed to perpetuate segregation by charging entrance fees to historically free public beaches, steering blacks to less desirable beaches farther away from the city and not providing adequate public transit to beaches. Furthermore, he allowed the Metropolitan Life Insurance Company to build two segregated housing developments—one downtown for whites (Stuyvesant Town) and another uptown for blacks (Riverton). All too often, housing renewal meant "Negro removal." Moreover, neighborhood-based swimming pools simply replicated existing housing segregation patterns because, suggests one historian, Moses thought that racially mixed pools would arouse fears of amalgamation[11] (see Unit 3-1 and Unit 9-3).

This negative portrait has been challenged in several ways. One interpretation is that Moses built the most pools in the most crowded neighborhoods because those were the most neglected areas with the fewest facilities for public recreation. Thinking broadly, he placed pools near parks and schools in order to create a public service cluster in each community. The pools were huge, attractive structures that inaugurated a new era of public architecture and a new commitment to providing leisure facilities for both children and adults. Although initial construction was in white neighborhoods, Moses included black neighborhoods when he began to see the pools as tools for diffusing black unrest, especially after the 1943 riots[12] (see Unit 7-3).

In the area of transportation, Moses brought New York City into the twentieth century with a network of highways, bridges and tunnels. Although roads dwarfed mass transit and accelerated the exodus to the suburbs (including Staten Island), they also brought New York into the automobile era. The result was a technological revitalization of the city that was essential to its future economic development. So too, Moses' urban renewal program was designed to modernize the city by eradicating its nineteenth-century slums. If slums were the problem, super blocks were the solution. Eliminating through streets would supposedly create oases of decent apartments amidst green space protected from traffic. In addition to public housing, Moses promoted public–private partnerships for middle-class housing, as reflected in the deal with Metropolitan Life as well as in his support of union-sponsored cooperative housing.[13]

In many ways, Moses was a visionary himself, but he scorned urban planners as "egotists" absorbed with abstract ideas and incapable of making the practical daily decisions essential for real change. Instead, Moses took advantage of opportunities as they presented themselves by moving on many different fronts simultaneously and manipulating the political power structure. Above all, he refused to tolerate, as he put it, the "partisans, enthusiasts, crackpots and fanatics" who got in his way. Although Moses was the ultimate pragmatist, he was motivated by an abiding faith that "the city, rebuilt, modernized and humanized, will always be the great magnet which draws from the hinterland the eager, the young, the curious, the ambitious, the talented."[14]

By the same token, Moses' driven sense of purpose and ruthless use of power proved his undoing. Over time, community opposition to his bulldozing approach grew. Moses never understood or cared to understand the human dislocation caused by his projects. To him, relocation was an administrative matter to be handled efficiently and firmly. He was incensed when ordinary citizens protested the elimination of their Lincoln Square community to build Lincoln Center or the destruction of their East Tremont neighborhood by the Cross Bronx Expressway or the replacement of a favorite Central Park playground by a fancy restaurant's parking lot. Although Moses won those battles, his reputation was tarnished. Moreover, he lost several subsequent battles over demolishing a section of Greenwich Village, running traffic through Washington Square Park and building an expressway across lower Manhattan.

For a long time, Moses' philosophy prevailed because his projects were widely supported as needed public improvements and the source of many jobs. Moreover, he was an effective publicist who constantly claimed to be *Working for the People,* which was the title of his 1956 book. However, Moses really did "not love the people," observed the New York City social worker and New Deal Secretary of Labor Frances Perkins (see Unit 6-3). "He'd denounce the common people terribly," she reported. "To him they were lousy, dirty people, throwing bottles all over Jones Beach."[15]

Jane Jacobs (1916–2006), a housewife turned activist, disagreed with Moses' attitude towards the city's people and places. In *The Death and Life of Great American Cities* (1961), she explained how neighborhoods functioned as vibrant social units. Jacobs criticized the sterility of super blocks, high-rise buildings and public housing. She insisted that many densely populated areas that Moses called "blighted" were nothing of the sort. To her, each street was a little community—enriched, not diminished, by its small scale, mixed uses, and diverse users.[16]

Jacobs' grassroots resistance to Moses' Greenwich Village plans helped burst the bubble of Moses' omnipotence. Her plea for maintaining the integrity of neighborhoods and the traditional fabric of the city provided an alternative urban vision that reinforced other people's concerns about demolition and development. So too, the growing dismay over Moses' bulldozing spurred efforts to preserve the past, most notably when New York's magnificent Pennsylvania Station was demolished in 1962, albeit not by Moses. The result was the nation's first historic preservation policy that, like New

York's 1916 zoning law, became a model for other states and marked a turning point in American attitudes towards modernization. New was not necessarily better.

Be that as it may, for almost all of his 44 years in power, Moses was the acknowledged master of urban redevelopment whose advice was sought from other cities in America and abroad. When questioned by a mayor, Moses' favorite tactic was to threaten resignation. However, because he was considered indispensable, the resignations were never accepted. Efforts by Mayors Wagner and Lindsay to reduce Moses' power failed miserably because Moses constantly outfoxed them and because so many influential men benefited from his various projects through construction contracts.

The situation was different with Governor Nelson Rockefeller who was less susceptible to pressure and more interested in controlling the development of roads and parks himself. As tension mounted, Moses typically suggested that he might resign from several state posts. Much to his surprise and dismay, Rockefeller quickly accepted the offer. The governor then reorganized the state's transportation administration so as to remove Moses from his remaining jobs. At age 79, after four decades of public service, Moses was out of power. [17]

The length of Moses' public service was outstanding; the scope of his power was unparalleled; the quantity and quality of his projects were exceptional. Serving under four mayors, he tackled daunting problems with controversial strategies that, for better or worse, had a permanent impact on urban planning, policy and politics. New Yorkers remain indebted to him as the master builder of the modern city.

To his detractors Moses was an elitist abuser of power; to his defenders he was the most effective of all city boosters. In the end, perhaps he was just a typical New Yorker—aggressive and arrogant, innovative and determined, ruthless and resourceful. As he once explained, "some of us like tough jobs. We like resistance and we don't think the task is impossible. We don't believe New York is going back. There is of course, another reason, far more influential, but, like most deep emotions, hard to explain. You see, we love the town."[18]

---

1. Why should Moses be praised?
2. Why should Moses be criticized?
3. Why was Moses so powerful?
4. How was Robert Moses similar to but different from Boss Tweed and Fiorello La Guardia?

8-4-1. CHANGING THE CITY: ROBERT MOSES, PUBLIC SERVANT, 1968

Traffic was one of the greatest challenges of the new automobile era. Although he never owned or drove a car himself, Moses understood the complexity of the problem and tried to modernize New York City accordingly. With the rise of the suburb in the post-World War II era, the need for roads was ever increasing. It is unclear whether roads were the cause or the effect of the suburbanization that drew the tax-paying middle classes out of the city. It is clear, however, that roads promoted the development of the four outer boroughs and facilitated automobile travel around Manhattan. In a 1968 interview, Moses' conveyed his goals, methods and style.

Source: Robert Moses, "What the Big Cities Must Do To Stay Alive," *U.S. News and World Report* [Nation and World], January 8, 1968, 66–68.

Q: Mr. Moses, are the giant central cities of the U. S. doomed to be strangled by traffic and swarms of people?

A: No, not if steps are taken now to meet and anticipate problems. We can make room for large numbers of people more comfortably. We can eradicate the old, densely populated slums, though the cost will be great. Our road system can be improved to handle traffic efficiently at all times, except perhaps during occasional peak hours. These results will be attained by tried, practical, conventional methods—not by the gaudy pronouncements of revolutionary planners.

Q: Where do these planners go wrong?

A: Many are too visionary. They forget that today's problems have to be solved with today's means, and with money that is available now. We are all getting a little sick of planning lingo, clichés, slang and metaphors—"city blight," "ghettos," "suburban mess," "suburban sprawl,"—all rich and poor, and nothing in between; steel and stone as against grass roots, and so on. Basically, many planners don't believe in the city at all. They condemn the noise and discomfort and crowding of the city, comparing it with the peaceful existence of a Walden Pond. Well, when it got cold, Thoreau moved from Walden Pond back to town. Planners seem to overlook the fact that most people like the city the way it is. Cities, however, can be vastly improved; there's no question about that. ...

Q: How, then, do you cope with overcrowding in central cities?

A: To accommodate large numbers of people more comfortably, the answer is vertical construction on less land. Instead of a building four or five stories high, covering 80 or 85 per cent of the land, you go up four or five times as high on 20 per cent coverage. This will leave plenty of open space, playgrounds for the kids, and better views.

Q: Mr. Moses, is there any practical solution to the concentration of low-income people in the city slums?

A: There's only one answer. That is to tear down every building in the slums and put up new ones on less land, then bring the people back. That doesn't go for all slum areas. There are some where you can still repair buildings rather than tear them down. ...

Q: Will big cities always be crime-ridden and riot prone?

A: No. The main job of the chief executive of a city ... is to preserve outward order and decency. This means adequate, trained, uncompromising, guaranteed police protection and respect for law and order. Any community can achieve this end if at the same time, other problems involving jobs and decent living conditions are met.

Q: How can city streets and parks ever be made safe?

A: By reasonable rules constantly enforced, by adequate policing and by tried recreation programs, tested by experience—not wild events and happenings which surrender parks to irresponsible "beatniks," vandals, "hippies" and agitators. The objective must be to preserve the parks for the 95 per cent of orderly citizens.

Q: Can freeways or throughways provide an answer to the problems of mushrooming traffic?

A: Yes, in part. But even with the most imaginative building of roads and improved use of streets, there will still be occasional and formidable peaks of traffic. We have to accept that.

Q: Aren't people complaining more and more about tearing up streets and buildings to make room for freeways?

A: Yes, but we have always had such protests. What big undertaking, anywhere, didn't involve tearing up something?"

---

1. What were the advantages and disadvantages of Moses' solutions for overcrowding, slums, safety and traffic?
2. What was Moses' attitude toward his critics?
3. What did this interview reveal about Moses' personality and power?
4. In what ways was Moses a pragmatist and/or a visionary?

8-4-2. PRESERVING THE CITY: JANE JACOBS, URBANIST, 1961

Jane Jacobs opposed Moses' emphasis on building roads and widening streets in order to make the city more accessible for cars. She believed that people were more important than parkways and explained what human factors made the city work best.

Source: Jane Jacobs, *The Death and Life of Great American Cities* (New York: Random House, 1961/1989), 29–32, 34–37.

This book is an attack on current city planning and rebuilding. It is also, and mostly, an attempt to introduce new principles of city planning and rebuilding.
...

Automobiles are often conveniently tagged as the villains responsible for the ills of cities and the disappointments and futilities of city planning. But the destructive effects of automobiles are much less a cause than a symptom of our incompetence at city building. ... The simple needs of automobiles are more easily understood and satisfied than the complex needs of cities. ... Cities have much more intricate economic and social concerns than automobile traffic. How can you know what to try with traffic until you know how the city itself works, and what else to do with its streets? You can't. ...

Streets and their sidewalks, the main public places of a city, are its most vital organs. Think of a city and what comes to mind? Its streets. If a city's streets look interesting, the city looks interesting; if they look dull, the city looks dull.

More than that, and here we get down to the first problem, if a city's streets are safe from barbarism and fear, the city is thereby tolerably safe from barbarism and fear. When people say that a city, or a part of it, is dangerous or is a jungle, what they mean primarily is that they do not feel safe on the sidewalks.

But sidewalks and those who use them are not passive beneficiaries of safety or hapless victims of danger. Sidewalks, their bordering uses, and their users, are active participants in the drama of civilization versus barbarism in cities. To keep the city safe is a fundamental task of a city's streets and its sidewalks.

This task is totally unlike any service that sidewalks and streets in little towns or true suburbs are called upon to do. Great cities are not like towns, only larger. They are not like suburbs, only denser. They differ from towns and suburbs in basic ways, and one of these is that cities are, by definition, full of strangers. ...

The first thing to understand it that the public peace—the sidewalk and street peace—of cities is not kept primarily by the police, necessary as police are. It is kept primarily by an intricate, almost unconscious, network of voluntary controls and standards among the people themselves, and enforced by the people themselves. In some city areas—older public housing projects and streets with very high population turnover are often conspicuous examples—the keeping of public sidewalk law and order is left almost entirely to the police and special guards. Such places are jungles. No amount of police can enforce civilization where the normal, casual enforcement of it has broken down. ...

A well-used city street is apt to be a safe street. A deserted city street is apt to be unsafe. ... A city street equipped to handle strangers, and to make a safety asset, in itself, out of the presence of strangers, as the streets of successful city neighborhoods always do, must have three main qualities:

First, there must be a clear demarcation between what is public space and what is private space. Public and private spaces cannot ooze into each other as they do typically in suburban settings or in projects.

Second, there must be eyes upon the street, eyes belonging to those we might call the natural proprietors of the street. The buildings on a street equipped to handle strangers and to insure the safety of both residents and strangers, must be oriented to the street. They cannot turn their backs or blank sides on it and leave it blind.

And third, the sidewalk must have users on it fairly continuously, both to add to the number of effective eyes on the street and to induce the people in buildings along the street to watch the sidewalks in sufficient numbers. Nobody enjoys sitting on a stoop or looking out a window at an empty street. ...

The safety of the street works best, most casually, and with least frequent taint of hostility or suspicion precisely where people are using and most enjoying the city streets voluntarily and are least conscious, normally, that they are policing.

The basic requisite for such surveillance is a substantial quantity of stores and other public places sprinkled along the sidewalks of a district; enterprises and public places that are used by evening and night must be among them especially. Stores, bars and restaurants, as the chief examples, work in several different and complex ways to abet sidewalk safety.

First, they give people—both residents and strangers—concrete reasons for using the sidewalks on which these enterprises face.

Second, they draw people along the sidewalks past places which have no attractions to public use in themselves but which become traveled and peopled as routes to somewhere else. ...

Third, storekeepers and other small businessmen are typically strong proponents of peace and order themselves; they hate broken windows and holdups; they hate having customers made nervous about safety. They are great street watchers and sidewalk guardians if present in sufficient numbers.

Fourth, the activity generated by people on errands, or people aiming for food or drink, it itself an attraction to still other people. ...

A lively street always has both its users and pure watchers. ... "

1. Why were city streets so important to Jane Jacobs?
2. According to Jacobs, what qualities made a city street safe?
3. According to Jacobs, who had "eyes on the street" and why were they valuable?
4. How does this excerpt help explain the title of Jacobs' book? What did she believe was killing the city and what would revive it?
5. Explain the major difference between Moses and Jacobs.

8-4-3. FIGHTING MOSES: LINCOLN SQUARE, 1956

Lincoln Center was the most ambitious urban redevelopment project masterminded by Robert Moses. It was the culmination of his plan to rescue Manhattan's west side from the slums while making the city attractive for the middle classes, promoting education in New York, and elevating Gotham to world-class status as a cultural center. Moses successfully accomplished all of these goals. Constructed from 1959–1966, the new complex not only housed Philharmonic Hall, the Metropolitan Opera House and two theaters, but also an elementary school, a high school, a performing arts library and museum, the Juilliard School of Music and a new campus for Fordham University.

The project had its critics. Jane Jacobs objected to the super-block concept which replaced eighteen square blocks with a large plaza defined by monumental buildings that were separated from the city by steps and walls. Moreover, 7,000 low-scale, low-rent apartments and 800 small businesses were eliminated in the community of Lincoln Square, which Moses considered a slum. Of the new 4,400 apartments completed in 1964, 4,000 would be high-rent units in six uniform 28-story buildings. The community protested, but its voice was drowned out by Moses' supporters including the press, Mayor Wagner and the Rockefellers. As Lincoln Square became history so that Lincoln Center could make history, the debate over urban planning loomed large.[19]

Source: Phil Staniolza, "Lincoln Square Residents Picket, 1956," *New York Work-Telegram and Sun.*

1. The woman with the baby carriage represented the Lincoln Square Residents Committee. Her sign read "You Don't Tear Down Homes in a Housing Shortage." How did the "Shelter before Culture" slogan reinforce her point and explain the distance between Moses and the community?

2. The third sign read "World-famous musicians, singers and artists want to save Carnegie Hall." The last sign asked "Why not build five new theaters in Times Square?" How did these signs reflect the larger context of the arts in New York City and question the entire Lincoln Center concept?

3. How would Robert Moses and Jane Jacobs each have completed the sign that started with "Humane Progress means...?"

4. In terms of size, strategy and significance, how did this protest compare with other protests discussed in this book such as any of the riots or strikes, the 1850 Hamlet case, the 1860 petition for the vote, the 1917 women's food protests, the UNIA parade or the *Ladies Home Journal* sit-in?

8-4-4. CRITICIZING MOSES: ROBERT A. CARO, BIOGRAPHER, 1974

The title of Caro's 1975 biography, *The Power Broker: Robert Moses and the Fall of New York*, accurately reflected his assessment of Moses as an abuser of power and destroyer of city life. Rather than focus on traffic as a problem of moving vehicles, Caro examined the socio-economic impact of building roads. Like Jacobs, Caro criticized Moses' road policies. However, like Moses, Caro emphasized the city as a whole, not just its individual streets or small neighborhoods. Note that Caro referred to Moses as "the Coordinator" because Moses held the job of N.Y.C. Coordinator of Construction through which he consolidated his control over state and federal monies spent on highways. In Caro's hands, the label was not complimentary.

Source: Robert A. Caro, *The Power Broker: Robert Moses and the Fall of New York* (New York: Alfred A. Knopf, 1974), 900–901.

The Coordinator's proposed highways and garages were designed to help automobile-owning families. But in 1945 two out of three residents of New York City belonged to families that did not own automobiles. Many of these families did not own them because they could not afford to. The Coordinator's subway-fare-increase proposals being advanced at that very moment in Albany would force poor New Yorkers to devote more—in many cases, more than they could afford—of their slender resources to getting around the city. The Coordinator's grabbing of the lion's share of public funds for highways and garages meant that public resources would be poured with a lavish hand into improving the transportation system used by people who could afford cars. Only a dribble of public resources would go into the transportation system used by people who could not—and who therefore rode subways and buses. While the city and state were providing car users with the most modern highways, they would be condemning subway users to continue to travel on an antiquated system utterly inadequate to the city's needs.

While highways were being extended into "suburban" areas of the city in which highways were needed—and, in fact, into areas of the city in which highways were not needed, in which the need for highways would be created by highways—subways would not be extended into areas of the city in which subways were needed. There were subway plans, too, just as there were highway plans: some, such as the proposal for a Second Avenue subway (for Manhattan's far east side and the Bronx) and the Hillside Avenue subway extension (for northeastern Queens), were advanced enough so that construction could have begun immediately if funds were provided. But the Coordinator's monopolization of public funds made subway construction impossible. By building transportation facilities for the suburbs, he was insuring that no transportation facilities would be built for the ghettos. Therefore, planners saw, in the transportation field, the portion of the public helped by the use of public resources would not be the portion of the public that needed help most.

For the well-to-do residents of the "suburban" areas of northeastern Queens, not having a subway nearby meant having to take a bus or drive a car to the end of the line in closer to Manhattan or having to drive all the way into Manhattan and back every working day. This was a hardship. But for the impoverished residents of the southeastern Bronx, not having a subway and not owning a car meant taking a bus to the subway and that meant paying a double fare each way—twice a day, five days a week—and that meant paying money that many of these residents simply could not afford. And *that* meant that often these residents walked to the subway, walked a mile or more, in the morning and home in the evening when they were tired. And it meant that on weekends, families that would have liked to take their children on trips—to a museum or a movie downtown or Coney Island or some other park (particularly to a park, since Moses had built few in "lower class" neighborhoods) or to visit a friend who lived in another neighborhood—stayed home instead. The Coordinator's policies were doing more than simply not helping these people. They were hurting them.

They were even limiting their freedom to choose a place to live. His denial of funds for the extension of mass transit lines into outlying sections of the city and into the suburbs meant that the new homes and apartments there would be occupied only by car-owning families. Whether by design or not, the ultimate effect of Moses' transportation policies would be to help keep the city's poor trapped in their slums. They were in effect policies not only of transportation but of ghettoization, policies with immense social implications. ...

---

1. According to Caro, what was the impact of Moses' car policy on mass transit?
2. According to Caro, what was the impact of Moses' car policy on the middle classes and on the working classes?
3. How were Caro's conclusions supported or refuted by Moses' own account in Document 8-4-1 above?
4. How does this excerpt help explain the title of Caro's book?

8-4-5. DEFENDING MOSES: KENNETH T. JACKSON, HISTORIAN, 2007

Caro's negative interpretation of Robert Moses has been reassessed by a variety of scholars including the urban historian, Kenneth Jackson who credited Moses for the rise of New York, not its fall. Jackson critiqued Caro's most powerful arguments by placing Moses into the larger context of urban development nationwide. Without denying Moses' limitations, Jackson emphasized his contributions.

Source: Kenneth T. Jackson, "Robert Moses and the Rise of New York," in Hillary Ballon and Kenneth T. Jackson (eds), *Robert Moses and the Modern City: The Transformation of New York* (New York: W. W. Norton, 2007), 68–71.

The Power Broker exaggerates Moses's influence on American life and makes him too much of an evil genius. For example, despite the many miles of roadway attributed to Moses, New York never became as hospitable to the motorcar as other American cities. In Caro's narrower context, we do not learn that Detroit voters chose the highway over public transportation in the 1920s or that the city of Cincinnati built a subway line in the 1930s and never opened it. Similarly, *The Power Broker* ignores Los Angeles's construction of nine hundred miles of highways and twenty-one thousand miles of paved streets in the twentieth century, both totals substantially eclipsing those of New York. The great builder was simply swimming with the tide of history. During most of his lifetime, the question was not whether to build highways or heavy rail systems; virtually everyone believed that the private car was the greatest invention since fire or the wheel. Public transportation seemed to be nothing more than a relic of the past. ...

The evidence does not support Caros's claims that racism was a defining aspect of Moses's character, or that his actions had a disproportionately negative effect upon African-Americans. When he first came to a position of great responsibility in the 1920s, prejudice based upon skin color was an established fact of the metropolitan region. In the middle of Harlem, for example, the most famous black neighborhood in all the world, restaurants, theaters and stores routinely treated African-Americans as second-class citizens. But Moses did try to place swimming pools and park facilities within reach of black families and accessible by convenient public transportation. He did not build bridges too low to accommodate buses so that black families would stay away from Jones Beach, nor did he control the water temperature so as to discourage black patronage.

Moses had contempt for the poor and rarely expressed admiration for African- Americans. But he did have a consistent and powerful commitment to the public realm: to housing, highways, parks, and great engineering projects that were open to everyone. While Moses was in power, the word "public" had not yet become a pejorative, and the power broker was willing to override private interests in order to enlarge the scope of public action. In the twenty-first century, when almost anything "public" is regarded as second-rate, and when the city cannot afford to repair—let alone construct—grand edifices, that alone is a remarkable achievement.

I wish that Robert Moses had been in charge of the subways instead of the highways. I wish that he had been as concerned about African-Americans as he was about the importance of open spaces and beaches. I wish that he had been as attentive to neighborhoods as he had been to highway interchanges and gigantic bridges. But he was what he was, and on balance he was a positive influence on the city. In fact, he made possible New York's ability to remain in the front rank of world cities into the twenty-first century. Had Moses never lived, America's greatest city might have deteriorated beyond the capabilities of anyone to return it to prosperity. As it is, the power broker built the infrastructure that secured New York's place among the greatest cities in the history of the world. ...

---

1. According to Jackson, was Moses' transportation policy as bad as Caro suggested?
2. How successfully did Jackson counter Caro's claim that Moses was racist?
3. According to Jackson, what was the significance of Moses' commitment to "the public realm"?
4. According to Jackson, how did Moses make the rise of New York possible?
5. Overall, what were the most positive and negative aspects of Moses' legacy?

SELECTED RESOURCES

Ballon, Hillary, and Kenneth Jackson (eds). *Robert Moses and the Modern City: The Transformation of New York*. New York: W. W. Norton, 2007.

Bellush, Jewel, and Stephen David (eds). *Race and Politics in New York City*. New York: Praeger, 1971.

Cannato, Vincent J. *The Ungovernable City: John Lindsay and His Struggle to Save New York*. New York: Basic Books, 2001.

Caro, Robert A. *The Power Broker: Robert Moses and the Fall of New York*. New York: Vintage Books, 1975.

Duberman, Martin. *Stonewall*. New York: Dutton, 1993.

McNickle, Chris. *To Be Mayor of New York: Ethnic Politics in the City*. New York: Columbia University Press, 1993.

Podair, Jerald E. *The Strike That Changed New York: Blacks, Whites and the Ocean Hill-Brownsville Crisis*. New Haven, CT: Yale University Press, 2002.

Schwartz, Joel. *The New York Approach: Robert Moses, Urban Liberals and the Redevelopment of the Inner City*. Columbus, OH: Ohio State University Press, 1993.

Shapiro, Fred, and James W. Sullivan. *Race Riots, New York 1964*. New York: Thomas Y. Crowell, 1964.

Tygiel, Jules. *Baseball's Great Experiment: Jackie Robinson and His Legacy*. New York: Oxford University Press, 1987.

www.chnm.gmu.edu/hardhats: 1970s riots

www. laguardiawagnerarchive.lagcc.cuny.edu: Robert F. Wagner, Jr.

CHAPTER 9

1970–1993

During the last quarter of the twentieth century, New York City confronted huge challenges with characteristic grit and energy. The 1975 fiscal crisis brought the city to its knees. Racial and ethnic strife during the 1980s and 1990s tore it apart from within. Industrial jobs declined, crime grew and grafitti spread. The South Bronx burned. Beset by chaos, conflict and confusion, New York became the symbol of the urban crisis.

At issue was the city's sense of identity. Throughout its history, New York had been proud of its political liberalism, social diversity, cultural creativity and economic prowess. Now those very strengths seemed to be weaknesses. In the 1970s people asked whether the city could survive. On September 17, 1990, *Time* magazine answered "no" with a special issue called "The Rotting of the Big Apple." It predicted the demise of the city due to rampant crime, high rents, lousy schools, pervasive filth, super rats and a frantic pace of life. Some people did flee the city, but most did not and more arrived. The city not only survived, but flourished. In the process, however, it was tested to the core.

This chapter explores those challenges. Unit 9-1 examines the fiscal crisis, which shocked the city and the nation into a major reassessment and realignment of urban priorities. Unit 9-2 deals with the image of New York as an urban jungle due to the rise of crime as well as the decline of poor neighborhoods through redlining and arson. Unit 9-3 discusses different mayoral strategies for coping with urban problems. Unit 9-4 focuses on the changes heralded by the Puerto Rican politician, Herman Badillo, and the Latino quest for influence in New York City politics.

UNIT 9-1. ECONOMICS AND THE PUBLIC INTEREST: THE FISCAL CRISIS

In 1975 New York City faced bankruptcy. It was a devastating prospect for the nation's most prominent city and the world's most important financial center. But the crisis had been building for decades. Liberal commitments to the public good generated costly labor contracts, the nation's largest urban public university plus a network of public hospitals. The city wanted to promote the public good through public services, but the sheer scale of New York made good deeds expensive.

To further complicate the situation, industries and middle-class taxpayers were leaving the city just as new groups of the aspiring poor were arriving. With federal and state aid lagging behind expenditures, the city borrowed money, floated municipal loans and hid deficits in budget tricks. When the banks refused to fund any more municipal bonds, disaster loomed. New York State set up fiscal monitors for the city and demanded retrenchment. The federal government scorn for the city's plight exposed not only the precarious political and economic situation of cities in the nation but also the negative image of New York City in the American mind.[1]

9-1-1. DECRYING DEFAULT: ABRAHAM D. BEAME, MAYOR, 1975

The mayor during the fiscal crisis was Abraham D. Beame (1906–2001), a dedicated public servant whose lifetime dream was realized by his 1974 inauguration as leader of the city he loved. Beame desperately wanted to avoid municipal default. Nonetheless, he may have contributed to it as the former budget director and city controller who helped camouflage the city's financial plight through various legitimate but deceptive accounting gimmicks. In defending himself and his city, Beame suggested that New York's financial burdens were partly the result of state and national policies, not just urban profligacy. He tried to postpone the day of reckoning and was truly pained when that day finally dawned.

Source: Speech by Mayor Abraham D. Beame, July 31, 1975, *The New York Times*, August 1, 1975.

My Fellow New Yorkers:

Today, we face the most serious economic challenge to the City's future. We are struggling to overcome a crisis of confidence in our fiscal integrity. Its roots trace back more than a decade.

The role of our cities has changed dramatically in response to national trends, heightened aspirations, and shifting policies. We have seen the demand for City services soar—outstripping our ability to pay for them with local dollars. The very national and State programs which help defray some of the cost of providing these services also *add* to their cost because they require matching local contributions.

For example, welfare and medical assistance this year will cost New York City taxpayers approximately $1 billion—a legal obligation no other municipality in the nation remotely shares. ...

To make up the difference between its modestly growing revenues and rapidly escalating demands, the City ... had resorted increasingly to borrowing for the cash required to stretch the budget. This kind of financing is questionable at best even when the economy is strong. But the economy did not remain solid. The City, in effect, gambled against a future which did not come.

Instead of economic expansion, we have deep recession.

Instead of stability, we have runaway inflation.

Instead of an enlightened political will to share national obligations more equitably, we have been told to go it alone.

That is why we must act today, and act decisively. We have exhausted the possibilities for negotiation and discussion. Now our options and time are running out. There must be financial restraint and service cutbacks. There must be fiscal reform and management resolve. Our program of austerity must be accelerated. There must be immediate steps to restore our credit. ...

There is nothing I have done in public life that has been more bitter than recommending these slashing economies that effect each and every one of us.

I recognize the problems and difficulties a wage freeze brings to the families of our workers. ... I know the hardship that a [mass transit] fare rise can cause.

I am a product of the City University system. I not only received my training, but a deep and abiding appreciation of the value of free education at City College. And now I must demand slashing economies from the university which gave me—and so many others—the opportunity for a full and more rewarding life.

My program may not make good politics, but there can be no politics as usual when the survival of the City as we know it is at stake.

My fellow New Yorkers, we are a diverse people who speak many languages and respect different traditions. But we are capable of pulling together. In times of crisis this City has shown its great strength and great heart. The demands upon us are real. We must respond with boldness, understanding and determination. I know we will not be found wanting. ...

To those who have demanded sharp evidence of reform, I say, we have cut to the bone—but we cannot and will not cut into the bone. We will sacrifice and change our lifestyle—but we will not cripple or hobble our great City.

1. According to Beame, what six factors helped create New York's fiscal crisis?
2. According to Beame, what was the city forced to do in order to address the fiscal crisis?
3. How did Beame feel personally about adopting those strategies?
4. According to Beame, what made New York City great? Did those qualities cause the fiscal crisis? Could they survive the fiscal crisis?

9-1-2. DENIGRATING NEW YORK CITY: FRANK VAN RIPER, JOURNALIST, 1975

President Gerald R. Ford did not sympathize with New York City's plight. From his perspective, New York had only itself to blame for spending more than it could afford. When Beame requested federal aid, Ford's response was so harsh that it inspired the *Daily News* headline "Ford to City: Drop Dead." However, Ford was not alone in disparaging Gotham. In fact, his perspective was widely shared and reflected America's long-term ambivalence toward cities in general, and New York City in particular. The fiscal crisis underlined the difference between rural and urban realities, conservative and liberal priorities.

Source: Frank Van Riper, "How Come They Hate Us In Omaha?" *New York Sunday News*, November 9, 1975, 10–12, 20.

Last month in Omaha, President Ford asked an audience of 1,000 Middle Americans like himself to stand up if they wanted the federal government to "bail out New York City." When the laughter died down, there was only one person on his feet. One week later, before a well-scrubbed group of Tennesseans in Knoxville, Ford asked the same question. This time out of an audience of more than 1,300, maybe a dozen rose. In both places, the lonely few who stood up for New York told Ford something he already knew: Out there, in the small towns and villages that still comprise so much of the country, New York is a city scorned. ...

"Let's face it," said [New York Conservative] Sen. James L. Buckley, "there is an anti-New York bias out there. It's inevitable, and it's reflected most vividly in Congress. For years the nation has been preached to from New York. For years, New York has done things on a large scale. New York has always seemed more adventuresome, and people on the outside have felt looked down upon because of it. Under the circumstances, it's understandable that they feel some glee when the 'king' is finally having it hard. It's not necessarily mean; it's just human nature."

Long before the current furor over its finances, New York seemed too large, too liberal, too rich, too poor, too ethnic, too everything for many members of Congress and their constituents. ... Why such a visceral feeling against the city, not only in the past but now when New York is in such grave need of friends? Perhaps, quite simply, because New York was—and to a large extent is—different from the rest of the country.

It is more crowded, for one thing. In Nebraska, where Ford conducted his bailout poll, the entire state has about 1.5 million compared to more than 8 million in New York City alone. Not only that, but unlike the population across the nation, it is still a multicolored, multi-ethnic crowd that fills the five boroughs. We've a huge black population, and a mammoth Puerto Rican one. ... There are more Jews in New York State than in all of Israel, more Irish in the city than in Dublin. And that is to say nothing of the Italians, the Greeks, the Polish, and everyone else who came over here in a wave of immigration that began more than a century ago and has never really stopped.

Still, the one thing that seems to rile New York's congressional critics most ... is the special kind of chutzpah the city seems to breathe into all of its offspring. ... "You know," said a New York congressional aide, pointing out the obvious, "One of the big things going against us is that we haven't really been good in selling our case for financial assistance. The fact is, our guys are aggressive and pushy and they piss everybody off."

Perhaps. But it's not quite the whole story. Equally important is the fact that, despite New York's undisputed role as a communications center of the nation, if not the world, the picture many Americans get of the city is often distorted. "It's a frightening place to a lot of people who never read or hear anything about New York's beauty," said Hubert Humphrey [former Democratic mayor of Minneapolis and U.S. vice-president] ... "When you thought of crime, you thought of New York, where years ago you thought of Chicago," said

Humphrey. "When you thought of new, often bizarre life styles, you thought of New York where once you thought of Hollywood or San Francisco."

One of the "bizarre life styles" most frequently jumped on by the city's critics has been that of the "welfare cheats and chiselers" who rip the city off for millions each year, all under the collective nose of muddle-headed local officials. ... [In addition,] Texas Republican Sen. John G. Tower, charged that the city is "in the grip of the trade unions" which have held it up for monstrously large pension benefits which, in turn, have pushed the city into "profligate spending beyond what its tax base or federal aid will support." Tower, it should be remembered, engineered the Lockheed bailout.

Add to these favorite themes the perennial rap at the City University's open admissions and free tuition policy, and you have a broad brush picture of a city whose liberal-leaning officials wanted nothing more than to spend their taxpayer's money and who now want to continue their spendthrift ways at the expense of taxpayers nationwide.

"I am the first to admit that there has been waste, on occasion extensive," [New York Democratic] Sen. Jacob K. Javits told the Senate Banking Committee as it opened hearings on legislation to provide the city with federal loan guarantees and other assistance. "But these evils are not the major cause of the crisis confronting New York City today. Rather, New York's problems are primarily the result of attempting to cope with enormous social problems, including welfare, unemployment and skyrocketing costs of decent housing, education, medical care and senior citizen care. They are," Javits went on, "the very same kind of problems which confront every city that attempts to grapple with human needs in our increasingly urbanized society." The only difference, he added later, is that New York is once again taking the heat for taking the lead. ...

---

1. Why was New York "a city scorned"?
2. What was the relationship between the criticisms of New York and the fiscal crisis?
3. Who best explained the widespread antipathy for New York?
4. Who offered the best defense of New York?
5. What were the similarities and/or differences between the national response to New York's 1975 fiscal crisis and the Wall Street versus Main Street response to the 2008 fiscal meltdown?

9-1-3. THE SINKING SHIP, 1975

The nation's attitude towards New York's plight was captured by the following drawing.

Source: Drawing accompanying Frank Van Riper, "How Come They Hate Us In Omaha?" *New York Sunday News*, November 9, 1975.

---

1. What stereotypes of New York City were represented by the people on the boat?
2. What stereotypes of America were represented by the people cheering the sinking of the boat?
3. Suggest at least three reasons why the artist made the New York City boat so big.
4. Who was steering the ship? Why was there no life preserver or lifeboat?
5. How could the drawing have been changed to reflect a pro-New York City perspective?
6. Explain why this drawing was both funny and sad.

9-1-4. UNMASKING THE FISCAL CRISIS: JOSHUA FREEMAN, HISTORIAN, 2000

To the historian Joshua Freeman, the fiscal crisis undermined New York City's historic commitment to the health, education and welfare of its citizens. In his opinion, the damage was not just in the details, but in the broad redirection of urban resources away from the good of the general community to the good of the business community. In other words, Freeman suggested that, although the fiscal crisis was partly about the immediate matter of balancing the books, it also was part of a long-range, multi-layered political, economic and social agenda.

Source: Joshua B. Freeman, *Working Class New York: Life and Labor Since World War II*. (New York: The New Press, 2000), 256, 258, 270–272.

For New Yorkers of a certain age, the phrase "fiscal crisis" has a very special meaning, the extended moment in the mid-1970s when the city seemed on the verge of bankruptcy and social collapse, when daily life became grueling and the civic atmosphere turned mean. As a recession settled over the country, a municipal budget squeeze became the occasion for a broad reordering of city life as bankers, financiers, and conservative ideologues made an audacious grab for power. Normally opaque class relations became shockingly visible. So did a national distaste for the city, its residents, and their way of life. Though working-class resistance slowed the counterrevolution from above, it could not stop it. Within a few years, many of the historic achievements of working-class New York were undone. ...

In the recession and the budget crisis, financial leaders saw an opportunity to undo the past, to restructure New York along lines more to their liking than those drawn by decades of liberalism and labor action. They wanted less and less costly government, fiscal probity, and the desocialization of services and protections for the working class and the poor. They also wanted humbled municipal unions that no longer would enable government workers to have superior benefits and a less intense pace of work than private-sector workers. The banks had not been able to affect such a program during the post-World War II years, a testament to the strength of labor and its allies. But as the city began sliding toward insolvency, they saw a greater need and a greater possibility of carrying out their financial and social agenda. ...

The fiscal crisis of the 1970s affected all New Yorkers, but the poor and working class were hit hardest. For one thing, they depended more on public services—schools, parks, public transportation, and neighborhood police—than the well-off who could afford private schools, health and country clubs, automobiles, and private security. For another thing, any diminishment in the quality of life, be it from higher taxes or reduced services, had greater effect on those living close to the margins than those with a cushion of ease and security.

City employees took the most severe blow. During the first three years of the crisis, the city laid off twenty-five thousand employees. ... With funding and manpower levels dramatically decreased, the level and quality of city services plummeted. The Board of Education suffered some of the worst cuts. Between 1974 and 1976 it reduced its teaching force by nearly 25 percent, while the number of students remained steady. The system-wide teacher-pupil ratio shot up, and classes of forty or more students were not unusual. With most young teachers laid off, the average age of the instructional staff soared. The staff also became much whiter; layoffs reduced the percentage of African American and Spanish-surnamed teachers from 11 to 3 percent, setting back the long effort to integrate the school system. Guidance counselors, crossing guards, sports programs, adult education, summer school, and bilingual education became luxuries, reduced or eliminated. ...

CUNY [the City University of New York] suffered even more grievous harm. The imposition of tuition, in spite of tuition assistance programs, led to a 62,000 student decline in enrollment. By 1980 the university had 50 percent fewer black and Hispanic freshmen than four years earlier. The university halted capital construction, stopped all library and laboratory acquisitions, and laid off 3,294 faculty members. ... Business leaders who once saw CUNY as a boost to the economy now saw it as an unneeded luxury, a squandering of tax money, a giveaway to the poor.

The fiscal crisis constituted a critical moment in the history of privatization, spreading the belief that the market could better serve the public than government, that government was an obstacle to social welfare rather than an aid to it, that the corporate world, if left alone, would maximize the social good. Because New York served as the standard-bearer for urban liberalism and the idea of a welfare state, the attacks on its municipal services and their decline helped pave the way for the national conservative hegemony of the 1980s and 1990s. Working-class New York led the way in both the rise and the fall of social democracy in America.

1. According to Freeman, how did the fiscal crisis lead to a counterrevolution? Against what?
2. According to Freeman, how successful was the counterrevolution?
3. According to Freeman, who won and who lost from the fiscal crisis? In what ways?
4. According to Freeman, what was the long-range significance of the fiscal crisis?

UNIT 9-2. CITY BUILDING: DESTROYING AND SAVING THE CITY

New York City's fiscal plight was paralleled by physical deterioration. The situation was so bad that many neighborhoods looked like war zones. The general sense of despair mounted as crime mushroomed, garbage piled up and graffiti covered walls and subway cars. Then in the summer of 1977, the city was horrified by a serial murderer who targeted couples parked in cars and by Blackout Riots which spurred significant looting after a power failure darkened the city. Armageddon had arrived. As in the fiscal crisis, New York seemed doomed by its own deviance.

9-2-1. ROTTING: ROGER BROWN, ARTIST, 1990

Time magazine's cover of September 17, 1990, drawn by Roger Brown, captured prevailing attitudes towards New York City during and after the crises of the 1970s. The image dramatized anxieties about the city that cut across classes and were felt by New Yorkers and non-New Yorkers alike. Everyone seemed to agree that Gotham was a forbidding cesspool.

Source: Roger Brown, "New York City," *Time*, September 17, 1990.

1. Explain the message of each of the three tiers of city life that are depicted in this drawing.
2. Explain the plight of the people in both the lower and middle tiers.
3. What positive and negative stereotypes about the city were reinforced by this drawing?
4. Explain how and why the artist revised the "I Love NY" slogan.

9-2-2. REDLINING: THE NEW YORK PUBLIC INTEREST RESEARCH GROUP, 1976

The physical and social decline of some neighborhoods, especially poor neighborhoods, was exacerbated when banks and other financial institutions decided to stop lending money to businesses and individuals in neighborhoods deemed financially risky. Because these areas were marked on maps with a red line, the policy of not granting loans or mortgages in them was called redlining. Redlining doomed a neighborhood to economic death. The process was hastened by vandals who set fires after ripping out marketable materials from abandoned buildings, or because they were hired by real estate owners seeking fire insurance money.

The whole situation was disastrous for residents and small business owners in low-income areas. As the crisis mounted, so did opposition from homeowners who wanted mortgage policies to be publicized and reviewed. However, redlining was hard to fight because it was hard to see. Rather than being a public policy, it was the result of private decisions by private companies (the banks) determined to make mortgage requirements almost impossible to meet. The discrimination was so cleverly camouflaged that it required time and painstaking research to expose it.

The New York Public Interest Research Group (NYPIRG), a non-profit organization with a civic service mission, rose to the challenge and, in 1976, published an important study of redlining. Focusing on Brooklyn with Brooklyn College students as researchers, NYPIRG demonstrated that, although Brooklyn banks were happy to take Brooklyn residents' money, they granted very few Brooklyn mortgages and most of those were in white, higher-income neighborhoods like Bensonhurst. NYPIRG's hard evidence proved that the banks' policy was, as the title of their study stated, to *Take the Money and Run!* The report aroused such public outrage that it led to laws banning redlining as discriminatory.

Source: The New York Public Interest Research Group, *Take the Money and Run! Redlining in Brooklyn* (New York: The New York Public Interest Research Group, 1976), 85–85.

Bank	% of all mortgages issued	% of total assets	Average dollar value of mortgages issued
Greenpoint Savings Bank	3.58	2.87	34,509
Dime Savings Bank	0.25	0.14	29,048
Metropolitan Savings Bank	0.36	0.28	43,278
Williamsburgh Savings Bank	0.15	0.01	28,553
Brooklyn Savings Bank	0.25	0.17	36,869
East New York Savings Bank	0.28	0.21	38,886
Greater New York Savings Bank	0.10	0.01	26,105

Dollar value of mortgages issued on Brooklyn properties during 1975 as percentage of total value of mortgages reported at close of the 1975 fiscal year (including conventional, VA, FNHA, GNMA, and FHA mortgages) and as a percentage of total assets at close of the 1975 fiscal year.

1. Based on the percent of mortgages and the percent of total bank assets, how willing were the banks to grant mortgages to Brooklyn residents in 1975?
2. If the average value of houses in Brooklyn in 1975 was $25,400, what is significant about the average dollar value of the mortgages granted by the seven banks in Brooklyn in 1975? What does it reveal about the type of neighborhood in which the mortgages were granted?
3. Use the material in all three columns of this chart to explain in what ways the banks agreed and disagreed about granting Brooklyn mortgages in 1975.
4. Based on the introduction to and information in this chart, explain why redlining was a problem and for whom.
5. What is the relationship between the controversies over redlining and Stuyvesant Town? (see Unit 7-3) How do those controversies also relate to the map in Document 9-3-4 below?

9-2-3. BURNING: JILL JONNES, JOURNALIST, 2002

Redlining took a particularly terrible toll on the South Bronx where the situation was compounded by an epidemic of arson. At one point there were over 12,000 fires a year resulting in the ruin of over 5,000 apartment buildings displacing at least 100,000 families. The abandoned buildings then became a haven for criminals, drug dealers and drug users. When President Jimmy Carter visited Charlotte Street in 1977, the South Bronx became a national symbol of the urban crisis. Yet, as journalist Jill Jonnes reported, the community refused to die.[2]

Source: Jill Jonnes, *South Bronx Rising: The Rise, Fall and Resurrection of an American City.* (New York: Fordham University Press, 2002), 230–233, 235, 298–300.

Although the Charlotte Street neighborhood was experiencing more fires, there was no official reaction except to increase the number of firemen in the firehouse. All through the 1960s and early 1970s, there was no press coverage, and there were no denunciations by Model Cities officials or expressions of concern by politicians. As the Bronx began to burn, no one said anything. ...

As the arson increased, firemen began to categorize it. There was arson commissioned by landlords out for their insurance. (A Lloyd's of London syndicate was to lose $45 million on fire insurance written in the South Bronx.) Arson was set by welfare recipients who wanted out of their apartments and into something better (preferably public housing), but knew they could only do so if they got onto a priority list. Large signs in the welfare centers stated very clearly in Spanish and English, "The only way to get housing priority is if you are burned out by a fire." The welfare department also paid out two or three thousand dollars to burned-out families for their destroyed goods. Many fires were deliberately set by junkies—and by that new breed of professional, the strippers of buildings, who wanted to clear a building so they could ransack the valuable copper and brass pipes, fixtures and hardware. A roaring fire in an already-vacant building made their job much easier. Fires were set by firebugs who enjoyed a good blaze and by kids out for kicks. And some were set by those who got their revenge with fire, jilted lovers returning with a can of gasoline and a match to annihilate entire buildings and teach one person a lesson.

Fire and arson became a way of life around Charlotte Street, another variable to be reckoned in. One mother who lived near Engine Company 82 says, "The firehouse was right down the block, and if my kids had any lullaby to go to sleep, it was the fire engines." One fifth-grade teacher at PS 61 remembers her students coming into class smelling like smoke. Sometimes they told her, "We have our suitcases packed. This week is the fire." (The word had been thoughtfully sent around beforehand, so people could escape with little loss of life or property.) When students said this, the teacher knew those kids would indeed soon disappear from class.

The firemen could never quite get over the scenes they saw again and again: a building consumed by flames and the families to the side, fully dressed and with suitcases and cartons neatly arranged on the sidewalk. Not all arsonists were that thoughtful, however, and the firemen saw other, terrible scenes as the fires burned away the neighborhood. Once they found three boys, paid to burn down the building, trapped in a fire of their own making. Said one man, shaking his head, "One kid was caught in it and he was a crispy critter when we got to him. The other two kids were badly burnt." In that rare instance, the landlord was prosecuted and convicted. Even the local antipoverty agency, the neighborhood's sole governmental presence, was torched. ...

The fires, the false alarms, the drugs, the apathy, and the violence waiting to erupt were constant, day in, day out. The firemen, like the cops, were called upon to staunch the endless flow of disasters besetting this disintegrating world. ...

Roger Starr, the housing and urban expert, was administrator of the City's housing department. On January 14, 1976, he gave a speech to the real estate industry lodge of the B'nai B'rith, where he astounded his audience by suggesting that the City should "accelerate the drainage" of the worst parts of the South Bronx by what he called "planned shrinkage," or the deliberate emptying out of largely destroyed neighborhoods. Starr said the City, deep in the throes of a financial crunch, should consider closing subway stations, police and fire houses, and hospitals and schools as a means of saving money and consolidating services. ...

The truth was that for many years City officials had responded to the precipitous collapse of neighborhoods like the South Bronx by talking about programs and big bucks that would turn things around. The Nixon White House had turned off the federal spigot, and now New York itself was broke. There could be no more consoling talk about programs. Everyone knew there was barely enough money to pay the cops or the garbage men. Those who believed the government could save the South Bronx if only it tried began to realize that the public officials had no idea what to do, and no money to do it with.

As the City government faltered, grassroots groups sprouted. Since no one had yet devised an antidote for crumbling neighborhoods, anyone crazy enough even to try reviving a building or a block commanded the grudging respect accorded doomed idealists. Although the neighborhoods around

Charlotte Street were almost completely cleared out by 1976, a few unusual people began to contemplate this vast urban wasteland in a new light, as a land of opportunity. They reconnoitered the territory and devised their own individual notions of what could be made out of the South Bronx."

---

1. Why were so many different people motivated to ignite the South Bronx?
2. What were the most tragic tolls of the arson epidemic?
3. Who would have gained and who would have lost from "planned shrinkage"?
4. Based on this account, how many factors spelled doom for the South Bronx? How many factors offered hope? What were the odds for saving the South Bronx in the 1970s?

9-2-4. RECLAIMING: BANANA KELLY, 1979

Faced with disaster, some ordinary people took matters into their own hands and organized to rebuild their neighborhoods. Banana Kelly was one of those groups. After successfully completing its first 21 units of affordable housing, Banana Kelly incorporated itself so that it could rehabilitate and manage thousands more units. In addition, it expanded its mission to provide a shelter for homeless youth, housing-related job-training programs and a small high school. Banana Kelly is still a community-run advocacy organization and is part of a strong network of self-help groups in the South Bronx.

Source: Robert Jensen and Cathy A. Alexander, "Resurrection: The People Are Doing It Themselves," in Robert Jensen (ed.), *Devastation/Resurrection: The South Bronx* (New York: The Bronx Museum of the Arts, 1979), 84–85.

Banana Kelly is named after a curving block-long section of Kelly Street— just south of 163rd Street—which has been referred to as "the banana" since the early twentieth century. "I live at the banana" might have been the proud proclamation of the 1920s residents of these once elegant duplex row houses. In August 1977 a group of residents on this street banded together and refused to move when the city wanted to demolish the buildings in which some of them lived. Their motto became: "Don't move, improve."

The group entered 936, 940 and 944 Kelly Street and gutted their interiors with eventual rehabilitation in mind. They had no money of their own and no funding from others. They sold the pipes and appliances from the building to raise some cash. The landlord, who was getting his building cleaned free of charge, brought the group five containers for refuse. Eventually, the Self-help Neighborhood Awards Program—SNAP Award for short—provided $900 for additional refuse bins. (SNAP Awards are start-up grants, and this was the largest award ever given.) On this foundation, Banana Kelly began.

In the spring of 1978 it sponsored a series of block parties and dances to unite the neighborhood and focus attention on its work. Banana Kelly's first substantial funding came through a Youth Conservation Community Improvement Program grant (a city-funded program) that permitted the organization to employ twenty-six youths, age sixteen to nineteen, to continue interior demolition of the three buildings. Meanwhile, with the aid of the

Open Space Task Force and the Pratt Institute Center for Community and Environmental Development, a garden was created. ...

Banana Kelly was not launched with an impressive board of directors or with large grants. It had energy and sweat to see tasks through until others recognized their potential. Today, Banana Kelly has funding under the federal Comprehensive Employment Training Act (CETA) program to hire fifty-six people for training and employment in construction; fifteen of the participants will learn to install a solar-heated hot water system and to weatherize buildings. Three crew chiefs, two youth supervisors and one construction supervisor oversee the work.

Banana Kelly has received a mortgage commitment of $576,000 from Community Development Block Grant funds to complete the work on 936, 940 and 944 Kelly Street. The Urban Homesteading Assistance Board (UHAB) helps sweat equity groups to obtain these funds from the city's Department of Housing Preservation and Development (HPD). ...

The renovation of Banana Kelly's original three buildings is nearing completion, and occupancy of their twenty-one units is scheduled for spring 1980. Twelve families that had moved from the area will return to cooperative apartments, for which they "sweated," to share in the neighborhood's renaissance. The garden has flourished for three years. Planning has begun on the sweat equity rehabilitation of three additional buildings.

---

1. What was significant about the way in which Banana Kelly got started and funded?
2. How was "sweat equity" a clever (albeit difficult) response to redlining?
3. How did "sweat equity" reflect the importance of community and civic activism?
4. How could the Banana Kelly example be used to support or criticize the concept of positive government?
5. Would Robert Moses and Jane Jacobs have supported Banana Kelly? (See Unit 8-4.)
6. Assume that you could travel back in time to study the Five Points, Weeksville, the Lower East Side, Harlem, Chinatown and the South Bronx. Whom would you want to interview? What key questions would you ask? What kind of answers would you expect to get? What conclusions could you draw about how New Yorkers handle conflict? (See Units 4-2, 4-4, 5-3, 7-1, and 7-2.)

9-2-5. SQUEEZING: THE NEW YORK PUBLIC INTEREST RESEARCH GROUP, 1976

The drawing on the facing page captures the realities of redlining.

Source: Cover of *Take the Money and Run! Redlining in Brooklyn* (New York: The New York Public Interest Research Group, 1976).

1. Who is squeezing?
2. Who is being squeezed?
3. How could this graphic be reinterpreted by different people covered in this book such as Adrien van der Donck, John Jacob Astor, Bishop John Hughes, Thomas Nast, Jay Gould, Rose Schneiderman, Emma Goldman, Fiorello La Guardia, W. E. B. Du Bois, Adam Clayton Powell Jr,, Robert Moses, Jane Jacobs, Abraham Beame or Herman Badillo?

UNIT 9-3. POLITICS AND THE PUBLIC INTEREST: THE UNGOVERNABLE CITY

Considering eight million inhabitants and three million daily commuters, a diversity of cultures spread across five boroughs in 59 different neighborhoods, plus many competing economic and political interests, it was a miracle that New York City worked at all. It was even more surprising that anyone wanted to lead it. Yet, there was never a shortage of people drawn to the second hardest job in America. The mayor's task was always great, but it was particularly difficult in the period of intense racial and ethnic strife between 1970 and 1993.

In *Governing New York City: Politics in the Metropolis* (1960), Wallace S. Sayre and Herbert Kaufman optimistically concluded that the complexity of New York City's politics was its strength. In comparison to a political system dominated by a uniform, uncontested and, therefore, undemocratic ruling elite, they thought that New York's diversity promoted "bargaining and accommodation among participants." Always in flux, New York's government functioned well and remained responsive precisely because it had to serve so many different groups.[3] The period between 1970 and 1993 tested that hypothesis.

9-3-1. REACHING OUT: JOHN V. LINDSAY, MAYOR, 1969

Keeping the city calm and functioning was a daunting challenge for a young, handsome, Yale-educated former congressman named John V. Lindsay (1921–2000). From the very start of his two terms in office (1966–1973), he confronted strikes, riots and protests concerning mass transit, education, housing, prisons, women's rights, gay rights, race relations and the Vietnam War. He may have understood the problems, but he never conquered them. Therefore, in contrast to Sayre and Kaufman, the historian Vincent Cannato concluded that, under Lindsay, New York was ungovernable. In the face of urban poverty, social pathology and racial conflict, wrote Cannato, Lindsay was too much talk and too little action. He symbolized the hollowness of liberalism.[4] However, Lindsay believed that, with enlightened policies and a personal approach, the city could be governed and that his liberal values would prevail.

Source: John V. Lindsay, *The City* (New York: W. W. Norton, 1970), 58–61, 86, 88–89, 104.

The mayor of New York presides over a city of 8 million people. During the working hours that population swells by several million people and tens of thousands of cars as the suburbanites flock to the core of Manhattan to work and shop and play. He presides over a city budget soon to go over $7 billion—greater than the budget of any single state. His city builds almost $2 billion a year in facilities. It employs 350,000 people. It teaches a million elementary and secondary school pupils every day. It puts 32,000 policemen on its streets each day to help protect safety. It tows away 100,000 illegally parked cars a year from midtown Manhattan alone, and hauls away 60,000 more cars that have simply been abandoned by their owners. It runs a court system that rivals that of any state.

The numbers are staggering. Each of them, in one way or another, touches my life every day. Each of them defines a small part of the job that a mayor of New York has; each of them poses new demands on an overtaxed, undernourished city treasury; each of them demands more productivity from a governmental structure that can barely keep pace with outmoded definitions of its job.

For beyond these numbers are the cold, hard facts of city life. With such an enormous number of people, with such a disparate collection of facilities, a statistically small fraction can mean tremendous burdens. … In New York, in other words, every problem … [is] large. And in cases where the problems are relatively large—such as in the achievement levels of city school children or the number of people on welfare—you have a crisis of major proportions on your hands. Then, too, you begin to recognize what may be the prime fact of municipal life—the essential interdependence of problems and solutions. ...

Take traffic congestion. For years, people have been urging New York to shut down midtown Manhattan to private automobiles. ... But you cannot shut Manhattan to cars unless you are sure you are providing alternative transportation. That means mass transit. ... Further, before you ban cars from midtown, you must listen to the arguments of the handicapped, United Nations diplomats and foreign consuls, garage operators, commuting businessmen, department store owners, merchants of every variety, the Automobile Association of America, and other powerful interests. ... Thus the act of banning autos from midtown Manhattan is far from a unitary act of planning. It raises a wide range of other political, economic and planning questions that are difficult to answer. ...

We realized when we came into office that the city government was in urgent need of basic structural reorganization. But this takes time. You may plant new roots, or redesign ways of producing buildings, but the citizenry won't be convinced that City Hall has changed, that it is becoming more responsive to legitimate demands of citizens for better municipal services, unless something more immediate, more dramatic occurs. Roots take time to grow; buildings take years to build. For people to regain hope, something visible is needed, now ...

It seemed to me critical, then, that the mayor, having promised a basically new attitude in city government, demonstrate by a personal act of commitment that he meant what he said and that his concern would not cease after the election. ... And thus the personal participation in the city came to be the start of the most urgent, basic effort the city has ever made to structure contact between citizen and government. Many have read far too much into these visits to ghetto areas. They have been credited with single-handedly stopping the riots, which is not true, and they have also been regarded as symbolically "buying off" black communities by promising to be permissive with law breakers and criminals, which is not true either.

I think these visits did, however, offer some sign that the city government cared. They did suggest that the administration did not intend to exclude any group from the business of the city. And they did force all of us to listen to voices of angry discontent in every neighborhood. They did make us begin looking toward new ways of linking government and citizen. And to the extent that we began moving to break down the business-as-usual approach to running the city, I think that what we did was important and necessary. ...

In September 1967, the city created the Urban Action Task Force on a year-round basis. And a few months later the task forces began to work in middle-income communities as well as in the ghettos. These communities— with serious problems of their own—had seen in ghetto neighborhoods a new source of community organization and direct access to the city, and they began to complain that city resources were being diverted from their neighborhoods to those in which the task forces were operating. It was a false assumption, but it did indicate the extent to which the task forces— direct contact between the neighborhoods and the city—had achieved success. ...

It can be said, then, that this whole program grew out of an initial decision to become a visible, accessible mayor whose administration was at work in the neighborhoods of New York. ... "

---

1. How perceptive was Lindsay's analysis of New York City's problems and the challenge of governing?
2. How practical were Lindsay's solutions to New York City's problems?
3. Was Lindsay a realist or an idealist?
4. Explain how Lindsay's approach supported the ideas of Sayre and Kaufman and/or of Cannato.

9-3-2. GOVERNING: EDWARD I. KOCH, MAYOR, 1990

Edward I. Koch (1924–), a graduate of City College and New York University Law School, entered New York City politics through the reform wing of the Democratic Party. In 1963, Koch defeated Carmine De Sapio, the last Tammany boss, in an election for Greenwich Village district leader. Koch then served as a city councilman for two years, a congressman for ten years and mayor for twelve years (1978–1989). Associated with liberal politics in the 1960s, Koch moderated his views in the 1970s and redefined himself as a "liberal with sanity."[5]

Koch's long public career was shaped by his personality. Witty, exuberant and outspoken, Koch often became the issue himself—a situation that he seemed to enjoy, but that sometimes backfired. That was especially true in the area of race relations when Koch antagonized African Americans by closing a hospital in Harlem and by criticizing marchers protesting the deaths of two African American young men in the white neighborhoods of Howard Beach, Queens in 1986 and Bensonhurst, Brooklyn in 1989.

The Reverend Al Sharpton (1954–) led several protest marches on "Days of Outrage" after the deaths at Howard Beach and Bensonhurst. Fearing that Koch would try "to quiet things down, chill them out, make it look good, and then let it drift away," Sharpton kept media attention on the incidents. The larger the protests were, the more controversy they aroused and the more they made the city ungovernable. Sharpton defended marching as an essential grassroots political strategy "because we could not live in a city where blacks were barred from traveling through or spending time in certain neighborhoods."[6]

Of course, Koch understood that the marches challenged his leadership. Moreover, he deplored the disorder and the tension that Sharpton created. In response, Koch spoke out at the time and published several books later to set the record straight.

Source: Edward I Koch, *All the Best: Letters from a Feisty Mayor* (New York: Simon & Schuster, 1990), 104, 231–232, 245–246.

ON GOVERNING: I've also come to realize that not every issue or problem is best addressed by glum expressions, somber tones, and predictions of gloom. If people think you think a problem is impossible to solve, they'll not want to waste their time trying to help. Will they?

On the other hand, if people have a little fun, relax a bit, and notice that you think a problem you've presented to them can be solved, they'll be much more ready to help. Enthusiasm, as my mother and probably your mother used to say, is contagious.

Above all else, that's what New York City needs. People enthusiastically helping people to help people. As a city, we've had good times and bad times, solved big problems and small ones. When all is said and done, however, in getting the job done we haven't been averse to having fun.

That's what makes New York exciting and what makes New York hum.

ON HOWARD BEACH: What happened at Howard Beach will scar the memory of every New Yorker for years to come. But we should not indict an entire community or an entire city because of the bestial and brutal actions of a few of its residents. "I personally believe it would be wrong to hold up Howard Beach and its citizenry as illustrative of racism," I told the press. ... "You could find punks in every part of this town. Every white community, every black community, every Hispanic community has punks in it. To hold up a particular area as racist because of the actions of a few punks, in my judgment, is unfair.

ON BENSONHURST: In the days that followed the murder of Yusef Hawkins, a number of militant black activists called for a protest march through Bensonhurst. Undoubtedly, many of those who joined the march did so out of anger as well as sorrow over the death. But others intended to exploit the killing and to use it to shame an entire community for the wrongful deeds of a few of its members. When I heard of the plans for the march, I was certain it would exacerbate an already tense situation.

The television pictures shown the Sunday evening of the march confirmed my worst fears. As the thirty marchers, almost all of them black, walked through Bensonhurst, crowds of neighborhood residents lined the sidewalks, separated from the protestors by a thin line of police officers. "Niggers go home!" was yelled again and again and again. Teenagers held water-melons over their heads as a symbolic insult to the marchers. It was so vile, so awful.

The next morning, a Monday, at City Hall, reporters asked if I had seen the TV reports and what I thought. "I believe the people who engaged in taunting are doing the city a great disservice when they engage in vile epithets or signage," I replied. "Those people have to be condemned. Communities ought not to be condemned. You cannot brand a community that way."

"While you have a right to march," I continued, "if you are interested in quieting the passion, then you are not quieting the passion by marching into Bensonhurst. There is nothing wrong or illegal about a protest march. The question is whether you want to be helpful to reduce the tensions or do you want to escalate the tensions? At this particular moment, if you want to lower the passions the thing to do is to find the people who committed the vile acts, make sure that their trials are expeditious, speedy, and that when and if the evidence is there, and they're convicted, they go to jail for a long period of time.

1. What was Koch's general approach to governing and making the city more governable?
2. Why did Koch think that marching made the city less governable?
3. How effectively did Koch answer Sharpton?
4. Explain whether or not these excerpts support Koch's claim to be a "liberal with sanity."
5. In what ways was Koch an idealist or a realist?

9-3-3. REASONING: DAVID N. DINKINS, MAYOR, 1992

David N. Dinkins (1927–) became Gotham's first African American mayor in 1990. A graduate of Howard University and a moderate Democrat, Dinkins promised racial and ethnic peace after twelve years of Koch's polarizing personality. Instead, his mayoralty was haunted by conflicts between Koreans and African Americans in Flatbush, Jews and African Americans in Crown Heights, the police and Dominicans in Washington Heights. Sincere as he was, Dinkins' mild manner could not tame the passions of the times. In one of his strongest statements, Dinkins confronted the racial and ethnic implications of the Crown Heights riots, which erupted in 1991 after a Jewish driver struck and killed a West Indian boy. In the subsequent melee, an African American youth stabbed a Jewish man who later died. The three-day riot motivated Dinkins to call for "Reason, Respect and Reconciliation in New York City."

Source: David N. Dinkins, "Reason, Respect and Reconciliation in New York City," *The New York Amsterdam News*, November 28, 1992.

Those who would seek to split our city apart by race or religion or sexual orientation are delighted to suggest that we New Yorkers do not have the will or the way to continue to live side by side in peace—that groups in conflict will never recognize or embrace their shared history of persecution and enslavement.

That in a city peopled by immigrants from every world culture and creed, there can only be chaos.

I will not accept that poisonous philosophy. ...

A few have suggested that someone made a political decision to deprive the people of Crown Heights of police protection. That charge is false and irresponsible and has been so firmly refuted by the police commissioner.

By their own accounts, though, the police department did make tactical errors in judgment and deployment of police officers in the early hours of the disturbance, which may have delayed a return to normalcy.

I know and I accept that when a mistake is made that it is the mayor who is called to account ... I'm proud to be accountable because the buck does stop here at this desk. That's why there are more cops on the beat. That's why crime is down across the board for the first time in almost 40 years.

I'm proud to say that I have never nor will I ever tolerate or sanction or allow disorder or lawlessness by any group toward any other. By the same token, I cannot allow a quiet riot of words and epithets to poison our children's minds. ...

Unlike some before me, I will never use code words and subliminal messages to create mistrust between groups.

I have never nor will I ever play favorites or pit one group against another for political advantage. In pandering, in playing favorites, in pitting group against group we only sow the seeds of our city's disunion. ...

In a city which prides itself on its ability to get along, too many groups come too close to upsetting the delicate balance by talking first and thinking later, by shouting without listening and by providing answers before asking the questions.

New Yorkers do not want or need this.

The luxury of hate is paid for in installments of fear and persecution and violence. We must never forget that no crime is more odious than the hate crime. ...

Never again should a life in this city be extinguished because of race or religion or sexual orientation. We must pray and work so that it will not occur. ...

Over the next few weeks, I will be implementing a dramatic government action plan to increase the peace. The plan includes: ... the creation of the first-ever curriculum against hate and bias ... the establishment of a program pairing religious institutions, community organizations and schools to promote the free exchange of culture and ideas. ... We will double the Stop the Violence Fund ... [and] the peace volunteer corps, the community service organization I created. These volunteers are trained in conflict resolution and cultural differences and proved themselves to be effective in Washington Heights last summer.

If we trust in the truth and in each other, then the cement that binds our gorgeous mosaic will remain seamless and strong.

---

1. How did Dinkin's envision the city and his role as mayor?
2. How did Dinkins plan to solve the problems of the city?
3. In what ways was Dinkins an idealist and/or a realist?
4. How do the documents by Lindsay, Koch and Dinkins suggest that New York City was and/or was not governable between 1970 and 1993?
5. Which mayor's leadership style and strategies seemed best suited to address the racial and ethnic conflicts of the time?

9-3-4. MAPPING SEGREGATION: NEW YORK CITY DEPARTMENT OF CITY PLANNING, 1987

The conflicts of Howard Beach, Bensonhurst and Crown Heights raised questions about urban neighborhoods. As subdivisions of the city, neighborhoods acquired distinct identities based on class, race, ethnicity or function. By breaking down the impersonal metropolis into personal, small-scale units, they balanced the need for community with the anonymity of the city. According to the sociologist Herbert Gans, the prevalence of the neighborhood proved that city dwellers were just "urban villagers."[7]

Whereas neighborhoods could provide a positive sense of place and identity among its residents, they could also breed hostility towards non-residents, as happened in Howard Beach and Bensonhurst. Moreover, turf wars could erupt between different groups within a neighborhood, as happened in Crown Heights or East Harlem (see Document 8-1-2). These incidents undermined New York's self image as a haven for "practical tolerance." They became particularly volatile when complicated by race. In fact, one cause of these conflicts may have been the resurgence of residential segregation after the 1960s.

Perhaps residential segregation was a result of the white backlash against the civil rights movement or perhaps it was just a continuation of historic racial tensions. Nonetheless, the fact remains that black renters and homeowners, including those with substantial incomes, seem to have been steered away from white neighborhoods during the 1960s and 1970s. In addition, there was a flight of white homeowners away from neighborhoods that blacks were able to enter. As always, isolation reinforced prejudice and opened the door to conflict. Consequently the following map, which was originally issued in 1987 using the 1980 census, provides an important backdrop for understanding the challenge to leadership posed by the conflicts in Howard Beach, Bensonhurst and Crown Heights. [8]

Source: "Patterns of Segregation: Percentage of nonhispanic whites living in each section of New York City, according to the 1980 census," New York Department of City Planning.

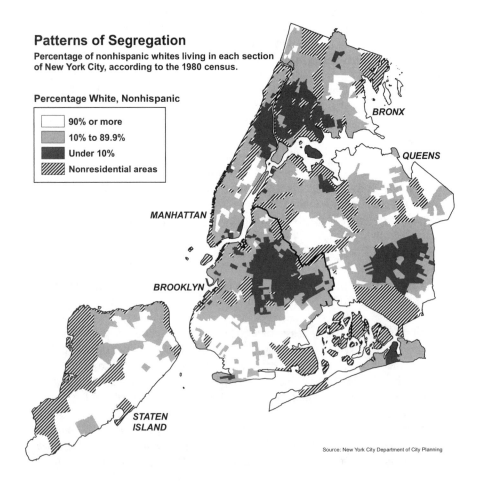

Patterns of Segregation

Percentage of nonhispanic whites living in each section of New York City, according to the 1980 census.

Percentage White, Nonhispanic

- 90% or more
- 10% to 89.9%
- Under 10%
- Nonresidential areas

BRONX

QUEENS

MANHATTAN

BROOKLYN

STATEN ISLAND

Source: New York City Department of City Planning

1. To what degree did this map suggest that New York City in 1980 was a unified whole or a compilation of "urban villages"? Was it one city or two or three?
2. How would focusing on the grey areas in the map affect your answer to question 1?
3. How does this map help explain the comments of Lindsay, Sharpton, Koch and Dinkins on the subjects of racial tension and neighborhood?
4. Explain the connection between this map and redlining (see 9-2 above).
5. Based on this map, was New York City ungovernable in 1980?

UNIT 9-4. BREAKING BARRIERS: HERMAN BADILLO, PUBLIC SERVANT

Herman Badillo's life story could have been written by Horatio Alger (see Unit 5-3): impoverished orphan works hard, gets education, succeeds professionally, becomes influential. It was a remarkable trajectory for anyone, but even more so for a Puerto Rican in an era when minorities were excluded from the national power structure. Indeed, Badillo's biography is a catalogue of firsts—first Puerto-Rican member of a prestigious New York City law firm, first Puerto-Rican commissioner in New York City government, first Puerto-Rican borough president, first Puerto-Rican congressman, first Puerto-Rican candidate for mayor, first Puerto-Rican deputy mayor, first Puerto-Rican chairman of the Board of Trustees of the City University of New York. He defied, and still defies, limits.

In fact, defiance could be Badillo's middle name. Born in 1929 in Caguas, Puerto Rico, Badillo faced hardship when, at age five, his parents and grandmother died from tuberculosis. For the next six years, he lived with relatives and ate mainly rice. Although his cousins begged in the streets, Badillo refused to join them. "I would rather starve," he explained. "I was stubborn even then." Instead, at age seven he got a job cleaning floors in a theater in order to earn enough money to support his meager diet. Four years later, at age 11, he migrated to New York City to live with an aunt whose own struggles forced her to shuttle Badillo between relatives in New York, Chicago and Burbank, California. Everywhere he went, he worked—selling newspapers, washing dishes, mowing lawns. During his two years in California, Badillo enrolled himself in junior high school, taught himself English and became class president.[9]

Back in New York City again, he completed junior high school, studied airplane mechanics in high school and worked as a short-order cook. He also wrote for the student newspaper where he met another boy (like Frank in *Ragged Dick*), who informed him that the vocational curriculum was an inferior curriculum "for blacks and Puerto Ricans." The boy suggested that Badillo was smart enough to be in the academic curriculum after which he could attend college in New York City for free.

This revelation changed Badillo's life. At a time when there were almost no minorities in the municipal colleges, Badillo graduated first in his high school class and met the stiff entrance requirements for what was then the Baruch School of the City College of

New York (CCNY). Studying business and accounting, he graduated magna cum laude and passed the difficult test to become a certified public accountant. While working as an accountant during the day, Badillo attended Brooklyn Law School at night to earn his second professional degree. It was a stunning accomplishment.[10]

Badillo's next education came in New York's Puerto Rican community where, combining degrees, he worked as a tax lawyer and often helped poor Spanish-speaking clients for free. The more cases he handled, the more he saw the larger context of the problems his clients faced. Politics beckoned. From the start, Badillo was a maverick. In 1960, he challenged the Italian-dominated East Harlem Democratic party by registering Puerto Ricans and blacks to vote for John F. Kennedy. When the regulars tried to thwart his efforts by closing registration places early, Badillo filed a lawsuit with the Board of Elections and won. He was already a man to be reckoned with.[11]

Mayor Robert Wagner Jr. recognized that fact and, in 1962, named Badillo commissioner of housing relocation, making him the first Puerto Rican to hold such a high appointive office. In 1965, he became Bronx borough president, making him the first Puerto Rican to hold such a high elective office and a hero in the Puerto Rican community. The future seemed bright.[12]

In 1969, Badillo sought the Democratic mayoral nomination in a crowded field of candidates. *The New York Times* endorsed him and observed that, as a light-skinned Puerto Rican of the Protestant faith with Spanish and Italian heritage plus a Jewish wife, Badillo was "the most extraordinary ethnic mix since the late Fiorello La Guardia" (see Unit 7-4). Badillo campaigned for better health care and schools in minority neighborhoods. At times he called his opponents "stupid" for making unrealistic promises and chastised white middle-class audiences for ignoring the poor. On the one hand, wrote the journalist Jack Newfield, these kinds of comments may have reflected Badillo's "pride, anger and independence." On the other hand, Newfield warned that they could "easily be misunderstood as rigidity and arrogance."[13]

The Democratic primary vote was disappointing. City controller, Mario Procaccino won with only a third of the votes, but more than any other candidate. The rest of the votes were split between Badillo, a comeback attempt by former Mayor Wagner, and an irreverent campaign by the writers Norman Mailer and Jimmy Breslin who proposed that New York City become the 51st State. To this day, Badillo asserts that the 42,000 votes for Mailer and Breslin cost him the nomination and the chance to beat Lindsay. "I would have been mayor, absolutely," he declared in 2001.[14]

Declining to run for a second term as borough president, Badillo joined a prestigious downtown law firm, the first Puerto Rican to do so. His next goal was to become the nation's first Puerto-Rican Congressman. His timing was perfect. In the wake of several divisive racial conflicts in the 1960s, many New Yorkers were looking for a moderate minority leader to heal the wounds. Badillo projected himself as an ethnic broker between Puerto Ricans, blacks and whites. As he explained, "The sad reality is that there is very little understanding or communication among these groups. The Bronx, as well as New York City, is a melting pot only when looked at from an airplane. On the ground, it is more of a boiling pot."[15]

Badillo served in Congress from 1970 through 1977. Annoyed by being shunted to an agriculture committee, he got reassigned to the education and labor committee, which better reflected his district's needs. From there he promoted funding for bilingual education. Back in the South Bronx, the City University of New York (CUNY) created

Eugenio Mario de Hostos Community College, an innovative bilingual institution that Badillo championed in the 1970s, but excoriated in the 1990s.[16]

Badillo was part of a small group of New York State leaders asked to negotiate a truce during the four-day uprising at Attica prison in 1971. The prisoners' demands for better living conditions were rejected by Governor Nelson Rockefeller whose state troopers ended the stand-off by killing 34 prisoners and 9 hostages. In response, Badillo advocated a complete reassessment of America's prison system with a shift from punishment to rehabilitation. He criticized "our tendency to discard human beings like beer cans" and insisted that prisoners be granted basic human and civil rights. His liberal credentials seemed solid.[17]

In 1973, while still in Congress, Badillo sought the Democratic mayoral nomination. When he was endorsed by neither the reform nor the regular Democrats, he blasted both as racist. The historian Chris McNickle suggested that Badillo "appeared so certain of himself that many delegates found his bearing arrogant." Nonetheless, he was praised by the *New York Times* and the *New York Post*, doing well enough in the primary to force a run-off with city controller, Abraham D. Beame. Badillo campaigned hard, but confronted opposition within the party and a series of damaging ads targeted to the white backlash. He didn't help his cause when, in a televised debate, the 6' 1" Badillo called the 5' 2" Beame "a vicious little man." Beame carried 61 per cent of the votes in the Democratic primary run-off and won the general election.[18]

Badillo ran for mayor again in 1977. When he got only 11 percent of the vote in a hotly contested Democratic Party primary, he backed Ed Koch. In 1981, Badillo considered another candidacy, but realized that Koch was too popular to defeat. In 1985, he floated his candidacy through a minority coalition that fell apart when black politicians, wary of Badillo's independence, backed someone else. After five tries, Badillo was becoming the perennial candidate and his base of support was shrinking, particularly as other politicians emerged from the Puerto-Rican community. The more he ran, the less he won; but he was far from finished.[19]

Frustrated in Congress and eager to build a base beyond the Latino community, Badillo resigned his seat, a move that the journalist Jack Newfield considered a "titanic blunder." Badillo then joined the new Koch administration as a deputy mayor charged with rebuilding the South Bronx. Badillo supported a middle-class housing plan, but when the plan was abandoned in 1979 as too costly, he was furious and resigned. Although Badillo blamed Koch for the debacle, Koch blamed Badillo for not lining up critical support. "That is Herman's problem," wrote Koch. "He is very shrewd politically, but in the end he is always by himself. He could have led the Hispanic constituency in New York to terrific heights. They wanted him to. But no one could work with him. He is a one-man band, not an orchestra leader."[20]

Badillo's second task under Koch was to improve public education. The son of a teacher and someone who often recounts his own educational success, Badillo made education his central crusade. He criticized "social promotion" by which weak students were moved from grade to grade in order to avoid stigmatizing them socially. Instead, Badillo wanted the weak students to be held back and given remedial assistance. The idea was implemented briefly in 1978 but, claimed Badillo, was dropped due to opposition from the teachers union. Nonetheless, Badillo ultimately prevailed when "back-to-basics" testing became a national movement in the 1990s.[21]

Badillo's public role diminished during the 1980s but resurged in the 1990s. Meanwhile, he wielded influence behind the scenes through his law firm, which is a New York City lobbying powerhouse. In 1993, Badillo challenged David Dinkins for the Democratic mayoral nomination, but, lacking support, quickly withdrew. Instead, he ran for city controller on a fusion ticket with Republican Rudolph Giuliani who won, even as Badillo lost. However, he joined Giuliani's team and officially became a Republican in 1998. "After forty years as a liberal Democrat, I'd had enough. ... " Liberalism, he contended, was stagnant. "The city of New York desperately needed a new direction."[22]

Badillo was in tune with national conservative Republicanism which was echoed locally by Mayor Giuliani during the 1990s. As Giuliani's point man on education, Badillo attacked social promotion in the public schools and open admissions at CUNY. Badillo had opposed open admissions since it started in 1970 after student protests demanded that CUNY serve more minorities. At the time, only 13 percent of all New York City high school graduates and only 5 percent of minority graduates were admitted to CUNY. The new policy guaranteed all New York City high-school graduates a seat in one of CUNY's colleges and actually benefited more white working-class students than minorities. Because remediation programs were developed to help poorly prepared students adapt to college, some saw open admissions as a noble experiment in democratizing higher education. To Badillo, it meant lower standards, unqualified students, a waste of resources and the devaluation of his cherished degree.[23]

In 1990, Badillo was appointed to CUNY's Board of Trustees and immediately began a campaign to end open admissions. Opposed by liberals and minorities, but supported by Giuliani, many CUNY alumni and a conservative think-tank, the Manhattan Institute for Policy Research, Badillo derided remediation and castigated the low "on-time" graduation rates at both the community and senior colleges. Badillo particularly criticized Hostos Community College where, he said, students were graduating without mastering English.[24]

When the governor and the mayor appointed more conservatives to CUNY's Board of Trustees, Badillo moved from the minority to the majority and from member to vice-chairman. In 1998, his motion to abolish open admissions in the senior colleges finally passed. Remediation was barred from the senior colleges even though 75 percent of American colleges offered it. Becoming chairman of CUNY's Board of Trustees in 1999, Badillo used his power to install university administrators who would perpetuate his policies. From his perspective, he had saved CUNY. [25]

In the process, however, Badillo's relations with the Latino community had become strained. The tension increased when he declared in 1999 that "the problem we have is that we are getting hundreds of students 12, 13, 14 years old from the hills of Mexico and the Dominican Republic who have never been to any school." Moreover, he asserted "that in Mexico and Central America there has never been a tradition of education. They have education in some of the cities, but they don't in the hills." Instantly, Badillo was labeled a "racist" and a traitor to Latinos. In response, Badillo compared himself to Clarence Thomas, the conservative black Supreme Court Justice, and Ward Connerly, the anti-affirmative action black entrepreneur. They too, said Badillo, were vilified for refusing to toe the usual liberal line for minority leaders.[26]

Ever restless and optimistic, Badillo resigned from CUNY's Board of Trustees to run for mayor again in 2001, this time as a Republican. At age 72, he was buoyed by his CUNY victory and believed, as he put it, that "Now my time has come." Nonetheless, he was outspent and outpolled by the billionaire businessman Michael Bloomberg, who promised to heal the civic wounds left by Giuliani. Curiously enough, Badillo was not endorsed either by New York State's Republican governor, George Pataki, or by the city's Republican mayor, Rudy Giuliani. After the election, however, Badillo became an education advisor to Bloomberg and continued to influence public policy while maintaining ties with his law firm and the Manhattan Institute.[27]

Badillo's four decades in public life have been full of crusades and controversies. Although he shifted from liberal to conservative, from Democrat to Republican, basically he remained the same. Through it all, he was a confirmed independent who never avoided saying what he meant, even if it alienated potential allies. This was particularly true in the Latino community where he lost support as he became more conservative and they became more diverse. Today, Puerto Ricans compete for power with Dominicans, Mexicans, Columbians and others. These new groups seek the same opportunities that Badillo advocated long ago and are dismayed by his current policies. As a result, notes the author James Traub, Badillo has increasingly become, "a minority of one."[28]

It may not be a position that Badillo regrets because he enjoys swimming against the tide and overcoming obstacles. He is a fighter. Significantly, his favorite quote is Robert Frost's "I have a lover's quarrel with the world." Above all, he would have loved to be mayor, a quest that both friend and foe consider his obsession. No, he insists, "My obsession is to solve the urban crisis in this country." Never a man of small ambitions, Badillo views himself as an agent of change, a lone voice of reason, a leader of lesser men. Some call him "driven" and his son wisely warns, "This is a man who is not easily deterred." [29]

---

1. What are the most inspiring aspects of Badillo's life story?
2. What are the most surprising and/or disturbing aspects of Badillo's life story?
3. What are Badillo's strengths and weaknesses?
4. What lessons could New York City's minorities draw from Badillo's life story?

9-4-1. DEFINING DEFIANCE: IRIS MORALES, ACTIVIST, 1998

The Young Lords was a controversial group of radical Puerto-Rican young adults who rejected mainstream politics and politicians like Badillo. Although committed to liberating Puerto Rico and oppressed peoples everywhere, their context was really the slums of New York.

After conventional strategies such as petitions, lawsuits, peaceful demonstrations and voting failed to produce results, they turned to unconventional ones. They went to jail after taking over a church for ten days when its minister refused to let them run a health clinic, a day-care center and a breakfast program on the premises. They set garbage on fire in the streets of El Barrio in order to get more frequent sanitation pick-ups. Their protests tied up traffic and infuriated officials, but they worked.

At the same time, the Young Lords reached out to the community in less spectacular ways by distributing free clothing, providing legal advice, exposing police brutality and denouncing prison conditions. Their efforts to help the poor and their willingness to stand up to authority won them admiration within the Latino community, but condemnation beyond it. Herman Badillo considered their strategies "outrageous."[30] The Young Lords lasted six years before succumbing to internal divisions.

Iris Morales was one of the Young Lords' founders. She has remained committed to social justice as a community organizer, educator, lawyer and documentary filmmaker. Her film about the Young Lords has won awards and is shown across the United States and in the Caribbean. Here she explains the motivation and methods of the Young Lords and their relationship to other grassroots movements of the era.

Source: Iris Morales, "Palante, Siempre Palante: The Young Lords," in Andres Torres and Jose E. Velazquez (eds), *The Puerto Rican Movement* (Philadelphia, PA: Temple University Press, 1998), 212–214.

At a significant historical moment, Puerto Rican youth entered a national and worldwide movement that said, in no uncertain terms, the status quo must change. Inspired by liberation struggles worldwide, in the United States, and in Puerto Rico, the Young Lords militantly and proudly stood up for the Puerto Rican community. It was a stand against economic exploitation, social injustice, and colonial dependency that resonated throughout the communities in the United States. It was a call for revolution!

The Young Lords said, "We're tired of injustice, and we're not going to take it lying down." That was the first step toward a very simple, popular appeal, reflected in the garbage offensive. The squalor of the barrio was the most visible and physical manifestation of oppression and neglect. Streets overflowed with garbage because the people of El Barrio were not a high priority for New York City sanitation services. When the Young Lords swept the streets and set fire to the garbage throughout the summer of 1969, they pressured the sanitation department to clean up the barrio streets. From East 110th Street, the garbage offensive spread to other blocks in the neighborhood and established the Young Lords as street fighters willing to confront the police and government authority to get results.

On another level, we reclaimed our identity, our heritage, our place in society. Although we were living in the United States, we declared, "We're Puerto Rican and proud." We were now here in mass numbers, and our generation asked, "Where do we go next? Our mothers have worked in sweatshops; our fathers have been dishwashers. We want better jobs and doors opened to quality educational opportunities. We were trying to figure out our situation without too many role models. ...

The militant spirit and commitment to work directly in the community attracted some of the best organizers. Activists who had participated in the Civil Rights, Black liberation and cultural Nationalists movements joined. Others were community organizers with experience fighting for education, jobs, housing, and health issues. Some united from the student protest movements including the Columbia University and City College takeovers.

We were convinced that we could make the world a better place for all of humanity. After all, the richest country in the world had resources to provide food, clothing, housing, and health care for everyone. It was unconscionable to have so few with so much and so many people with so little. We believed that the most disfranchised segment of our community, the most oppressed—the street people—would play a revolutionary role because they had nothing to lose. For us, "community" included these people, who today are considered part of the "underclass." We identified completely with the most oppressed sectors because we came from those sectors. "

---

1. What sentences best summarize the Young Lords' goals?
2. How radical and/or dangerous were the Young Lords' goals and methods?
3. How idealistic and/or realistic was Morales?
4. How were the Young Lords similar to but different from Herman Badillo?

9-4-2. REALIGNING LATINO POLITICS: MICHAEL JONES-CORREA, POLITICAL SCIENTIST, 1998

The rise of Sonia Sotomayor from a Bronx public housing project to the Supreme Court marked a milestone for Puerto-Rican political legitimacy. Nonetheless, in an immigrant city like New York, ethnic politics are always in flux. After the 1965 Immigration Act, the Puerto-Rican struggle for political power, difficult in itself, was complicated by the arrival of new Spanish-speaking groups from the Caribbean, Central and South America. As the political scientist Michael Jones-Correa observed, when these groups jockeyed with each other, they redefined Latino politics.

Source: Michael Jones-Correa, *Between Two Nations: The Political Predicament of Latinos in New York City* (Ithaca, NY: Cornell University Press, 1998), 114–116.

The instrumental use of Hispanic ethnic identification is readily apparent in the case of Latinos in New York City. Puerto Ricans were the first Latino group to enter city politics in any numbers and have dominated Hispanic politics since. They began building up political power through government-funded nonprofit organizations founded in the 1960s and then challenging Democratic incumbents in districts with heavily Puerto Rican populations. (Herman Badilllo, for example, used the experience and connections gained in the nonprofit service organization ASPIRA to form his own political club in the Bronx as an alternative to the Democratic machine. ...) Having built alternative electoral organizations and captured various political positions, Puerto Ricans have kept them ever since. ...

Through the 1980s, Puerto Rican politics *were* Latino politics. All the while, Puerto Rican leaders benefited from the Hispanic label—pointing to the growing numbers of Latinos in the city to argue for increased benefits to the community while occupying almost all the elected and appointed positions set aside for Hispanics. Today, however, the shifting demographics of the Latino population have created something of a dilemma for Puerto Rican leaders. Puerto Ricans now constitute less than 50 percent of the Hispanic population in the city (though they are still the single largest Hispanic group). Puerto Rican political success, combined with the rapid growth of other Latino groups, has led to considerable tensions among the various Latino groups.

There are accusations that Puerto Ricans have jealously guarded their position as gatekeepers to Hispanic politics in the city. The sense of injustice this belief provokes is only aggravated by the feeling that Puerto Ricans do not fully represent the views of other Latinos. Many of these Latinos, a good portion of whom cannot vote because they are not citizens, feel that Puerto Ricans, who are automatically citizens upon arrival, do not fully sympathize with the barrier that lack of citizenship poses to full participation, and are not sensitive to the differences among the newer immigrants. Colombian activists conducting a voter registration drive among recent immigrants in Queens, for example, had to throw out boxes of registration materials borrowed from a Puerto Rican organization, all of which were emblazoned with the Puerto Rican flag. For their part, Puerto Rican leaders, echoing other New York politicians, say that they will deal with other Latinos as full partners only when they begin to vote in sizable numbers.

This situation has begun to change as the wave of immigrants who arrived in the city in the 1960s and '70s begin to organize, naturalize as American citizens, and enter the political process. First Dominicans, then other groups, have begun to replicate or simply take over the organizations and networks built by the Puerto Ricans on their way to political representations and power. In 1991 Guillermo Linares, a Dominican, was elected to the New York City Council. For the first time, a Latino from another national group could claim to represent Hispanics in the city, and this has weakened Puerto Rican assertions (though not their desire) to be speaking for Latinos as a whole.

To counter this shift, the Puerto Rican leadership has made emphatic use of the label "Puerto Rican/Latino" at events in which they present themselves as the spokespersons for Latinos in the city. The label sends the clear message, both to other Latinos and to non-Hispanic politicians across the city, that Puerto Ricans are still the key players in Latino politics. It succeeds in emphasizing communality and difference, precedence and subordination, all at the same time. Other Latinos often have the impression that Puerto Ricans are using the term "Latino" cynically, to leverage more power and inflate their numbers. ... The rivalry and maneuvering between Puerto Ricans and other Latinos illustrates the way ethnic groups can manipulate identities in the political sphere to further their various interests as national groups within a government-sanctioned pan-Hispanic identity.

---

1. How did Puerto Ricans acquire political power in New York City?
2. Why are Puerto Ricans losing political power in New York City?
3. According to Jones-Correa, what were the strengths and weaknesses of the Puerto Rican response to change?
4. How did Herman Badillo's career reflect these changes?

9-4-3. MAKING A LATINO IDENTITY: XAVIER F. TOTTI, ANTHROPOLOGIST, 1987

To the anthropologist Xavier F. Totti, the increased diversity of Latino immigrants since 1965 could promote cultural cooperation instead of political conflict. On the one hand, he acknowledged the existence of real differences and tensions between Latino groups. On the other hand, Totti thought that the common cultural experiences of Latino immigrants in the United States could override their separate national identities and create a common Latino ethnicity. Like immigrants who preceded and followed them, Latinos used culture to bridge their old and new lives. (see Units 4-2 and 10-1)

Source: Xavier F. Totti, "The Making of a Latino Ethnic Identity," *Dissent* (Fall, 1987), 539–540.

Given these different and disparate migratory processes, what, then, unites Latinos? How do they constitute a group? I believe two things serve to induce the formation of the Latino ethnic identity. One, of course, is the perceived shared cultural background in contrast to the larger American culture, with the Spanish language at the center. The other is the structural position of most Latinos within American society, and, as its consequence, their relationship to the state apparatus and politics.

The shared cultural background, even if it is a superficial construct that leaves out the heterogeneous nature of the groups, has a tremendous force in identifying Latinos across national boundaries. That background, nurtured in common values, is constantly reinforced in the mass media, both in the U.S. Latino press and in that of the separate countries of origin. The notion is further solidified by the immediate, traditional presence of the "colossus of the North" in the life of Latin America. The Spanish language serves as more than a *lingua franca* among groups; it is the most visible and immediate mark of their shared distinction from the rest of the society. The language is also a *living* force since, unlike other migrants in the United States, Latinos are followed by a powerful and complex system of Spanish-language mass media. ...

The maintenance of Spanish and the ideal of bilingualism and formal bilingual education are, as recent surveys indicate, immutable tenets of identity for most Latinos. In 1980 eight out of ten Hispanics interviewed in the New York metropolitan area favored formal bilingual education. ... In ordinary everyday discourse, even among fully bilingual or English-dominant Latinos, Spanish continues to preserve a special notion of self. Like Guarani among bilingual Paraguayans, it's the voice of the soul; uttering a few words of Spanish signifies a separation from the dominant culture and a symbolic unity. The force of Spanish among Latinos, in intraethnic and interethnic encounters, lies in its ability to compress many contradictory symbols in the search for power, reflecting exclusivity, nostalgia, and/or respect among speakers.

Especially important in the process of creating a new ethnic identity are those occasions when shared "culture" leaves the remembrances of the old country and is used to adapt to and describe life in the present environment. Among migrants and their descendants, these are the creative moments of forging new interpretations and future traditions. Within the process of Latino ethnic formation, the music of composer-singer Ruben Blades ... [uses] expressive culture in forging a new unity based on common traditions and a present similarity within the new polity. Blades, the most popular Latino singer of the moment, sings to a unified Latino group in America, composed of those from the "south," of a different color, of a strange tongue, united by a common origin and their present situation in the United States.

For Blades, those situations are generally the products of exploitation, discrimination, and poverty (both here and in Latin America). In the song *Siembra*, he urges Latinos to use their *conciencia*, in this case their identity and pride, to improve their situation. He warns assimilated Latinos of the pitfalls in their quest for the American dream. The song *Plastico* categorizes those who unequivocally assimilate into the complacent middle class as shallow, "plastic" individuals preoccupied with the latest fashions and willing to mortgage their future in the name of "social status." Both *Siembra* and *Plastico* urge Latinos to unite and through education, hard work, and the inner strength of the group create their own better future. ...

As expressed by ... Blades ... the uncertainties lie not between assimilation and the maintenance of the traditional culture. They do not present two or more static, all-or-nothing cultures, but interaction and creativity within new situations. They speak of poor, working-class and street Latinos who are forging a new consciousness out of their shared past and present conditions.

1. Why was bilingualism so important to Latinos? What is "a language of the soul"? Why is bilingualism so controversial today?
2. According to Totti, how did Ruben Blades confront the perils and possibilities of the American dream for Latinos? Do the same issues apply to other immigrants?
3. According to Totti, would the development of a Latino ethnic identity be un-American?
4. Imagine that Badillo, Morales, Jones-Correa and Totti were on a panel entitled "a new Latino consciousness." What would be each person's main point? In what ways would they agree and disagree? Who would be most convincing?

9-4-4. SEEKING "JUSTICE EVERYWHERE": GROUNDSWELL COMMUNITY MURAL PROJECT, 2004

If the anthropologist Roger Sanjek is correct, the issues of Puerto-Rican politics and a Latino ethnic identity might be moot. Looking at the Elmhurst-Corona community in Queens, he found that common concerns crossed cultural boundaries. Because Elmhurst-Corona may be "the most ethnically mixed community in the world," Sanjek offered it as a model of what America can become. His study demonstrated how multi-ethnic cooperation prevailed over conflict in the midst of rapid social change.

The statistics are striking. Elmhurst-Corona was 98 percent white in 1960 but only 18 percent white in 1990, by which time it was 45 percent Latino, 26 percent Asian and 10 percent Black. The resulting tensions were gradually mitigated by a variety of grass-roots leaders, often women, who participated in community politics and created civic organizations to address local problems. In politics, through religion, in schools, at public cultural events, on their blocks or in their apartment houses, different groups learned to work together because no single group held a majority. Sanjek hopes that this development may hold *The Future of Us All*. [31]

As the following section of a mural in Brooklyn suggests, the experience of Elmhurst-Corona is being echoed in other neighborhoods. It is one of 50 murals citywide created by artists, community groups and at-risk youth committed to grass-roots activism. Significantly, the mural is called "Justice Everywhere."

Source: "Justice Everywhere," Groundswell Community Mural Project, c. 2004. Lead artists: Amy Sananman and Belle Benfield.

1. Explain the symbolism of the fist and the key.
2. Explain how this mural advocates pluralism across class, age, race, ethnicity and gender lines.
3. Explain how this mural advocates grass roots activism.
4. How would Badillo, Morales, Jones-Correa and Totti react to this mural?

SELECTED RESOURCES

Auletta, Ken. *The Streets Were Paved with Gold: The Decline of New York—An American Tragedy*. New York: Random House, 1980.

Cannato, Vincent J. *The Ungovernable City: John Lindsay and His Struggle to Save New York City*. New York: Basic Books, 2001.

Freeman, Joshua B. *Working Class New York, Life and Labor Since World War II*. New York: The New Press, 2000.

Jonnes, Jill. *South Bronx Rising: The Rise, Fall and Resurrection of an American City*. NewYork: Fordham University Press, 1986.

Koch, Edward I. *Mayor: An Autobiography*. New York: Warner Books, 1984.

McNickle, Chris. *To Be Mayor of New York: Ethnic Politics in the City*. New York: Columbia University Press, 1993.

Morris, Charles R. *The Cost of Good Intentions: New York City and the Liberal Experiment, 1960–1975*. New York: McGraw Hill, 1980.

Sanchez-Korroll, Virginia E. *From Colonia to Community: The History of Puerto Ricans in New York City*. Berkeley, CA: University of California Press, 1983.

Traub, James. *The Devil's Playground: A Century of Pleasure and Profit in Times Square*. New York: Random House, 2004.

www. laguardiawagnerarchive.lagcc.cuny.edu: Abraham D. Beame and Edward I. Koch

CHAPTER 10

1993–2008

Moving from the late twentieth century to the twenty-first century, New York was impacted by three unrelated, but pivotal developments that altered its sense of self. They are examined in this chapter. First was the arrival of new immigrants who changed the city's ethnic and racial identity. Second was the mayoralty of Rudolph Giuliani who challenged the city's liberal traditions. Third was the World Trade Center tragedy which forced the city to rethink its most cherished assumptions. Because these events raised old questions in new forms, the last unit tries to tie the book together by exploring some of the lasting dilemmas posed by New York City's restlessness.

UNIT 10-1. BREAKING BARRIERS: THE NEW IMMIGRANTS

New York is an immigrant city and proud of it. As the Statue of Liberty constantly reminds us, New York has long been the gateway to America. In every era, the restlessness that brought new people to New York constantly reinvigorated and redefined the city.[1] Immigration also redefined the immigrants. The pressure to assimilate into a cultural melting pot was strong. New groups were expected to "Americanize" by abandoning their native languages in favor of English and by submerging, if not losing, their old customs.

While some immigrants voluntarily relinquished their pasts, others held onto them and combined them with mainstream cultural norms. Thus developed the hyphenated American (Irish-American, etc.) and the concept of the salad bowl in which immigrants retained their separate identities as lettuce, tomatoes and peppers, but shared the same salad dressing in a common salad bowl. The result was pluralism or multiculturalism.

The urban ethnic mix was further enriched (and complicated) after immigration restrictions were liberalized in 1965. By 1990 whites were no longer the statistical majority of New York City residents. New groups meant new challenges and new coping strategies that reshaped urban life for everyone.

10-1-1. DEMONSTRATING DESINESS: SUNITA S. MUKHI, PERFORMANCE SCHOLAR, 2000

One of the shocks of immigration is suddenly becoming an ethnic minority in a multicultural city where diversity is the norm. Much to their surprise, people from one nation are often lumped together with other people from the same general geographic area but from nations with which their country of origin has often been at odds. For example, the Chinese, Japanese and Koreans have a long history of antagonism, but in the United States, they are all labeled East Asian.

Immigrants have taken advantage of this situation by creating political alliances that give them visibility and influence. Some have turned those alliances into bold self-assertion, as in the West Indian American Day Carnival. Others have turned diversity into profit through fusion restaurants that blend different culinary traditions, such as Chinese and Cuban. All of these combinations are hybrids, that is, new entities created out of different old entities.

As the performance scholar Sunita S. Mukhi explains, the term 'Desi' reflects this dynamic process. In Hindu culture, it refers to popular forms of entertainment that do not follow formal rules. That flexibility and openness has been applied to the development of a flexible and open form of mixed South-Asian identity in the United States. It can even lead to integrating South-Asian with European traditions, as in the following recipe, which celebrates New York's diversity.

Source: Sunita S. Mukhi, *Doing the Desi Thing: Performing Indianness in New York City*, (New York: Garland, 2000), 188–191.

The complex, exciting, new emerging Desi Hybrid identity is shared by those of South Asian origin who feel committed in the hereland they find themselves in and acknowledge the similarities in the colonial histories, in the multicultural politics of their present, and the pleasure they derive from the mélange of American, African, and South Asian expressive forms that they share with others like them. Caste, region, religion, national origins hold no bar in coming together to advocate for an issue, to party, to represent, to coalesce. This Desi Hybridity is shared among ourselves whereas we may call ourselves South Asian when we speak to other non-South Asians, or speak officially about our coalition.

Following are excerpts of a recipe of Lasagna Keema—a hybrid blend of an Italian-American dish with some typically Desi ingredients. … Though New York City can boast of having the most varied and at times delicious array of ethnic foods, preparing and eating an ethnic food is an important form of performing and participating in Desiness, and reassuring Desis in America that despite being here, they have maintained their 'taste' for their homelands by preferring and yearning for Desi spice. And also that in their sojourn here, Desis are 'American' enough to enjoy food that is not 'native' to them. This recipe is also an act of appropriation—taking a foreign artifact and making it one's own, adjusting it to the Desi palate, and in doing so, overpowering its distance and otherness. Thus, here are excerpts of this amalgam, an attempt to create a transnational cuisine.

Ingesting Hybridity While Being Hospitably Desi …

This is an arduous dish because it takes time to prepare. It is not a diet dish either. … Do not fall into the trap of "Indian woman means cooking." Such nonsense! I insist you include your partner, your family, your friends in the preparation of this dish, in shopping for the ingredients, in assembling the dish, in eating it—making it a communal, egalitarian affair. Hey! A party!

Much of the recipe can be followed by reading the directions off the box of lasagna. I present here only the variations, especially the secrets in the sauce …

[Use] two pounds of goat meat ground and cleaned by any of the Muslim halal butchers in Elmhurst or Jackson Heights, [Queens] … I am not a Muslim, but I feel that halal meat is lean, clean, fresh and tasty. …

[Add] one big red onion. Its pungency makes the meat fragrant.

[Mix] one tablespoon each of garlic powder, ginger powder, cumin powder, coriander powder, chili powder, garam masala, mango powder. I prefer that you purchase these spices from any Desi grocery store rather than from general supermarkets. …

So that the spices are more pungent, you can purchase them in seed form and grind them yourself using a coffee bean grinder. To perform the ultimate in folksiness, you may want to pound these spices with a pestle and mortar instead...

Corn oil for sautéing will do but you can up the notch of 'authentic' Desiness by using ghee—clarified butter. Most Desis in the U.S.A. use corn oil. It is healthier and easily available. …

For the cheeses, [add] one tablespoon each of cumin seeds, dried red peppers, ground black pepper to the 1.5 pounds of ricotta and 1.5 pounds of mozzarella.

Most of the procedure can be followed from the lasagna box. However, goat meat may take longer to cook so add ten minutes if you are not convinced of its doneness. The sauce must be fragrant and not smell of meat.

Then with gusto serve, eat and relish this hybrid dish which will win the hearts of both your Desi buddies, American colleagues, multi-culti chums, and all those in between.

---

1. What are the characteristics of Desi Hybridity?
2. How does Desiness differ from Indian traditions?
3. How does Lasagna Keema bridge the homeland and the hereland?
4. Which sentences best express the spirit of Desiness?
5. Explain whether and how Desiness represents assimilation and/or pluralism.

10-1-2. EXAMINING HAITIAN ADAPTATION: MICHEL LAGUERRE, ANTHROPOLOGIST, 1984

The dilemmas of ethnic minorities were clarified by the experience of Haitians in New York City. Fleeing political repression in the poorest nation of the Western hemisphere, Haitians settled first in Miami but soon migrated to other major U.S. cities, especially New York. Although Haitians confronted many of the same problems as other Caribbean immigrants regarding race, their French heritage made them unique and created barriers between Haitian and English- or Spanish-speaking Caribbean immigrants. (Tensions between Haitians and Dominicans on their shared island of origin are longstanding.) The anthropologist Michel Laguerre described the various survival strategies that Haitians adopted to handle this situation. One measure of their success was the election of New York City's first Haitian-born city councilman in 2007.

Source: Michel S. Laguerre, *American Odyssey: Haitians in New York City.* (Ithaca, NY: Cornell University Press, 1984), 106-107, 156–159.

Ethnic awareness is played out in the adaptive strategies that Haitian-Americans develop to secure employment. Sometimes they identify with Afro-Americans; at other times it is wiser to put forth their Haitian origins. … Haitian-American job seekers, for example, may try to convince an Anglo-American employer that their minority status and their fluency in more than one language will be beneficial to the employer. A different strategy may be followed with a Haitian-American employer. Here job applicants are likely to stress the importance of ethnic solidarity for the well-being of the community, their personal interest in the employer's success, and the lack of communication problems between them.

Ethnicity is also used as a strategic factor in other economic endeavors. Organizers turn to co-ethnics to develop rotating credit associations in order to minimize the chance of default. Borlette [numbers game] operators recruit players among their compatriots, assuming that they are less likely than others to denounce them to the police. The players, too, find it more convenient to deal with co-ethnics than with others. Ethnicity is clearly a factor in the establishment and success of businesses in the Haitian-American community. … Haitian-American entrepreneurs are well aware of the consumer behaviors of their co-ethnics. They maintain their clientele by selling the kinds of goods and products that Haitian-Americans need and desire. …

Despite the divergent cultural and ideological orientations of immigrants to the United States, they all seem to share some similarities. For Oscar Handlin, … "the history of immigration is a history of alienation and its consequences." Most immigrants, whether black or white, tend to experience multiple miseries during the resettlement and adaptation process. They also share the will to improve their lot and that of their children. Black and white immigrants, however, have not fared equally in their pursuit of economic opportunity. The racial barrier adds a dimension to the everyday problems immigrants usually face. Skin color suddenly becomes a problem, and one that cannot be overcome. European immigrants who had to start life in America at the bottom of the socioeconomic ladder knew that their children, at least, had a realistic hope of improving their situation; even economic improvement does not solve the black immigrant's problem. Whether an intellectual, a bourgeois, or a beggar, the Haitian-American remains black.

It is often argued that all immigrants generally start at the bottom and over the years are able to improve their economic situation. But this is not always true. The stigmatization of some immigrant groups has made their adaptation more severe than others. The Chinese were the first people whose presence was interdicted by exclusion acts. The Japanese were the one group declared an internal enemy and rounded up in concentration camps. ...

The ambiguity of the situation of more recent black immigrants is obvious. They are perceived as blacks by the wider society and are relegated to the same racial status as Black Americans. ... They consider themselves Haitians, Jamaicans, Trinidadians, and the like. Black Americans lump them all together as foreigners, though in Harlem, Haitians are often singled out as "French fries." In the context of these perceptions, West Indian immigrants develop adaptive strategies to improve their opportunities and achieve upward mobility. They introduce themselves as West Indians in interactions with whites, for example, but identify themselves as blacks when they run for political office. ...

The Haitian-American experience has demonstrated that ethnicity must be understood in its situational context, that is, the ecological and historical circumstances that help explain ethnic awareness. Ethnicity is used in a tactical manner to maintain and protect individual and group interests. In the Haitian-American case, it is used as a response to a situation of dependency. Each ethnic identity taken by the immigrants (black, West Indian, Haitian) is manipulated in the context of their minority status in a white-dominated society. Their dependency situation obliges them to use their ethnicity as a means of survival. The awareness of such a situation is but one factor in ethnic consciousness. Haitian-American consciousness of their dependency arises in large part with their passage from majority status in Haiti to minority status in the United States. ...

Ethnic consciousness is not static; it is adaptable to external circumstances. ...

---

1. What adaptive strategies have Haitians used in dealing with non-Haitians?
2. What adaptive strategies have Haitians used in their own communities?
3. How has race complicated the process of Haitian adaptation?
4. Explain the implications of Laguerre's last sentence for the future of assimilation or pluralism in New York City.

10-1-3. CONSIDERING IMMIGRANT ENTREPRENEURS: THE CENTER FOR AN URBAN FUTURE, 2007

Many immigrants come to the United States for economic opportunity. They are a self-selected group of people who are ambitious enough and restless enough to leave their ancient roots behind and try to plant new ones. Writing for the non-profit research organization, The Center for an Urban Future, urbanists Jonathan Bowles and Tara Colton explored the challenges facing immigrants who tried to enter the American economy by opening small businesses. Some came equipped with money; others pooled resources with co-ethnics to finance their ventures. Different groups found different ethnic economic niches such as the grocery store, a sector which is now Korean, but was previously dominated by Italians who took it over from the Irish. These small businesses were crucial to the economic health of ethnic neighborhoods as well as of the larger city, but they suffered from the general marginalization of minority groups. Their struggles hold up a mirror to urban economic realities and the obstacles to immigrant adaptation.

Source: Jonathan Bowles and Tara Colton, *A World of Opportunity* (New York: The Center for an Urban Future, 2007), 3, 7, 9–12, 26, 32–33.

During the past decade, immigrants have been the entrepreneurial sparkplugs of cities from New York to Los Angeles—starting a greater share of new businesses than native-born residents, stimulating growth in sectors from food manufacturing to health care, creating loads of new jobs, and transforming once-sleepy neighborhoods into thriving commercial centers. And immigrant entrepreneurs are also becoming one of the most dependable parts of cities' economies. While elite sectors like finance (New York), entertainment (Los Angeles), and energy (Houston) fluctuate wildly through cycles of boom and bust, immigrants have been starting businesses and creating jobs during both good times and bad.

Two trends suggest that these entrepreneurs will become even more critical to the economies of cities in the years ahead: immigrant-led population growth and the on-going trend of large companies in many industries moving to decentralize their operations out of cities and outsource work to cheaper locales. But despite this great and growing importance, immigrant entrepreneurs remain a shockingly overlooked and little understood part of cities' economies, and they are largely disconnected from local economic planning. ...

No American city has been more central to the immigrant experience, or benefited more from successive generations of newcomers, than New York. Particularly during the late 19th and early 20th centuries, ... immigrant entrepreneurs from Italian bakers to Eastern Europeans in the garment trade helped power the city's incredible economic expansion. One hundred years later, history might be poised to repeat itself. ...

Census data shows that immigrants are starting businesses in the city at a considerably higher rate than New Yorkers who were born in this country. ... In addition to mere volume, New York City's immigrant entrepreneurs can boast a number of remarkable success stories. ...

More commonly, immigrants in New York start out by opening small family-run businesses, from flower shops and accounting offices to newsstands, day care centers and construction companies. Many become street vendors, taxi owners or sole proprietors selling everything from makeup to real estate. Others work out of their homes, making tamales or cakes and selling them primarily to friends and neighborhood businesses. Some bring in suitcases full of products from their home country and sell them on the streets to local shop owners. ...

But despite the increasing significance of immigrant-run businesses, city economic development officials have hardly begun to incorporate them into their overall economic development strategy. ... Indeed, immigrants face all kinds of hurdles when attempting to start or grow a business in the five boroughs, causing some to go bankrupt after a short existence and others to toil in an endless struggle to stay afloat. Many are tripped up by the same factors that hamstring other businesses in New York, from the high cost of commercial real estate and insurance to the city's overzealous regulatory enforcement agents. Others find it difficult to survive simply due to the intense competition or because their business model isn't sustainable. But immigrants also encounter a long list of problems unknown to most native-born entrepreneurs: unfamiliarity with how business is done in this country, lack of awareness about local regulations, limited financial literacy, and, often, no credit history. ...

Language and cultural barriers exacerbate these problems. Unable to communicate effectively, immigrant entrepreneurs are less likely to attempt to sell goods and services in markets beyond their own ethnic communities, or to seek help from government agencies and nonprofit economic development organizations. Without such help, many immigrant business owners take bad advice from friends, family or accountants, and make costly mistakes. Others turn to professionals who speak their language but take advantage of them. ... Too few of the city's mainstream economic development organizations have made genuine attempts to reach out to immigrant entrepreneurs. ...

Microenterprise organizations like the Business Outreach Center Network and the New York Association for New Americans and some of the city's federally funded small business development centers—such as the one at La Guardia Community College—have been aggressive in trying to work with immigrant entrepreneurs. Yet, these groups generally aren't as well funded as the more mainstream business assistance organizations. Many immigrant communities aren't served by these organizations at all. ...

Going forward, it's critical for groups with sufficient expertise and funding ... to penetrate immigrant communities. On this front, the last few years have seen some progress. For example, classes offered by the Queens Economic Development Corporation on how to start a business, formerly offered only in English, are now held in Spanish and Chinese, and they are usually overbooked.

---

1. Identify at least four ways in which immigrant entrepreneurs strengthen the urban economy.
2. How many obstacles do they face? Which obstacles are most difficult to overcome?
3. Should immigrant entrepreneurs be better served? If not, why not? If so, how and by whom?

10-1-4. SPEAKING THROUGH SIGNS

Immigrants from over 120 nations make northwestern Queens the most diverse neighborhood in the world. Accordingly, the federal government has designated the #7 elevated train line the International Express because each station stop reflects the culture of different ethnic groups including Argentinians, Colombians, Filipinos, Irish, Indians, Italians, Mexicans, Romanians, Trinidadians and Turks, just to name a few. By the same token, none of these groups lives in isolation and every neighborhood is a potpourri of different ethnicities. For example, one store in Corona, Queens advertises itself as an American, Spanish, Bangladeshi, Indo-Pak Grocery!

Many of these groups came to the United States fairly recently. For example, Korean immigration to the United States is a post-1965 development. From about 70,000 in 1970, they increased to over 800,000 in 1990. Although most Koreans settled on the West Coast, a sizable group came to New York City, especially Queens, where over 70 percent of New York City's Koreans live. Starting with small businesses serving their own community, family members worked together, thereby lowering labor costs and avoiding the language barrier.[2]

When Koreans opened stores in non-Korean communities, they sometimes encountered hostility, as seen in the nine-month boycott of the Korean-owned Red Apple grocery store in Flatbush, Brooklyn during 1990. In response, Koreans formed a businesses advocacy group to defend their interests, influence urban politics and develop strategies for reducing interpersonal conflict in business settings.[3]

One example of this process of conflict and adaptation was the fight over Korean store signs in Flushing, Queens from 2001 to 2004. Historically, Flushing was a white ethnic neighborhood dominated by Irish, Italians, Germans and Jews. After 1965, it became a key destination for Chinese and Korean immigrants seeking an alternative to Manhattan's Chinatown, which was overcrowded and where rents were high. By 2000, Flushing was more than 50 percent Asian and had a larger Asian population than Manhattan's Chinatown. In 2001, Flushing elected John C. Liu to the New York City Council, making him New York's first Asian American elected official. [4]

Demographic change created conflict between old and new residents as well as between Chinese and Korean immigrants. Historic hostility between Chinese and Koreans in their homelands spilled over to America. When Koreans who had stores on Flushing's Main Street found their rents raised or their leases terminated by Chinese landlords they moved to nearby Union Street, which became dominated by Korean businesses with Korean language signs. Then, however, tensions increased between Koreans and white ethnic residents to whom the Korean language signs spelled exclusion and the decline of their own dominance.

A nasty conflict ensued. The Koreans were criticized as "colonizers" and white ethnic politicians called for laws requiring signage in English. Actually there already was such a New York State law dating from 1905, when residents were angry about signs in Yiddish and Italian on the Lower East Side. Like today's English-only advocates, they too claimed that foreign language signs were un-American. But, like the earlier immigrants, today's immigrants pointed out that none of their customers spoke English. The debate raged for years and polarized the Flushing community until Korean business and civic groups helped store owners learn what English words to put on their signs. Albeit a seemingly small controversy, the issue captured the volatile nature and enduring challenges of perpetual change in the city of immigrants.[5]

Sources: "Male Workers on Strike Holding Signs in Different Languages," c. 1918. Lawrence H. Rushing, "Signs on Union Street, Flushing NY, 2009."

---

1. How do the signs in these photos reflect New York City's historic role as the gateway to America?
2. In what ways could these signs be considered un-American and/or very American?
3. Do these signs prove that New York City is a melting pot and/or a salad bowl?
4. How was the experience of Korean immigrants similar to and/or different from the experiences of other groups discussed in this unit as well as throughout the book, such as African Americans, Irish, Chinese, Europeans and Puerto Ricans? (see Units 1-1, 1-2, 4-2, 4-4, 6-3, 7-, 8-1 and 9-4)

UNIT 10-2. LAW AND ORDER: RUDOLPH W. GIULIANI, MAYOR

As mayor from 1994 to 2001, Rudolph W. Giuliani had a profound effect on New York City. Born in 1944, Giuliani graduated from Manhattan College and New York University Law School, after which he served in the U.S. Attorney's office for the New York area and the Justice Department in Washington, D.C. His policy of detaining Haitian refugees as well as his prosecutions of the Mafia and Wall Street traders won him national attention. Originally a Democrat, he became an Independent in 1975 and a Republican in 1980.

In 1989, Giuliani narrowly lost the mayoral election to David Dinkins, but beat Dinkins in 1993. Giuliani's mission was to challenge and change the city's long-term liberal policies. Even though he polarized the city and his popularity plummeted, he was strikingly successful in accomplishing his goals. Moreover, after September 11, 2001, Giuliani became a national and international hero.

The debate over Giuliani's mayoral legacy revolves largely around his approach to policing through which he intended to make the city governable. He abandoned David Dinkins' use of community policing whereby cops worked with neighborhood residents to stem crime. Accepting the "Broken Windows" theory that small infractions bred general lawlessness, Giuliani declared zero tolerance for quality of life violations. Increasing numbers of people were arrested for jaywalking, loitering, begging, sleeping or urinating in public as well as riding bicycles without lights or walking dogs without leashes. The courts were swamped with minor cases and many ordinary people were arrested and jailed overnight.

Giuliani was particularly proud of a new computer-based system of counting police arrests called CompStat, which, he said, made policing more effective. Others claimed that it pressured the police to make more arrests and created a climate of fear. Giuliani also expanded the Street Crimes Unit (SCU), which focused on getting guns off the street through an increased use of stop and frisks, especially of minority men.[6]

As these strategies affected more and more New Yorkers, critics called them authoritarian. In response, Giuliani explained that "Freedom is about authority. Freedom is about the willingness of every single human being to cede to lawful authority a great deal of discretion about what you do and how you do it." To Norman Siegel, then director of the New York Civil Liberties Union, Giuliani's statement was "antithetical to tradition and our rich history of freedom" in New York.[7]

Giuliani's reliance on law and order was tested in three cases. First was the 1997 violent internal assault of Abner Louima, an unarmed Haitian immigrant, by a policeman in a police station using a toilet plunger. Second was the 1999 death of an unarmed West African immigrant named Amadou Diallo when four SCU officers mistook him for a criminal and shot him 41 times in his own doorway Third was the 2000 shooting to death by a policeman of another unarmed Haitian immigrant, Patrick Dorismond, after he objected to being accused of selling drugs.

New Yorkers of every age, race, ethnicity, religion and class responded with outrage and sustained weeks of protest led by the Reverend Al Sharpton, a controversial civil rights activist who achieved national and international prominence in this struggle. At issue was the long debate over the relationship between minorities and the police set in the larger context of the relationship of freedom to authority in a dense, dynamic, free-wheeling city.

10-2-1. TAMING THE CITY: RUDOLPH W. GIULIANI, MAYOR, 2000

During his two terms as mayor, Giuliani frequently defended his law-enforcement policies in speeches, statements to the press and weekly radio addresses. The following selection from his January 2000 State of the City address summarized Giuliani's position on law and order. It was delivered within the context of the public outcry against police brutality and the trial of the four Street Crimes Unit policemen involved in the Diallo shooting. The 1990 *Time* cover that he mentioned is reproduced Unit 9-2.

Source: Rudolph W. Giuliani, "The State of the City Address," January 13, 2000. ww.NYC.gov

I want to show you, as a way of symbolizing what we have been able to accomplish, two different covers of *Time Magazine*. This one is from September 17, 1990, at the beginning of the decade. This is where our City was in the estimation, I think, of most people: [holding up cover] "The Rotting of the Big Apple": "I [broken heart instead of a heart] New York." And I think many of us had a broken heart.

The artwork on this cover is a picture of a City which our fellow Americans thought of as the crime capital and the welfare capital of America . . . a city which, if you read the article, had seen its best days and had no prospect of being in the shape it's in now, in the year 2000. Ten years later, this is the cover of *Time Magazine*. [Holds up cover showing Times Square at midnight, January 1, 2000.] ...

Because the changes from 1990 to 2000-the things that represent why the *Time Magazine* covers are so different-aren't about hype, and they're not about sound bites, or anything else. They're about real ideas that changed the way we did things.

We need to understand those changes and the ideas behind them. Otherwise, there's no question in my mind that the City will go back to the way it was before-with high crime, swelling welfare rolls, cyclical bankruptcy, fleeing jobs, and all the rest. After all, that's the way the City was for most of the last half-century. And human societies tend to recede to the way they usually operate, unless they can understand what caused their problems and also understand the philosophy that can change their direction.

Let me give you a couple of quick examples, and then I'll discuss this in more detail.

Crime. The reduction in crime has been dramatic ... tremendous ... greater than any other city in America. When that first *Time* cover was published, we were the crime capital of America. We were averaging 2,000 murders per year, and 550,000 serious crimes per year. Now we're averaging under 700 murders, we have 55 percent less crime, and we are unquestionably the safest large city in America.

That didn't happen by accident. It happened because new and better ideas replaced old ideas that weren't working.

Maybe the most important new idea is the "Broken Windows" theory, which says that you have to pay attention to small crimes, because if you don't, neighborhoods will get out of control and serious crimes will get even worse.

That idea replaced the old notion that the Police Department and the City didn't have enough time for small crimes. We can't ever think like that again, because if we do crime will go up in the City and quality of life will deteriorate.

Another new idea is the CompStat program, and shifting the Police Department's emphasis from arresting people to reducing crime. That requires collecting crime statistics compulsively. It requires always coming up with new strategies to reduce crime. It requires responding to trends. And most of all, it requires holding the Police Department accountable. If we stop doing any of these things, crime is going to go up again.

And we have to support the Police-in the right way, in the appropriate way-but we have to support the Police. Not long ago, the politicians of this City would run out on the Police whenever things got tough. When that happens, then the Police hold back, because they see that doing what they are supposed to do puts their careers and lives at risk.

We saw that happen last year when Police Officers got involved in a terrible and tragic shooting-the final resolution of which is going be determined in a courtroom. However, one court came to the conclusion that "the carnival-like atmosphere" in our City created a threat to those officers' civil rights. …

For any Mayor, this simple rule has to be followed in periods like that: the Police should be supported and given the benefit of the doubt. Because, overwhelmingly, the Police of our City are out there trying to protect people and save lives. And in the neighborhoods where crime is the highest, their activity is most important.

So supporting the police is not some political thing, in the cynical meaning of that word. Supporting the police is a way to save lives. But you have to be willing to withstand criticism and ignore public opinion polls that say you're unpopular when you're doing it. If we're going to continue to reduce crime and save lives, then the political leaders of the City have to understand this principle.

---

1. What policing strategies did Giuliani advocate to tame the city?
2. What evidence did Giuliani provide to demonstrate the success of his policies?
3. Why did Giuliani say that the Diallo protests created a "carnival-like atmosphere" in the city?
4. What was the relationship between Giuliani's analysis of the effect of the Diallo protests on police behavior and the debate over the Civilian Review Board in Unit 8-3?
5. What grade would this speech have earned from Stuyvesant, La Guardia, Wagner, Lindsay, Koch and Dinkins? Why?

10-2-2. TAMING THE MAYOR: *THE NEW YORK DAILY NEWS,* 2000

The shooting of Patrick Dorismond on March 15, 2000 was the third high-profile death of an immigrant of color by the NYPD during Giuliani's administration. The three deaths horrified the city and coalesced a diverse, ever-growing opposition to Giuliani. Moreover, Dorismond's death followed the acquittal of the policemen involved in the Diallo case, thereby turning the mounting communal discontent into anger.

As he had during the Koch administration (see Unit 9-3), the Reverend Al Sharpton assumed leadership of the protest movement. For three weeks after the Diallo death, he held daily demonstrations at Police Plaza where he orchestrated the civil disobedience arrests of almost 12,000 local citizens and national celebrities cutting across barriers of race, class, age, religion and ethnicity. The protestors included former mayors David Dinkins and Ed Koch, Sharpton's old enemy. Koch supported many of Giuliani's policies but opposed his confrontational leadership style and, in 1999, published a book about him titled *Nasty Man*. Through it all, Giuliani defiantly defended his policing strategies and scornfully denigrated the protestors.[8]

When Giuliani released Dorismond's police records and his sealed juvenile records, many people, including some of his allies, believed that the mayor had crossed legal and ethical boundaries. In fact, Dorismond's trangressions had been minor, but Giuliani's main objective was defending the police. Claiming the public's right to know, he insisted that dead men have no right to privacy. The tactic backfired and calls for Giuliani's impeachment rang louder than ever.[9]

In addition to the massive public demonstrations, one barometer of public furor was the following editorial in the *New York Daily News*. Even this staunch supporter of the mayor had to recognize the negative ramifications of aggressive policing and the limitations of Giuliani's leadership style.

Source: *The New York Daily News*, March 26, 2000.

Taken at a time when New York is safer than it has been in decades, today's *Sunday News*/New York 1 News poll, which focuses on the police shooting of Patrick Dorismond, reflects a crisis of confidence that Mayor Giuliani, Police Commissioner Howard Safir and the entire NYPD cannot ignore.

A majority of all New Yorkers—whites and African-Americans, Democrats and Republicans, Protestants, Catholics and Jews, even respondents from the GOP stronghold of Staten Island—believes that the NYPD is out of control, according to the poll. That is a startling indication that concern and anger over the killing of the unarmed black man, laid to rest yesterday amid incidents of bottle-tossing and scuffles with police, is wider than anyone thought possible.

More important, the data are the clearest expression yet of a serious disconnect between the perception of an out-of-control police force and the reality that it is one of the most restrained in the nation. The poll of 504 New York City adults (45% white, 27% black, 19% Latino) had a margin of error of plus or minus 4.5 percentage points.

That's a small sample of the city, taken March 22, at the height of the Dorismond controversy.

It's a snapshot taken in the heat of the moment. Nevertheless, the results are distressing. Nearly half the respondents (47%) believe Safir is doing a bad job and should be replaced. An overwhelming 61% want federal monitoring of the NYPD. And pollsters Blum and Weprin point out that "a majority of all demographic subgroups and even a plurality of Giuliani approvers (48%) say the mayor should not have released Dorismond's [police] record."

But here is the most troublesome statistic from the poll—72% of the respondents believe the following statement: "The use of deadly force by the NYPD has gotten out of hand because in the past 13 months there have been three police shootings of unarmed men."

Call it the triumph of perception over reality.

By now, we know the statistics. There were 41 fatal police shootings in 1990, compared with 11 last year. That's the lowest incidence since records have been kept. New York's rate of fatal shootings per 1,000 officers was .28 or a 10th of the 3.0 level reported in Miami.

Indeed, the NYPD consistently has been one of the least trigger-happy forces in the country.

In 1993, Temple University criminologist James Fyfe reported that when compared to Atlanta, Chicago, Dallas, Houston, Kansas City, Los Angeles and Philadelphia, the "NYPD's rate of [police shootings resulting in injury or death] per 1,000 officers was the lowest" in 17 of the 22 years from 1970 through 1991. In fact, from 1983 to 1991, the Big Apple had the lowest rate. As it does today.

Yet, the perception-reality chasm remains. New Yorkers must not only be safe, they must also feel safe. That many, particularly black New Yorkers, don't is unacceptable. Sadly, Giuliani's response to the Dorismond shooting seems to have widened the gulf.

Saying he wanted to prevent riots, Giuliani released Dorismond's police record. When he was criticized for doing so, the mayor blasted critics as "political." This is New York, where everything is political—particularly when the mayor is running for the U.S. Senate.

But empathy in a time of pain is not political. Nor is it weakness. It's what a troubled populace has a right to expect from its elected leader.

As *The News'* poll shows, the city as a whole is unnerved by Dorismond's death. The mayor must heal the wound.

---

1. What was the "crisis of confidence" that concerned the *Daily News* and why did it matter?
2. What evidence did the *Daily News* offer in Giuliani's defense?
3. According to the *Daily News,* how could Giuliani have been a better mayor?
4. Based on this editorial, why did Giuliani's emphasis on law and order end up causing so much disorder?

10-2-3. TAMING CRIME: JOHN F. ECK AND EDWARD R. MAGUIRE, CRIMINOLOGISTS, 2000

The *Daily News* editorial and three weeks of Diallo demonstrations reflected widespread concerns about Giuliani's law and order policies. In fact, the issues were serious enough to motivate the U.S. Commission on Civil Rights to investigate and write a critical report about police brutality in New York City. Questions also came from policemen who were unhappy about being demonized by the press and the public. One third-generation policeman even feared that Giuliani's policies were promoting a "police state mentality."[10]

Although the decline in New York City's crime rate under Giuliani was undeniable, criminologists wondered whether it was unique to New York and therefore attributable, as Giuliani claimed, to CompStat and aggressive policing. Interestingly enough, they found that San Diego, California, which used community policing, actually had a larger crime rate drop than New York. Moreover, it appeared that there was a national reduction in crime during the 1990s, which correlated with the expansion of jobs in a strong economy and the contraction of the crack-cocaine epidemic of the late 1980s and early 1990s. Criminologists John F. Eck and Edward R. Maguire graphed these trends using data from crime reports issued by the Federal Bureau of Investigation between 1986 and 1999.[11]

Source: Homicides per 100,000 population for 10 largest cities from 1986–1998 in John E. Eck and Edward T. Maguire, "Have Changes in Policing Reduced Violent Crime? An Assessment of the Evidence," Alfred Blumstein and Joel Wallman (eds.), *The Crime Drop in America* (New York: Cambridge University Press, 2000), 234.

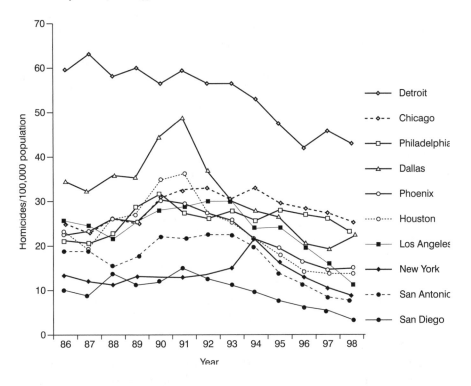

1. According to this chart, what was the overall trend in homicides for America's ten largest cities from 1986 to 1998?
2. How does this chart support Giuliani's claim that aggressive policing was successful during his mayoralty (1994–2000)?
3. Considering that most of the other cities in the chart used less aggressive policing strategies and that none used CompStat, how can this chart be used to challenge Giuliani's claim that his policies were responsible for New York City's crime reduction?
4. How does this chart prove that big cities are and are not inherently dangerous?

10-2-4. TAMING THE POLICE: MARILYNN JOHNSON, HISTORIAN, 2003

Focusing on the issue of police brutality, the historian Marilynn Johnson provided a long-range perspective on the role of the police in New York City.

Source: Marilynn Johnson, *Street Justice: A History of Police Violence in New York City* (Boston, MA: Beacon Press, 2003), 2–3.

The New York Police Department (NYPD) has attracted considerable historical attention over the years, and for good reason. Since its founding in 1845, the NYPD has been the nation's largest police department, one that has been a model for other cities. Like many urban departments in the nineteenth and early twentieth centuries, the NYPD had an unsavory reputation for corruption and close ties with the city's Democratic political machine, known as Tammany Hall. Beginning in the Progressive Era, however, periodic waves of reform made the department more centralized, bureaucratized, and highly regulated. Indeed, it sometimes pioneered efforts to reduce police violence, establishing the first regularly functioning police review board as well as the first panel to monitor police discharge of firearms. Compared with police agencies in Los Angeles, Chicago, and Miami, for example, New York has not been an especially abusive department.

Moreover (and relatedly), New York has historically been the epicenter of antibrutality organizing. Both the American Civil Liberties Union and the National Association for the Advancement of Colored People, two organizations that led protracted campaigns against abusive police practices, had their headquarters in New York and paid close attention to the local scene. As a case study, then, New York offers particularly rich documentation of police brutality in a city that was sometimes a pacesetter, though not always a successful one, in efforts to curb police violence.

New York's experience with police brutality dates back to the founding of the force and has taken many different forms. Urban residents in the late nineteenth century, for example, complained mainly about "clubbing"— the routine bludgeoning of citizens by patrolmen armed with nightsticks or blackjacks. With the rise of Prohibition and organized crime in the 1920s, reformers targeted the so-called "third degree," in which police detectives in the precincts used violent interrogation tactics to elicit confessions. During periods of social and political unrest in the 1870s, 1930s, and the 1960s, public attention centered on violent mass action policing—incidents in which the police used physical force to control or suppress strikes, demonstrations, or other public political events. In recent years, the emphasis has once again returned to cases of street brutality, though involving a wider range of police weapons and tactics.

While the definition of police brutality has continually shifted, the relationship between police perpetrators and their victims has remained roughly the same. Like criminal suspects generally, victims of police brutality were mainly poor and working class, often immigrants or newcomers to the city. Jews and other southern and eastern Europeans were common complainants at the turn of the century, while African Americans and Latinos gradually replaced them by the mid-twentieth century. The overrepresentation of these groups was not just a result of economic and demographic trends; it was also aggravated by racial tension and bias.

With the NYPD drawn mainly from the upper ranks of the white working class (often Irish Americans), class and racial resentments made violent conflict more likely. Such conflicts were usually between police and lower class immigrants or African Americans, but on occasion—as in the clashes between police and antiwar demonstrators in the 1960s—they also flowed upward. Finally, gender has also been implicated in police violence, as notions of manhood and male prowess have contributed to numerous conflicts between predominantly male suspects and male officers. Even in the less common incidents involving female victims, ... police violence against women have also reflected dominant gender relations. ...

Historically, public outcry against police brutality has followed a cyclical pattern that bears no simple or direct relationship to the crime rate. The episodic nature of this history is based on a constantly shifting balance between official efforts to ensure public order on the one hand and public demands for the protection of civil rights and civil liberties on the other. City authorities have responded to outbreaks (or perceived outbreaks) of crime and disorder with stepped up enforcement efforts. ... Whether the strong-arm squads of the late-nineteenth century, the prohibition and gunmen's squads of the 1920s, the Tactical Police Force of the 1960s, or the Street Crime Unit of the 1990s, these specialized anticrime and civil defense units repeatedly swept through the city's poor neighborhoods with a mandate to clear the streets and round up the thugs. In the process, they bred fear and resentment among local residents, some of whom ardently desired increased law enforcement but soon found their own safety and civil rights sacrificed in the process. ...

As police historians have noted, public scandals and investigations into police misconduct have recurred roughly every twenty years and have been followed by periods of reform. In succeeding decades, however, the reform impulse usually ebbed as new political and law enforcement priorities took hold. As abuses continued or mounted and new police authorities became less responsive to citizen concerns, new scandals erupted and a new round of investigation, reform and retrenchment ensued.

Although such exposes and investigations were sporadic and yielded only short-term benefits, they constituted the first crude forms of citizen oversight—a means of penetrating the closed and self-protective police bureaucracy and providing an outside citizens' perspective on police practices. Initially, these exposes were provided by police reporters, reform-minded magistrates, and legislative investigations led by oppositional political parties. In the twentieth century, new civil rights and civil liberties organizations practiced more consistent monitoring of police through legal defense and advocacy work. Ultimately, these groups helped build broader coalitions that waged a protracted struggle to create more permanent, institutionalized forms of citizen oversight—a struggle that continues to this day.

1. According to Johnson, how has the definition of police brutality changed over time?
2. According to Johnson, what groups have most often been the victims of police brutality?
3. According to Johnson, what factors bred tensions between the police and the public?
4. According to Johnson, what has been the pattern of police abuse and civic reform?
5. Explain why Johnson would or would not support the Civilian Review Board (see Unit 8-3).

UNIT 10-3. CITY BUILDING POST-9/11

The destruction of the two World Trade Center towers by terrorists on September 11, 2001 had a profound effect on the American mind. In New York City, the physical and psychological toll was particularly great—almost 3,000 dead, mountains of rubble, acrid smoke and simmering fires. Although the crisis created "a citizenship of common loss,"[12] it also stoked anger, fear and a renewal of nativism (see Unit 4-2). Some of America's most basic civil liberties were questioned and constrained. Many people considered these changes necessary adaptations to new circumstances; others believed that undermining democracy was capitulating to terrorism. For New Yorkers, the dilemma was personal and political, immediate and historical. It struck at the core of the New York experience and challenged the city to reassess its values.

10-3-1. LOVING GOTHAM: FELICIA LEE, JOURNALIST, 2001

For the journalist Felicia Lee, the agonies of the moment reaffirmed her faith in the traditions of the past and the promise of the future as symbolized by New York City.

Source: Felicia R. Lee, "A Letter to a Child in Difficult Times," *New York Times*, October 21, 2001.

My Dear Son:
You are only 3 years old, and have only a vague sense of the tumult and sadness in the city since Sept. 11. I imagine that the passage of a decade will let you read this with maturity and perspective ...

For now, your father, your brother and I have decided we want to stay in the city. The only way we know how to help heal New York's bruised spirit is to turn inward, to take the long view. This is not just a battle against terrorism or even a test of bravery. It is about life's fragility and uncertainty suddenly writ large. So here we are, trying to balance self-preservation and the desire to continue the life we came to New York to create.

Unlike me and your father, you are a native New Yorker. This has been your only home. By the time you were 2, you knew how to hail a taxi. When the doorbell rings, you ask if dinner is being delivered, the food made with recipes that come from places like Japan, Mexico and India. Everybody and everything is here in this city, which has a spirit of adventure, defiance and eccentricity unlike anywhere else. ...

This is a wonderful city, son, because there are enough people here who try to get along, who try to understand one another. In our family, in which your father and I have different skin colors and different religions and your older brother was born of your father's former marriage, difference is more than a notion. We have friends who are gay, who have fled war, whose parents were in concentration camps. In this city, with its critical mass of outsiders, survivors and strivers, many of us find a measure of comfort that is lacking in most places.

Your maternal grandparents are refugees from the Deep South. They fled the back of the bus, inferior schools, physical brutality. They settled in Chicago, but your mother was determined to conquer New York. None of your grandfather's five brothers learned to read and write because of educational apartheid, but here I sit off Times Square, a staff writer for one of the best newspapers in the world.

Your father spoke only serviceable English when he came her from Italy 20 years ago, lured by everything from J. D. Salinger's books to the myth of the melting pot. But this city allowed him to thrive as a psychotherapist.

Our triumphs are not simply self-congratulation. Rather they reflect a collective triumph of New York's brand of American reinvention. Reinvention of law, custom, self.

If we flee the city, family by family, who will be left? And will we be targets somewhere else? New York is more than where we live. It represents our guts, our idealism, our loathing for cookie-cutter living. As your brother says, the men who flew into the twin towers that Tuesday morning as you sat at home watching cartoons will win if we retreat. We will only leave if there is a strong chance that our lives are at stake.

Despite what happens, and despite where we make our home by the time you read this letter, son, remember that we are New Yorkers.

Love Always, Mommy

---

1. What characteristics originally drew Lee to New York and compelled her to stay?
2. How did Lee's family reflect New York City's historic character? (see Unit 2-2)
3. According to Lee, what is the "collective triumph" of New York?
4. Did 9/11 make Lee sadder and/or stronger?

10-3-2. FEARING GOTHAM: MAX PAGE, CULTURAL HISTORIAN, 2001

Why has New York City repeatedly evoked images of disaster in American literature, film and even video games? This is the question that the cultural historian Max Page asked in examining the psychological trauma of 9/11. His answer revolves around America's long love–hate relationship with New York City, an anxiety that was heightened by 9/11 and the anthrax scare that followed it.

Source: Max Page, "On Edge, Again," *New York Times*, October 21, 2001.

New York is still the city that never sleeps. Fear will do that.

Fear of death borne in the air: a jet, a microbe. In Lower Manhattan, the dust has been scraped away. Night and day trucks rumble off with more rubble. But the fear persists: there are letters to open, cross-country trips to take. The fear is a psychic anthrax, an almost invisible powder creeping under the windowsills of thought, sifting into the corners of each mind.

Fear and this city are no strangers. History reminds us that New York has burned and been occupied by soldiers. It has been besieged by epidemics and riots. Our popular culture has been in dress rehearsal for the city's destruction for decades: in books, at the movies, in computer games, although no amount of rehearsals could prepare New Yorkers for Sept. 11 and the days of grief and worry that followed.

It was the most perfect demolition job. Two quarter-mile high towers exploding, then imploding, one-acre floors falling through the next one, 200 times over. The survivors, blanketed in the gray mist of urban disaster, headed north and east. The attacks' human spores bearing their stories, their fear, throughout the city. That unleashed energy was finally absorbed by each resident here, metastasizing into a malaise that has lingered as the country has gone to war and the specter of bioterrorism has grown. ...

Perhaps Sept. 11 has not created a new city, but in many respects ferried us back to an older, more visceral New York, where it was understood that the city was at risk. And while today the rest of the country is on edge, New York is even more so. New Yorkers understand that their city is a target.

To 19th-century New Yorkers, who may have been told stories of the city's burning during the seven-year British occupation in the Revolutionary War, or who lost family members to the cholera epidemics of the 1830's, who perhaps watched the burning of much of Lower Manhattan in 1835, or who later saw rioting mobs rage through the city in 1863, the notion that the city was forever was absurd. Even the city of the 1940's and 1950's was not immune to fears of sudden catastrophe, the distinct possibility of nuclear attack. Sept. 11 bombed us back into the atomic age, when a roar in the sky could instantly evict daydreams from New Yorkers' minds and substitute apocalyptic visions.

Fear and New York are words that have often gone together. Usually, it has been the rest of the country fearing New York, rather than New Yorkers fearing their city. New York, ascending to dominance by the early 19th century, became the most feared city of all. In New York, Americans saw the poor, the immigrants, people of all races. In New York, crowding, crime, disease and radicalism were not only found, but nurtured and propagated.

American movies and television, books and newspapers have projected images of urban fear for more than a century. Urban catastrophe movies and novels, paintings and comic books—have used New York to try to reveal the dangers of the American city. America's popular culture has returned to the theme of New York's destruction time and again, almost as a leitmotif that resonates with some of the most longstanding themes in American history: the ambivalence towards cities, the troubled reaction to immigrants and racial diversity, fear of technology's impact, and the tension between natural and human made disasters.

In a nation as religious as the United States, with a strong apocalyptic strain in its popular culture, it is not surprising to find so many examples of catastrophe. But more regularly than any other, New York—not only our largest city but "the city" of the platonic ideal—has repeatedly met its death by art. In moments of social upheaval, visions of how New York would be demolished, blown up, swallowed by the sea, or toppled by monsters have proliferated in films and in science fiction novels as well as in photography, painting and the graphic arts.

In Joaquin Miller's 1886 novel, *Destruction of Gotham*, a great fire engulfs the city as lower-class mobs attack the homes and stores of the wealthy. Only when Manhattan had "burned and burned and burned to the very bed-rock" was the apocalypse complete.

Jacob Riis, the photographic chronicler of the slums of the Lower East Side, encapsulated the fears of many Americans in 1890 with his metaphors of the waves of radical immigrants flooding onto the beaches of Brooklyn in his landmark book, *How the Other Half Lives*.

At the nearby immigrants' paradise, Coney Island, tenements were routinely set on fire at Dreamland, giving those same immigrants a chance to witness from afar the tenuous world they inhabited on the Lower East Side.

In paintings by the futuristic artist Chesley Bonestell from the cold war 1950's, in popular magazines like *Fortune* and *Collier's*, Manhattan is repeatedly devastated by atomic bombs.

In the SimCity software of the 1990's, users could pick what disaster would strike New York, or just watch past disasters play out before their eyes.

And in movie after movie, ... Hollywood has found inspiration in destroying New York: through earthquake (*Deluge*), tsunami (*Deep Impact*), asteroid (*When Worlds Collide* and *Armegeddon*), and monster (*Godzilla* and *King Kong*). ...

[However,] it's important to remember that New York has always been better at celebration than fear. ... Ticker tape parades down Broadway, the tall ships at the Bicentennial, that memorable V-J Day Kiss (caught by Eisenstaedt) in Times Square: these are New York's emotional landmarks. ...

All this is why we continue to destroy New York in books, on canvas, on movie screens and on computer monitors: because it is so unimaginable for us, in reality, not to have this city. We have played out our worst fears on the screen and in our pulp fiction because, as the city's oracle, [E. B.] White wrote in the shadow of the atomic bomb, "If it were to go, all would go—this city, this mischievous and marvelous monument which not to look upon would be like death."

Maybe fear is the wrong word for what New Yorkers feel now. There is anxiety, there is uncertainty. New York is no longer an invulnerable porcupine of skyscrapers that can never be attacked. Instead, the city has been rediscovered as a fragile community. ...

E. B. White wrote: "New York is to the nation what the white church spire is to the village—the visible symbol of aspiration and faith, the white plume saying the way is up!" The white plume we saw on Sept. 11 was the cloudy debris of two massive towers collapsing, shrewdly demolished to turn gleaming symbols of the city into burning signs of terror. ... Still, in this time of New York's haunting, I think White was right. New York will remain the way up for us all, the home of our ideals, and the place to which the world looks for ideas, for success, for art and for a new start.

---

1. According to Page, in what ways has New York City always been vulnerable?
2. According to Page, why have Americans feared and admired New York City in the past?
3. How did "death by art," or the destruction of Gotham in popular culture, reflect America's long-term attitude toward New York City?
4. Which images in this book support and/or contradict Page's thesis?
5. According to Page, what message about New York City should we draw from 9/11?

10-3-3. DISPERSING GOTHAM: *THE WALL STREET JOURNAL,* 2002

Wall Street and New York City are interchangeable terms; each reinforces the other's positive and negative attributes. Located just north of Wall Street, the Twin Towers were targets because they symbolized American capitalism and culture. In that sense, Wall Street is less a physical place than a concept. In fact, Wall Street's role in the American economy has always been in flux and reports of its demise have been frequent, if always premature. After the New Deal, people predicted that economic power would shift to Washington, D.C. After the 1975 fiscal crisis, people assumed that economic power had passed from the city to the state. After 9/11, people feared that financial institutions would all flee lower Manhattan. After the financial meltdown of 2008, people expected London or Beijing to replace New York as the center of the world's economy. But while Wall Street has undergone constant revision, like its city it has always rebounded.

Source: Randall Smith and Kate Kelly, "Rebuilding Wall Street—Everywhere," *The Wall Street Journal*, September 11, 2002, C1.

The terrorist attacks a year ago left a hole in the heart of lower Manhattan, and also accelerated a movement: the long-term exodus from the financial center known as Wall Street, with thousands of jobs moving elsewhere.

Actually, Wall Street has always been something of a misnomer. Indeed, few securities firms that remain in Manhattan's financial district literally are located on Wall Street, But more than at any other time in the 210-year history of the U.S. financial markets, "the term 'Wall Street' is more descriptive of an industry than a geographic location," Mr. [David] Komansky [Merrill Lynch chairman and CEO] says. ...

The securities industry's exodus from lower Manhattan dates back to the advent of computers and electronic trade processing during the 1960s. Before that, "every firm had to have a location" in the vicinity of Wall Street so their messengers, known as runners, could physically deliver stock certificates to one another or to a central depository, says Hardwick Simmons, chairman and chief executive of the Nasdaq Stock Market. ...

Once offerings were speeded up and firms amassed enough capital to assume more risk by themselves, the choice of firms to participate in stock and bond sales was driven more by capital and research capability. Firms that moved to midtown Manhattan, Mr. Simmons believes, did so to get closer to corporate clients who either worked there or visited because of the area's choice of hotels, restaurants, entertainment and cultural attractions, and even its greater proximity to La Guardia airport. ...

Meanwhile, some Wall Street CEOs brush off the entire issue of migration from Manhattan's financial district. "The essential question is: "Is New York the financial center or not?" Morgan Stanley's [chairman and chief executive Philip] Purcell says. "And I think it is. The question of midtown, downtown, Brooklyn or New Jersey—it's the same metropolitan area."

---

1. What long-term changes were already decentralizing Wall Street before 9/11?
2. What typically New York advantages did midtown have over downtown?
3. For all practical purposes, has Wall Street become an anachronism?
4. If Wall Street survives as a symbol, what positive and negative messages would it convey? (see Units 5-4 and 7-2)
5. How were those messages reinforced by the 2008 economic crisis?

10-3-4. GREENING GOTHAM: MICHAEL BLOOMBERG, MAYOR, 2007

Michael Bloomberg (1942–) became New York City's mayor right after the 9/11 tragedy and immediately began thinking about rebuilding the city. He suggested that downtown Manhattan should be less exclusively a business district dependent on big Wall Street firms and more open to start-up businesses set in a mixed-use environment with enough residential, recreational and cultural components to keep it alive beyond the workday.

At the same time, Bloomberg thought boldly about the city as a whole and advocated major, albeit controversial, development projects in land use and transportation. One ambitious proposal was a long-range vision for greening Gotham by 2030. Invoking the city's innovative traditions, Bloomberg presented a 127-point plan for making New York the world's first environmentally sustainable city. The occasion was Earth Day of 2007; the message was aggressive; the tone was urgent.

Source: "Mayor [Michael] Bloomberg Delivers PLANYC: A Greener, Greater New York," (April 22, 2007) www.NYC.gov

You might have seen [a plaque] when you walked in. It is stamped with a Kenyan proverb: "The earth was not given to you by your parents, it was loaned to you by your children." I think that sentiment has particular resonance today, Earth Day, when hundreds of millions of people around the globe are making an extra effort to conserve and promote our natural resources. And the proverb has also been the driving force behind our efforts over the past year—to create a comprehensive plan for a brighter, healthier, more economically prosperous city. ...

There are now 8.2 million New Yorkers—more than at any time in our history. And more are coming—probably almost a million more by 2030.

This growth will bring vibrancy, diversity, opportunity, jobs (some 750,000 of them) and billions of dollars in new revenue. But it will also pose challenges that—if left unmet—could be paralyzing: infrastructure stretched beyond its limits, parks bursting at their seams, streets choked with traffic, trains packed beyond capacity, and climate change that is real and worrisome. As a coastal city, we're on the leading edge of one of the most dramatic effects of global warming: rising sea levels and intensifying storms. The science is there. It's time to stop debating it and start dealing with it. Of course, no city or country can address this issue alone. But that doesn't mean we can walk away from the responsibility to do our part and to show others it can be done in ways that will strengthen the economy's long-term health. ...

Leadership is about recognizing challenges and seizing opportunities. And we are going to seize this opportunity to lead the way forward and create the first environmentally sustainable 21st century city. ...

That's our vision: a city that finds creative solutions to the need for more housing and parks. That has much cleaner air—the cleanest of any large city in the nation—[and] that protects the purity of its drinking water—and opens virtually all of our rivers and creeks and coastal waters to recreation. It is the vision of a city that produces more energy more cleanly, more reliably, and more cheaply, and that offers New Yorkers more choices to get around town more quickly. A 21st Century City that makes the most of our wealth of natural resources so that New Yorkers can make the most of their lives. ...

But let me conclude, not by gazing at the future, but by asking you to put yourself back in time. It's the early 1850s. Plans are being drawn up for an enormous Central Park at a time when much of Manhattan was open fields and forest. Some propose a much smaller park. Where do you stand?

Skip forward to the 1890s. Plans are drawn up for a subway system that goes all the way into Northern Manhattan. Some say it will cost too much. And who needs a subway in the countryside. What do you say?

Now on to 1931, the middle of the Great Depression. Plans are drawn up for a new midtown mega-project. As [George] Gershwin wrote, "They all laughed at Rockefeller Center ... " Are you laughing too?

Our great water supply system, our arterial highway network, our bridges and tunnels, our parks, all of them were built by a city of people who were looking forward. That has been our heritage. Time and again, New Yorkers have taken the big steps that require political courage and a belief that the future can and should be better than the present.

Our city has come back from the abyss of the 1970s and from the attacks of 9/11, and we have come back stronger than ever. Our economy is humming, our fiscal house is in order, and the near-term horizon looks bright. If we don't act now, when? And if we don't act, who will?... This is our opportunity to look forward and to step forward. ... Together, as the Kenyan proverb suggests, we can "return" this city to our children. And it will be stronger, healthier, cleaner, greener, and greater than ever.

1. What were the most important aspects of Bloomberg's proposal?
2. How realistic and/or idealistic was Bloomberg's proposal?
3. How was Bloomberg's vision of New York City's future rooted in his understanding of its past?
4. What would John Jacob Astor, John Griscom, Frederick Law Olmsted, Boss Tweed, Jacob Riis, Mary White Ovington, Robert Moses, Banana Kelly and Rudy Giuliani think about "greening" New York City?

UNIT 10-4. CHANGE AND CHALLENGE: THE RESTLESS CITY

The restless city is a busy city noted for its fast pace, big crowds, varied activities, rich resources, and diverse people. It is a magnet for those seeking refuge, change, rebellion, freedom, anonymity and opportunity. It is fascinating but frightening, tense but tolerant. All cities possess these characteristics; yet, all cities are not the same. If they differ by degree, then New York City's temperature must be very high.

Over time, Gotham has confronted its own complexity. In 1948, the writer E. B. White noted that New Yorkers had a "sense of belonging to something unique, cosmopolitan, mighty and unparalleled." That sense, said White, compensated for the frustrations, disappointments and struggles of life in the city—all of which also reflect its restlessness. The following documents capture many sides of New York City's character and ask whether or not restlessness was its greatest asset.

10-4-1. RUNNING: YORK, A SLAVE, 1758

From the start, slaves resisted bondage; they were restless. In the city, where slaves were often sent out alone on errands and had contact with free blacks, flight was easier than on an isolated plantation. The colonial era newspapers were full of appeals for the capture of escaped slaves. The wording illuminates the nature of slavery in the city. Note that slaves often played musical instruments as a way of preserving their culture, participating in social events and earning income as entertainers.

Source: *New-York Gazette and Weekly Post-Boy*, #811, July 17, 1758.

New York, July 16, 1758: RUN away on the 10th of this inst. July from James Swan, of this city, [river] pilot; a negro man named York, about 5 feet 8 inches high, of a slender make, talks pretty good English, is a good cook, can play on the violin, and shave and dress wigs. He had on when he went away old shoes and carved silver buckles, blue and red worsted plush breeches, old trowsers, check shirt, a blue jacket, a small-cropped hat, with yellow worsted binding around it; and steps pretty long. He formerly belonged to Lawrence Lawrance, of this city, merchant. Whoever takes up the said negro, and secures him so that his master may have him again, shall have, if within the city, 20s; if between it and Kingsbridge, 30s; and 40s if farther, and all reasonable charges paid by James Swan.

All masters of vessels, and captains of privateers, are forewarned from carrying him to sea, or harbouring him on board their vessels, as they may expect to answer it at their peril.

---

1. Did York's skills, possessions and employment history fit the stereotype of a slave?
2. How did the reward schedule reflect patterns of escape and the likelihood of capturing York?
3. Why might ship captains have helped York?
4. How did York's skills, possessions, employment history and escape reflect the nature of slavery in the city?
5. How did this ad reveal the complexity of restlessness among blacks and whites in colonial New York City?

10-4-2. MOVING: LYDIA MARIA CHILD, REFORMER, 1845

Lydia Maria Child was an American reformer who opposed slavery and promoted rights for women as well as for Native Americans. Born, raised and educated in Massachusetts, she was an influential novelist and journalist. Just as her popular book, *The American Frugal Housewife* (1829) was full of practical advice, so too her *Letters From New York* (1845) provided a no-nonsense analysis of urban life.

Source: Lydia Maria Child, *Letters From New York* (New York: C. S. Francis and Company, 1845), 285–288.

May-day in New York is the saddest thing, to one who has been hunting mosses by the brook, and paddling in its waters. Brick walls, instead of budding trees, and rattling wheels in lieu of singing birds, are bad enough; but to make the matter worse, all New York moves on the first of May; not only moves about, as usual, in the everlasting hurry-scurry of business, but one house empties itself into another, all over the city. ...

Do you want an appropriate emblem of this country, and this age? Then stand on the sidewalks of New York, and watch the universal transit on the first of May. The facility and speed with which our people change politics, and move from sect to sect and from theory to theory, is comparatively slow and moss-grown. ...

That people should move so often in this city is generally a matter of their own volition. Aspirations after the infinite lead them to perpetual change, in the restless hope of finding something better and better still. But they would not raise the price of drays, and subject themselves to great inconvenience, by moving all on one day, were it not that the law compels everybody who intends to move at all, to quit his premises before twelve o'clock on May morning. Failing to do this, the police will put him and his goods into the street, where they will fare much like a boy beside an upset hornet's nest. This regulation, handed down from Dutch times, proves very convenient in arranging the Directory with promptness and accuracy. ...

However, human beings are such creatures of habit and imitation, that what is necessity soon becomes fashion, and each one wishes to do what everybody else is doing. A lady in the neighborhood closed all her blinds and shutters on May-day. Being asked by her acquaintance whether she had been in the country, she answered, "I was ashamed not to be moving on the first of May, and so I shut up the house that the neighbors might not know it." One could not well imagine a fact more characteristic of the despotic sway of custom and public opinion in the United States and in the nineteenth century. ...

O, for one of those old German homes, where the same stork, with his children and grandchildren, builds on the same roof generation after generation; where each family knows its own particular stork; and each stork knows the family from all the world beside. ...

But after all, this is a foolish, whining complaint. A stork's nest is very pleasant, but there are better things. Man is moving to his highest destiny through manifold revolutions of spirit; and the outward must change with the inward.

---

1. According to Child, what were the advantages and disadvantages of May Day?
2. According to Child, what did May Day reveal about New York City's social class system?
3. According to Child, what did May Day reveal about New York City's character?

10-4-3. HUSTLING: THEODORE DREISER, AUTHOR, 1900

In *Sister Carrie*, a classic novel of Gilded Age America, Theodore Dreiser compared America's two largest cities, Chicago and New York. Although they were then competing for predominance, Dreiser suggested that there really was no contest between them.

Source: Theodore Dreiser, *Sister Carrie* (New York: Doubleday, Page and Company, 1900), 321.

Whatever a man like Hurstwood could be in Chicago, it is very evident that he would be but an inconspicuous drop in an ocean like New York. In Chicago, whose population still ranged about 500,000, millionaires were not numerous. The rich had not become so conspicuously rich as to drown all moderate incomes in obscurity. The attention of the inhabitants was not so distracted by local celebrities in the dramatic, artistic, social and religious fields as to shut the well-positioned man from view. In Chicago the two roads to distinction were politics and trade. In New York the roads were any one of a half-hundred, and each had been diligently pursued by hundreds, so that celebrities were numerous. The sea was already full of whales. A common fish must needs disappear wholly from view—remain unseen. In other words, Hurstwood was nothing."

1. According to Dreiser, what were the major differences between Chicago and New York City?
2. According to Dreiser, which city offered the most opportunity for economic success? Why?
3. Explain why Dreiser compared New York City to an ocean.

10-4-4. BUSTLING: THE LOWER EAST SIDE, c. 1907

In the late nineteenth and early twentieth centuries, the Lower East Side symbolized New York as a place of perpetual change. However, print and visual images of the neighborhood conveyed mixed messages. On the one hand, it was a gateway to America for new immigrants, a melting pot, a busy marketplace, a rich cultural center. On the other hand, it was a crowded, dirty, dangerous slum full of foreigners speaking strange languages, eating strange foods and practicing strange religions. Fascination with and fear of the Lower East Side (and New York City) justified turning this early-twentieth-century photograph into a postcard.

Source: "Hester Street, postcard c. 1901–1907, Detroit Publishing Company.

1. How did this photographer capture the density, activity and diversity of the Lower East Side?
2. How did the buildings in this photograph reflect change over time?
3. How did this photograph convey both positive and negative images of the Lower East Side (and New York City)?

10-4-5. BUILDING: ARTHUR GUITERMAN, POET, 1920

After emigrating from Vienna, Austria to the United States with his parents, Arthur Guiterman (1871–1943) attended the City College of New York. An editor of the *Woman's Home Companion* and the *Literary Digest,* Guiterman was also a founder of the Poetry Society of America. Noted for their humor, Guiterman's poems used simple language to analyze common subjects.

Source: Arthur Guiterman, "New York," *Ballads of Old New York* (New York: Harper and Brothers, 1920), 287.

The city is cutting a way,
The gasmen are hunting a leak,
They're putting down asphalt today,
To change it for stone in a week.

The builders are raising a wall,
The wreckers are tearing one down,
Enacting a drama of all
Our changeable, turbulent town.

For here is an edifice meant
To stand for an eon or more,
And there's a gospeler's tent,
And there is a furniture store.

Our suburbs are under the plow,
Our scaffolds are raw in the sun,
We're drunk and disorderly now,
But—'Twill be a great place when it's done.

1. How did Guiterman suggest that building the city is really destroying the city?
2. How did Guiterman's emphasis on physical change complement Child's emphasis on social change?
3. Did Guiterman and Child agree with Bender (see Ducument 1-4) that the unfinished city is the best city?
4. How was Guiterman's city similar to and/or different from Dreiser's city?

10-4-6. BURSTING: CHARLES HANSON TOWNE, WRITER, 1931

Charles Hanson Towne (1877–1949) was a prominent member of New York City's literary world during the first half of the twentieth century. In addition to being a magazine editor, literary agent and literary critic, he was a prolific writer of novels, poems and travel books. His observations help explain why the city is both loved and hated.

Source: Charles H. Towne, *This New York of Mine* (New York: Cosmopolitan Book Company, 1931), 5–11.

The spell of Manhattan is irresistible. And the pathos of our love for it is one of the amazing manifestations of our modern times. For we love the evil along with the good; we cherish the cruelty that clings to so great a city as we cherish the kindness that hides within it. We are bound, we are chained; yet all of us long for the moment when we can escape from the shackles that surround us. Though we are bruised and torn; though we feel … that we would rather bleed in New York than be happy elsewhere, always there is the urge to leave the siren city. But, paradoxically, the urge to come back is even stronger. So there is a constant battle of emotion being waged in the hearts of the dwellers in New York, and that seething tide within us, those cross-currents forever whirling in our breasts, are what give the town its spiritual Hell Gate, and make it the force and power that it is. …

Metropolitan centers become great factors in any country, because the best young blood of the provinces seeks the lure and lights and opportunities that await the newcomer. … And that spirit of bravado, merging its young strength in the whirlpool, creates new ripples, until the caldron bubbles anew, overfilled as it is with the intensity of youthful dreams.

In every great city, too, beggar and prince may walk side by side. Before the millionaire's palace the meanest mendicant may hover. Contrasts such as these, like the battling tides, only serve to enrich the daily drama that is played on the agate stage of Manhattan. It is a fiery story that is unfolded here; only it is not one story, it is eight million stories. They may be sordid, they may be sad, they may be mean, or they may be beautiful; but certainly not one of them is ever dull. …

The "rush hour" is a slogan peculiar to New York. No wonder that foreigners, coming to us for the first time, stand aghast. …

The lure of New York! Our city has been a magnet to draw unto itself the flotsam and jetsam of the whole world. … Thus, by degrees, we came to absorb this foreign population: Russian Jews, … Germans, Irish, Poles, Slovaks, Italians, French, Greeks and Slavs, Spanish, Swedes, Norwegians and Danes—every possible element that the Old World sent to our shores. A vast cosmopolitan city is the result today, a town bursting with every known nationality, our streets echoing with the chatter of foreign tongues.

And Asia, too, has sent us its full quota of Chinese and Japanese. … Conglomerate, sprawling, shimmering New York! Everything is here: Armenians, Turks, Egyptians—yes, and even a few Americans!

If there is Rivington Street, there is likewise Park Avenue. If there is Hester Street, there is also Fifth Avenue. If there is MacDougal Alley, there is Harlem with its Negroes. If there is the squalor of the Bowery, there is, a long way from it, the aristocracy of Sutton Place. It is a far cry from the Battery to the Bronx. Yet it is not so far from Riverside Drive to the crowded tenements of Second and Third Avenues. And Avenue A and Avenue B. And in between, huddling together to preserve some sort of decorum, there are the side streets, enriched now with fine residences. If Washington Square has lost no little of its old glamour and grandeur, the fine facades there have been transported to thoroughfares further uptown; and if something has been lost, something also has been gained in neighborhoods that were once shabby and poor.

"The old order changeth," but nowhere on earth does it change so rapidly, as in conglomerate, restless New York. A city of moods. A city of energy and hope and despair. A city of terror too; and yet, for almost every one of us, a city that we cannot leave.

---

1. What are the positive and negative qualities of the "spiritual Hell gate" and "the siren city" that Towne described?
2. According to Towne, what were New York City's most distinctive historical traits?
3. What is the relationship between a city of contrasts and a "conglomerate, restless" city?
4. For all of its negative qualities, why is New York "a city that we cannot leave"?

10-4-7. WRESTLING: DAVID HALBERSTAM, JOURNALIST AND AUTHOR, 1972

David Halberstam (1934–2007) was a renowned journalist, editor, author and historian. Starting out as managing editor for the *Harvard Crimson,* Halberstam worked for the *New York Times* during the 1960s, covered the civil rights movement and won a Pulitzer Prize for his Vietnam War reports. He wrote 22 highly acclaimed books on politics, foreign policy, media, cars and sports. He also chronicled the life and death of 12 firemen from his local firehouse on 9/11. Tragically, at age 73, Halberstam was killed in a car accident on his way to an interview for another book. Fortunately, he left a rich legacy of work that will continue to inspire readers over time. One small sample of Halberstam's lively, perceptive writing style was his 1972 comment on the restlessness of New York.

Source: David Halberstam, "In Defense of New York," *Harper's Bazaar* (February 1972), 102–103.

And I think whatever its faults, it is a great city, the international city. The faces and the styles are magnificent, and it teems with a special kind of driving energy, everyone running, pushing, scratching to get ahead. It is not a city to retire in or to coast in.

The energy is a special kind. Nervous energy, I think—the energy of the insecure and the rootless, which makes the city at once so neurotic and so creative. The true New Yorker does not control his environment. He is in fact at war with it, and it is this war which makes him interesting and may produce his talent.

It is restless here. This is above all not a company town. If anything, it is the anti-company town. The people who have made it here have not made it in the typical American success pattern, but instead because they rebelled against that pattern.

It is a critic's town, not a booster's town. Its values are not the abiding trusting values of Protestant America; they are the darker, more suspicious values of people who have nothing going for them except themselves. ...

In New York you cannot rely upon your title and your position to get you through. It is what you are yourself and I think the result of this is that energy, that restless quality of the city. It is not a city for people to stand still, but it also abounds in people from whom you can learn. Which also means that it is a tough town.

1. How did Halberstam define the restless city?
2. According to Halberstam, what were the advantages of a city full of insecure, rootless, neurotic, rebellious, suspicious and competitive people?
3. How are all of the documents in this unit similar but different?
4. Which topics, events, or individuals in this book best captured the positive and negative qualities of a restless city?
5. Considering all of its manifestations from colonial times to the present, was restlessness New York City's greatest strength or its greatest weakness?

SELECTED RESOURCES

Barrett, Wayne assisted by Adam Fifiel. *RUDY! An Investigative Biography of Rudolph Giuliani.* New York: Basic Books, 2000.

Chernick, Howard (ed.). *Resilient City: The Economic Impact of 9/11.* New York: Russell Sage Foundation, 2005.

Foner, Nancy. *New Immigrants in New York.* New York: Columbia University Press, 1987.

—— (ed). *Wounded City: The Social Impact of 9/11.* New York: Russell Sage Foundation, 2005.

Johnson, Marilynn. *Street Justice: A History of Police Violence in New York City.* Boston, MA: Beacon Press, 2003.

Kessner, Thomas, and Betty Boyd Caroli. *Today's Immigrants, Their Stories.* New York: Oxford University Press, 1982.

Kirtzman, Andrew. *Rudy Giuliani, Emperor of the City.* New York: William Morrow, 2000.

Lardner, James, and Thomas Repetto. *NYPD: A City and Its Police.* New York: Henry Holt and Company, 2000.

Min, Pyong Gap. *Changes and Conflicts: Korean Immigrant Families in New York.* Boston, MA: Allyn and Bacon, 1998.

Mollenkopf, John (ed.). *Contentious City: The Politics of Recovery in New York City.* New York: Russell Sage Foundation, 2005.

Ricourt, Milagros. *Hispanics in Queens: Latino Panethnicity in a New York City Neighborhood.* Ithaca, NY: Cornell University Press, 2003.

Siegel, Fred, with Harry Siegel. *Prince of the City: New York and the Genius of American Life.* San Francisco, CA: Encounter Books, 2005.

Sorkin, Michael, and Sharon Zukin (eds). *After the World Trade Center: Rethinking New York.* New York: Routledge, 2002.

Sutton, Constance, and Elsa M. Chaney. *Caribbean Life in New York City: Sociocultural Dimensions.* New York: Center for Migration Studies of New York, 1992.

www.911digitalarchive.org

NOTES

Chapter 1: Introduction

1 Morris Dickstein, "Neighborhoods," *Dissent* (Fall, 1987), 606.
2 *The Restless City, A Short History of New York from Colonial Times to the Present* (New York: Routledge, 2006)
3 Peter L. Berger, "In Praise of New York: A Semi-Secular Homily," *Commentary* (February, 1977), 59–62.
4 Chiang Yee, *The Silent Traveller in New York* (London: Methuen, 1950), 48–59, 280.

Chapter 2: 1609–1799

1 Thomas Bender, "New York as a Center of 'Difference': How America's Metropolis Counters America's Myth," *Dissent* (Fall 1987), 429–435; Thomas Bender, *The Unfinished City: New York and the Metropolitan Idea* (New York: The New Press, 2002), 185–192.
2 Joyce D. Goodfriend, "Burghers and Blacks: The Evolution of a Slave Society in New Amsterdam," *New York History* 59 (1978), 125–144.
3 Milton M. Klein, *The Politics of Diversity: Essays in the History of Colonial New York* (Port Washington, NY: Kennikat Press, 1974), 183–201.
4 Henry H. Kessler and Eugene Rachlis, *Peter Stuyvesant and His New York* (New York: Random House, 1959), 169–196.
5 Klein, *The Politics of Diversity*, 183.
6 Kessler and Rachlis, *Stuyvesant*, 3–23; Oliver Allen, *New York, New York: A History of the World's Most Exhilarating and Challenging City* (New York: Atheneum, 1990), 23.
7 Edwin G. Burrows and Mike Wallace, *Gotham: A History of New York City to 1898* (New York: Oxford University Press, 1999), 43–49, 57–58; Kessler and Rachlis, *Stuyvesant*, 63–77; Oliver A. Rink, *Holland on the Hudson: An Economic and Social History of Dutch New York* (Ithaca, NY: Cornell University Press, 1986), 94–116, 160–164; Edward Robb Ellis, *The Epic of New York City* (New York: Old Town Books, 1966), 43–46; Henri and Barbara van der Zee, *A Sweet and Alien Land, The Story of Dutch New York* (New York: Viking, 1978), 170–172.
8 Burrows and Wallace, *Gotham*, 46–48, 59–61; Kessler and Rachlis, *Stuyvesant*, 67, 179–186.
9 Kessler and Rachlis, *Stuyvesant*, 51–52.
10 van der Zee, *A Sweet and Alien Land*, 161–167, 180–192; Kessler and Rachlis, *Stuyvesant*, 68–77, 95–108; Russell Shorto, *The Island at the Center of the World, The Epic Story of Dutch Manhattan and the Forgotten Colony that Shaped America* (New York: Doubleday, 2004), 170–179, 197–203, 216–232, 240–245.
11 Shorto, *The Island at the Center of the World*, 262–265; Burrows and Wallace, *Gotham*, 64–66.

12 Shorto, *The Island at the Center of the World*, 268; Burrows and Wallace, *Gotham*, 66; van der Zee, *A Sweet and Alien Land*, 345–6.

13 Kessler and Rachlis, *Stuyvesant*, 118–24; Burrows and Wallace, *Gotham*, 67–70.

14 William R. Shepherd, *The Story of New Amsterdam* (New York: Alfred A. Knopf, 1926), 111; Kessler and Rachlis, *Stuyvesant*, 259–269.

15 Burrows and Wallace, *Gotham*, 190–204; Richard M. Ketchum, *Divided Loyalties: How the American Revolution Came to New York* (New York: Henry Holt, 2002), 95–159.

16 Larry Gerlach (ed.), *The American Revolution: New York as a Case Study* (Belmont, CA: Wadsworth, 1972), 17.

17 Carl Becker, *The History of Political Parties in the Province of New York, 1760–1776* (Madison, WI, University of Wisconsin Press, 1909); Staughton Lynd, "The Mechanics in New York Politics, 1774–1788," *Labor History* V (1964), 225–246.

Chapter 3: 1800–1840

1 Washington Irving, *Diedrich Knickerbocker's A History of New York* (New York: Harcourt, Brace and Company, 1927), 128–129.

2 Elizabeth Blackmar, *Manhattan for Rent, 1785–1850* (Ithaca, NY: Cornell University Press, 1989), 94–99; Isaac S. Lyon, *Recollections of an Old Cartman: Old New York Street Life* (New York: New York Bound, 1984), 8–9.

3 Carl E. Prince, "The Great Riot Year: Jacksonian Democracy and Patterns of Violence in 1834," *Journal of the Early Republic* 5 (Spring 1985), 1–20.

4 Linda K. Kerber, "Abolitionists and Amalgamators: The New York City Race Riots of 1834," *New York Historical Society Quarterly* 48 (1967), 28–39; Paul A. Gilje, *The Road to Mobocracy: Popular Disorder in New York City, 1763–1834* (Chapel Hill, NC: University of North Carolina Press, 1987), 165–170; John M. Werner, *Reaping the Bloody Harvest: Race Riots in the United States During the Age of Jackson, 1824–1849* (New York: Garland, 1986), 119–137, 265–288; Paul O. Weinbaum, *Mobs and Demagogues: The New York Response to Collective Violence in the Early Nineteenth Century* (Ann Arbor, MI: University of Michigan Press, 1979), 5–14, 25–30.

5 Graham Russell Hodges, "David Ruggles: The Hazards of Anti-Slavery Journalism," *Media Studies Journal* (Spring/Summer, 2000), http://www.freedomforum.org.

6 Timothy J. Gilfoyle, *City of Eros: New York City, Prostitution, and the Commercialization of Sex, 1790–1920* (New York: W. W. Norton, 1992), 92, 96; Patricia Cline Cohen, "The Helen Jewett Murder: Violence, Gender and Sexual Licentiousness in Antebellum America," *National Women's Studies Association Journal* 2 (Summer 1990), 374–389; Marilynn Wood Hill, *Their Sisters' Keepers: Prostitution in New York City, 1830–1870* (Berkeley, CA: University of California Press, 1993), 9–17.

7 Mary P. Ryan, *Womanhood in America from Colonial Times to the Present* (New York: New Viewpoints, 1979), 75–117.

8 Cited in Lori D. Ginzberg, "Fanny Wright," in Mari Jo Buhle, Paul Buhle and Harvey Kaye (eds), *The American Radical* (New York: Routledge, 1994), 22; A. J. G. Perkins and Theresa Wolfson, *Frances Wright, Free Enquirer: The Study of a Temperament* (New York: Harper and Brothers, 1939), 233, 292; Edwin G. Burrows and Mike Wallace, *Gotham: A History of New York City to 1898* (New York: Oxford University Press, 1999), 538–541.

9 *New York Herald*, April 30, 1836; Burrows and Wallace, *Gotham*, 525–527; Ric Burns and James Sanders, *New York: An Illustrated History* (New York: Alfred A.

Knopf, 1999), 80–81; Richard O'Connor, *The Scandalous Mr. Bennett* (Garden City, NY: Doubleday and Co., 1962).

10 Burrows and Wallace, *Gotham*, 596–602.

11 Sean Wilentz, *Chants Democratic: New York City and the Rise of the American Working Class, 1788–1850* (New York: Oxford University Press, 1984), 286–293.

12 Burrows and Wallace, *Gotham*, 609–618.

13 Arthur D. Howden Smith, *John Jacob Astor: Landlord of New York* (Philadelphia, PA: J. B. Lippincott, 1929), 13–64.

14 Ibid, 67–190; Edward Robb Ellis, *The Epic of New York City* (New York: Old Town Books, 1966), 208–10.

15 Ellis, *The Epic of New York City*, 211–214.

16 Smith, *John Jacob Astor*, 255–9; Axel Madsen, *John Jacob Astor, America's First Multimillionaire* (New York: John Wiley, 2001), 244–55.

17 Burrows and Wallace, *Gotham*, 447; Elizabeth Blackmar, *Manhattan for Rent*, 33: Smith, *John Jacob Astor*, 259–61.

18 Madsen, *John Jacob Astor*, 254–5; Gilje, *Mobocracy*, 220–222.

19 Ellis, *The Epic of New York City*, 183; Blackmar, *Manhattan for Rent*, 204; Smith, *John Jacob Astor*, 256–258; Madsen, *John Jacob Astor*, 252, 257; Kenneth W. Porter, *John Jacob Astor, Businessman* II (Cambridge, MA: Harvard University Press, 1931), 1186–90.

20 Smith, *John Jacob Astor*, 283–284; Madsen, *John Jacob Astor*, 6.

21 Burrows and Wallace, *Gotham*, 600–601; Gilfoyle, *City of Eros*, 67, 96; Madsen, *John Jacob Astor*, 250–51; Justin Kaplan, *When the Astors Ruled New York* (New York: Viking, 2006), 15–26.

22 Smith, *John Jacob Astor*, 267; Burrows and Wallace, *Gotham*, 273, 337–338, 411, 434–436, 447–449.

Chapter 4: 1840–1865

1 "City of Ships," in Mark Van Doren (ed.), *The Portable Walt Whitman* (New York: The Viking Press, 1973), 217.

2 Roy Rosenzweig and Elizabeth Blackmar, *The Park and the People: A History of Central Park* (Ithaca, NY: Cornell University Press, 1992), 15–54; Elizabeth Barlow, *Frederick Law Olmsted's New York* (New York: Praeger, 1972), 17–19; Eric Homberger, *Scenes in the Life of a City: Corruption and Conscience in Old New York* (New Haven, CT: Yale University Press, 1994), 212–293; Ian R. Stewart, "Politics and the Park: The Fight for Central Park," *New York Historical Society Quarterly* LXI (1977), 124–155; Edward K. Spann, *The New Metropolis, New York City, 1840–1857* (New York: Columbia University Press, 1981), 159–173.

3 Donald MacLeod, *Biography of Fernando Wood* (New York: D. F. Parsons, 1856), 307–312; Jerome Mushkat, *Fernando Wood, A Political Biography* (Kent, OH: Kent State University Press, 1990), 47–48; Stewart, "Politics and the Park," 151–153; Rosenzweig and Blackmar, *The Park and the People*, 56–58.

4 Albert Fein, editor, *Landscape into Cityscape: Frederick Law Olmsted's Plans for a Greater New York City* (Ithaca, NY: Cornell University Press, 1967), 98–102; Rosenzweig and Blackmar, *The Park and the People*, 95–205; Homberger, *Scenes in the Life of a City*, 253–293.

5 Rick Beard, "Calvert Vaux," in Kenneth T. Jackson (ed.), *The Encyclopedia of New York City* (New Haven, CT: Yale University Press, 1995), 1226.

6 Edwin G. Burrows and Mike Wallace, *Gotham: A History of New York City to 1898* (New York: Oxford University Press, 1999), 1104; Hasia R. Diner, *Erin's Daughters in America: Irish Immigrant Women in the Nineteenth Century* (Baltimore, MD: Johns Hopkins University Press, 1983), 72–73.

7 Paul A. Gilge, *The Road to Mobocracy: Popular Disorder in New York City, 1763–1834* (Chapel Hill, NC: University of North Carolina Press, 1987), 267–288; James F. Richardson, "To Control the City: The New York Police in Historical Perspective," in Kenneth T. Jackson and Stanley Schultz (eds), *Cities in American History* (New York: Knopf, 1972), 272–289.

8 Joel Tyler Headley, *The Great Riots of New York, 1712–1863* (New York: Dover, 1873/1971), 111–128; Richard Moody, *The Astor Place Riot* (Bloomington, IN: Indiana University Press, 1958); James F. Richardson, *The New York Police, Colonial Times to 1901* (New York: Oxford University Press, 1970), 28–68.

9 Iver Bernstein, *The New York City Draft Riots: Their Significance for American Society and Politics in the Age of the Civil War* (New York: Oxford University Press, 1990); Headley, *The Great Riots of New York*, 136–288; Ernest A. McKay, *The Civil War and New York City* (Syracuse, NY: Syracuse University Press, 1990); Adrian Cook, *The Armies of the Streets: The New York City Draft Riots of 1863* (Lexington, KY: University of Kentucky Press, 1974); Edward K. Spann, *Gotham at War: New York City, 1860–1865* (Wilmington, DE: Scholarly Resources, 2002); Graham Russell Hodges, *Root and Branch: African Americans in New York and East Jersey, 1613–1863* (Chapel Hill, NC: University of North Carolina Press, 1999), 263–270.

10 John H. Hewitt, "The Search for Elizabeth Jennings, Heroine of a Sunday Afternoon in New York City," *New York History* (October 1980), 386–415.

11 Ibid, 389–390.

12 Ibid, 399–406.

13 Ibid, 390–393.

14 Ibid, 393–397.

15 Ibid, 406.

16 Ibid, 412; Craig Steven Wilder, *A Covenant with Color: Race and Social Power in Brooklyn* (New York: Columbia University Press, 2000), 70.

17 Hewitt, "The Search for Elizabeth Jennings," 405–412.

18 Ibid, 413–415; Carla L. Peterson, "Black Life in Freedom: Creating an Elite Culture," in Ira Berlin and Leslie M. Harris (eds), *Slavery in New York* (New York: The New Press, 2005), 183–214.

19 Hewitt, "The Search for Elizabeth Jennings," 390–392.

20 Glyndon Van Deusen, *Horace Greeley, Nineteenth Century Crusader* (New York: Hill and Wang, 1953).

21 Philip S. Foner, *Business and Slavery: New York Merchants and the Irrepressible Conflict* (Chapel Hill, NC: University of North Carolina Press, 1941), 1–14, 144–168; Wilder, *Covenant with Color*, 74–75; Graham Russell Hodges. *Root and Branch: African Americans in New York and East Jersey, 1613–1863* (Chapel Hill, NC: University of North Carolina Press, 1999), 256–257.

22 Leslie M. Harris, *In The Shadow of Slavery: African Americans in New York City, 1626–1863.* (Chicago, IL: University of Chicago Press, 2003), 267–270; Wilder, *Covenant with Color*, 74–79.

23 Craig Steven Wilder, "Black Life in Freedom: Creating a Civic Culture" and Manisha Sinha, "Black Abolitionism: The Assault on Southern Slavery and the Struggle for Racial Equality," in Ira Berlin and Leslie M. Harris (eds), *Slavery in New York* (New York: The New Press, 2005), 215–262.

24 Wilder, *Covenant with Color*, 78–9; Herbert Aptheker, *A Documentary History of the Negro People in the United States from the Colonial Times through the Civil War* vol. I (New York: Citadel Press, 1951), 454–58.

25 Wilder, *Covenant with Color*, 21–41, 113–114.

Chapter 5: 1865–1900

1 Bayard Still, *Mirror for Gotham, New York as Seen by Contemporaries from Dutch Days to the Present* (New York: New York University Press, 1956), 213.

2 Bayard Still, *Urban America, A History with Documents* (Boston, MA: Little, Brown and Company, 1974), 198.

3 Still, *Mirror for Gotham,* 209, 220.

4 Alan Trachtenberg, *Brooklyn Bridge, Fact and Symbol* (Chicago, IL: University of Chicago Press, 1965/1979), 139.

5 David C. Hammack, *Power and Society, Greater New York at the Turn of the Century* (New York: Columbia University Press, 1982), 188–229.

6 Alexander B. Callow, Jr. *The Tweed Ring* (New York: Oxford University Press, 1965), 168, 241, 253–278; Kenneth D. Ackerman, *Boss Tweed: The Rise and Fall of the Corrupt Pol Who Conceived the Soul of Modern New York* (New York: Carroll and Graf, 2001), 105–109.

7 Callow, *The Tweed Ring,* 198–206; M. R. Werner, *Tammany Hall* (Garden City, NY: Doubleday, Doran and Company, 1928), 164–168; Oliver E. Allen, *The Tiger: The Rise and Fall of Tammany Hall* (Reading, MA: Addison-Wesley1993), 80–143; Eric Homberger, *Scenes from the Life of a City: Corruption and Conscience in Old New York* (New Haven, CT: Yale University Press, 1994), 141–211; Lincoln Steffens, *The Shame of the Cities* (New York: Hill and Wang, 1904/1957).

8 Callow, *The Tweed Ring,* 8–9, 110–114, 208–213.

9 Ibid, 254.

10 Ibid, entire.

11 Louis F. Post and Fred C. Leubuscher, *Henry George's 1886 Campaign* (New York: John W. Lovell, 1886/1961), 28–29.

12 Gunther Barth, *City People: The Rise of Modern City Culture in Nineteenth-Century America* (New York: Oxford University Press, 1980), 110–147; M. Christine Boyer, *Manhattan Manners, Architecture and Style, 1850–1900* (New York: Rizzoli, 1985), 87–96; Thomas Kessner, *Capital City: New York City and the Men Behind America's Rise to Economic Dominance, 1860–1900* (New York: Simon and Schuster, 2003), 86; Stephen N. Elias, *Alexander T. Stewart: Forgotten Merchant Prince* (Westport, CT: Praeger, 1992).

13 Jacob A. Riis, *How the Other Half Lives: Studies Among the Tenements of New York* (New York: Dover Publications, 1971), 134.

14 John Dizikes, *Opera In America: A Cultural History* (New Haven, CT: Yale University Press, 1993), 216–219.

15 Robert W. Snyder, *The Voice of the City: Vaudeville and Popular Culture in New York* (Chicago, IL: Ivan R. Dee, 1989), 12–24; David Nasaw, *Going Out: The Rise and Fall of Public Amusement* (Cambridge, MA: Harvard University Press, 1993), 23–27; Edwin G. Burrows and Mike Wallace, *Gotham: A History of New York City to 1898* (New York: Oxford University Press, 1999), 1144–1146.

16 Robert H. Bremner, *From the Depths: The Discovery of Poverty in the United States* (New York: New York University Press, 1956), 16–30.

17 Ibid, 31–66.

18 Edward J. Renehan, Jr., *Dark Genius of Wall Street: The Misunderstood Life of Jay Gould, King of the Robber Barons* (New York: Basic Books, 2005), 21–43; Maury Klein, *The Life and Legend of Jay Gould* (Baltimore, CT: The Johns Hopkins University Press, 1986); 11–41.

19 Renehan, *Dark Genius,* 69–93; Klein, *Jay Gould,* 63–75.

20 Renehan, *Dark Genius,* 95–161; Klein, *Jay Gould,* 76–98; Ron Chernow, *The House of Morgan: An American Banking Family and the Rise of Modern Finance* (New York: Grove Press, 1990), 30–32; Burrows and Wallace, *Gotham,* 914.

21 Renehan, *Dark Genius,* 163–178; Klein, *Jay Gould,* 99–115.

22 Renehan, *Dark Genius*, 163–213; Klein, *Jay Gould*, 1–3, 11–12, 99–115, 122.

23 Renehan, *Dark Genius*, 163–213; Klein, *Jay Gould*, 11–12, 99–136, 205–207, 316.

24 Renehan, *Dark Genius*, 215–246.

25 Renehan, *Dark Genius*, 259–266; Klein, *Jay Gould*, 195–205, 394–395.

26 Renehan, *Dark Genius*, 266–273; Klein, *Jay Gould*, 281–291, 474–475.

27 Renehan, *Dark Genius*, 247–258, 275–296; Klein, *Jay Gould*, 441–497; Robert Irving Warshow, *Jay Gould, The Story of a Fortune* (New York: Greenberg, 1928), 182.

28 Renehan, *Dark Genius*, 232.

Chapter 6: 1900–1920

1 Bayard Still, *Mirror for Gotham: New York as Seen by Contemporaries from Dutch Days to the Present* (New York: New York University Press, 1956), 257–282; Elizabeth Sussman, *City of Ambition: Artists and New York, 1900–1960* (New York: Whitney Museum of American Art, 1996), 10; John H. Girdner, MD, *NewYorkitis* (New York: The Grafton Press, 1901), 35–36.

2 Clifton Hood, *722 Miles: The Building of the Subways and How They Transformed New York.*(Baltimore, MD: The Johns Hopkins University Press, 1993), 21–74.

3 Michael W. Brooks, *Subway City: Riding the Trains, Reading New York* (New Brunswick, NJ: Rutgers University Press, 1997), 59–62; Hood, *722 Miles*, 66–74.

4 Brooks, *Subway City*, 62–69; Hood, *722 Miles*, 75–98.

5 Brooks, *Subway City*, 69–105; Hood, *722 Miles*, 112–132.

6 Judith Dupre, *Skyscrapers* (New York: Black Dog and Leventhal, 1996), 28–29.

7 Kenneth D. Revell, *Building Gotham: Civic Culture and Public Policy in New York City, 1898–1938* (Baltimore, MD: The Johns Hopkins University Press, 2003), 185–226.

8 David Levering Lewis, *When Harlem Was in Vogue* (New York: Oxford University Press, 1989), 92, 200, 296–297.

9 William R., Taylor (ed.), *Inventing Times Square: Commerce and Culture at the Crossroads of the World* (Baltimore, MD: The Johns Hopkins University Press, 1991); James Traub, *The Devil's Playground, A Century of Pleasure and Profit in Times Square* (New York: Random House, 2004).

10 Christine Stansell, *American Moderns: Bohemian New York and the Creation of a New Century* (New York: Henry Holt, 2000); Ross Wetzsteon, *Republic of Dreams, Greenwich Village: The American Bohemia, 1910–1960* (New York: Simon and Schuster, 2002).

11 John F. Kasson, *Amusing the Million, Coney Island at the Turn of the Century.* (New York: Hill and Wang, 1978); Michael Immerso, *Coney Island: The People's Playground* (New Brunswick, NJ: Rutgers University Press: 2002).

12 John F. McClymer, *The Triangle Strike and Fire* (Orlando, FL: Harcourt Brace, 1998); Leon Stein, *The Triangle Fire* (New York: J. B. Lippincott, 1962); David Von Drehle, *Triangle: The Fire That Changed America* (New York: Grove Press, 2003).

13 Nancy Schrom Dye, *As Equals and as Sisters* (Columbia, MS: University of Missouri Press, 1980).

14 Carolyn Wedin, *Inheritors of the Spirit: Mary White Ovington and the Founding of the NAACP* (New York: John Wiley and Sons, 1998), 1–51; Ralph E. Luker (ed.), *Black and White Sat Down Together: The Reminiscences of an NAACP Founder* (New York: The Feminist Press at the City University of New York, 1995), 7–12; Mary White Ovington, *The Walls Came Tumbling Down* (New York: Schocken Books, 1947/1970), 3–12.

15 Wedin, *Inheritors of the Spirit*, 53–78; Luker, *Black and White Sat Down Together*, 14–25; Ovington, *The Walls Came Tumbling Down*, 4–33.

16 Wedin, *Inheritors of the Spirit*, 79–104; Luker, *Black and White Sat Down Together*, 26–31; Ovington, *The Walls Came Tumbling Down*, 33–43.

17 Wedin, *Inheritors of the Spirit*, 105–135; Luker, *Black and White Sat Down Together*, 56–60.

18 Wedin, *Inheritors of the Spirit*, 96–100; Luker, *Black and White Sat Down Together*, 3–6, 32–36; Ovington, *The Walls Came Tumbling Down*, 43–47.

19 Wedin, *Inheritors of the Spirit*, 91–93; Luker, *Black and White Sat Down Together*, 66–71; Ovington, *The Walls Came Tumbling Down*, 100–112.

20 Wedin, *Inheritors of the Spirit*, 137–198, 229–274; David Levering Lewis, *W. E. B. Du Bois, Biography of a Race, 1868–1919* (New York: Henry Holt, 1993), 495–496.

21 Lewis, *Du Bois*, 419; Luker, *Black and White Sat Down Together*, 94–98.

22 Wedin, *Inheritors of the Spirit*, 293–302; Luker, *Black and White Sat Down Together*, 129–134.

23 Lewis, *Du Bois, 1868–1919*; David Levering Lewis, *W. E. B. Du Bois: The Fight for Equality and the American Century, 1919–1963* (New York: Henry Holt, 2000); Manning Marable, *W. E. B. Du Bois: Black Radical Democrat* (Boston, MA: Thayne, 1986).

24 Harriet Stanton Blatch and Alma Lutz, *Challenging Years: The Memoirs of Harriet Stanton Blatch* (New York: G.P. Putnam's Sons, 1940).

25 Ronald Schaffer, "The New York City Woman Suffrage Party, 1909–1919," *New York History* 43 (July 1962), 268–287.

26 Richard Drinnon, *Rebel in Paradise: A Biography of Emma Goldman* (New York: Harper and Row, 1976).

27 Hyman, Paula. "Immigrant Women and Consumer Protest: The New York City Kosher Meat Boycott of 1902," *American Jewish History* 70 (September, 1980), 96–103.

28 *The New York Times*, May 23, 1902; William Freiberger, "War, Prosperity and Hunger: The New York Food Riots of 1917," *Labor History* 25 (Spring, 1984), 217–239.

Chapter 7: 1920–1945

1 Thomas G. Aylesworth and Virginia L. Aylesworth, *New York, The Glamour Years, 1919–1945* (New York: Gallery Books, 1987), 98–103.

2 Ric Burns and James Sanders, *New York, An Illustrated History* (New York: Alfred A. Knopf, 1999), 347.

3 Elton Fax, *Garvey, the Story of a Pioneer Black Nationalist* (New York: Dodd Mead, 1972); E. David Cronon, *Black Moses: The Story of Marcus Garvey and the Universal Negro Improvement Association* (Madison, WI: University of Wisconsin Press,1964).

4 James L. W. West III (ed.), *My Lost City, Personal Essays, 1920–1940: F. Scott Fitzgerald* (Cambridge: Cambridge University Press, 2005), 106–115.

5 Jervis Anderson, *This Was Harlem: A Cultural Portrait, 1900–1950* (New York: Farrar Straus Giroux, 1981), 272–275; Schomburg Center for Research in Black Culture, *The Black New Yorkers* (New York: John Wiley and Sons, 2000), 440.

6 Peter Kwong and Dusanka Miscevic, *Chinese America: The Untold Story of America's Oldest New Community* (New York: The New Press, 2005), 186–188. Also see Peter Kwong, *Chinatown: New York Labor and Politics, 1930–1950* (New York: Monthly Review Press, 1979), 61–67 and Renqui Yu, *To Save China, To Save Ourselves: The Chinese Hand Laundry Alliance of New York* (Philadelphia, PA: Temple University Press, 1992), 31–36.

7 Arthur Mann, *La Guardia Comes to Power 1933* (Chicago, IL: University of Chicago Press, 1965), 26.

8 Fiorello H. La Guardia, *The Making of an Insurgent, An Autobiography: 1882–1919* (New York: Capricorn Books, 1948/1961), 17–33; Arthur Mann, *La Guardia: A Fighter Against his Times, 1882–1933* (Chicago, IL: University of Chicago Press, 1959), 19–42; Thomas Kessner, *Fiorello La Guardia and the Making of Modern New York* (New York: McGraw Hill, 1989), 3–23.

9 La Guardia, *Autobiography*, 34–75.

10 La Guardia, *Autobiography*, 74–107; Ronald H. Bayor, *Fiorello La Guardia: Ethnicity and Reform* (Wheeling, IL: Harlan Davidson, 1993), 18–26.

11 La Guardia, *Autobiography*, 106–133.

12 La Guardia, *Autobiography*, 134–209; Kessner, *La Guardia*, 41–80.

13 Howard Zinn, *La Guardia in Congress* (Ithaca, NY: Cornell University Press, 1958), viii, 270; Bayor, *La Guardia*, 51–81; Mann, *La Guardia*, 181–230; Kessner, *La Guardia*, 81–133.

14 Mann, *La Guardia Comes to Power*, 37–65; Charles Garrett, *The La Guardia Years: Machine and Reform Politics in New York City* (New Brunswick, NJ: Rutgers University Press, 1961), 64–79.

15 Mann, *La Guardia Comes to Power*, 66–88; Garrett, *The La Guardia Years*, 80–113.

16 Mann, *La Guardia Comes to Power*, 89–159; Kessner, *La Guardia*, 233–253; Robert Moses, *Working for the People* (New York: Harper and Brothers, 1956), 30.

17 Bayor, *La Guardia*, 95,112; Kessner, *La Guardia*, 248, 260, 271; Garrett, *The La Guardia Years*, 142–151.

18 Kessner, *La Guardia*, 292–341; Garrett, *The La Guardia Years*, 178–219.

19 Bayor, *La Guardia* 110–118; Kessner, *La Guardia*, 257–262, 508–517.

20 "Campaign Battle Page, Provided by the Citizens' Committee for Mahoney-Taylor-Schneider" (October 31, 1937), Fiorello H. La Guardia Papers, Box 2762, folder 02, La Guardia-Wagner Archives, La Guardia Community College, CUNY.

21 Dominic J. Capeci, Jr, *The Harlem Riot of 1943* (Philadelphia, PA: Temple University Press, 1977); Cheryl Lynn Greenberg, *"Or Does It Explode?" Black Harlem in the Great Depression* (New York: Oxford University Press, 1991).

22 Anderson, *This Was Harlem*, 307–314.

23 Capeci, *The Harlem Riot of 1943*, 138–139, 156–168; *New York Amsterdam News*, May 15, 1943.

24 Barry Singer, *Black and Blue: Life and Lyrics of Andy Razaf* (New York: Schirmer Books, 1992).

25 *New York Amsterdam News*, June 12, 1943.

26 Ibid; Charles V. Hamilton, *Adam Clayton Powell Jr: The Political Biography of an American Dilemma* (New York: Atheneum, 1991); Dominic J. Capeci, "From Different Liberal Perspectives: Fiorello H. La Guardia, Adam Clayton Powell, Jr., and Civil Rights in New York City, 1941–1943," *Journal of Negro History*, 62 (1977), 160–173.

27 *New York Amsterdam News*, June 26, 1943.

28 Kessner, *La Guardia*, 531–532.

Chapter 8 1945–1970

1 Jules Tygiel, *Baseball's Great Experiment: Jackie Robinson and His Legacy* (New York: Oxford University Press, 1987); Arnold Rampersad, *Jackie Robinson, A Biography* (New York: Ballentine Books, 1997).

2 "Harlem's Plea," *New York Amsterdam News*, July 25, 1964.

3 Vincent J. Cannato, *The Ungovernable City: John Lindsay and His Struggle to Save New York* (New York: Basic Books, 2001), 155–183; Joseph P. Viteritti, *Police,*

Politics and Pluralism in New York City: A Comparative Case Study (Beverly Hills, CA: Sage Publications, 1973), 25–34; Marilynn S. Johnson, *Street Justice: A History of Police Violence in New York City* (Boston, MA: Beacon Press, 2003), 241–254.

4 *New York Daily News*, November 3, 1966.

5 Roy Wilkins, "A Sly Campaign Against Negroes," *New York Amsterdam News*, October 15, 1966 and "The People Must Have A Say," *New York Amsterdam News*, October 29, 1966; Whitney M. Young, Jr. "The Civilian Review Board," *New York Amsterdam News*, October 22, 1966.

6 Robert Moses, "What's the Matter With New York?" *New York Times Magazine*, August 1, 1943, 8–9, 28–29.

7 Robert A. Caro, *The Power Broker: Robert Moses and the Fall of New York* (New York: Vintage Books, 1975), 52–55.

8 Ibid, 317–319, 413, 827, 1122.

9 Ibid, 5–12, 571, 633.

10 Ibid. 12–16, 218; Joel Schwartz, *The New York Approach: Robert Moses, Urban Liberals and the Redevelopment of the Inner City* (Columbus, OH: Ohio State University Press, 1993), 107.

11 Caro, *The Power Broker*, 319, 513–514, 968; Jack Newfield and Paul DuBrul, *The Permanent Government: Who Really Runs New York?* (New York: The Pilgrim Press, 1981), 131; Martha Biondi, "Robert Moses, Race, and the Limits of the Activist State," in Hilary Ballon and Kenneth Jackson (eds), *Robert Moses and the Modern City: The Transformation of New York* (New York: W. W. Norton, 2007), 116–121.

12 Marta Gutman, "Equipping the Public Realm: Rethinking Robert Moses and Recreation," in Ballon and Jackson, *Robert Moses and the Modern City*, 72–85.

13 Owen D. Gutfreund, "Rebuilding New York in the Auto Age," in Ballon and Jackson, *Robert Moses and the Modern City*, 86–93; Hilary Ballon, "Robert Moses and Urban Renewal, The Title 1 Program," in Ballon and Jackson, *Robert Moses and the Modern City*, 94–115.

14 Hilary Ballon, "Robert Moses and Urban Renewal," 105; Robert Moses, *Working for the People* (New York: Harper and Brothers, 1956), 61, 90; Joel Schwartz, "Robert Moses and City Planning," in Ballon and Jackson, *Robert Moses and the Modern City*, 130–133.

15 Caro, *The Power Broker*, 318.

16 Jane Jacobs, *The Death and Life of Great American Cities* (New York: Vintage, 1961).

17 Caro, *The Power Broker*, 800, 1117–1131.

18 Robert Moses, "What's the Matter With New York?"

19 Caro, *The Power Broker*, 1013–1016; Jacobs, *Death and Life*, 168; "Title I Developments," Ballon and Jackson, *Robert Moses and the Modern City*, 279–289.

Chapter 9: 1970–1993

1 Roger E. Alcaly and David Mermelstein (eds), *The Fiscal Crisis of American Cities: Essays on the Political Economy of Urban America with Special Reference to New York* (New York: Vintage, 1977); Ken Auletta, *The Streets Were Paved with Gold: The Decline of New York—An American Tragedy* (New York: Random House, 1980); Charles R. Morris, *The Cost of Good Intentions: New York City and the Liberal Experiment, 1960–1975* (New York: McGraw Hill, 1980); Martin Shefter, *Political Crisis, Fiscal Crisis: The Collapse and Revival of New York City* (New York: Basic Books,1987).

2 Jill Jonnes, *South Bronx Rising: The Rise, Fall and Resurrection of an American City* (New York: Fordham University Press, 1986), 7–8.

3 Wallace S. Sayre and Herbert Kaufman, *Governing New York City: Politics in the Metropolis* (New York: W. W. Norton and Company, 1960/1965), 738.
4 Vincent J. Cannato, *The Ungovernable City: John Lindsay and His Struggle to Save New York* (New York: Basic Books, 2001).
5 Edward I. Koch with Leland T. Jones, *All the Best: Letters from a Feisty Mayor* (New York: Simon and Schuster, 1990), 17; Edward I. Koch with William Rauch, *Mayor: An Autobiography* (New York: Warner Books, 1985); Edward I. Koch with Daniel Paisner, *Citizen Koch: An Autobiography* (New York: St. Martins, 1992).
6 Al Sharpton and Anthony Walton, *Go and Tell Pharaoh: The Autobiography of the Reverend Al Sharpton* (New York: Doubleday, 1996), 99–100.
7 Herbert Gans, *Urban Villagers: Groups and Class in the Life of Italian Americans* (New York: The Free Press, 1982).
8 Ronald Smothers, "Housing Segregation: New Twists and Old Results," *New York Times*, April 1, 1987.
9 Herman Badillo, *One Nation, One Standard: An Ex-Liberal on How Hispanics Can Succeed Just Like Other Immigrant Groups* (New York: Sentinel, 2006), 9–13; *New York Times*, June 25, 1973.
10 Badillo, *One Nation, One Standard*, 14–15.
11 Badillo, *One Nation, One Standard*, 22, 39–49.
12 Badillo, *One Nation, One Standard*, 23, 97–9; *New York Times*, November 9, 1969; Jonnes, *South Bronx Rising*, 155–59; Herman Badillo, Keynote Speech, "Puerto Ricans Confront the Problems of the Complex Urban Society: A Design for Change," *Conference Proceedings* (New York City, April 15–17, 1967), 10–19.
13 *New York Times*, April 1, 1969, April 4, 1969, May 8, 1969, June 9, 1969; Jack Newfield, "Garcia and Badillo: Tale of Two Compadres," *Village Voice*, March 24, 1987, 13–14.
14 Chris McNickle, *To Be Mayor of New York: Ethnic Politics in the City* (New York: Columbia University Press, 1993), 223–229; Cannato, *The Ungovernable City*, 409–411; *New York Times*, June 9, 2001.
15 Badillo, *One Nation, One Standard*, 149, 173; *New York Times*, January 29, 1969, November 9, 1969, June 14, 1971; McNickle, *To Be Mayor of New York*, 226; Jose Ramon Sanchez, *Boricua Power: A Political History of Puerto Ricans in the United States* (New York: New York University Press, 2007), 131.
16 Badillo, *One Nation, One Standard*, 58–63, 122–124; Sanchez, *Boricua Power*, 164.
17 Herman Badillo, *A Bill of No Rights: Attica and the American Prison System* (New York: Outerbridge and Lazard, 1972), 172.
18 McNickle, *To Be Mayor of New York*, 244–252.
19 Sherrie Baver, "Puerto Rican Politics in New York City: The Post-World War II Period," in James Jennings and Monte Rivers (eds), *Puerto Rican Politics in Urban America* (Westport, CT: Greenwood Press, 1984), 45–56.
20 Baver "Puerto Rican Politics," 52; Jonnes, *South Bronx Rising*, 324–325; *New York Times*, November 30, 1977; Wayne Barrett, "Runnin' Scared," *Village Voice*, June 18, 1979, 3; Koch, *Mayor: An Autobiography*, 166; Pablo "Yoruba" Guzman, "The Decline of Herman Badillo," *Village Voice*, June 18, 1979, 41, 43, 45, 101; Newfield, "Garcia and Badillo."
21 Badillo, *One Nation, One Standard*, 73–108.
22 Badillo, *One Nation, One Standard*, 166–167, 174; Guzman, "The Decline of Herman Badillo."
23 Badillo, *One Nation, One Standard*, 109–138; James Traub, *City on a Hill: Testing the American Dream at City College* (Reading, MA: Addison-Wesley, 1994). Note that this author participated in the struggle to save open admissions; Joanne Reitano, "CUNY's Community Colleges: Democratic Education on Trial," in Raymond C. Bowen and Gilbert H. Muller (eds), *Gateways to Democracy: Six Urban Community College Systems* (San Francisco, CA: Jossey-Bass, 1999), 23–40.
24 Badillo, *One Nation, One Standard*, 63–71, 122–124.

25 Badillo, *One Nation, One Standard*, 128–38; *New York Times*, May 31, 1999; *New York Daily News*, May 30, 1999.

26 Badillo, *One Nation, One Standard*, 79–80; 128–32; James Traub, "A Minority of One," *New York Times Magazine* (October 31, 1999), 56–59; *New York Times*, October 9, 1999, October 2, 1999, November 30, 1999.

27 *New York Times*, May 9, 2001, July 5, 2001, July 6, 2001, August 31, 2001.

28 Traub, "A Minority of One," 56–59; *New York Daily News*, May 22, 2001; Earl Shorris, *Latinos: A Biography of the People* (New York: W. W. Norton, 1992), 412.

29 Traub, "A Minority of One," 59; *New York Daily News*, August 31, 2001.

30 *New York Times*, October 15, 1970, June 14, 1971.

31 Roger Sanjek, *The Future of Us All: Race and Neighborhood Politics in New York City* (Ithaca, NY: Cornell University Press, 1998), 1–14.

Chapter 10: 1993–2008

1 Nancy Foner, "How Exceptional is New York? Migration and Multiculturalism in the Empire City," *Ethnic and Racial Studies* 30:6 (November 2007), 999–1023.

2 Pyong Gap Min, *Changes and Conflicts: Korean Immigrant Families in New York* (Boston, MA: Allyn and Bacon, 1998), 9–24; Illsoo Kim, *New Urban Immigrants: The Korean Community of New York* (Princeton, NJ: Princeton University Press, 1981), 101–146.

3 Jean Claire Kim, *Bitter Fruit: The Politics of Black-Korean Conflict in New York City* (New Haven, CT: Yale University Press, 2000); Pyong Gap Min, *Caught in the Middle: Korean Merchants in America's Multiethnic Cities* (Berkeley, CA: University of California Press, 1996).

4 *New York Times*, September 30, 2004.

5 *New York Times*, August 5, 2001, February 24, 2002, January 10, 2004; *New York Daily News*, August 27, 2001, September 3, 2003, December 2, 2003; *The Washington Post*, July 29, 2002.

6 Wayne Barrett assisted by Adam Fifiel, *RUDY! An Investigative Biography of Rudolph Giuliani* (New York: Basic Books, 2000), 331–333, 344–345; Rudolph W. Giuliani, *Leadership* (New York: Hyperion, 2002), 41–43, 72–82; Andrew Kirtzman, *Rudy Giuliani, Emperor of the City* (New York: William Morrow, 2000), 39, 91, 223–226; Fred Siegel with Harry Siegel, *Prince of the City: New York and the Genius of American Life* (San Francisco, CA: Encounter Books, 2005), 142–150.

7 *New York Newsday*, April 20, 1998.

8 Marilynn Johnson, *Street Justice: A History of Police Violence in New York City* (Boston, MA: Beacon Press, 2003), 294–301; Edward I. Koch, *Giuliani: Nasty Man* (New York: Barricade Books, 1999).

9 Barrett, *RUDY!* 335–337; Kirtzman, *Rudy Giuliani*, 272–275; Siegel, *Prince of the City*, 273–274; *Newsday*, March 21, 2000; *New York Times*, March 22, 2000.

10 *Newsday*, April 15, 1999; *New York Times*, April 2, 2000; Johnson, *Street Justice*. 294–301.

11 *New York Times*, April 4, 1999, March 4, 2000.

12 Michael Sorkin and Sharon Zukin (eds), *After the World Trade Center: Rethinking New York* (New York: Routledge, 2002), viii.

CREDITS

The author and publisher are grateful to the following organizations and individuals for permission to reprint material in this Reader. Every effort has been made to credit completely the original source material for each document used in this collection. In the event that something has inadvertently been used or credited incorrectly, every effort will be made in subsequent editions to rectify the error.

Chapter 1: Introduction

1-1.   The Rushing City: Theodore Dwight, *Things As They Are; or, Notes of a Traveller through some of the Middle and Northern States.* New York: Harper and Brothers, 1834.

1-2.   The Crushing City: "A Nineteenth-Century Traffic Jam," in Henry Collins Brown (ed.), *Valentine's Manual of Old New York* (Hastings-on-Hudson, NY: Valentine's Manual, 1928), 397.

1-3.   The Thrilling City: "Mannahatta" by Walt Whitman, *New York Herald*, February 27, 1888. Reprinted in the "Sands at Seventy" annex to *Leaves of Grass*. Philadelphia, PA: D. McKay, 1888.

1-4.   The Evolving City: Thomas Bender, *The Unfinished City: New York and the Metropolitan Idea,* New York: The New Press, 2002. © 2002 The New Press. Reprinted by permission of The New Press, www.thenewpress.com

1-5.   The Living City: Chiang Yee, *The Silent Traveller in New York.* London: Methuen, 1950. Used by permission from Chien-Fei Chiang.

Chapter 2: 1609–1799

2-1-1.   Struggling to Survive: "Memorial of the Eight Men at the Manhattan to the States General," in E. B. O'Callaghan (ed.), *Documents Relative to the Colonial History of the State of New York Procured in Holland, England and France by John Romeyn Brodhead*, vol. I. Albany, NY: Weed, Parsons and Company, 1856.

2-1-2.   Drawing the First Settlement: Dingman Versteeg, *Manhattan in 1628.* New York: Dodd Mead, 1904, frontispiece from Joost Hartger, *Beschrijvinghe van Virginia, Nieuw Nederlandt, etc.* Amsterdam, 1651.

2-1-3.   Freeing Slaves: E. B. O'Callaghan (ed.), *Laws and Ordinances of New Netherland, 1638–1674.* Albany, NY: Weed, Parsons and Company, 1868.

2-1-4.   Baptizing Slaves: State of New York, Report of the Commissioners of Statutory Revision, *The Colonial Laws of New York from the Year 1664 to the Revolution* vol. I. Albany, NY: James B. Lyon, 1894.

2-1-5.   Prosecuting Slaves: Daniel Horsmanden, *Journal of the Proceedings Against the Conspirators, at New York, in 1741.* New York: James Parker, 1744.

2-1-6.   Executing Slaves: "Slave Being Burned at the Stake in Colonial New York," Courtesy of Brown Brothers, Sterling, PA.

2-2-1.   Promoting Tolerance: E. B. O'Callaghan, *History of New Netherland or New York Under the Dutch,* vol. II. New York: D. Appleton and Company, 1848.

2-2-2.   Debating Education: *The Independent Reflector,* Numbers xvii, xviii, xx (1753).

2-2-3.   Defining New York: Milton M. Klein, "Shaping the American Tradition: The Microcosm of Colonial New York," *New York History* 59 (1978), 173–197. Reprinted by permission of *New York History* and Mrs. Margaret Klein.

2-2-4.   Thomas A. Janvier, *In Old New York: A Classic History of New York City.* New York: Harper and Brothers, 1894.

2-3-1.   Ruling New Amsterdam: Bertold Fernow (ed.), *The Records of New Amsterdam from 1653 to 1674 Anno Domini,* vol. I. New York: Knickerbocker Press, 1897.

2-3-2.   Opposing Stuyvesant: J. Franklin Jameson (ed.), *Narratives of New Netherland, 1609–1664.* New York: Charles Scribner's Sons, 1909.

2-3-3.   Surrendering to the British: E. B. O' Callaghan, *History of New Netherland or New York Under the Dutch,* vol. II. New York: D. Appleton and Company, 1848.

2-3-4.   Dramatizing Surrender: "'Old Silver Nails' was persuaded not to fire and New Amsterdam surrendered to the English' in The Manhattan Company," *"Manna-hattin:" The Story of New York.* Port Washington, NY: Ira J. Friedman, Inc., 1929.

2-4-1.   Condemning the Riots: G. D. Scull (ed.), *The Montresor Journals/New York Historical Society Collections,* vol. XIV. New York: New York Historical Society, 1882.

2-4-2.   Seeking Peace: *The Letters and Papers of Cadwallader Colden* vol. VII. New York: New York Historical Society, 1923.

2-4-3.   Reconsidering the Riots: Jesse Lemish, "The American Revolution Seen from the Bottom Up," in Barton J. Bernstein (ed.),*Towards A New Past: Dissenting Essays in American History*, (New York: Pantheon Books), 19–21. © 1968, Random House, Inc. Used by permission of Pantheon Books, a division of Random House.

2-4-4.   Representing New York: "Advertisement. At a general Meeting of the Committee of Mechanicks, 1774," Broadsides and Other Printed Ephemera Collection. Courtesy of Library of Congress Prints and Photographs Division.

Chapter 3: 1800–1840

3-1-1.   Denouncing Riots: *New York Evening Post,* July 12, 1834.

3-1-2.   Deploring Amalgamation: *New York Commercial Advertiser,* July 10, 1834.

3-1-3.   Ridiculing Amalgamation: Edward W. Clay, "The Fruits of Amalgamation," Item #00167-0001, Collection of the American Antiquarian Society. Courtesy of the American Antiquarian Society.

3-1-4.   Debating Amalgamation: David Ruggles, A Man of Color, *"The 'Extinguisher' Extinguished! Or David M. Reese, M.D. 'Used Up'."* New York: D. Ruggles, Bookseller, 1834.

3-1-5.   Appealing for Help: Miscellaneous Manuscripts, Riots, 1834. Courtesy of the New York Historical Society.

3-2-1.   Publicizing the Jewett Case: Murder of Ellen Jewett, pamphlet printed in New York, 1836. Negative #712912, collection of the New York Historical Society. Courtesy of the New York Historical Society.

3-2-2. Observing the Trial: Allan Nevins (ed.), *The Diary of Philip Hone, 1828–1851*, vol. I. New York: Dodd Mead, 1927.

3-2-3. Questioning Sin City: *New York Herald*, April 13, 1836.

3-2-4. Analyzing Gender Roles: Timothy J. Gilfoyle, *City of Eros: New York City, Prostitution ,and the Commercialization of Sex, 1790–1920* (New York: W. W. Norton). © 1992, Timothy J. Gilfoyle. Used by permission of W. W. Norton & Company, Inc.

3-3-1. Condemning Strikes: *New York Evening Post*, June 13, 1836.

3-3-2. Defending Strikes: *New York Herald*, June 7, 1836.

3-3-3. Questioning the Sick City: *The New York Herald*, February 25, 1836.

3-3-4. Depicting the Depression of 1837: Edward W. Clay, "The Times." Item #29.100.2355 Collection of the Museum of the City of New York. Courtesy of the Museum of the City of New York.

3-4-1. Assessing Astor: Allan Nevins (ed.), *The Diary of Philip Hone, 1828–1851*, vol. 1. New York: Dodd Mead, 1927.

3-4-2. Criticizing Astor: *New York Herald*, April 5, 1848.

3-4-3. Reconsidering Rags to Riches: Edward Pessen, *Riches, Class and Power in America Before the Civil War*. New Brunswick, NJ: Transaction, 1973/1990. Reprinted with permission from Transaction Publishers.

3-4-4. Framing Broadway: Augustus Köllner, "Broadway." Item #52.100.13 Collection of the Museum of the City of New York. Bequest of Mrs. J. Insley Blair in memory of Mr. and Mrs. J. Insley Blair. Courtesy of the Museum of the City of New York.

Chapter 4: 1840–1865

4-1-1. Opposing Central Park: *New York Times,* June 30, 1853.

4-1-2. Promoting Central Park: *New York Times*, March 24, 1855.

4-1-3. Planning Central Park: Frederick Law Olmsted, "Public Parks and the Enlargement of Towns," *Journal of Social Science* (1871).

4-1-4. Envisioning Central Park: Board of Commissioners of the Central Park, *Third Annual Report, January 1860*. New York: William C. Bryant Co., 1860.

4-1-5. Questioning Central Park: Edward K Spann, *The New Metropolis, New York City, 1840–1857*. New York: Columbia University Press, 1981. © 1981 Columbia University Press. Reprinted with permission of the publisher.

4-2-1. Touring the Five Points: James D. McCabe, Jr., *Lights and Shadows of New York Life; or the Sights and Sensations of the Great City*. Philadelphia, PA: National Publishing Company, 1872.

4-2-2. Illustrating the Five Points: George Catlin, "Five Points, 1827, Intersection of Cross, Anthony and Orange Streets," *Valentine's Manual.* (New York, 1885). Same as #35910. Negative no. 44668 Collection of the New York Historical Society. Courtesy of the New York Historical Society.

4-2-3. Expanding Religious Freedom: *New York Tribune*, May 22, 1844.

4-2-4. Limiting Religious Freedom: *New York Commercial Advertiser,* June 6, 1844

4-2-5. Charting Jobs in 1855: Richard B. Stott, *Workers in the Metropolis: Class, Ethnicity and Youth in Antebellum New York City*. Ithaca, NY: Cornell University Press, 1990. Used by permission of Cornell University Press.

4-2-6. Describing the Irish Struggle: Hasia R. Diner, "The Most Irish City in the Union: The Era of the Great Migration, 1844–1877," in Ronald H. Bayor and Timothy J. Meagher (eds), *The New York Irish*. Baltimore, MD: Johns Hopkins

University Press. © 1996,The Johns Hopkins University Press. Reprinted with permission of The Johns Hopkins University Press.

4-3-1.   Protesting the 1849 Riots: *New York Tribune*, May 12, 1849.

4-3-2.   Defending the 1863 Riots: *New York Times*, July 15, 1863

4-3-3.   Defending the Police: George W. Walling, *Recollections of a New York Chief of Police*. New York: Caxton Book Concern, 1887.

4-3-4.   Battling the Barricades in 1863: George W. Walling, *Recollections of a New York Chief of Police*. New York: Caxton Book Concern, 1887.

4-4-1.   Asserting Equality: *Frederick Douglass' Paper*, July 28, 1854.

4-4-2.   Subverting Slavery: *New York Daily Tribune*, October 1 and 7, 1850.

4-4-3.   Petitioning for the Vote: James McCune Smith, James P. Miller and John J. Zuille, "The Suffrage Question in Relation to Colored Voters in the State of New York," Respectfully submitted by the New York City and County Suffrage Committee of Colored Citizens, September, 1860.

4-4-4.   Cherishing Weeksville: Judith Wellman, "Weeksville" in Ira Berlin and Leslie M. Harris (eds), *Slavery in New York*. New York: The New Press, 2005. © 2005, Judith Wellman. Reprinted by permission of The New Press. www. thenewpress.com

Chapter 5: 1865–1900

5-1-1.   Praising the Brooklyn Bridge: Board of Trustees of the New York and Brooklyn Bridge, *Opening Ceremonies of the New York and Brooklyn Bridge, May 24, 1883*. New York: Brooklyn Eagle Job Printing Dept, 1883.

5-1-2.   Honoring the Statue of Liberty: Emma Lazarus, "The New Colossus," *Catalogue of the Pedestal Fund Art Loan Exhibition*. New York: De Vinne, 1883.

5-1-3.   Fearing for Liberty: Thomas Nast, "The Rise of the Usurpers, and the Sinking of the Liberties of the People," 1889. Miriam and Ira D. Wallach Print Collection, Division of Arts, Prints and Photographs, The New York Public Library, Astor, Lenox and Tilden Foundations.

5-1-4.   Opposing Consolidation, Brooklyn League of Loyal Citizens, *Letters Worth Reading*. Pamphlet #4. New York: n.p., 1894. Collections of the New York Historical Society.

5-1-5.   Supporting Consolidation, Albert E. Henschel, *Municipal Consolidation: Historical Sketch of the Greater New York*. New York: Stettiner, Lambert and Co., 1895. Collections of the New York Historical Society.

5-2-1.   Explaining Bossism: "Testimony of William M. Tweed, January 4, 1878," in Board of Aldermen, *Tweed Ring Investigation. Report of the Special Committee of the Board of Alderman Appointed to Investigate the "Ring" Frauds, Together with the Testimony Elicited During the Investigation*. Document No. 8, 208–209.

5-2-2.   Attacking Bossism: Thomas Nast, "The City Treasury," *Harper's Weekly*, October 14, 1871. Courtesy of the Rutherford B. Hayes Presidential Center.

5-2-3.   Justifying Bossism: William L. Riordon, *Plunkitt of Tammany Hall: A Series of Very Plain Talks on Very Practical Politics*. New York: McClure, Phillips and Company, 1905.

5-2-4.   Assessing Bossism: Theodore Roosevelt, *An Autobiography*. New York: Macmillan, 1914.

5-3-1.   Comparing Rich and Poor—Fifth Avenue and Poverty Gap: "A. T. Stewart Mansion," in Henry Collins Brown (ed.), *Valentine's Manual of Old New York*. New York City: Chauncey Holt, 1924. Jacob Riis,"Poverty Gap," 1889. Courtesy of the Library of Congress, Prints and Photographs Division.

5-3-2. Satirizing Wealth: Tony Pastor, "The Upper and Lower Ten Thousand," in *New Comic Irish Songster*. New York: Dick and Fitzgerald, 1863.

5-3-3. Preaching Social Darwinism: Horatio Alger, *Ragged Dick: Street Life in New York with the Bootblacks*. Boston: Loring, 1868.

5-3-4. Preaching Social Reform: Jacob A. Riis, *How the Other Half Lives: Studies Among the Tenements of New York*. New York: C. Scribner's Sons, 1903.

5-4-1. Scorning Strikes: "Testimony of Jay Gould," U.S. Senate, Committee on Education and Labor, Report on the Relations Between Capital and Labor. Washington, DC: U.S. Government Printing Office, 1084–1090.

5-4-2. Defending Strikes: "Testimony of Samuel Gompers ," U.S. Senate, Committee on Education and Labor, Report on the Relations Between Capital and Labor. Washington, DC: U.S. Government Printing Office, 366–373.

5-4-3. Castigating Jay Gould: *The New York Times*, December 3, 1892.

5-4-4. Rehabilitating Jay Gould: Maury Klein, *The Life and Legend of Jay Gould*. Baltimore, MD: The Johns Hopkins University Press, 1986. © 1986, Maury Klein. Reprinted with permission of The Johns Hopkins University Press.

5-4-5. Caricaturing Jay Gould: Frederick Opper, "Jay Gould's Private Bowling Alley," *Puck*, March 29, 1882. Courtesy of the Rutherford B. Hayes Presidential Center.

Chapter 6: 1900–1920

6-1-1. Praising the Subway: *New York Times*, October 28, 1904.

6-1-2. Criticizing the Subway: Ray Stannard Baker, "The Subway Deal: How New York City Built Its New Underground Railroad," *McClure's Magazine*, March 1905.

6-1-3. Observing the Subway: Reginald Marsh, "The Melting Pot," *New York Daily News*, June 26, 1923. © 2009, Estate of Reginald Marsh/Arts Students League, New York/Artists Rights Society (ARS), New York. Reprinted with permission.

6-1-4. Praising the Skyscraper: William George Fitzgerald, *America's Day: Studies in Light and Shade*. New York: Dodd, Mead, 1919.

6-1-5. Criticizing the Skyscraper: Clement Wood, "Woolworth Cathedral," *The Masses*, April, 1916.

6-2-1. Seeing Coney Island: "Seeing Coney Island: An Official Guide." Original repository, Brooklyn Historical Society.

6-2-2. Celebrating Coney Island: Lindsay Denison, "The Biggest Playground in the World," *Munsey's Magazine* 33 (August 1905).

6-2-3. Condemning Coney Island: Maxim Gorky, "Boredom," *The Independent*, August 8, 1907.

6-2-4. Interpreting Coney Island: *Amusing the Millions: Coney Island at the Turn of the Century* by John F. Kasson. © 1978 by John F. Kasson. Reprinted by permission of Hill & Wang, a division of Farrar, Straus and Giroux, LLC.

6-3-1. Working: Miriam Finn Scott, "The Spirit of the Girl Strikers," *The Outlook* 94 (February 19, 1910).

6-3-2. Dying: *New York Times*, March 26, 1911.

6-3-3. Falling: Boardman Robinson, "In Compliance with Law?" *New York Daily Tribune*, March 28, 1911.

6-3-4. Mourning: *New York Times*, March 3, 1911.

6-3-5. Evaluating: Frances Perkins, *The Roosevelt I Knew*. New York: Viking, 1946. ©1946, Frances Perkins. Reprinted by permission of Curtis Brown Ltd.

6-4-1. Advocating Activism: W. E. B. Du Bois, "Editorial," *The Crisis: A Record of the Darker Races*, November 1910.

6-4-2. Marching for the Vote: *The New York Times*, February 17, 1908.

6-4-3. Defending Birth Control: *The Masses*, June 1916, 27.

6-4-4. Pleading for Food: News Photo Service, "Crowd of Women, 1917," *The Independent*, 12 March 1917 and *International Socialist Review* April 1917. Courtesy of the Library of Congress, Prints and Photographs Division.

Chapter 7: 1920–1945

7-1-1. Contemplating Harlem: Edward Silvera, "Harlem," *The Crisis: A Record of the Darker Races*, December 1928. Used with permission of the Crisis Publishing Co., Inc., the publisher of the magazine of the National Association for the Advancement of Colored People

7-1-2. Parading for Pride: Report of UNIA Parade in *Negro World Convention Bulletin*, August 3, 1920, cited in Robert A. Hill (ed.), *The Marcus Garvey and Universal Negro Improvement Association Papers,* vol. II. Berkeley, CA: University of California Press, 1983. Reprinted with permission from the University of California Press.

7-1-3. Defying Prohibition: Ernest W. Mandeville, "The Biggest City and Its Booze," *The Outlook*, March 4, 1925.

7-1-4. Debating the Flapper: Helen Bullitt Lowry, "Mrs. Grundy and Miss 1921," *New York Times*, January 23, 1921.

7-1-5. Depicting the Flapper: Illustration accompanying Helen Bullitt Lowry, "Mrs. Grundy and Miss 1921," *New York Times*, January 23, 1921.

7-2-1. Crashing: James N. Rosenberg, "October 29, Dies Irae," 1929. Courtesy of the Library of Congress Prints and Photographs Division.

7-2-2. Struggling: Michael Gold, *Jews Without Money*. New York: Carroll & Graf, 1930. © 1930 Horace Liveright, Inc.; Copyright renewed 1958 by the estate of Michael Gold.

7-2-3. Surviving: Excerpts from Jeff Kisseloff, *You Must Remember This: An Oral History of Manhattan from the 1890s to World War II*, San Diego, CA: Houghton Mifflin, 1989. ©1989, Jeff Kisseloff. Reprinted by permission of Houghton Mifflin Harcourt Publishing Company.

7-2-4. Organizing: Peter Kwong, *Chinatown, New York Labor and Politics, 1930–1950,* New York: The New Press, 2000. © 2000, Peter Kwong. Reprinted by permission of The New Press. www.thenewpress.com

7-3-1. Championing Change: "Mayor's Final Report," in Rebecca B. Rankin (ed.), *New York Advancing: Victory Edition*. New York: Municipal Reference Library, 1945.

7-3-2. Opposing La Guardia: "There are Two Kinds of Dishonesty," The Citizens' Committee for O'Dwyer, Church and Fertig (October 21, 1941), Fiorello H. La Guardia Papers, Box 2762, Folder 02, La Guardia-Wagner Archives, La Guardia Community College.

7-3-3. Working With La Guardia: Newbold Morris, *Let the Chips Fall: My Battles Against Corruption*. New York: Appleton-Century-Crofts, 1955.

7-3-4. Assessing La Guardia: Thomas Kessner, *Fiorello H. La Guardia and the Making of Modern New York*. New York: McGraw-Hill, 1989. Reprinted by permission of Thomas Kessner.

7-4-1. Defining the Savoy: *The People's Voice*, May 22, 1943.

7-4-2. Deploring Stuyvesant Town: *The People's Voice*, June 12, 1943. Used with the consent of Adam Clayton Powell III.

7-4-3. Responding to the Riots: "Broadcast made by Mayor F. H. La Guardia from his desk at City Hall, August 2, 1943," Fiorello H. La Guardia Collection,

Harlem 1943 Race Riots: Box 3531, Folder 11. La Guardia-Wagner Archives, La Guardia Community College, CUNY. Original repository: New York City Municipal Archives.

7-4-4. Clarifying the Riots: Letter from the Metropolitan Chapter of the National Council of Negro Women to Mayor Fiorello H. La Guardia, August 6, 1943, Fiorello H. La Guardia Collection, Harlem 1943 Race Riots: Box 3532 Folder 01. La Guardia-Wagner Archives, La Guardia Community College, CUNY. Original repository: New York City Municipal Archives.

Chapter 8: 1945–1970

8-1-1. Desegregating Baseball: Jackie Robinson, *I Never Had It Made: An Autobiography.* New York: HarperCollins, 1972/1995. © 1995, Rachel Robinson. www.JackieRobinson.com

8-1-2. Crossing Third Avenue: Humberto Cintron, "Across Third Avenue: Freedom" in Edward Mapp (ed.), *Puerto Rican Perspectives.* Metuchen, NJ: The Scarecrow Press, 1974. Reprinted by permission from Rowman and Littlefield Publishing Group.

8-1-3. Analyzing Stonewall: David Eisenbach, *Gay Power: An American Revolution.* New York: Carroll & Graff, 2006. Reprinted by permission of DeCapo/ Carroll & Graff, a member of the Perseus Group.

8-1-4. Asserting the New Feminism: *Ladies Home Journal,* August, 1970.

8-2-1. Contemplating the Harlem Riots: Langston Hughes, "Harlem," *The New York Post,* July 23, 1964. ©1964 Langston Hughes. Reprinted by permission of Harold Ober Associates Incorporated.

8-2-2. Curbing the Harlem Riots: Remarks by Mayor Robert F. Wagner, Jr on CBS-TV, July 22, 1964. Robert F. Wagner, Jr Collection, Box 060054W, Folder 8, La Guardia-Wagner Archives, La Guardia Community College, CUNY.

8-2-3. Assessing the Riots: Arthur Poinier "What Do I Have to Lose?" *The Detroit News.* Reprinted with the permission of *The Detroit News.*

8-2-4. Assessing the Riots: Al Leiderman, "Grist For The Mill," *The Long Island Daily Press,* 1964, Rothco.

8-3-1. Opposing the Civilian Review Board: Independent Citizens Committee Against Civilian Review Boards, "The Civilian Review Board Must Be Stopped," *New York Times,* September 26, 1966.

8-3-2. Supporting the Civilian Review Board: M. F. Dubin, *The New York Amsterdam News,* October 22, 1966.

8-3-3. Evaluating the Civilian Review Board: Edward T. Rogowsky, Louis H. Gold, and David W. Abbott, "Police: The Civilian Review Board Controversy," in Jewel Bellush and Stephen M. David (eds), *Race and Politics in New York City: Five Studies in Policy-Making.* New York: Praeger, 1971. Used with permission from Jewel Bellush.

8-4-1. Changing the City: "What the Big Cities Must Do To Stay Alive," *U.S. News and World Report* [Nation and World], January 8, 1968, 66–68. © 1968, *U.S. News and World Report.* Reprinted with permission.

8-4-2. Preserving the City: From *The Death and Life of Great American Cities* by Jane Jacobs. © 1961, 1989 by Jane Jacobs. Used by permission of Random House, Inc.

8-4-3. Fighting Moses: Phil Stanziola, "Lincoln Square Residents Picket, 1956," *New York World-Telegram and Sun.* Courtesy of the Library of Congress Prints and Photographs Division.

8-4-4. Criticizing Moses: Robert A Caro, *The Power Broker: Robert Moses and the Fall of New York*. New York: Alfred A. Knopf, 1974. © 1974, Robert A. Caro. Used by permission of Alfred A. Knopf, a division of Random House, Inc.

8-4-5. Defending Moses: Kenneth T. Jackson, "Robert Moses and the Rise of New York," in Hillary Ballon and Kenneth T. Jackson (eds), *Robert Moses and the Modern City: The Transformation of New York*. © 2007, Queens Museum of Art, Hillary Ballon and Kenneth T. Jackson. Used by permission of W. W. Norton & Company, Inc.

Chapter 9: 1970–1993

9-1-1. Decrying Default: Speech by Abraham D. Beame, July 31, 1975, printed in full in the *New York Times*, August 1, 1975.

9-1-2. Denigrating New York City: Frank Van Riper, "How Come They Hate Us In Omaha?" *New York Sunday News*, November 9, 1975. Used with permission of New York Daily News, L.P.

9-1-3. The Sinking Ship: Drawing accompanying Frank Van Riper, "How Come They Hate Us In Omaha?" *New York Sunday News*, November 9, 1975. Used with permission of New York Daily News, L.P.

9-1-4. Unmasking the Fiscal Crisis: Joshua B. Freeman, *Working Class New York, Life and Labor Since World War II*. New York: The New Press, 2000, 256, 258, 270–272. © 2000, Joshua B. Freeman. Reprinted by permission of The New Press. www.thenewpress.com.

9-2-1. Rotting: Roger Brown, "New York City," *Time*, September 17, 1990. Reprinted by permission of Time, Inc.

9-2-2. Redlining: The New York Public Interest Research Group, *Take the Money and Run! Redlining in Brooklyn*. New York: The New York Public Interest Research Group, 1976. Used with permission from NYPIRG.

9-2-3. Burning: Jill Jonnes, *South Bronx Rising: The Rise, Fall and Resurrection of an American City*. New York: Fordham University Press, 2002. Used by permission from Fordham University Press.

9-2-4. Reclaiming: Robert Jensen and Cathy A. Alexander, "Resurrection: The People Are Doing It Themselves," in Robert Jensen (ed.), *Devastation/Resurrection: The South Bronx*. New York: The Bronx Museum of the Arts, 1979. Used by permission from the Bronx Museum of the Arts.

9-2-5. Squeezing: Cover of *Take the Money and Run! Redlining in Brooklyn*. New York: The New York Public Interest Research Group, 1976. Used with permission from NYPIRG.

9-3-1. Reaching Out: John V. Lindsay, *The City*. New York: W. W. Norton, 1970. © 1969, 1970, W. W. Norton & Company, Inc. Used by permission of W. W. Norton & Company, Inc.

9-3-2. Governing: Edward I. Koch, *All the Best: Letters from a Feisty Mayor*, New York: Simon & Schuster, 1990. © 1990, WNYC Foundation. Reprinted with the permission of Simon and Schuster, Inc

9-3-3. Reasoning: David Dinkins, "Reason, Respect and Reconciliation in New York City," *New York Amsterdam News*, November 28, 1992. Used by permission of David Dinkins.

9-3-4. Mapping Segregation: New York City Department of City Planning, "Patterns of Segregation: Percentage of nonhispanic whites living in each section of New York City, according to the 1980 census." Used with permission of New York City Department of City Planning. All rights reserved.

9-4-1.   Defining Defiance: Iris Morales "Palante, Siempre Palante: The Young Lords," in Andres Torres and Jose E. Velazquez (eds), *The Puerto Rican Movement*. Philadelphia, PA: Temple University Press, 1998. Used by permission from Iris Morales.

9-4-2.   Realigning Latino Politics: Michael Jones-Correa, *Between Two Nations: The Political Predicament of Latinos in New York City*. Ithaca, NY: Cornell University Press, 1998. © 1998, Cornell University Press. Used by permission of Cornell University Press.

9-4-3.   Making a Latino Identity: Xavier F. Totti, "The Making of a Latino Ethnic Identity," *Dissent*, Fall 1987. Used by permission from the University of Pennsylvania Press and Xavier F. Totti.

9-4-4.   Seeking "Justice Everywhere:" Groundswell Community Mural Project, © 2004. Lead artists: Amy Sananman and Belle Benfield. Photograph courtesy of Lawrence H. Rushing.

Chapter 10: 1993–2008

10-1-1.   Demonstrating Desiness: Sunita S. Mukhi, *Doing the Desi Thing: Performing Indianness in New York City*. New York: Garland, 2000, 188–191. Used by permission from Sunita S. Mukhi.

10-1-2.   Examining Haitian Adaptation: Michel S. Laguerre, *American Odyssey: Haitians in New York City*. Ithaca, NY: Cornell University Press, 1984. © 1984, Cornell University. Used by permission of the publisher, Cornell University Press.

10-1-3.   Considering Immigrant Entrepreneurs: Jonathan Bowles and Tara Colton, *A World of Opportunity*. New York: The Center for an Urban Future, 2007. Used by permission from The Center for an Urban Future.

10-1-4.   Speaking Through Signs: "Male Workers on Strike Holding Signs in Different Languages," © 1918. Courtesy of Brown Brothers, Sterling, PA. Lawrence H. Rushing, "Signs on Union Street, Flushing NY, 2009." Courtesy of Lawrence H. Rushing.

10-2-1.   Taming the City: Rudolph W. Giuliani, "The State of the City Address," January 13, 2000. The Rudolph W. Giuliani Archives, New York City Municipal Archives.

10-2-2.   Taming the Mayor: *The New York Daily News*, March 26, 2000. Used with permission of New York Daily News, L. P.

10-2-3.   Taming Crime: John E. Eck and Edward T. Maguire, "Have Changes in Policing Reduced Violent Crime? An Assessment of the Evidence" in Alfred Blumstein and Joel Wallman (eds), *The Crime Drop in America*. New York: Cambridge University Press, 2000, 234: Chart: homicides per 100,000 population for 10 largest cities from 1986–1998. Reprinted with the permission of Cambridge University Press.

10-2-4.   Taming the Police: Marilynn Johnson, *Street Justice: A History of Police Violence in New York City*. Boston, MA: Beacon Press, 2003. © 2003, Marilynn Johnson. Reprinted by permission of Beacon Press, Boston.

10-3-1.   Loving Gotham: Felicia R. Lee, "A Letter to a Child in Difficult Times," *The New York Times*, October 21, 2001. © 2001, *The New York Times*. All rights reserved. Used by permission. and protected by the Copyright Laws of the United States. The printing, copying, redistribution, or retransmission of the Material without express written permission is prohibited.

10-3-2.   Fearing Gotham: Max Page, "On Edge, Again," *The New York Times*, October 21, 2001. © 2001 *The New York Times*. All rights reserved. Used by permission. and protected by the Copyright Laws of the United States. The printing, copying, redistribution, or retransmission of the Material without express written permission is prohibited.

10-3-3. Dispersing Gotham: Randall Smith and Kate Kelly, "Rebuilding Wall Street—Everywhere," *The Wall Street Journal*, September 11, 2002. © 2002, Dow Jones & Company. Used by permission of DJ Reprints.

10-3-4. Greening Gotham: "Mayor [Michael] Bloomberg Delivers PLANYC: A Greener, Greater New York, 2007," www.nyc.gov

10-4-1. Running: *New-York Gazette and Weekly Post-Boy*, #811, July 17, 1758.

10-4-2. Moving: Lydia Maria Child, *Letters From New York*. New York: C. S. Francis and Company, 1845.

10-4-3. Hustlng: Theodore Dreiser, *Sister Carrie*. New York: Doubleday, Page and Company, 1900.

10-4-4. Bustling: "Hester Street, c. 1901–1907," Detroit Publishing Company. Courtesy of the Library of Congress, Prints and Photographs Division.

10-4-5. Building: Arthur Guiterman, "New York, " in *Ballads of Old New York*. New York: Harper and Brothers, 1920.

10-4-6. Bursting: Charles H. Towne, *This New York of Mine*. New York: Cosmopolitan Book Company, 1931.

10-4-7. Wrestling: David Halberstam, "In Defense of New York," *Harper's Bazaar*, February 1972. Published with permission from the author's estate.

INDEX

eBooks – at www.eBookstore.tandf.co.uk

A library at your fingertips!

eBooks are electronic versions of printed books. You can store them on your PC/laptop or browse them online.

They have advantages for anyone needing rapid access to a wide variety of published, copyright information.

eBooks can help your research by enabling you to bookmark chapters, annotate text and use instant searches to find specific words or phrases. Several eBook files would fit on even a small laptop or PDA.

NEW: Save money by eSubscribing: cheap, online access to any eBook for as long as you need it.

Annual subscription packages

We now offer special low-cost bulk subscriptions to packages of eBooks in certain subject areas. These are available to libraries or to individuals.

For more information please contact webmaster.ebooks@tandf.co.uk

We're continually developing the eBook concept, so keep up to date by visiting the website.

www.eBookstore.tandf.co.uk